100 Projects for Beginning Astronomers
EXPLORING THE * SKY

Richard Moeschl

CHICAGO REVIEW PRESS

LIBRARY OF CONGRESS
Library of Congress Cataloging-in-Publication Data

Moeschl, Richard.
    Exploring the sky: 100 projects for beginning astronomers/
Richard Moeschl.
        p.   cm.
    Includes bibliographies and index.
    Summary: Presents 100 astronomy projects, with information on related mythology and
pertinent history, cultures, and people.
    ISBN 1-556-52039-5 (pbk.): $14.95
    1. Astronomy projects—Juvenile literature.   2. Astronomy—
Observers' manuals—Juvenile literature.   [1. Astronomy projects.
    2. Astronomy.   3. Science projects.]   I. Title.
    QB64.M6 1988
    523'.007'8—dc19   88-21485
                                                                   CIP
                                                                   AC

Printed in the United States by McNaughton & Gunn

CONTENTS

INTRODUCTION

This book will help you understand the stars, planets, and the universe they occupy, even if you've tried to figure it all out before and got lost. More important, I hope it helps you understand the Earth and how it fits into the picture. It took me more than 10 years to put this book together. I am a teacher, not an astronomer. One day I was asked to teach astronomy to a class of high-school seniors. The person who asked me knew that I was interested in the stars and had been studying them on my own for awhile. When I went to find material for the class I discovered that there was nothing out there for people the age of my students. There was plenty of material for the college student and the very young child, but when it came to high-school students, "the cupboard was bare." The following years I taught astronomy to juniors and seniors, then eighth graders, seventh graders, and finally sixth graders. If I thought the cupboard was bare for high-school students, there was *no* cupboard for middle-school students. So I began collecting what I could find for older and younger people and tailoring it for my students. As I did more research, I found one or two excellent books for this age group. They are mentioned in this book at the end of each Chapter Section. None of these books, however, had everything in it that I felt my students would want to know.

After awhile I had collected a great deal of information. Remembering how hard it was to find everything, I decided to put together a resource book for teachers so they could use the material to teach astronomy, especially if they had no real science background. The idea was for me to be an editor, to collect my favorite projects and articles and put together an anthology. It soon became clear that the book would be for students as well as teachers and that I would have to rewrite everything in my own words, do the illustrations, and develop a number of projects on my own.

Here we are, 10 years, many classes, and a lot more information later. I have cut the book in half but kept my original goals which included the following:

1. Refer to the northern *and* southern hemispheres in all the material.
2. Mention contributions from people of all nations, from women, and from people from other fields besides science.
3. Describe how real people made discoveries and increased our understanding of the universe and tell a little about their lives in the process.
4. Bring in art, literature, poetry, math, science, history, physics, language, etc.—all the ways people have looked at the sky.
5. Present lots of projects recreating the original experiments performed throughout history so that people doing the projects today can experience the same sense of wonder and accomplishment.
6. Write a friendly, factual book, one full of interesting information so that anyone 11 years and older (including adults) will enjoy reading and learning about the sky.
7. Design the book so that it will also be suitable for classroom use without feeling like a textbook.

Some of the projects and concepts in this book are fairly simple, others are more complicated, but they are all fun and educational. The more complex material may be a little difficult for some readers. I did this deliberately in order to serve the goals of science and the spirit of inquiry which require that in order to learn, we must keep stretching the boundaries of our knowledge beyond the limits of our present understanding. The information in this book comes from many places: old, new, and out-of-print books; magazine articles; primary sources; conversations with astronomers, science teachers, and students; classroom activities; my own imagination; and many, many hours in libraries. When I was sure of the source of a project, I have given credit in the text. If you find one I missed, please let me know and I will be glad to give credit to the author in the next edition. I have not given credit for those projects which have appeared in one form or another in several books since it is not clear who the original author was. I have rewritten, changed or combined each of the projects. I have also invented many of them. That has been the most fun. Experiment with them all and come up with your own versions. Use the space in the margins to add your own comments or to include new discoveries to keep your book up to date. At the back of this book in a section called "Sky Files," are charts, lists, a glossary, and an index to help you find whatever information you need quickly. There is also a listing of where to get some of the less common materials for the projects.

To the many people who have helped and encouraged me, thank you. My special thanks to: my advisory board who encouraged and assisted me in the early days of the manuscript: Heidi Keller-von Asten, George Benner, Anne Charles, LeRoy Doggett, Stephen Edelglass, Johannes Hardorp, Will Kyselka, George Lovi, Norman Macbeth, Robert A. McDermott, Guy Ottewell, George K. Russell, Douglas M. Sloan, and Sheldon Stoff; to my friend Bruce King who lent his support; to the writers, publishers, and photographers who so generously allowed me to adapt and adopt their ideas; to Ise Hogan and Linda DeGraw for cheerfully and beautifully typing the manuscript; to Linda's husband Dennis for taking some of the photographs; to Roy Kindell for reviewing parts of the text; to Amy Teschner, my editor, for her incredible patience and thoroughness; and to my wife Joanne, my sons, and our relatives for believing in me and this book.

I dedicate this book to my two wonderful sons, Christopher and Joel who were three and five when this all began. As I have told them and my students over the years, you don't have to be an astronomer to enjoy and learn about the stars and the universe. They belong to everyone. Just look up.

Cone Nebula. *Photo courtesy of Observatoire de Haute Provence*

Chapter 1:   CELEBRATING THE SKY

Section 1:   THE CHANGING FACE OF THE HEAVENS

The Dome of the Sky   How do you feel when you're out camping or just going for a walk alone and you find yourself under the night sky surrounded by darkness and thousands of points of light overhead? You probably can't hear anything except the sounds of nature and the whisperings of your own inner thoughts. You might wonder how many people in how many ages have stood under the stars just as you are standing now, looking up, asking questions and thinking.

Your ancient ancestors learned a great deal about the sky without telescopes and space probes, simply by looking. You can too. You don't have to be an astronomer to understand the world of the stars. The sky and its treasures belong to everyone.

Imagine yourself like your ancestors, without any information about the sky except what you find out yourself, with your own eyes, your imagination, and your ability to figure things out. When you look up, you can imagine that the sky wraps around you like a great blanket of stars. Being under this blanket feels like being inside a tent, shaped like an upside-down bowl. The stars are on the inside of this bowl, so are the Sun, the Moon, and the planets. In the daytime, the bowl becomes a blue dome, filled with light, clouds, and birds. Each person is in the center of this dome. No matter where you walk, the dome is around you. In this next project, you can stand under the dome of the sky and begin to get to know it.

———————— **Project 1: Observing the Night Sky** ————————

MATERIALS
   a clear night

PROCEDURE
   1. Go outside to the same spot for a few minutes several times a night for a week.
   2. Select a group of stars that you can easily recognize.
   3. Find something near the stars that you can use as a landmark, such as the branch of a tree, a telephone pole, the roof of your house, a distant mountain, etc.
   4. Look for your landmark when you come out every night to check on your stars. Stand in the exact same place each time.

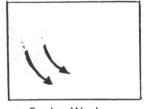

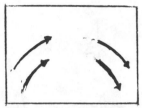
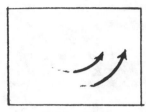

| Facing West | Facing North | Facing South | Facing East |

OBSERVATIONS

Did your group of stars stay where you left them the night before? Did all the stars in your group remain more or less in the same group? **Leonardo da Vinci** used to look at the stars through a sheet of glass and draw a tree or building on the glass as a landmark. He would then draw the changing positions of the star on different nights.

Your observations have given you enough information to begin to see what is happening in the sky. The stars are moving. They move together and they all move in the same direction, making curves across the sky.

It depends on which direction you faced when looking at the stars, which way the curve they made will be going. You can combine all four views in the drawing above and see what trails stars leave by doing the next project.

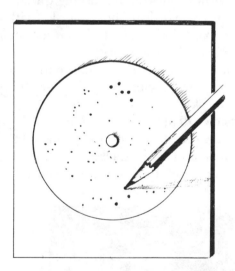

Project 2: Drawing Star Trails

MATERIALS

circumpolar star chart (in book)   cardboard or stiff paper
sheet of plastic   paper fastener
grease pencil or crayon   pencil
straight pin

PROCEDURE

1. Cut out a 4-inch (11 centimeters) circle from the plastic sheet.

2. Place the circle on the star chart so that the pole star is in the center. For the southern hemisphere, the center is the 90° mark (the line where it says 12^h).

3. Mark the star positions onto the circle using the grease pencil.

4. Remove the plastic circle and, using the straight pin, make holes through the plastic for each star.

2

5. Attach the plastic circle to a piece of cardboard or stiff paper by pushing the paper fastener through the pole star. Be sure the plastic circle can rotate freely.

6. Starting with the innermost star, put the point of a pencil through the pole and move the plastic circle counterclockwise (northern hemisphere) or clockwise (southern hemisphere) so you end up drawing a circular "star trail."

7. Draw trails for each star.

OBSERVATIONS

What do these star trails tell you about the movement of the stars? What did the Pole Star do?

Looking at star trails can give you a sense that the sky is moving. In this next project you can see how the sky moves by making a model of it.

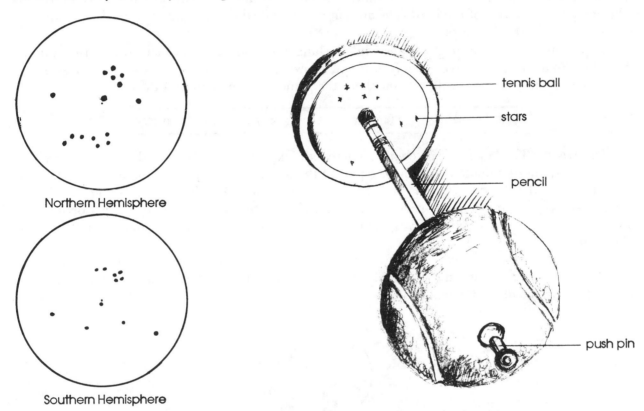

Northern Hemisphere

Southern Hemisphere

—————————————— **Project 3: Making a Tennis Ball Sky Dome** ——————————————

MATERIALS
an old tennis ball
felt-tip pen
knife (or razor blade)

dowel (about the size of a pencil)
2 push pins

PROCEDURE
1. Cut the tennis ball exactly in half with the knife (or razor blade).
2. Draw the stars inside each half just as they appear in the illustration using the felt-tip pen.
3. Attach the dowel to the inside center of each half using push pins.

USING THE TENNIS BALL SKY DOME
1. Hold the dowel in one hand with your fingers and thumb.
2. Choose which half you are going to look at—north or south. Move your fingers and thumb as close as you can toward the half you are not looking at.

3. Hold the dowel in front of you so that one half of the sky dome blocks the other half.

4. Move the half nearest your eye down until you can see the stars on the other half just like they look where you live. The half nearest you is the Earth and your horizon.

5. Turn the dowel slowly so that the tennis ball halves move from right to left (counterclockwise) for viewing the northern hemisphere, and left to right (clockwise) for the southern hemisphere.

OBSERVATIONS

Do any of the stars set below the horizon level so that you can't see them for awhile until they rise? What paths do the stars follow as they move? What does the star in the middle do?

The Planets   If you were a regular skywatcher, as your ancestors were, you would get to know what the stars look like and which ones belong where. You would also notice some "stars" that do not stay fixed to the sky dome. After awhile, you would be able to easily spot these five mavericks who stray from the rest of the herd. The ancient Greeks called them wanderers. So do we using the same word the Greeks did: **planet.**

The planets move with the sky dome while inching along on curves of their own in the opposite direction. Some of them move quite fast. If you know where to look, you can see them traveling a little each night. Chapter 6 will tell you about the planets and how to find them.

---

planet comes from the Greek word πλανητης *(planetes)* = wanderer

---

The Moon   The Moon has its own path across the sky which it follows in the opposite direction from the way the sky dome is turning. As part of the heavenly family, it also moves with the stars and planets as the sky dome turns. The Moon is easy to spot and, unlike the stars and the planets, can be seen clearly in the daylight or at night. Looking at the Moon, you notice it can be found in various places in the sky and with varying degrees of brightness. See Chapter 6, Section 2 for more about the Moon.

The Movement of the Sun   From our point of view, the Sun appears to rise every morning, travel across the sky during the day, and set in the evening replacing daylight with night. You can mark this movement in the next project.

—————— **Project 4: Marking Sunrise and Sunset** ——————

MATERIALS

hammer	pen or pencil
9 sticks the size and strength of tent pegs	newspaper, almanac, or radio

PROCEDURE

1. Mark the sticks as follows: R1, S1, R2, S2, R3, S3, R4, S4. Leave the last stick unmarked.

2. Find a place where nothing blocks your view of the sunrise in the east. This should also be a place no one will disturb for a month.

3. Drive the unmarked stick in the ground to mark where you will stand to observe.

4

4. Find out from the newspaper, almanac, or radio when the Sun will rise each day for a month.

5. Stand at your premarked observing place with your hammer and the stick labeled R1. (R stands for *Rising*.) As soon as the complete ball of the Sun has risen, drive stick R1 in the ground about 10 feet (3 meters) in front of you, right in the middle of your view of the Sun. You might want a friend along to help. One of you sights the Sun telling the other person the exact positioning for the stick.

6. Return to your observing spot that same night and mark the sunset with S1 in the same way.

7. Repeat this process with the remaining sets of sticks, one set each week for four weeks (one month).

OBSERVATIONS

Where are sticks 2–4 compared to the first set of sticks? On which side of the first sticks did you have to place the others? Are the rising and setting sticks in the same order and on the same side as the first ones? What do you notice is happening? How do you think your sticks would look if you did this project for 12 months?

Since the Sunrise and Sunset positions keep moving you can find out where they will be. By marking shadows, just as you did, your ancestors knew *exactly* where the Sun would rise and set throughout the year and how high it would be in the sky. You can see how the sun moves across the sky in one day by doing the next project. Putting the information from the Sunrise and Sunset Project with the information from this next project will give you a clearer picture of how the Sun moves.

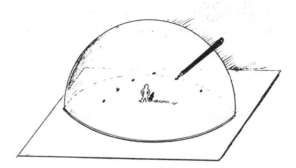

———— Project 5: Keeping Track of the Sun During the Day ————

MATERIALS

a clear glass or plastic bowl

sheet of stiff paper (larger than the
    diameter of the bowl)

grease pencil or crayon

regular pen or pencil

PROCEDURE

1. Place the bowl on the paper and trace a circle around the bowl. Remove the bowl and mark the center of the circle on the paper. Draw a little person (½ inch or about 1 centimeter) standing at the center mark. This person is you and the bowl is the sky dome that you are under.

2. Cut around the top and sides of the drawing of yourself. Bend it so you are standing straight up.

3. Take the bowl and paper outside to a place where they will be free of shadows and disturbances for 6 hours. Put the paper on the ground so the little drawing of you faces the Sun. Put the bowl on top of the paper so it lines up with the circle outline.

4. Place the point of the grease pencil on the bowl so the tip of its shadow touches the little drawing of you underneath. Put a dot on the bowl using the grease pencil to show where it was. Write the time of your observation next to the dot.

5. Repeat step # 4 every hour for the next 6 hours.

6. Draw a line through all 7 dots on the bowl to see how the Sun moved across the sky this day.

OBSERVATIONS

How much did the Sun move? Imagine that the line on the ground is an arrow, with the extra markings being the end with the feathers. What is the arrow pointing to? Where did it come from? It's tempting to answer "west" and "east" but you have no way of knowing that with the information you have. You can say, however, that it's likely that the arrow is pointing in the direction the Sun is traveling. It indicates the place where the Sun rose and the place where it will set. If you can, see if the arrow helps you find the sunrise and sunset points for the Sun tomorrow.

About what angle does the Sun make with east when it rises? About what is the highest angle of the Sun from the south at noon? Try this project in each of the 4 Seasons. See Chapter 6, Section 1 for more about the Sun.

To notice the changing positions of the Sun and the planets you would need to keep records for several months, preferably for a whole year. That seems like a long time for us, but serious students of the sky make many observations over long periods of time. This was easy to do in early civilizations which lasted for thousands of years. One generation of observers would hand their list of sky watches to the next. You would end up with long, uninterrupted lists of observations which you could study.

The ancients could see that the sky was constantly changing. They learned that if they watched carefully, they could see patterns in these changes. These patterns occurred at regular intervals or cycles. The Sun rose and set once a day. The Moon changed its brightness from dark to light every month. The planets moved across the night sky at different times during the year. It wasn't long before people figured out how to measure all of these rhythms and predict them. It soon became possible to plan ahead for the seasons by relying on detailed permanent records of continuous observation. Astronomy, the first science, had begun.

READING MORE

Jobb, Jamie. *The Night Sky Book: An Everyday Guide to Every Night.* Boston: Little Brown and Company, 1977.
Simon, Seymour. *Look to the Night Sky: An Introduction to Star Watching.* New York: Penguin Books, 1977.

Section 2: SEASONS AND FESTIVALS

The Four Directions   The sky dome is a hemisphere, half of a sphere or globe. Since the sky dome is located in the heavens and not on the Earth we call it the **celestial hemisphere.** It spins around carrying the stars with it.

North and south tend to be directions up and down, while east and west are directions going across. People in the United States talk about their relatives "up" north, "down" south, "out" west and "back" east. You need the Earth and the sky together to find the four directions. The four basic directions, north, south, east, and west, are called the **cardinal** points.

---

celestial comes from the Latin word *caelestis* = of the heavens, heavenly
hemisphere comes from the Greek word ἡμι (hemi) = half, and σφαιρα (sphaira) = ball
cardinal comes from the Latin word *cardinalis* = basic
Imagine that there are no calendars, no months, no days of the week.
How could you predict the coming of important events like the seasons?

Write down the four directions as you would find them on a map, North on top, South on the bottom, East to the right, and West to the left. Now draw two lines, one connecting the North to the South and one connecting the East to the West. You now have a cross, which, when you place a circle around it is the astronomical symbol for the Earth. This symbol often appears in paintings and sculptures of kings and queens holding in their hands a round globe marked with a cross. Each point of the cross represented the "four corners of the Earth" (N,S,E,W), symbolizing the power of the king.

If you take the first letter of each word *N*orth, *E*ast, *W*est, and *S*outh you'll find that you have the name for the information that the reporters gather from the four corners of the Earth: NEWS.

The four directions were especially important to our ancient ancestors. It was crucial to have the places where people worshipped lined up along these directions. The ancients were able to orient their buildings with great precision without using a compass. You can find directions without a compass in the next project.

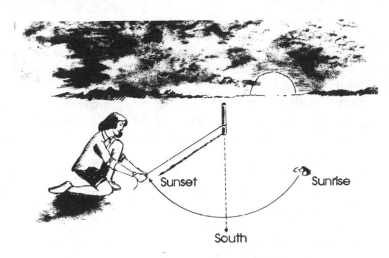

Project 6: Finding Directions From a Shadow Stick

MATERIALS
a stick   rocks
a piece of string with a nail tied to
   one end

PROCEDURE
1. Find a spot where the ground is level and free from disturbances.
2. Drive the stick into the ground. Make sure it is straight up and down by checking it all around using the weighted string as a guide.
3. Use rocks to mark the tip of the stick's shadow a few hours before noon. Tie the end of the string to the bottom of the shadow stick. Use the string and the nail to draw a long arc on the gound from the stick to the tip of the shadow.
4. Use rocks to mark the tip of the stick's shadow a few hours *after* noon when it again touches the arc. Halfway between the two marks on the arc facing *away* from the stick is **north** in the northern hemisphere (south in the southern hemisphere).

OBSERVATIONS
What does this project tell you about the directions in which sunrise and sunset occur? When the shadow is at its shortest, around noon, it also points north in the northern hemisphere (south in the southern hemisphere). Why?

7

Looking down the hall in the Temple of Karnak.

A straight stick used in this way is one of the earliest astronomical instruments. The sundial is a relative of this instrument. You can build sundials and tell time with straight sticks in Section 3 of this chapter (Project 10, Making A Sundial).

The Great Pyramid in Egypt, built around 2600 B.C. displays a tremendous understanding of engineering and astronomy. Its sides line up precisely along the north–south, east–west lines. One of the shafts inside the pyramid pointed to the star Thuban which was the pole star at that time. Another shaft pointed to the star Sirius.

The ancient Chinese were able to figure out the four directions N, S, E, W very precisely. Which direction a house or temple faced was very significant. Therefore the Chinese carefully arranged their buildings to line up with the four directions and included their knowledge of the directions in yearly rituals.

Cathedral builders in the middle ages built their churches along an east–west line. The entrance was from the west. The people and the priest faced the east, the place from which the Sun rises and the direction from which Christ, as the Sun-Being, having risen, would return.

Throughout the world, builders often used the east–west, sunrise–sunset equinox line to set up their buildings. The most dramatic example of this plan was in the temple of Amon-Ra in Karnak, Egypt, built around 2000 B.C. Its main hallway was about 600 yards (500 meters) long and built so that the farther you went inside the temple, the narrower the passageway became. The line through the middle of the building (axis) passed through 17 or 18 stages, each with the floor, ceiling, and columned walls closing in. This made the space smaller and smaller until you reached the darkened sanctuary. Here, where only the priests were allowed to go, was an opening through which for only a few moments on the day of the solstice you could behold the rising midwinter Sun. Such an alignment made it possible for the Egyptians to determine the length of the solar year. Their calculations were only about one minute off.

The Egyptian temple builders arranged other temples along lines pointing to stars such as Sirius, which traveled around the pole star. Because of the pharaoh's responsibility to maintain the calendar, people expected each of the early kings to build a new temple. When the position of the star changed over many years and the temple no longer pointed to it exactly, the pharaoh added on a new temple with its axis changed.

---

archaeology comes from the Greek word $\dot{\alpha}\rho\chi\eta$ (arche) = beginning and $\lambda o\gamma o\varsigma$ (logos) = that which is spoken or thought of
astronomy comes from the Greek word $\dot{\alpha}\sigma\tau\eta\rho$ (aster) = star and $\dot{o}\nu o\mu\alpha$ (onoma) or the Latin word nomen = a way of knowing or a name

---

The Four Seasons, Equinoxes, and Solstices People who study ancient history mainly by examining the ruins and remains left behind by earlier cultures we call **archaeologists.** Those who combine this study with a particular interest in the astronomical significance of these early structures we call **archaeoastronomers.** One of the pioneers in archaeoastronomy was **J. Norman Lockyer** (1836–1920).

Archaeologists and archaeoastronomers have found many examples of buildings, including major temples, built along the east–west lines of the equinoxes.

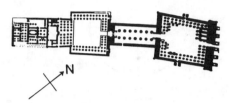

The Temple of Luxor plan shows how builders altered its axis to keep it aligned with the changing rising position of the star toward which the temple faced.

In section 1 you discovered that the Sun's rising and setting positions move during the year. With what you know now, you can make a north–south, east–west line on the ground to see where exactly the Sun does rise during the year.

You'll find that only twice does the Sun rise exactly in the east and set exactly in the west: on March 21st and September 23rd. On these two dates, the Sun rises at about 6 in the morning and sets at about 6 at night (local Sun time or apparent time). Because day and night are equal (12 hours each) on these two dates, we call each date the **equinox.** In the northern hemisphere, March 21st is the spring equinox and September 23rd is the autumn equinox. In the southern hemisphere, March 21st is the autumn equinox and September 23rd is the spring equinox.

Double the Sun's *rising* gives the approximate length of the *night.* For example, if the Sun rises at 8, 2 x 8 = 16; the time from sunset to sunrise = 16 hours. Double the time of the Sun's *setting* gives the approximate length of the *day.* For example, if the Sun sets at 7, 2 x 7 = 14; the time from sunrise to sunset = 14 hours.

On the two equinox dates, the line joining the tips of the daily shadows of the shadow stick is a straight line.

---

equinox comes from the Latin words *aequi* = equal, and *nox* = night
season comes from the French word *saison,* which comes from the Latin word *satio* = sowing
The word for **spring** in French is *printemps* which comes from the Latin words *primus* = the first or best and *tempus* = time.
The word for **spring** in Latin is *ver* or *vernus. Vert* in French means green.
Spring means to shoot forth.
Summer comes from the Middle English word *sumer* = half year.
Autumn comes from the Latin word *autumnus* = changeable.
Fall means to drop to the ground.
Winter comes from the Old English word *wintar.*

If you draw a line in between each section of the cross, you now have eight marks or points on the outside of your circle. Each of these points represents a date starting with March 21st and proceeding counterclockwise. Because you make these four dates by drawing lines across the four quarters of your circle, we call them **cross-quarter days.** The season of spring is an on-going process, like a wave, which begins gradually, grows in intensity, and then fades. The cross-quarter days mark the gradual beginning and fading periods of the seasons. The equinox dates mark the peak intensity of spring and autumn, or the middles of the two seasons.

Spring Nature's year begins with spring. Light and darkness are in balance. Growth and renewed life are everywhere. Our calendars used to begin the year at this time, at the Green or Vernal equinox, the morning of the year. In Section 4 of this chapter you can find out why the new year now begins in January.

Spring—"Comes in like a lion, goes out like a lamb."

February 2	First cross-quarter day Candlemas	Beginning of Spring—night wanes. Celebrated by the blessing of candles for sacred use.
	Purification or Presentation	Feast of the Purification of the Virgin Mary or Presentation of the child Jesus in the temple.
	Groundhog Day	The groundhog (woodchuck) comes out of his burrow, if he sees his shadow, he goes back inside & back to sleep for the 6 weeks remaining until the equinox.
		"If Candlemas be bright and clear we'll have two winters in the year." "If Candlemas be fair and bright, Come, Winter, have another flight; If Candlemas bring clouds and rain, Go, Winter, and come not again." "Don't use up more than half your provisions by Candlemas"
February 5 (approximately)	Chinese New Year	Celebrated on first new Moon when the Sun is in Aquarius.
February 29	Leap Year Extra Day	Occurs every four years. See Section 4 of this chapter for details.
March 14 (approximately)	Purim	Commemorates the deliverance of the children of Israel with the help of Queen Esther.
March 15	The Ides of March	The time of the full Moon in the first month of the Roman calendar. The date when Julius Caesar, the one mostly responsible for our calendar, was assassinated.
March 17	St. Patrick's Day	Feast of St. Patrick, missionary to Ireland & patron saint of that nation. The garden

		season starts today in Great Britain with the sowing of peas, the earliest of vegetables.
40 Days before Easter	Ash Wednesday	Beginning of Lent. People recognize Lent by having the sign of the cross marked on their foreheads with ashes remaining from the burned palms of last year's Palm Sunday.
	Lent	Days of preparation before Easter.
March 21	Vernal Equinox	Middle of Spring. Day & night are equal. The Sun is at mid-height angle from the Earth at noon, making the days not too warm, not too cool.
Sunday before Easter	Palm Sunday	Commemorates Christ's entry into Jerusalem when the crowds placed palm branches in his pathway.
March 22 to April 25	Easter	The festival of Christ's resurrection. Celebrated on the first Sunday following the full Moon after the Vernal Equinox. People often celebrate with sunrise services outside. Our word **Easter** comes from the time when missionaries introduced Christianity among the Saxons, who celebrated a spring festival to their goddess *Eoster.* People celebrate Easter by coloring eggs, a symbol of rebirth and joy.
	Passover	Pesach or the Passover is a Jewish holiday in memory of their deliverance from the bondage of Egypt. The name comes from the "passing over" of the houses of the children of Israel by the angel of death, after the people had marked the door posts and lintels of their houses with the blood of the Paschal lamb. People celebrate with a festival meal commemorating the meal held on the first passover night.
March 25	The Annunciation	The feast commemorating the announcement of the archangel Gabriel to Mary that she was chosen to become the mother of the Messiah. This was the beginning of the year in France and Great Britain until the calendar was changed in 1564 for France and 1752 for Great Britain. (See Section 4 of this chapter for details.)
40 Days after Easter	Ascension Day	The festival of Christ's ascending into heaven.
50 Days after Easter	Whitsun or Pentecost	Whitsunday commemorates the descent of the Holy Spirit in the form of tongues of fire above the heads of Christ's disciples and the beginning of the church.

11

		Pentecost comes from the Greek word $\pi\varepsilon\nu\tau\varepsilon$ (pente) = 50.
50 Days after Passover	Shabuoth or Pentecost	Also called the Festival of Weeks, commemorates the giving of the Law (Ten Commandments) from God to Moses on Mount Sinai.
Last Sunday in April	Beginning of Daylight Saving Time	The way to remember which direction to turn the hands of the clock is: "Spring forward, Fall back."

Summer—the noon of the year. For some people, this is their favorite time of the year.

April 30	Second cross-quarter day	Beginning of Summer. Days grow longer than nights.
	Walpurgisnacht, May Eve	Fertility Festival, celebrating the return of the goddess Flora to the Earth.
May I	Beltane or May Day	Sacred day to Brigit, the fairy queen. A great Celtic festival with bonfires. Later became May Day, celebrated by young men and maidens dancing around May poles, presided over by the May Queen.
June 21	Summer Solstice	Midsummer's Day. The longest day of the year. Short night. The Sun is at its highest angle from the Earth at noon, making the days hot. Light reigns.
June 23	St. John's Eve	People in Europe celebrate this night when the Sun sets late in the evening. They light a huge bonfire to encourage the Sun to shine and ripen the crops. In many parts of the world, bonfires still blaze at this time, while people sing songs around them. Young men leap across the flames to give them strength for the year ahead as people mark the half-way point of the year.
June 24	St. John's Day	The feast of St. John the Baptist. What it meant to have the Sun at its strongest and about to decrease again with the coming of Winter, reminded people of the words of St. John in reference to Christ, "He must increase, I must decrease." The light grows stronger again after the birth of Christ celebrated at Christmas.
July 3 to August 11	Dog Days	People associate these days of unbearable heat with strange behavior, including dogs going mad with the Dog Star Sirius in the constellation Canis Major (the Great Dog). These days occur 20 days before & 20 days after the time when Sirius is closest to the Sun.
Around July	Ramadan	Month of fasting for followers of Islam.

July 15	St. Swithin's Day	Feast of St. Swithin. "St. Swithin's Day, if thou dost rain, for forty days it will remain, St. Swithin's Day if thou be fair, for forty days 'twill rain nae mair." Swithin, Bishop of Winchester in England, died in 862. Before he died he asked to be buried outside the church. He was. A hundred years later, however, the monks decided to move the remains inside the church on July 15th. The Saint protested by causing a forty-day rain which persuaded the monks to leave the Saint buried outside.

Autumn—the evening of the year, when the trees are ablaze with color, the air is crisp, sometimes filled with the smell of burning leaves.

August I	Third cross-quarter day	Beginning of Autumn. Daylight wanes.
	Lammas	A wheat harvest festival dating from Saxon times. **Lammas** means loaf-mass from the practice of offering bread at Mass, made from the first fruits of the new wheat.
	Lagnasadh	Gaelic Summer **games of Lug,** the Sun-god. Sacred day of the Mother goddesses Kore and Ceres.
Weekend before Labor Day	Labor Day Weekend	Regarded in the U.S. as the end of Summer.
Around September	Succoth	The Feast of Tabernacles, celebrated for eight days in commemoration of the Israelites who dwelt in booths or tabernacles which they made from branches of trees & covered with leaves, during their forty years wandering in search of the Promised Land.
In September/ October	Rosh Hashana	The Festival of the New Year.
In September/ October	Yom Kippur	The Day of Atonement, a day of prayer to obtain forgiveness. "It never rains on the Day of Atonement."
September 11	Harvest Festival	A festive celebration to mark the harvest. Called **Harvest-Home** in England and the **Kern** in Scotland. The European Thanksgiving.
September 23	Autumnal Equinox	Middle of Autumn. Day & night are equal. The Sun is at mid-height at noon, making the days not too warm, not too cool.
September 29	Michaelmas	The Festival of the archangel Michael. A call to wake up from the drowsiness of Summer. The mood of this day appears in paintings of St. Michael (or St. George) overcoming the forces of darkness (the dragon) while gazing alertly ahead.

Winter—the night of the year.

Last Sunday in October	End of Daylight Saving Time	Return to Standard Time.
October 31	Fourth cross-quarter day	Beginning of Winter. Nights grow longer than days.
	Halloween	**All Hallows E'en.** The name means hallowed or holy evening, the eve before All Saints Day. Before that it was an old Druid festival which began at midnight and lasted throughout the following day. The festival was in honor of Crone Hecate the destroyer who brought death to all vegetation, returning the seed of life to the unconscious to sleep. To honor Pomona, the goddess of fruits & seed, people shared apples & nuts. Today children dress like souls of the dead and go around asking for food—mostly candy.
November I	Samhain (pronounced "savin")	Celtic New Year in honor of the departing Sun & beginning of new fires for a new year. At this time dark spirits visit the Earth until the good spirits can send them away. In the U.S. people celebrate a combination of Halloween and Samhain on the night of October 31.
November I	All Saints Day	A day to commemorate all the saints and holy ones who do not have a feast especially set for them. A day to reflect on their example.
November 2	All Souls' Day	A day of prayer to remember those who have died.
November 11	Martinmas	Feast of St. Martin, patron saint of farmers (at the end of the harvest), outcasts, and beggars (since he divided his cloak with one). On the evening of Martinmas, people in many French homes remember the Saint with a festival of lanterns, carrying the light through the darkened house. "If St. Martin's Day be bright & sun-shiny there will be a cold Winter, or if the trees & vines shall retain their foliage the same will follow. But if there be frost before Martinmas, the Winter will be mild." "A la Saint Martin l'hiver en chemin" (with St. Martin on the road is Winter)
Last Thursday in November	Thanksgiving	Harvest festival in the U.S. commemorating the help given by the Native Americans to the Pilgrim settlers in New England. People generally celebrated with family gatherings around a sumptuous feast usually featuring turkey. The turkey almost became the national bird of the U.S. instead of the eagle.

4 weeks before Christmas	Advent	Preparation for Christmas. The word **advent** comes from the Latin word *adventus* = a coming or approach. People place four candles on the Advent wreath, lighting one for each Sunday until all four are shining to announce the birth of the light at Christmas. People also use Advent calendars with windows to open on each day before Christmas.
December 6	St. Nicholas Day	The Feast day of St. Nicholas, the patron saint of children, Russia & merchants, and the model for Father Christmas and Santa Claus. This is the day children celebrate Christmas with presents in Holland, Belgium & parts of Germany. At this time, people in these countries observe many of the customs we associate with Christmas.
December 13	St. Lucy's Day	The Feast of St. Lucy formerly thought of as "the year's midnight" "Lucy light, shortest day, longest night." In Sweden, the festival is celebrated in the home. While the family sings a St. Lucy song, the eldest daughter serves a sweet roll to everyone in the house. She wears a white gown. On her head she wears a wreath with four lit candles.
December 19	Saturnalia	The Roman midwinter festival in honor of Saturnius. A celebration of light and darkness which the Romans used to mark with wild parties.
in Mid-December	Yule	Germanic celebration of the beginning of the year. *Yule* = wheel.
in December	Hanukkah	The Festival of Dedication, kept in memory of the purification and rededication of the temple. It is also the Feast of Lights in memory of the re-lighting of the perpetual lamp in the temple. People celebrate this festival in homes and synagogues by lighting the candles on the 8-branched Menorah.
December 22	Winter Solstice	Midwinter Day. The shortest day of the year. Long night. The Sun is at its lowest angle from the Earth at noon, making the days cold. Darkness reigns.
December 24	Christmas Eve	The night before Christmas. Many families in Europe celebrate Christmas on this night. Mass is celebrated at midnight; church bells ring out. Legend has it that the animals speak at midnight as they celebrate the birth of the Christ Child in a stable warmed by an ox, ass and sheep, many years ago.
December 25	Christmas	The festival celebrating the birth of Jesus,

bearer of the Christ.

Christmas = *Christes Masse* (the Mass of Christ). The Christmas customs used throughout the world are a mixture of local traditions and pre-Christian practices. Thus, Christmas is both a holy day and a holiday. Many decorations include stars made of shiny paper or straw. The celebration of Christmas lasts 12 days (the 12 Days of Christmas or the 12 Holy Nights).

December 26	St. Stephen	The feast of the first Christian to die for his faith. "Good King Wenceslas looked out on the feast of Stephen When the snow lay round about deep and crisp and even."
December 31	New Year's Eve	Called **Hogmanny** in Great Britain, it marks the last day of the year. Many people stay up to welcome in the New Year at midnight. There are a number of old European customs which people practice this night while waiting. They include a number of ways of telling fortunes.
January 1	New Year's Day	The first day of the New Year. This used to be celebrated on March 25.
January 6	Epiphany	The Twelfth Day of Christmas. *Epiphany* comes from the Greek word ἐπιφανεια (epiphaneia) = coming to light, appearance. This day commemorates the appearance of Christ to all peoples through the visit of the three wise men to Bethlehem. This day also commemorates the baptism of Christ in the Jordan River by John the Baptist when a voice from heaven recognized him publicly.
January 20	St. Agnes' Eve	The night before the Feast of St. Agnes. Considered a good time to tell fortunes.
January 21	St. Agnes	The Feast of St. Agnes.
January 25	St. Paul's Day	The Feast of St. Paul. "If St. Paul's Day be fair & clear it doth betide a happy year; But if it chance to snow or rain, there will be dear all kind of grain."

The calendar also includes other celebrations such as birthdates and days to remember a particular idea or group of people. In Project 16, Designing Your Own Calendar in Section 4 of this chapter, you can make your own calendar and add whatever celebrations you want.

As you can see, there are many moments to celebrate in the four seasons which have some connection with the rhythms of the Sun and Moon.

People needed to know in advance when these events were going to occur. How did they find out? One way was to figure out how long it would be between the same two events, from one equinox to the next or from Halloween to Halloween, etc. To do this you would use the shadow stick. Over the course of the year you would notice that the lengths of the shadows at noon weren't the same size every day. At one date the shadow was so short that it was hardly there. Six months later, the shadow was quite long. Watching the size of the shadow from one event until it became the same length again would tell you when that date would be.

The higher the Sun is on the celestial hemisphere, the shorter the shadows it casts on the Earth. "Higher" doesn't mean farther away, it just means the angle at which its rays strike the Earth—the higher the Sun, the greater the angle. This affects the amount of heat and light you receive each season. The next project shows why.

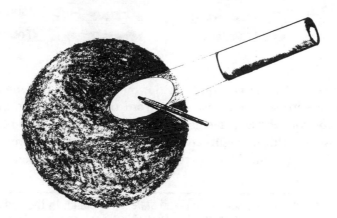

—— Project 7: Comparing the Intensity of the Sun from Different Angles ——

MATERIALS
a ball

black paint

paper tube

thermometer

paper and pencil

PROCEDURE
1. Paint the ball black.

2. Go outside. Put the ball on the ground. Hold the paper tube so the Sun shines through it casting a beam of light straight onto the ball. Notice the size and brightness of the circle of light on the ball and record its temperature.

3. Move the paper tube so that the beam of sunlight hits the ball at an angle. Be sure to keep the tube at the same height from the ball as in step #4. Observe and record the temperature of the lighted area.

OBSERVATIONS
As the tilt of the paper tube increases, what happens to the size and brightness of the light on the ball? When the same amount of light gets spread farther this way, what happens to its heat?

In the northern part of the world, summer is 4.5 days longer than winter. Spring is 3.8 days longer than winter. Autumn is 0.9 days longer than winter. The time differences are the opposite for those in the southern part of the world. (e.g., winter is 4.5 days longer than summer, etc.)

In the winter, on December 22nd, the Sun rises much later than it does in the summer. You get up before it does. The Sun rises at about 8:00 in the morning in the southeast, climbing at only a slight angle to slip quickly out of sight again as it sets in the southwest at around 4:00 in the afternoon after shining on the Earth for only eight hours. The night will last sixteen hours—just perfect for an astronomer.

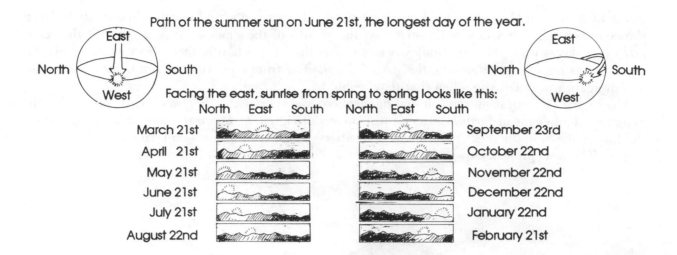

Path of the summer sun on June 21st, the longest day of the year.

Facing the east, sunrise from spring to spring looks like this:

	North East South		North East South	
March 21st				September 23rd
April 21st				October 22nd
May 21st				November 22nd
June 21st				December 22nd
July 21st				January 22nd
August 22nd				February 21st

Ancient Observatories   At the two points in the Sun's journey through the seasons (June 21 and December 22), when sunrise is farthest away from the east and the Sun is at its highest (or lowest) point from the horizon, the Sun seems to stop. Having climbed as high or descended as low in the sky as it could, the Sun now begins to change direction and make its way back towards a middle position in the sky. The name for the two dates when this happens is the **solstice.**

---

solstice comes from the Latin words *sol* = Sun, and *stare* = to stand. In the northern hemisphere, on June 21st the Sun seems to "stand still" at its highest point in the summer sky (summer solstice). On December 22nd the Sun seems to "stand still" at its lowest point in the winter sky (winter solstice). In the southern hemisphere, the winter solstice occurs on June 21st, and the summer solstice on December 22nd.

By watching the changing lengths of the shadows from the shadow stick in Project 6, Finding Directions From a Shadow Stick, you can tell what time of year it is and what season is coming next. You can do the same by noticing where the Sun rises and sets compared to the exact positions of the east and west. Without staring at the Sun you can get a good idea whether its path is at a high or low angle. With what you now know about how to predict the arrival of each season you can construct your own working version of one of the first astronomical observatories and calendars: Stonehenge.

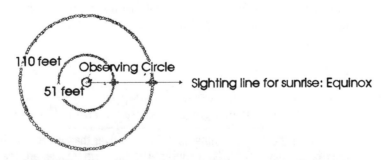

Project 8: Building a Stonewheel Observing Circle

MATERIALS

rope (or clothesline) over 60 (18 meters) feet long
piece of chalk
bag of lime

plenty of rocks
a clear field
at least 3 people

PROCEDURE

1. Find a site which has a clear view of the east and west horizons. Make a mark at the place that will become the center of a circle 110 feet (34 meters) in diameter.

2. Stand in the center holding on to one end of the rope. Another person holds the rope and using it as a drawing compass measures out a circle. Use 1½ normal walking steps from the center mark as the radius to make the circle. Knot the rope at this distance or mark it with chalk. A third person follows behind drawing the circle with lime. Cover the circle with rocks, the larger the better. This is the observing circle.

3. Make two more circles around the first one in the same way always measuring from the center mark. The second circle has a radius of 25½ feet (8 meters), the third circle has a radius of 55 feet (17 meters). The sizes of these circles come from the "megalithic yard" discovered by the British archaeologist **Sir Alexander Thom.** You can use any measurement. Instead of using a ruler, count one normal walking step as 2½ feet (1 meter).

USING YOUR STONEWHEEL OBSERVING CIRCLE

On the morning of the equinox, stand in the center of the observing circle and face the direction where the Sun will be rising. Have a companion stand on the outermost circle facing the same direction. When the Sun rises, whoever is standing in the observing circle has the other person stand directly in front of the Sun and mark that spot on the circle with sticks or a pile of stones. Keeping the Sun always in view and lined up with the person in the observing circle, mark the middle circle to help create a straight viewing line from the center. The ancients often included an additional point on the horizon: a tree, a notch in the mountainside, etc. You can too.

Use the sighting method described above to find and mark other points, such as:

a. North

b. Sunset on the equinoxes

c. Sunrise on the solstices

d. Sunset on the solstices

OBSERVATIONS

Your Stonewheel is a combination of Stonehenge built in England around 2000 B.C. and the Medicine Wheels built by the Native Americans of Wyoming around 1500 A.D. How do you think your Stonewheel works? Will it be accurate for the same positions next year? What other activities could you think of for the Stonewheel?

Stonehenge, Wiltshire, England. *Photo courtesy of Ministry of Public Buildings & Works, England*

The ancient Druids did not build Stonehenge, but they used it possibly to celebrate the Autumn festival of Samhain and welcome in the seasons of the Solstices and Equinoxes.

Legend has it that Merlin, the wizard friend of King Arthur, built Stonehenge. This becomes more believable when you find that the stones which make up this massive observatory, temple, and calendar, are not available anywhere locally.

The word **henge** means a circular enclosure, usually earthen with a bank and a ditch.

People made their observations at the Medicine Wheel by standing in one of the circles of stones on the outside of the main circle and sighting along the ground (horizontal) following the lines of stones. The observation points at Stonehenge included the rising and setting positions for the Moon as well as an eclipse calendar. The Medicine Wheel includes the rising positions of stars which observers used in addition to the rising of the Sun to indicate important seasonal points.

People made their observations at Stonehenge from inside the horseshoe-shaped group of stones looking through the outer circles, just as in your Stonewheel. An additional vertical stone stands beyond the outer circle to further mark the summer solstice point. When the Sun rises on June 21st, it stands on top of this "heel stone" just as it did for you when you marked the sunrise with a stick in our earlier projects. Stonehenge is not the only example of its kind. There are many other standing stones arranged in circles and avenues throughout Great Britain and parts of France.

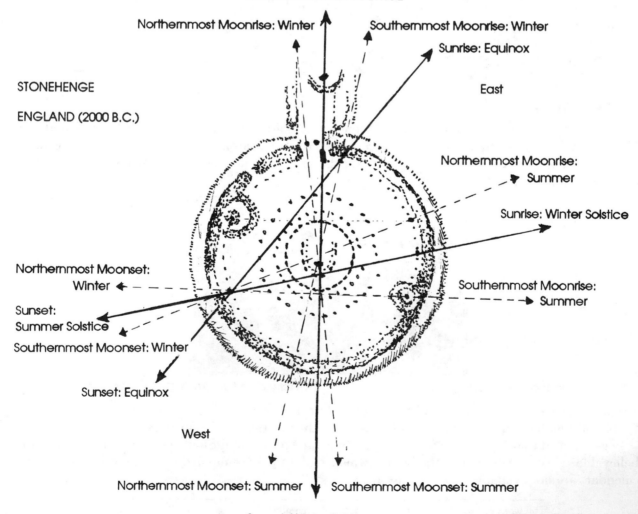

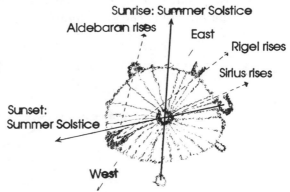

Medicine Wheel, Wyoming, U.S.A. *Photo courtesy of U.S. Forestry Service, Medicine Wheel Ranger District*

READING MORE

Allison, Linda. *The Reason for Seasons: The Great Cosmic Megagalactic Trip Without Moving from Your Chair.* Boston: Little Brown and Company, 1975.
Cary, Diana and Judy Large. *Festivals, Family and Food.* Stroud, Gloucestershire: Hawthorn Press, 1982.

Section 3: TIME

The Year, Month, and Day   When you stand outside in the dark under the stars or when you watch the sunrise bring in the morning light, you are experiencing the two most basic units of time: day and night. Two different times, two different worlds. A "day" used to mean the time when the Sun shone, that is from sunrise to sunset. A day now lasts from midnight to midnight. Thus we have created a "day" which doesn't depend on what we see and begins and ends in the night.

The kind of time most of us keep is for measuring "how long." How long until, how long since, how long from beginning to end. Nature offers us a number of events with which to measure the passing of time. Native Americans counted years by "winters" or "summers," months by "moons," and days by "sleeps."

The Year   The Sun and Moon were the first and most widely recognized means of measuring time. Their rhythms divided the year into the four seasons.

The Sun gives us time and direction. During the year, the noon position of the Sun changes. Sometimes it is higher, sometimes lower in the sky. It also moves a number of degrees north or south from a true east-west rising and setting position. The combination of the change in the Sun's noon positions and the different speeds of the Sun's movement in summer and winter creates a figure-eight pattern in the sky. Like the circle for the sky, there also is a signature for the Sun. We call this figure-eight pattern the **analemma**. It takes the Sun the whole year to etch its signature into the daytime sky.

Often scientists need to conduct ongoing experiments which may continue over the space of a year or longer. One astronomer aimed his camera toward the south and took a photograph of the daytime sky at the same time every 10 days for the whole year. As a reward for his patience he now has an amazing photograph of the analemma, the figure 8 pattern made by the Sun. There are several ways that you too can make the analemma visible. In this next project you can follow the path of the Sun and read its signature.

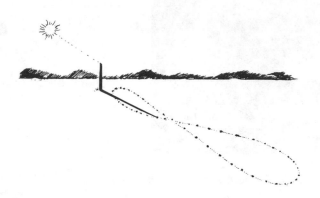

Project 9: Displaying the Path of the Analemma

MATERIALS

Shadow stick from Project 6   pencil and paper
rocks   (camera)
calendar

PROCEDURE

1. Find a spot where the ground is level and free from disturbances.

2. Drive the stick into the ground. Make sure it is straight up and down by checking it all around using the weighted string as a guide.

3. Use rocks to mark the tip of the stick's shadow at the same time and on the same day of the week every week for a few months.

4. Write yourself a reminder on the calendar when to mark the shadow. If it's cloudy, rainy, or you miss a day, mark the shadow on the next possible day.

5. Try to predict, as you go along, based on the marks you already have made:

a. Where the next mark will be.

b. What the finished figure 8 will look like and how big it will be.

Use the drawing on this page to help you make your predictions. Remember that in the northern hemisphere, the summer loop is smaller because the Sun appears to move faster. In the southern hemisphere, the winter loop is smaller.

6. Make a drawing or photograph of what you have marked so far and use it to help you map out where your predicted marks will be and what the final shape will look like. Write the dates next to each mark (actual and predicted). You may decide to change your predictions from time to time.

7. Keep marking the tip of the stick's shadow for the rest of the year. You will be rewarded with the Sun's signature for your patience! Fill in the spaces in between the rocks with a curved row of smaller rocks to show the figure 8 better.

8. Make a drawing or photograph of your finished analemma.

OBSERVATIONS

Notice the shape your marks are beginning to make. If you have been marking for six months, the rest of the year will produce a mirror image of what you already have marked. How close to the actual positions and shape were your predictions?

The Sun changes the angle of its height during the year. It also moves slightly north or south from a true east-west rising and setting position. The combination of these two movements creates the figure 8 pattern or the analemma.

Mechanical time-pieces such as watches do not change how they mark the hours from day to day. The time they give us indicates the time of the average or "mean" position of the Sun. Since the real Sun is neither mechanical nor average, our clocks are always a bit ahead or behind the real Sun in the sky. Only four times a year do our watches and the Sun (as shown on the sundial) agree: December 25th, April 15th, June 15th, and September 1st. On February 11th, for example, clocks are 14 minutes faster than the Sun. By November 3rd, clocks are behind the Sun by more than 16 minutes. The analemma can help make the necessary adjustments. These adjustments are referred to as the **Equation of Time.** See the Equation of Time Chart in Sky Files.

The Month During the year the Moon is busy moving around the celestial hemisphere. The fact that you can see the Moon both in the daylight and night, makes it a more convenient timekeeper than the Sun which you could only see during the day.

---

crescent comes from the Latin word *cresco* = to grow, increase, enlarge
Crescent is the name we give to a curved shape like half of the letter "O."

The time it takes for the Moon to go from one of its shapes all the way through the others and back to the first shape again, we call a **month,** after the Moon which measures it. In the time it takes the Sun to get from one of its places (solstice or equinox) back to the same place (one year), the Moon has gone through all of its shapes 12 times. You can now further divide the year into 12 parts.

The Week The time it takes the Moon to go from one shape to the next is about the same for each shape. While the shape and brightness of the Moon are constantly changing, four main shapes and brightness can be easily recognized = (1) when the Moon is not visible, (2) when half the circle of the Moon is lit, (3) when the full circle of the Moon is lit, (4) when the Moon is not visible again. The interval between each of these four we call a **week.** You can now divide the year into 52 parts.

---

week comes from the Middle English word *weke,* or *wike* which came from the Latin word *vici* = change or turn
Day comes from the Old English word *doeg* and the Latin word *dies.* Both words mean the time from daylight to night or from night to daylight.

The Day The interval between one sunrise or sunset to the next we call a **day.** There are seven days in one week. Although there are weeks of other lengths throughout the world ranging from five to ten days, the number seven has caught the attention of humankind as the signature or symbol of perfection. There are seven notes in the western musical scale. Christianity lists seven supreme virtues, seven deadly vices, and seven mansions of heaven. In Japan there are seven gods of happiness. In Rome there were seven hills. There are seven stars in the Pleiades and seven ancient and seven modern wonders of the world. You can divide one month into approximately thirty days.

The Saxon **King Edgar** in 958 A.D. ordered no work to be done from Saturday noon to Monday dawn, thus inventing the "weekend."

The ancient Babylonians who gave us our word for year, also gave us a convenient way to divide it. They noticed that circles keep showing up when we try to understand what is happening in the sky: the outer rim of the celestial hemisphere, star trails, the shape of the Sun and the Moon, etc.

Other places which have circles are Stonehenge, the Medicine Wheel and the Stonewheel, the spiral of the Anasazi, and the observing station in Caracol.

THE DAYS OF THE WEEK

English	Saxon Usage	Planet/Symbol	Gods & Goddesses Greek/Roman
Sunday	Sun's Day	Sun ☉	Helios/Apollo (Sol)
Monday	Moon's Day	Moon ☽	Artemis/Diana (Luna)
Tuesday	Tiw's Day	Mars ♂	Hermes/Mercurius
Wednesday	Woden's Day	Mercury ☿	Aphrodite/Venus
Thursday	Thor's Day	Jupiter ♃	Ares/Mars
Friday	Frigg's Day	Venus ♀	Zeus/Jupiter
Saturday	Saterne's Day	Saturn ♄	Kronos/Saturnus

German	French	Spanish	Latin
Sontag	Dimanche	Domingo	Dies Solis
Montag	Lundi	Lunes	Dies Lunae
Dienstag	Mardi	Martes	Dies Martis
Mitwoch	Mercredi	Miercoles	Dies Mercurii
Donnerstag	Juedi	Jueves	Dies Iovis
Freitag	Vendredi	Viernes	Dies Veneris
Samstag	Samedi	Sabado	Dies Saturni

The Babylonians recognized that the circle must be the "signature" of the sky. To be able to read that signature would make it possible for you to better understand the sky. The Babylonian priest-astronomers used the tools of geometry to divide the circle and the year first into twelve equal parts. Then they further divided each section into thirty smaller parts. Each part had an angle of one degree.

The Hour The shadow stick can measure time within the day. The shadow stick teams up with the circle to form a sundial. All over the world people have used various kinds of sundials. The Chinese were among the first to use them. The sundial only tells you the day-time intervals, however. People called these intervals **watches** (from the fact that certain people had the task of watching the time pass and in some cases, watching out for intruders or the enemy). In the earliest Hebrew day, there were six watches: three dark; from sunset to midnight, from midnight to three in the morning, and from three to sunrise. The three light watches were morning, from sunrise till about 10 in the morning; "the heat of the day," from 10 to about 2 in the afternoon; and the "cool of the day," from 2 until sunset.

In the New Testament years, people divided the night into four watches: from sunset to 9 at night; from 9 to midnight; from midnight to 3 in the morning; and from 3 to sunrise. There were four **hours** of daylight

---

hour comes from the Greek word ὥρα *(hora)* and the Latin word *hora* = time of day

---

Morning began with the "third" hour from sunrise to 9 in the morning, then came the "sixth" hour from 9 to noon, then the "ninth" hour from noon to 3 in the afternoon, ending with the "twelfth" hour from 3 to sunset.

The Chinese day began at 11 at night and had 12 periods of 2 hours each. Each of these double hours had 8 periods equal to 15 minutes each.

The ancient Egyptians in the 4th century B.C. were the first people we know of to divide the complete "day" (daylight and night time) into equal parts. They divided the night (from sunset to sunrise) into twelve parts. Astronomer-priests measured the passing of these parts by watching certain stars rise on the eastern horizon. They divided daylight (from sunrise to sunset) into 10 parts. A shadow clock like a sundial kept track of these 10 parts. There were 2 other parts which were neither day or night. One was dawn, just before sunrise. The other was dusk, just after sunset. These 2 parts, the 10 daytime and 12 nighttime parts made up their 24-part day.

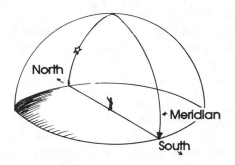

A Star Crossing the Meridian

---

meridian comes from the Latin word *meridiem* = mid-day

Noon and midnight become the dividing lines when you separate the day into two 12-hour parts. Time occurring after midnight is "morning." Time after mid-day is "afternoon." Remember that the Sun casts a shadow at noon which points to the north. Imagine a north-south line from this shadow continuing as far behind and as far in front of you as you can see and right overhead. Not only does the Sun cross the north-south line on the ground every day, it crosses the same line in the sky, at the same time. When it is right on the line, it is noon. The Sun at noon is in the middle of its daytime journey. For this reason, we call the extended north-south line in the sky the **meridian.**

If the Sun hasn't reached the meridian yet, the hours are called *ante **meridiem*** = before mid-day (A.M.). The "morning" hours which occur after midnight and before noon are A.M. hours. 12 A.M. = midnight. We call hours after noon *post **meridianus*** = after mid-day (P.M.). The "afternoon" hours which occur after mid-day and before midnight are P.M. hours. For example, 10 P.M. = 10 hours after noon, or 10 at night. In this next project you can make use of the Sun's movements to tell time by building a sundial.

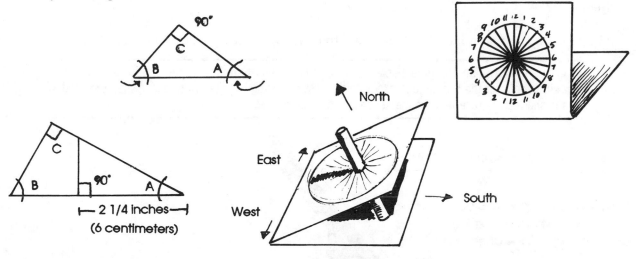

─────────── **Project 10: Making a Sundial** ───────────

MATERIALS

piece of cardboard 8½ x 11 inches or 22 x 28 centimeters (notebook-paper size)

map showing the latitude for where you live

protractor

drawing compass

tape

pair of scissors

drinking straw

pen or pencil

25

PROCEDURE

1. Cut a 4 x 8½ inch (10 x 22 centimeter) piece from the cardboard.

2. Fold the cardboard in half so that it sits up as shown. The part that is standing up is the FACE. The part underneath is the BASE.

3. Make a 3 inch (8 centimeter) diameter circle using the compass in the center of the front of the face.

4. Divide the circle into 24, 15° sections using the protractor and label the sections as shown. Be sure that your vertical line (12) is really straight up and down.

5. Poke a hole in the exact center of the circle drawing large enough for the straw to fit through.

6. Cut out one triangle with these dimensions and label it.

7. Draw a line on the triangle 2¼ inches (6 centimeters) from Angle A, this line should make a 90° angle.

8. Tape this triangle onto the back of the FACE next to the hole so that the line drawn on the triangle points to the hole and Angle A fits into the fold between the FACE and the BASE, and Angle B is on the top.

9. Push the straw through the hole so that it sticks out about 2 inches or 5 centimeters in the front and about 1½ inches or 4 centimeters in the back. The straw should match up with the line drawn on the triangle. Tape the straw in place onto the triangle and tape the triangle onto the base making sure it is vertical.

10. Place your finished sun dial on a flat, level surface with the straw pointing north.

---

gnomon comes from the Greek word γνωμων *(gnomon)* = that by which a thing is known

---

OBSERVATIONS

The stick in the shadow stick projects and in the sun dial "tells the time." For this reason we call it the **gnomon.** Note the position of the gnomon's shadow every hour on the hour. Be careful not to move the sundial. Compare your results with a clock. Why does the gnomon have to point to the north? Will this sundial be accurate in all seasons?

The Romans used sundials. In Elizabethan times, people used pocket sundials.

The gnomon in Egyptian Sun time markers was slightly different from the vertical ones in use elsewhere. At dawn, people set the Sun time marker with its crossbar facing the east. At midday, when the shadow was the shortest, they turned the marker around to face the west.

Egyptian shadow clock, circa 1000 B.C.

You place it with the cross-bar in the east during the morning and in the west in the afternoon.

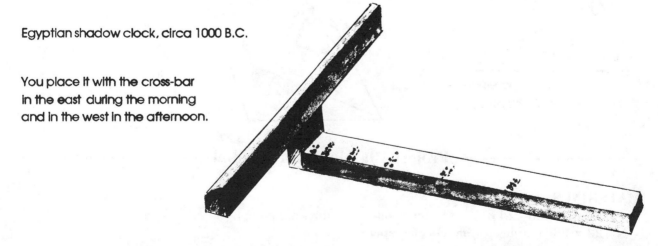

Here's a handy timepiece that combines the Egyptian time marker and the Sundial. Hold a pencil with your thumb while your hand is pointing horizontally. The angle of the pencil should be as close to that of your latitude as you can manage.

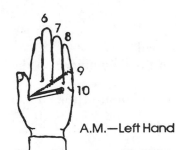

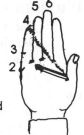

A.M.—Left Hand

P.M.—Right Hand

Hand pointing west, pencil pointing north

Hand pointing east, pencil pointing north

clock comes from the French word *cloche* = bell
o'clock means "of the hour."

One of the first clocks made its appearance around 1550 B.C. It was the creation of the Egyptian astronomer **Amenemhet** for **King Amenophis I** (c. 1545–1525 B.C.). The clock was a big bucket which was filled with water at nightfall up to a marked line. A small hole near the bottom of the bucket allowed the water to trickle out slowly into another container. On the inside of the big bucket were statuettes of gods and goddesses which appeared at certain times as the water level kept getting lower. At night the pharaoh could tell the time by feeling raised lines inside the bucket. Amenemhet noted that a winter night was 14 hours long and a summer night was 12 hours long. You can make your own version of this water clock in the next project.

We call water clocks **clepsydra** from two Greek words $\kappa\lambda\epsilon\pi\tau\eta\varsigma$ *(cleptes)* = a thief, and $\dot{\upsilon}\delta o\rho$ *(hydor)* = water.

Project 11: Making Water Clocks

MATERIALS

1 small paper cup

drinking straw

aluminum foil pie dish

1 gallon paper paint bucket

1 small container

stack of books

nail

toothpick

water

pencil

tape

PROCEDURE

1. Put a hole in the side of the paint bucket near the bottom with the nail.

2. Set the paint bucket on a stack of books on top of a table with the small container on the table below the large container to catch the water.

3. Decorate the upside-down paper cup and tape a toothpick on to the bottom of the cup so that the toothpick sticks out as a pointer.

4. Fill the paint bucket with water.

5. Set the paper cup inside a foil pie dish and float the dish on the water in the paint bucket so that the toothpick points to the rim of the paint bucket.

6. Pencil a line on the inside of the paint bucket after 5 minutes to show where the toothpick is pointing.

7. Repeat every 5 minutes until all the water has gone out.

OBSERVATIONS

How accurate and useful is your water clock? What problems might exist in very cold or very hot weather?

A Sand-Filled Hour Glass   Sand doesn't freeze, doesn't evaporate and is in a sealed glass container so no dirt can get in and block the flow. The French monk **Luiprand,** who lived at Chartres in the eighth century, invented the hourglass. In 807 **Charlemagne** (742–814) ordered a sandglass so large that he only needed to turn it once every 12 hours.

Archimedes (287-212 B.C.) made the first clock that didn't require water, sand, or Sun. Using a clock like the one **Cleopatra** may have used, Archimedes replaced the water and substituted a weight for the floating piston. In the fourteenth century people built large clocks of this type, replacing the piston and shaft with gears. The weights pulled at the gears from long ropes. Since the weights needed plenty of room to pull, these clocks were in tall towers. The big clock at Rouen in Normandy, France was built in 1389. It was there when **Joan of Arc** was on trial in that city. It is still in use today (its parts have had to be changed over the years). Cuckoo clocks work the same way. Grandfather clocks use a pendulum with the weights making the time more accurate by releasing the weight for a moment with one swing, then holding it up with the next. The device which held and released the weight is an **escapement.** The clicking sound of the escapement holding and releasing is the tick-tock we hear.

All clocks until 1687 had only the hour hand and counted only hours and quarter hours.

Clock showing only hours. German, 1643

How old are you in minutes? How old are you in hours?

28

The Minute   In the Babylonian division of a circle, you can divide each of the 360° into smaller sections called **minutes.** There are 60 minutes (60') in 1°. While these minutes are meant to measure space and not time, we have borrowed the term and its size. There are 60 minutes of time in an hour. In 1687, clocks started using the minute hand.

The Second   You can divide the degree in a circle even smaller than a minute. Each minute contains 60 **seconds** (60"). Just as there are 60 seconds of space to 1 minute of space, so there are 60 seconds of time to 1 minute of time.

---

minute comes from the Latin word *minuta* = small
second comes from the middle English and French word *second* taken from the Latin word *secundus* = the following, or next in order

---

Here on the face of a clock are: the 360° of the ancient Babylonians; the hours, minutes and seconds of several cultures; and on some versions, the calendar. Clocks we wear on our wrists are called **watches** because they tell us the time of the "watches" our ancestors used to observe.

Telling Time at Night   In one day, the celestial hemisphere makes one complete turn carrying the Sun with it bringing day and night. We can use the stars around the pole stars. In this next project you can use the circumpolar stars to help you tell time at night.

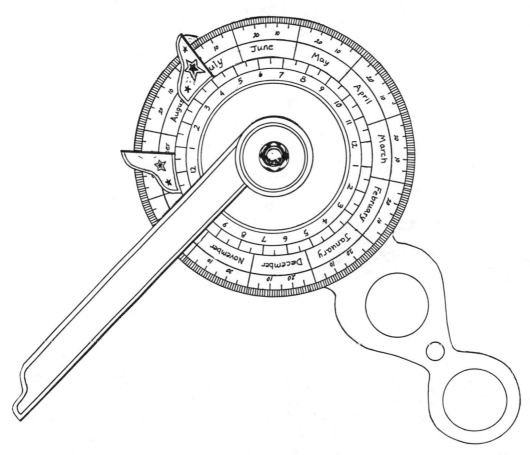

Project 12: Making a Night Clock (Nocturnal)

MATERIALS

thin, stiff cardboard
metal grommet
felt-tip pen
scissors

ruler
protractor
access to a photocopier with enlarger

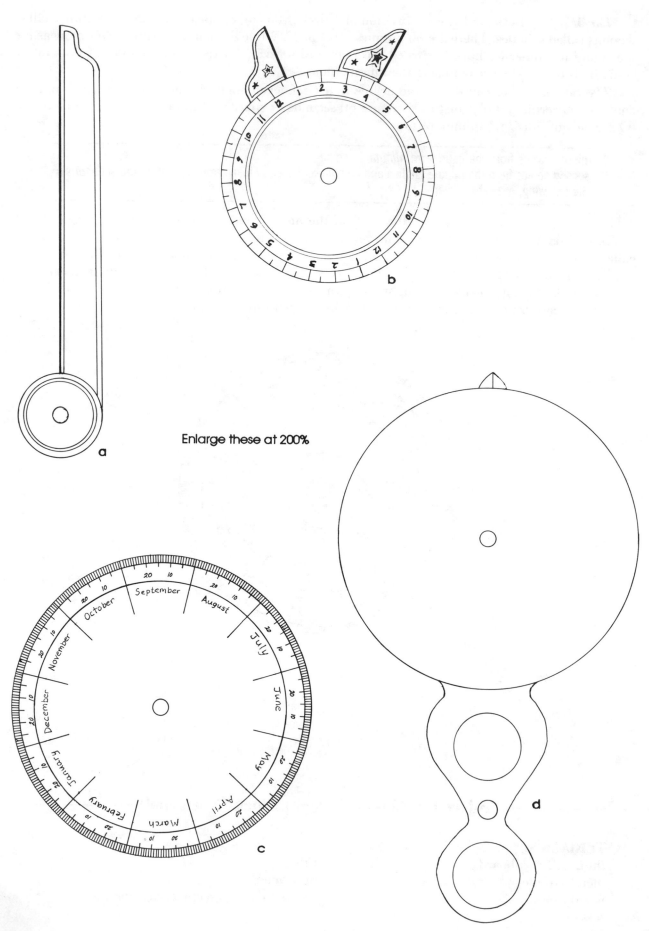

Enlarge these at 200%

PROCEDURE

1. Photocopy the three parts of the nocturnal, glue them onto the cardboard and cut them out. You may wish to enlarge the parts when you photocopy them.

2. Attach the time and date dial, then the pointer, with the metal grommet. Be sure the dial and pointer can move freely and that you can see through the sighting hole.

USING YOUR NOCTURNAL

Set the date by lining it up with the star at the top of the nocturnal (check the 2 stars and the shading on the handle). Hold the nocturnal so that it is vertical. Look at Polaris through the sighting hole. Line up the pointer with the two pointer stars, Dubhe and Merak in Ursa Major (the Big Dipper) or one of the two guardian stars Kochab and Pherkad in Ursa Minor (the Little Dipper). The top edge of the pointer will line up next to the correct time on the time and date dial. (Adjust for daylight-saving time, if necessary).

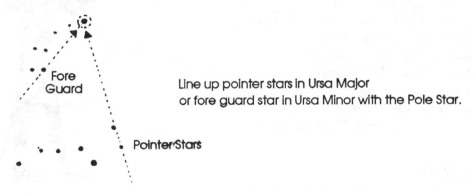

Line up pointer stars in Ursa Major
or fore guard star in Ursa Minor with the Pole Star.

OBSERVATION

With a combination of a sundial and a nocturnal you can keep up with the passing of time by making use of the movements of the heavens.

Sidereal Time Remember the experiment of Leonardo da Vinci in which you watched the stars move past a certain point on the landscape? If you were to do that experiment again, this time marking the first position of the star before it moves and waiting until the next night until it returns to that exact spot, you will have measured the length of one day, according to star time. A star day is 23 hours, 56 minutes, and 4 seconds long. We call this unit of time measurement **sidereal time.**

Synodic Time If instead you chose to measure the time from sunset to sunset or sunrise to sunrise, you would not need to wait for the Sun to return to its same place in the sky, like the star in sidereal time. You would need for the Sun to return to its same relationship to you—rising, setting, noon, etc. The length of this day, the time between the same relationships, is 24 hours.

If you see the Moon next to a certain star and you wait while it goes through its phases and comes back again to that star, it won't be quite in the phase it was when you first saw it. You will have measured a **sidereal month** which is 27 days, 7 hours, 43 minutes, and 11.5 seconds (27.32166 days).

A **synodic month** is the time it takes for the Moon to return to the same phase it left a month ago. This takes 29 days, 12 hours, 44 minutes, and 29 seconds, or 29½ days (29.53059 days).

---

sidereal comes from the Latin word *sidus* = star
synodic comes from the Greek word συνοδος *synodos* = coming together, meeting

---

You use the synodic amounts in calculating days and in producing calendars. You use the sidereal times for locating stars on the celestial hemisphere as you can see in Chapter 2.

The father of time is Cronos, the ancient one. He is the Sun of Ouranos (the Sky) and Gaea (Mother Earth). Cronos is also the god of agriculture, thus time and agriculture have always been connected.

From Cronos and Rhea (the daughter of Gaea) came Zeus (Jupiter). The Romans recognized in their god Saturnus (Saturn) many of the qualities of the Greek god Cronos, although they were two different beings. The Roman feast of Saturnalia held in his honor lasted from five to seven days in December. You often see Saturnus with a sickle or curved garden-knife as a sign that he was the first to teach the people how to trim the vine and olive. You also see Cronos as the god of the harvest with a sickle. Sometimes he has an hourglass with him and a long beard: "Father Time." From this god's name we get our words **chronological, chronicle, chronometer,** and **chronic.** (From this god's children we get most of our constellation stories, and the names of many of the days of the week.)

WHAT IS TIME?

The shadow on the dial
The striking of the clock
The running of the sand
Day and Night, Summer and Winter
Months, Years, Centuries—
These are but arbitrary and
outward signs, the measure
of time, not time itself.
Time is the life of the soul.
                    —H. W. Longfellow

Thoth

READING MORE
Burns, Marilyn. *This Book Is About Time.* Boston: Little, Brown and Company, 1978.

Section 4:   CALENDARS

Lunar and Solar Calendars, Ancient and Modern   Our word **calendar** comes from the Roman practice of announcing the new Moon and therefore the new month. A certain official had the task of watching for the first signs of the approaching new Moon in order for the sacrifices in the temple to take place which officially welcomed in the new month. To summon the common people to the Capitol, the high priest would cry out **"Calo"** which means in Latin, *"I call you to assemble."* The Romans called the first day of the month the **calends** after this custom.

A true solar year, where the Sun returns to its starting point in the seasons, is 365 days, 5 hours, 48 minutes, and 46 seconds long (or 365.242199 days) which is nearly 365¼ days. A lunar year of twelve synodic months of 29.5 days adds up to only 354 days—11¼ days too short. Since we rely both on the Sun and the Moon to determine our calendar, we have struggled over thousands of years to make the two different measurements work together. The ingredients don't fit. The year ends up being either too long or too short. To avoid this situation, calendar makers have added extra days or taken some away.

Lunar Calendars   The first calendar makers began their work around 3000 B.C.. They chose the Moon as the basis for their calendars, since a lunar month of 29½ days was an obvious measurement. But how could you have half a day? One solution was to have 6 months of 29 days each and 6 months of 30 days each. The months would alternate so that one month would have 30 days, the next 29, followed by one with 30 and so on. This is a typical lunar calendar. The early Babylonians used lunar years such as these. Jewish, Islamic, and Chinese calendars still use them.

The Solar Calendar   In Egypt, the god Thoth, the divine scribe and father of astronomy, kept watch over the calendar. Agriculture, time, the activity of the heavens, and religion all weave together in the calendar.

The Sun, as source of life and the seasons, became the source of the calendar for the ancient Egyptians. Their earliest calendars contained 12 months of 30 days each. Their calendar was 5 days too short, so they inserted the 5 missing days at the end of the year as holy days. These 5 days honored the birth of the five children of **Geb,** the god of Earth and **Nut,** the goddess of the sky: **Osirus, Horus, Set, Isis** and **Nepthys.**

Osiris was king of Egypt and the Lord of Life. His wife was Isis, who brought crops to the fields and children to the home. Set, the brother of Osiris and husband of Nepthys was jealous and plotted to murder his brother by having him sealed in a coffin and set adrift on the Nile. Isis set off in search of the casket and when she found it, she restored her husband to life. Again Set attempted to murder his brother by cutting him into 14 pieces and throwing them into the Nile. Horus, the son of Isis and Osiris, assembled all 14 of the parts of his father that his mother had found in the 14 days from the full moon to the last quarter. Horus then prepared his father to receive the gift of life. This gift would only be possible if the body had been preserved intact. Horus reunited the soul to his father's body. Osiris rose from the dead and ruled the world, crossing it in his Sun boat by day and at night on the Milky Way, the heavenly Nile. Osiris reigned as lord of the dead with his wife and son. There he presided over the judgment of the soul in the journey from death to new life.

The story of Isis and Osiris is one of the oldest and most important among the stories associated with the stars. There are celestial rhythms connected with this story which made it the source of a second Egyptian calendar. The Egyptians used this calendar along with the one containing 360 days and the five divine birthdays.

Practically all cultures, whether in the northern or southern parts of the world, can see the group of stars called **Orion.** In the north, you see this group in the winter; in the south, you see it in the summer. Orion stands on the Milky Way. So does another star group to its south, **Canis Major.** You can find Canis Major very easily because of the exceptionally bright star in it. This sparkling blue gem of a star is **Sirius,** the brightest star in the entire sky.

Orion and Canis Major

To the Egyptians, the Milky Way was the heavenly Nile, Orion was Osiris sailing on both the heavenly Nile and the one in Egypt. Following close behind on the Nile, as she had done so many times before, was the goddess Isis. Sirius is her star and its name in Greek is **Sothis** = Dog Star.

Just as we do, the Egyptians saw Sothis (Sirius) in the evening skies beginning in winter until she vanished from view with Osiris (Orion) in the spring. Just after the beginning of summer in June, Sothis would once again come into view just before sunrise. On that day the priests of ancient Egypt celebrated three risings: first the rising of Sothis, second the sunrise, and third, the gradual rise of the Nile River. These three events marked the beginning of the New Year. Sothis had come as the star of Isis to announce that Osiris had returned to his people. He had brought again the life-giving waters of the Nile. Egypt and her people would prosper for another year.

It took 70 days from the passing of Sothis from the night sky in spring to her heliacal rising in the summer. As part of the service for the dead, priests prepared the body for the soul's return, just as it had been when Horus prepared his father's body. It took 70 days for the soul to pass from death to reunion with the body at burial. During those 70 days, priests soaked the body in a brine solution as part of the embalming process.

Whenever a star or planet rises just before the Sun, we call that an **heliacal** rising, from the Greek word ἥλιος *(helios)* = the Sun.

The heliacal rising of Sothis as well as the flooding of the Nile were major events in the Egyptian calendar. However, since the calendar only had 365 days, the missing ¼ day would soon add up. The result was that date of the beginning of the year with its observance of the heliacal rising of Sothis and the flooding the Nile, was occurring weeks before the actual events. Once in a while, the Egyptian year of 365 days and the solar year matched the date and events perfectly.

The Egyptian Year = 365 days or 1460/4
The Sothis Year (the Solar Year) = 365¼ days or 1461/1

1,460 Sothis Years = 1,461 Egyptian Years. That means that after 1,460 solar years of 365¼ days, the events of the heliacal rising of Sothis and the rising of the Nile will occur on the date they are supposed to according to the Egyptian calendar of 365 days. Every 1,460 years this happens. This period is called the Sothic Cycle. The oldest date we have in history is the year 4241 B.C.. This date happens to be the beginning of a Sothic Cycle. The two calendars fit that year.

Our calendar shares its history with other calendars. It is the result of the effort of many people and various cultures. Originally it was a basic luni/solar calendar with all the strengths and problems that come with using the different rhythms of the Sun and the Moon. By the time it reached Rome, it looked like the calendar listed under Roman in the months of the year chart.

Leap year comes from the days when the year used to begin on the first day of the week. After a leap year, the year began on the second day of the week. This "leaping over" of a week day gave leap year its name.

Julius Caesar (102–44 B.C.) made the most far-reaching and long-lasting reforms in the calendar. The ideas suggested to Caesar by the astronomer **Sosigenes** from Alexandria in Egypt included some of the ideas put forth almost 200 years earlier by **Ptolemy II Euergetes.** One of them was his idea of a leap year. Caesar inserted the extra day between February 23rd and 24th, six days before the Calends of March. He also rearranged the months to start with Januarius instead of Martius. Januarius is the month sacred to the god **Janus** who has two faces, one looking ahead and one looking behind. In 44 B.C., two years after Caesar's death, **Mark Antony** renamed the fifth month **Quinctilis,** the month in which Caesar was born, **Julius** in honor of this great Roman leader. Caesar's calendar, served humanity faithfully for over 1,600 years. It was only 11 minutes and 14 seconds too long.

The next emperor **Augustus Caesar** (63 B.C.–14 A.D.) moved some of the days around from one month to another. He shortened February by one day, and increased Sextilis by two. Sextilis was the month which had the most dates celebrating the great deeds of the emperor. For that, the Senate renamed it **Augustus.** They took a day from September and added it to October. They also took a day that was in November and added it to December. In 321 A.D., the emperor **Constantine** (288–337 A.D.) changed the day of rest from Saturday to Sunday. He also made the seven-day week official.

The Gregorian Calendar In 1582, people used an analemma to show **Pope Gregory XIII** (1502–1585) that the exquinox and solstices did not occur on the dates given for them on the calendar. The extra 11 minutes and 14 seconds in Julius Caesar's calendar had been steadily adding up at the rate of one day extra in 128 years.

EGYPTIAN 4000 BC (Lunisolar)		MAYA		JEWISH (Lunar)		MOSLEM 622 AD (Lunar)	
Thoth	30	Pop	20	Nisan	30	Muharram	30
Paophi	30	Uo	20	Iyyar	29	Safar	29
Tybi	30	Zip	20	Sivan	30	Rabi 1	30
Mechir	30	Zotz'	20	Tammuz	29	Rabi 2	29
Pachons	30	Zec	20	Av	30	Jumada 1	30
Payni	30	Xul	20	Ellul	29	Jumada 2	29
Athyr	30	Yaxkin	20	Tishri	30	Rajab	30
Choiak	30	Mol	20	Heshvan	29	Sha'ban	29
Phamenoth	30	Ch'en	20	Kislev	30	Ramadan	30
Pharauithi	30	Yax	20	Tevet	29	Shawwal	29
Epiphi	30	Zac	20	Shevat	30	Dhu al-Qa'dah	30
Mesore	30	Ceh	20	Adar	29	Dhu al-Hijjah	29
Total Days	*360*	Mac	20	*Total Days*	*354*	*Total Days 354*	

EGYPTIAN: plus five days added to the end of one year and the beginning of the next to celebrate the birthdays of the gods:
1. Osiris
2. Horus
3. Set
4. Isis
5. Nephthye

MAYA (continued): Kankin 20, Muan 20, Pax 20, Kayab 20, Cumku 20, *Total Days 360* plus a month of five unlucky days (Uayeb) used with another calendar of 28 weeks with 13 numbered days each

MOSLEM: designed by Muhammed to replace the old luni-solar calendar of the Arabs. The Moslem calendar is totally lunar and does not relate to the Sun or the seasons.

ROMAN 746 AD (Solar Lunar)		JULIAN/AUGUSTAN (Solar Lunar)		GREGORIAN 1582 (Solar Lunar)	
Martius	31	Ianuarius	31	January	31
Aprilis	29	Februarius	29/30	February	28/29
Maius	31	Martius	31	March	31
Iunius	29	Aprilis	30	April	30
Quinctilis	31	Maius	31	May	31
Sextilis	29	Iunius	30	June	30
September	29	Iulius*	31	July	31
October	31	Augustus*	30/31	August	31
November	29	September	30/31	September	30
December	29	October	30/31	October	31
Ianuarius*	29	November	30/31	November	30
Februarius*	28	December	30/31	December	31
Total Days	*355*	*Total Days 365/366*		*Total Days*	*365*

ROMAN: *Added in 712 BC by King Numa. Even numbers were unlucky, so the months had odd numbers of days. The names of the months from Quinctilis through December begin with the Latin word for the numbers five through ten.

JULIAN/AUGUSTAN: *Names given by the emperors Julius and Augustus Caesar. Sosigenes of Alexandria designed the Julian calendar by order of Julius Caesar. This calendar replaced the lunar calendar and made the calendar function regularly by itself. The solar year had 365 ¼ days. The civil year had 365 days. Each fourth year had an extra day.

GREGORIAN: Designed by Pope Gregory XIII. Pope Gregory removed eleven days from the Julian calendar that was in use in order to restore the Vernal Equinox to March 21st. This calendar omits leap year three times in four centuries, provided that you can divide the century by 400. Each year begins on a different day of the week. After 400 years, the pattern repeats itself.

By 1582, the extra days meant that spring began around March 11th instead of March 21st. By papal decree, Pope Gregory removed 10 days from that year's calendar. The result was that October 4th, 1582 was followed by October 15th instead of October 5! This restored the vernal equinox to March 21st. In addition to having a leap year every four years, the Pope decreed that people should omit the leap year three times in four centuries.

A handy month reminder   Say the names of the months in order, counting on your left hand while you point with your right (do the opposite if you are left-handed). Point to the tips of your fingers for the long months, and in between for the short ones. February has the shortest journey for your pointing finger. Start again with August on the tip of your third finger and count backwards ending with December on the tip of your first finger.

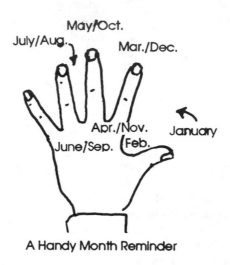

May/Oct.
July/Aug.
Mar./Dec.
Apr./Nov.
January
June/Sep.
Feb.

A Handy Month Reminder

Thirty days hath September, April, June, and November.
All the rest have thirty-one,
except February with twenty-eight and no more,
'till Leap Year comes and it gets one more.

The Julian Period

Joseph Justus Scaliger   (1540–1609), a French chronologist living at the time of Pope Gregory XIII, took three different calendar cycles of time and calculated when they would all begin together and when they would meet again. He found the interval between these two dates to be 7,980 years. This period he called the **Julian Period** after his father **Julius Scaliger** (1484–1558). Using the Julian Period, Joseph Scaliger established the date January 1st, 4713 B.C. as the beginning point of time reckoning. The end of the first Julian Period will be December 31st, 3267. In the Julian system, there are no weeks, months, or years, only day numbers, a day being from noon to noon. Parts of a day appear as decimals carried to as many places as needed depending on the degree of precision required. Individual day numbers show the number of days that have passed since the beginning of the period, that is, since January 1st, 4713 B.C. Here's how to figure out a particular day: e.g., September 21, 1988, the day of Mars' most recent close approach to Earth.

1) Multiply $4713 \times 365.24798 = 1721413.7$
2) Multiply $1988 \times 365.24798 = 726112.98$
3) Calculate the number of days since December 31st, 1988 = 265
4) Add all three figures together
   The Julian Day for September 21, 1988 = 2447791.6

Today, astronomers use Julian Day numbers to list computer-calculated dates of ancient eclipses, and other astronomical events, because by using simple subtraction you can find the interval between dates in different months and years.

A.D., B.C., A.U.C., Etc.   In the United States we abbreviate dates by writing 7/30/89 A.D. day, month, year. In Europe the date is abbreviated 30/7/89 A.D. month, day, year. The A.D. at the end stands for the Latin words **Anno Domini** = Year of Our Lord or the Christian Era. The earliest known use of A.D. was on a document written by Reginald, King of the Isle of Man in 1219. B.C. simply means **Before Christ.** Dates in B.C. are numbered backwards. Julius Caesar lived from 102 to 44 B.C. That means he was born 102 years before the Christian Era and died 44 years before it.

The Romans numbered their years after the founding of Rome which occurred in 753 B.C. The letters **A.U.C.** which stand for the Latin word **Ab Urbe Condita** = from the founding of the city, appeared at the end of the year number showing how long after the finding of the city, the date occurred.

The Islamic calendar gives dates for the Moslem Era starting from the Hegira or the date of the Flight of the Prophet Mohammed from Mecca in 622 A.D.

Counting the years from some point in the past to the present is called a **Long Count.** The Native Americans often used Long Counts to record their history.

Maya and Inca Calendars   In our twentieth century Long Counts, we use four counting positions:
  Weekday: (name of the day) One of seven names for a 7-day period
  Day Number: (day of the month) Number from 1 to 31
  Month: (name of the month) One of twelve names
  Year: (number of years in the Christian Era)
The Maya people of Central America had a unique calendar which calculated Long Counts. In this next project you can see how these calendars worked by making one for yourself.

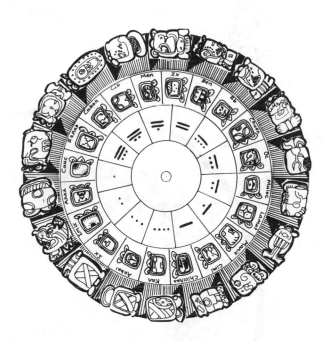

————————————— **Project 13: Making a Mayan Calendar** —————————————

MATERIALS

3 circles from book	paints
paper plate	yarn
stiff paper	scissors
paper fastener	glue
pencil	hole punch
colored pencils	access to a photocopier

PROCEDURE

1. Photocopy the three circles from the book. Cut them out and glue the two small ones onto stiff paper

2. Color in the designs.

3. Glue the large circle onto the paper plate.

4. Attach the two small circles to the paper plate with the paper fastener. Make sure they can move freely.

5. Cut a piece of yarn 1½ times the diameter of the plate. Loop the middle yarn around the paper fastener and bring both ends up to the top of the plate.

6. Punch a hole near the top of the plate. Thread both ends of the yarn through the hole, wrap them around the edge of the plate and through the hole again.

7. Tie the ends of the yarn together at the edge of the plate and a few inches from it so you can hang up your calendar.

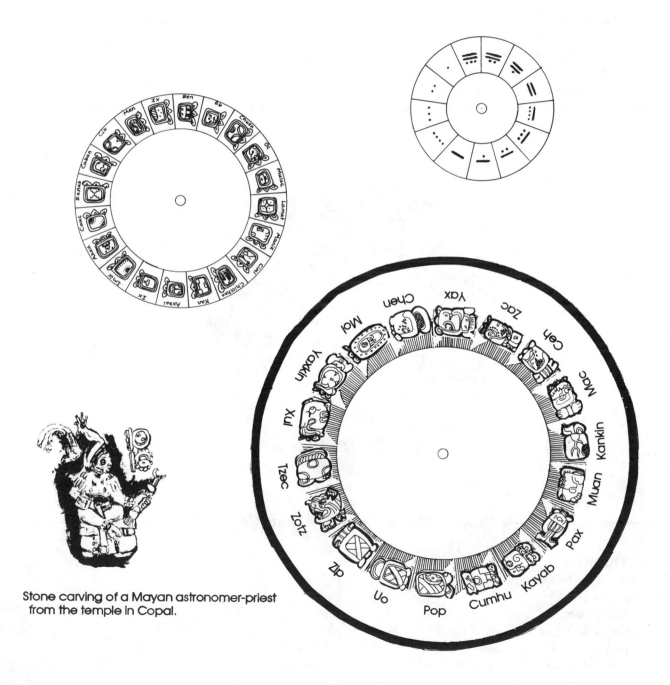

Stone carving of a Mayan astronomer-priest from the temple in Copal.

38

USING YOUR MAYA CALENDAR

Line up the three circles so that the date shown in the book lines up at the top of your calendar. To change the date, move each circle clockwise, one space for each day. To read the date, start with the day circle, then the month, then the year. The arrangement of a 260-day lunar cycle and a 360 + 5–day solar cycle is similar to the two Egyptian calendars, the 360 + 5–day lunar cycle and the 365¼ day Sothis/solar period. With all the combinations possible, the same exact combination would recur only every 19,980 days (52 years).

OBSERVATIONS

The 260-day calendar has been in existence at least since 800 B.C. and is still being used by the Quiche Maya. When **Hernando Cortez** (1485–1546) arrived in Mexico in 1518, the Spaniards were amazed that the Maya could have measured time so well. The Maya calendar agreed precisely with the Spaniards' calendar except that the Maya calendar was missing 10 days!

THE WORLD CALENDAR

First Quarter

	S	M	T	W	T	F	S
Jan.	1	2	3	4	5	6	7
	8	9	10	11	12	13	14
	15	16	17	18	19	20	21
	22	23	24	25	26	27	28
	29	30	31				
Feb.				1	2	3	4
	5	6	7	8	9	10	11
	12	13	14	15	16	17	18
	19	20	21	22	23	24	25
	26	27	28	29	30		
March						1	2
	3	4	5	6	7	8	9
	10	11	12	13	14	15	16
	17	18	19	20	21	22	23
	24	25	26	27	28	29	30

Third Quarter

	S	M	T	W	T	F	S
July	1	2	3	4	5	6	7
	8	9	10	11	12	13	14
	15	16	17	18	19	20	21
	22	23	24	25	26	27	28
	29	30	31				
August				1	2	3	4
	5	6	7	8	9	10	11
	12	13	14	15	16	17	18
	19	20	21	22	23	24	25
	26	27	28	29	30		
Sept.						1	2
	3	4	5	6	7	8	9
	10	11	12	13	14	15	16
	17	18	19	20	21	22	23
	24	25	26	27	28	29	30

Second Quarter

	S	M	T	W	T	F	S
April	1	2	3	4	5	6	7
	8	9	10	11	12	13	14
	15	16	17	18	19	20	21
	22	23	24	25	26	27	28
	29	30	31				
May				1	2	3	4
	5	6	7	8	9	10	11
	12	13	14	15	16	17	18
	19	20	21	22	23	24	25
	26	27	28	29	30		
June						1	2
	3	4	5	6	7	8	9
	10	11	12	13	14	15	16
	17	18	19	20	21	22	23
	24	25	26	27	28	29	30

Fourth Quarter

	S	M	T	W	T	F	S
Oct.	1	2	3	4	5	6	7
	8	9	10	11	12	13	14
	15	16	17	18	19	20	21
	22	23	24	25	26	27	28
	29	30	31				
Nov.				1	2	3	4
	5	6	7	8	9	10	11
	12	13	14	15	16	17	18
	19	20	21	22	23	24	25
	26	27	28	29	30		
Dec.						1	2
	3	4	5	6	7	8	9
	10	11	12	13	14	15	16
	17	18	19	20	21	22	23
	24	25	26	27	28	29	30

**Leap-year day follows June 30th in leap years.

*Year-end day follows December 30th every year.

The World Calendar   There is no calendar today that keeps perfect time. Somewhere along the line the differences between lunar and solar time are going to cause problems and require adjustments in the calendar. In 1914 the International Congress of Commerce asked that people study the possiblity of a new calendar. What this study came up with was the **World Calendar. Elizabeth Achelis** has been a leading supporter of this calendar in which the days of the month are the same every year. Holidays and birthdays fall on the same day of the week every year. Easter is always on Sunday, April 8th. Some people feel that the World Calendar doesn't show a living relationship with the rhythms of nature and the sky. The festivals and the seasons no longer shape the mood and course of the year. They are simply dates. Others feel that the calendar would make it much easier to serve religious, business, and community needs. Take a close look at the calendar yourself and see what you think.

The World Calendar has not been accepted yet. In the meantime in the next project you can make a calendar that you can use every year.

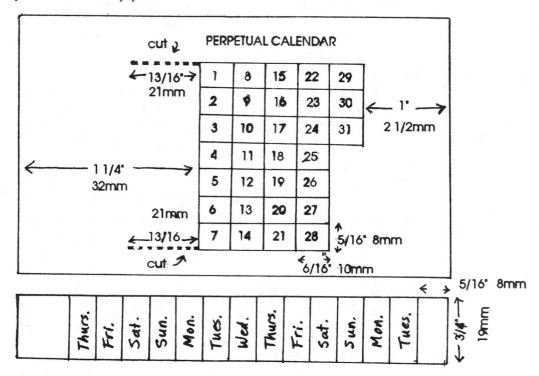

—————————— **Project 14: Making a Perpetual Calendar** ——————————

MATERIALS

2 3 × 5 inch (8 × 13 centimeters) index cards
ruler

colored pencils
razor blade or utility knife
regular pen or pencil

PROCEDURE

1. Copy the numbers shown on one of the index cards using your ruler to help you make the boxes the same sizes shown and to keep them straight.
2. Draw the long strip on the other index card, writing the days of the week in the exact order shown. Use your ruler to help you keep the days within spaces 5/16 inch (8 millimeters) wide.
3. Color in the days of the week using the chart in Section 3 of this chapter.
4. Cut the day strip out, ¾ inch (19 millimeters) wide.
5. Cut two slots along the dotted lines on the first card. If they are about 1³/16 inch (21 millimeters) long they will give the day strip enough room to slide freely.
6. Insert the day strip so the days show in the front.

USING THE PERPETUAL CALENDAR

Line up the day of the week with the day the month starts. If the month begins on Sunday, move the day strip next to Monday. The calendar also works if you know the day of any date in the month. Just line it up.

OBSERVATIONS

Does this calendar work? Why?

Chinese Calendars   The Chinese calendar is one of the world's oldest. While it may not have been the first, the Chinese calendar was thriving by the year 2357 B.C. More people past and present have used the Chinese calendar than any other calendar, including the Gregorian one. The Chinese divided their luni-solar calendar into 24 half months. The New Year began on the first new Moon after the Sun entered the zodiac constellation of Aquarius.

In this next project you can use all that you have learned about calendars to design one of your own.

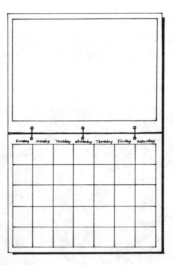

Project 15: Designing Your Own Calendar

MATERIALS

13 sheets of drawing or painting quality
   paper
pencil
ruler
drawing and painting supplies
magazines
fine point felt-tip pens (several colors)
scissors

paper glue
hole punch
perpetual calendar (from Project 14,
   Making a Perpetual Calendar)
almanac
yarn
access to a photocopier

PROCEDURE

1. Using your pencil and ruler, make a grid for 35 days (7 across and 5 down) with the names of the week at the top but no month name or dates. Make 12 photocopies of the grid. Photocopy onto the drawing or painting paper if you can. Otherwise glue the photocopies onto the paper.

2. Label each page with the name of the month. Use the perpetual calendar to fill in the dates.

3. Put all of the months in order, with the blank sheet on top. Punch three holes in the tops and one hole exactly in the middle of the bottom. Tie the pages together loosely with yarn so you can flip them.

4. Illustrate each month:

    a. Pick a color for each season and use it to shade the outer edges of the three months that are in that season.

    b. Color in the name of the days of the week at the top using the colors mentioned in this chapter.

    c. Check the almanac to find out the Moon phases and draw them on the days they occur.

    d. Write in the names of the major festivals of the year on the dates they occur. Include a drawing or symbol for each, if you wish.

    e. Write in important events (births, death, discoveries, etc.) on the dates they occur.

    f. Illustrate the months using the blank page on the back of the calendar for the previous month. Cut out pictures from magazines, take your own photographs or make drawings of things that happen during that month, either where you live or somewhere else in the world.

OBSERVATION

What else can calendars do for you besides simply recording dates?

READING MORE

Chase, William D. and Helen M. *Chase's Annual Events.* Chicago: Contemporary Books, Inc. (Published for each year).
Irwin, Keith G. *The 365 Days: The Story of Our Calendar.* New York: Thomas Y. Crowell Co., 1963.

Horsehead Nebula. *Photo courtesy of Observatoire de Haute Provence*

Chapter 2: LIKE DIAMONDS IN THE SKY

Section 1: THE ZODIAC

The Path of the Sun   The apparent journey of the Sun passes across the celestial hemisphere and therefore in front of some of the stars on it. When the Sun is "high" in the summer, it passes in front of the higher stars, in the winter, the lower ones and at the equinoxes, the middle ones. The star groups visited by the Sun remain the same year after year. There are 12 of them and because they alone are hosts to the visiting Sun, they have the honor of belonging to a unique collection of star groups. This band of stars is the **zodiac.** Stars which form a group we call a **constellation.**

The zodiac constellations form the backdrop against which the Moon and planets also travel. Since the Sun's light outshines the stars around it, you can't see where the Sun is so you have to calculate the Sun's position. During an eclipse you can see the Sun and the stars together. The royal path of the Sun, Moon, and planets is also the path of the eclipses. For this reason, we call the Sun's path the **ecliptic.**

---

zodiac comes from the Greek word ζωος *(zoos)* = living, since the Sun brings life
constellation comes from the Latin words **con** = with, and *stella* = star. There are 12 zodiac constellations and 76 other constellations, 88 in all
ecliptic comes from the Greek word ἐκλείπω *(ekleipo)* = to leave out

---

Armillary Sphere, Middle Ages.

Where do the Sun, Moon, planets, and stars go when they set and where do they come from when they rise? People once believed that the heavenly bodies entered the mountains in the west, traveled under the Earth, and re-emerged in the east. To the Egyptians, a goddess swallowed the Moon at night and gave birth to it at moonrise. For the Egyptians a boat carried the Sun across the sky; for the Greeks, a chariot carried the Sun. Soon people came to believe that the sky must be larger than half a sphere and that the Earth must also be more vast than one's own country. These ideas inspired the picture of the sky as a complete globe surrounded by stars. The stars set when the celestial sphere moved them out of your line of sight and into someone else's. In the same way, the celestial sphere carried the Sun across the sky causing sunrise and sunset. When it was day for you, those on the other side of the Earth's globe would be having night.

In this new picture, the zodiac was a band of constellations wrapped around the inside of the celestial sphere. The ecliptic passed along this band, right in its center. This next project will show you what the zodiac looks like as the celestial sphere moves it across the sky.

Zodiac Grid

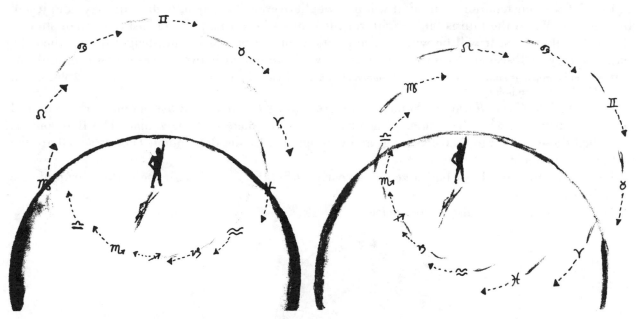

—————— **Project 16:   Sketching the Daily Movement of the Zodiac** ——————

MATERIALS

zodiac grid

7 Sheets of tracing paper

pen

colored pencils or crayons

PROCEDURE

1. Place a sheet of tracing paper over the zodiac grid.

2. Draw the horizon line using a colored pencil or crayon. This line does not represent the whole Earth. It shows only the part you are on so don't draw it as a complete circle.

3. Draw yourself standing just below the horizon line so your feet are above the center point of all the concentric circles and your head is below the two concentric circles close together above the horizon line.

4. Write the symbol for *Gemini* at the top where the seventh circle crosses the vertical line.

5. Write the symbol for *Sagittarius* where the first circle meets the vertical line.

6. Write the symbol for *Taurus* on the right where the sixth circle crosses the line on the right of the vertical line.

7. Write the symbol for *Cancer* on the left where the sixth circle crosses the line on the left of the vertical line.

8. Continue on in this way until you have written all the symbols as shown: *Leo* and *Aries* on the fifth, *Virgo* and *Pisces* on the fourth, right where the circle meets the horizon line. *Libra* and *Aquarius* go below the horizon line on the third circle and *Scorpius* and *Capricornus* on the second.

9. Draw little arrows from each constellation to the next, pointing counterclockwise. This is the daily east to west movement you saw in Chapter 1. Label this drawing #1.

10. Make six more drawings, but each time you make a new chart, move each constellation counterclockwise to the next line on the grid. Don't change the constellations from the circles they are on, just imagine that the circles are moving, carrying the constellations to a new spot.

11. Place all seven sheets in front of you and observe what has happened.

OBSERVATIONS

You have just made a record of the passage of the zodiac constellations in one 24-hour period. What has happened? The little figure of yourself is looking south into the daytime sky. Below the horizon line it is night. When a constellation is straight over your head, it is noon. Notice the difference between when Gemini is in the noon position and when Sagittarius is there. If the Sun is passing in front of the constellation Gemini, it will be straight overhead at noon, high in the sky, and it will be summer. When the Sun is "in" Sagittarius, it is at its lowest angle at noon rather than shining down directly on us. It will be winter. The positions of the Sun at its mid-height occur when the Sun is either in Pisces or Virgo. At these times we have our in-between seasons, spring and autumn.   This project is adapted from, *Sterne Schauen Dich An*, by Heidi Keller-von Asten, Dornach: Verlag Walter Keller, 1973. Used with permission.

The Zodiac Constellations   Sometime before 3000 B.C., Akkadian astronomer-priests moved into Syria bringing with them their ideas of the celestial sphere and the zodiac. The Babylonians absorbed these ideas into their teachings and writings such as the Babylonian Tablets which are the oldest written records we have.

The Egyptians may have had a zodiac as early as 5000 B.C., although the earliest example we have is from 250 B.C.

The Chinese zodiac is also quite ancient.

The Chinese Zodiac.

The constellations of the zodiac vary in size and brightness. Virgo is the largest, Cancer is the smallest. Leo and Taurus are the brightest, Cancer and Aquarius are the dimmest. Each constellation can just about fit into a space of 30°, or ¹⁄₁₂ of the complete circle around the inside of the celestial sphere. Thus, the Sun spends about one month (or ¹⁄₁₂ of a year) in front of each of these 12 constellations.

From your project you can see that the sphere of the heavens and the sphere of the Earth each have an upper half and a lower half. Both halves are equal. The line that divides them into two hemispheres (half spheres) is called the **equator** which means *equal*. In Chapter 3 you will find out how you can further divide and map the Earth and the sky.

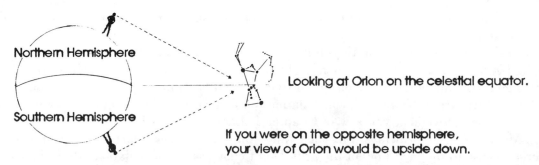

Looking at Orion on the celestial equator.

If you were on the opposite hemisphere, your view of Orion would be upside down.

The Earth equator is in the middle of our globe. It is 90° down from the top of the world, which we call the **North Pole** and 90° up from the bottom of the world, which we call the **South Pole.** Imagine that these poles point to the top and the bottom of the celestial sphere which also has a north and a south pole. **Polaris,** the North Star, marks the North Pole of the sky and Octanis marks the South Pole. Constellations which travel in small circles around these poles are called **circumpolar constellations.** Ursa Major (which contains the Big Dipper) and Crux (which contains the Southern Cross) are circumpolar constellations.

circumpolar comes from the Latin word *circum* = around, and the Greek word πολος *(polos)* = pivot around which something turns

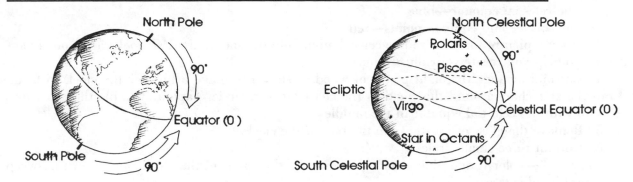

If you move 90° from the pole stars you will find the celestial equator. Pisces and Virgo are on that part of the ecliptic that crosses the celestial equator. Gemini is above the celestial equator for those living on the Earth's northern hemisphere, and Sagittarius is below the celestial equator. For southern hemisphere observers, the view is the opposite. In this next project you can track the Sun and Moon in the zodiac.

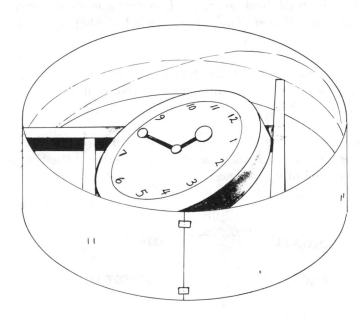

—— **Project 17: Showing How the Sun and Moon Move in the Zodiac** ——

MATERIALS

star chart from this book	saw
tape	staple gun
colored pencils	access to a photocopier, one with
books or charts with illustrations of	enlarging capabilities
zodiac constellations	paper
an old clock	
8 pieces of wood, approximately 1 foot	
(30 centimeters) long	

PROCEDURE

1. Photocopy the star chart from this book. Enlarge it so that the celestial equator is about 3 feet (1 meter) long.

2. Locate and color these places on the star chart:

    a. the **ecliptic**—orange

    b. the **celestial equator**—blue

    c. the **solstice** and **equinox points**—red

3. Draw a picture for each zodiac constellation onto the star chart. Use books and your imagination to help you create your illustrations.

4. Cut and arrange the eight pieces of wood as shown to make a box for the clock to fit in. Wrap the star chart around the wood so the chart forms a circle. Tape and staple the chart into position with the celestial equator in the middle.

5. Remove the glass or plastic from the face of the clock.

6. Cut out three small circles:

    a. *Earth*—color it and glue it onto the center of the hands of the clock (on top of the sweep second hand if there is one).

    b. *Sun*—color it and glue it onto the end of the hour hand.

    c. *Moon*—color it and glue it onto the end of the minute hand.

Be sure both hands can move freely when you turn the setting knob on the back of the clock.

7. Place the clock inside the wooden box at an angle so that the face of the clock is even with the ecliptic and the hands point to it.

8. Turn the setting knob on the back of the clock to demonstrate the movement of the Sun and Moon through the zodiac. For a slower demonstration wind or plug in the clock if it still works.

OBSERVATIONS

In your model of the zodiac, it takes the Sun one hour (month) to go through one zodiac constellation and twelve hours (year) to go through all twelve zodiac constellations. How long does it take the Moon to do the same?

To help you understand the combined motions of the daily movement of the zodiac as the celestial sphere turns and the monthly or yearly movement of the Moon and the Sun in front of the zodiac, you can make a moving model of the zodiac.

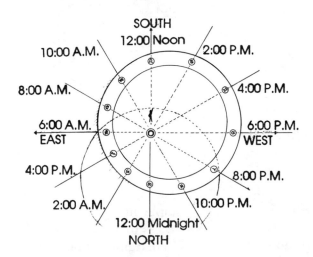

———— **Project 18: Making a Moveable Star Chart (Planesphere)** ————

MATERIALS

zodiac grid

clear plastic sheet

metal grommets

permanent ink felt-tip pens

12 self-adhesive paper dots
    approximately ¼ inch (60 millimeters)

cardboard or stiff paper, 8½ × 11
    inches (22 × 28 centimeters)

X-acto knife	grease pencil
glue	pen and colored pencils
ruler	access to a photocopier

PROCEDURE

1. Photocopy the zodiac grid and glue it to a piece of cardboard or stiff paper.

2. Draw yourself and color in the horizon on the project sheet just as you did on the blank page in Project 16, Sketching the Movement of the Zodiac. Do not write in the zodiac symbols or make any arrows.

3. Fill in the other information on the zodiac grid as shown:

   a. *times*—be sure to include A.M. and P.M.

   b. *cardinal directions*—these should be in a different color than the other writing.

   c. *celestial equator*—this can be shaded a bit with a color to make it more visible.

4. Cut a circle from the plastic sheet 4¾ inches (12 centimeters) in diameter, the same size as the horizon circle.

5. Place the plastic disk on the zodiac grid so that you position the *inner circle* with its top touching the top of the outermost circle on the zodiac grid. The bottom of the plastic disk should be touching the bottom of the innermost circle on the zodiac grid. The two points where the celestial equator meets the horizon on the zodiac grid should also touch the inner circle of the plastic disk. Keeping the plastic disk in place, carefully mark on it using the felt-tip pen:

   a. the point on the zodiac grid which is the center of all its circles.

   b. the lines from the first circle on the zodiac grid to the place where they meet the inner circle of the plastic disk. Use a ruler to help you.

   c. the point on the plastic disk in between its inner circle and its outer edge at the places where the lines on the zodiac grid continue beyond the lines you have drawn on the plastic disk. These points mark the positions of the zodiac constellations.

6. Place a paper dot on each of the zodiac positions.

7. Cut a hole with the X-acto knife in the plastic disk, the zodiac grid, and the cardboard where you have made mark a. on the plastic disk (where it meets the center of all the circles on the zodiac grid).

8. Place a metal grommet through the hole and bend its edges over so the plastic turns freely.

9. Turn the plastic disk until you position it as it was in step #4. On the top dot, write the symbol for Gemini. Turn the plastic disk clockwise until each dot and line below it overlaps the top vertical line. Mark the symbols on each dot in order following Gemini (Cancer, Leo, etc.).

OBSERVATIONS

Use the grease pencil to draw the symbol for the Sun or the Moon to answer the following questions. To erase, use your thumb or a piece of paper towel but don't smear the cardboard part of the planesphere.

1. What time does the Sun rise in June?

2. What time does the Sun set in June?

3. What time does the full Moon rise in March?

4. What time does the full Moon set in in March?

You can make up your own questions to answer with your planesphere. You will be using it to help you in this book from time to time. This project is adapted from *Sterne Schauen Dich An* by Heidi Keller-von Asten, Dornach: Verlag Walter Keller, 1973. Used with permission.

Remember, we tell time by the position of the Sun, not the Moon.

Constellations and Signs   You may have heard the term **signs of the zodiac,** and have wondered if they were the same as the **constellations of the zodiac.** They were the same once. In ancient Greece, spring began when the Sun reached the Vernal Equinox point. In those days, this point was in the constellation Aries. Today this point is in Pisces. What happened?

In its yearly journey around the zodiac the Sun does not return to the exact place where it began the journey one year ago. The Sun stops a little short of a complete 360° passage around the zodiac by about 50 inches. In 72 years, the Sun has fallen back in the zodiac by 1°. One degree in the sky is about the size of two full Moons side by side. The Babylonians gave each zodiac constellation the ideal boundaries of 30° (12 × 30° = 360°). In all ancient recorded zodiacs spring began in the constellation Taurus. Since that time, the number of degrees the Sun has fallen back has been adding up. After 2,160 years the Vernal Equinox falls back one whole constellation. By late Greek times, the Vernal Equinox point had entered Pisces. Today it is approaching the end of Pisces as it moves slowly towards Aquarius. This change to ever earlier constellations for the Vernal point is the **precession of the equinoxes.**

---

precession comes from the the Latin word *praecedo = to go before.* We associate each period in history with the constellation in which the Vernal equinox occurred. That is what people mean when they talk about the dawning of the Age of Aquarius.

March 21st now occurs in Pisces, not in Aries as it once did. The constellation Pisces which is visible to us in the night sky does not fit neatly into a boundary of 30° as it did on the Babylonian charts. For these reasons, when people speak of the **signs** of the zodiac, they mean the ideal arrangement in which there are 12 equal zodiac constellations of 30° each and the First point of Aries is the beginning of spring. This zodiac is also the one we use to map the Earth as you will see in the next chapter.

Notice that the names of the **signs** Scorpio and Capricorn are different from the **constellations** Scorpius and Capricornus.

Star Wisdom, Astrology, and Astronomy Almost every civilization ancient and modern has practiced some form of **star wisdom**. Although it is barely remembered or understood, star wisdom is the original source for most seasonal celebrations, many national customs, and a number of words in several languages. Star wisdom is the great-grandmother of astronomy and the mother of astrology.

Astrology came about as a calculating and interpreting task of the priesthood of ancient cultures who became the official representatives of what was then known about star wisdom. These astronomer-priests considered time sacred: the time of birth, the time of death, the time of founding a city or beginning a battle. These times were sacred because the gods were present at all important events. The priests could detect the presence of the gods at human events by making a chart showing exactly how the signposts of the gods (the stars and planets) were arranged at any moment in the past or the future. This chart is a **horoscope**.

Casting a baby's horoscope in ancient Rome.

The chart of a horoscope is similar to the planesphere you made. Preparing such a chart required careful mathematical reckoning, an understanding of the sky, and a sensitivity to the information it revealed. The three wise men or Magi who visited the Christ child were astronomer-priests.

---

horoscope comes from the Greek word ὥρα (hora) = time, and σκοπεω (skopeo) = to look at
magi comes from the Greek word μαγος (magos) = wise man, seer

---

The astronomer-priests made the information they gathered from the stars available only to the king, the pharaoh (or in China, the emperor). It was very late in the history of astrology, around 400 B.C., that this information became available to the general public.

The practice of astrology spread from Babylonia and Egypt into Greece and the rest of Europe. People also practiced astrology in China, India, and Central America. Today astronomer-priests are not the only ones who practice the ancient science of astrology. Computers often prepare the charts which an astrologer interprets. Many astrologers are no longer familiar with the night sky. Some astrologers, however, have helped advance the continued growth and relevance of their art and have, in the process, helped many people understand their lives better.

Astronomy is among the "Things fit to be learned" according to the ancient Greek definition of Mathematics. These "Things fit to be learned" were **Arithmetic** (numbering), **Geometry** (measuring the Earth), **Astronomy** (classifying the stars), **Optics** (light), and **Harmonics** (the theory of music and therefore sound).

Over the years astronomy has grown from being the daughter of astrology to become a separate scientific discipline which includes within it the other "Things fit to be learned." As a science astronomy makes use of experiments, technology, and intelligent guesses called hypotheses and theories. Many astronomers no longer go out and look at the night sky. Much of their information comes to them from telescopes, cameras, and computers. Modern astronomy is concerned with examining the physical nature of the objects in the universe to increase humanity's understanding of them. The work of astronomers has greatly advanced our knowledge of the physical makeup of our own planet and others.

READING MORE
Branley, Franklyn M. *Age of Aquarius.* New York: Harper and Row, 1979.
Knox, Richard. *Experiments in Astronomy for Amateurs.* New York: St. Martin's Press, 1977.

Section 2: CONSTELLATIONS

Stories in the Sky   By 270 B.C., people knew forty-four constellations by specific names and two more which were unnamed. When knowledge of what lived behind the constellations faded from memory, the starry sky became a connect-the-dots puzzle. Naming the shapes you found depended on when and where you lived. In early Judaeo-Christian lands, people chose biblical names like Camelopardalis (the camel that brought Rebecca to Isaac) and Columba (Noah's dove). In Renaissance times, explorers brought back descriptions of new creatures from the southern hemisphere such as Tucana (the Toucan) or Volans (the Flying Fish). People honored their leaders by naming stars after them: Scutum Scobiescianum (the shield of **John Scobiesci III,** king of Poland). Enlightenment France selected names from the tools of the arts and sciences: Pictor (the painter's easel) and Fornax (the chemist's furnace). **Augustin Delporte** (1844–1891) drew the boundaries of all the constellations.

In 1930, the International Astronomical Union (I.A.U.) declared that no one could name any more constellations. The I.A.U. would only recognize the names and boundaries of the 88 constellations known at that time. Astronomers still use this system of charting the constellations.

In early star maps, artists drew the constellations as you would see them on the *outside* of the celestial sphere instead of how they would look if you saw them from inside the celestial sphere. That is why their drawings appear backwards from the view you have from Earth. The drawing of Leo on the cover of this book is from one of these old star maps. It appears backwards from the way it is shown on modern star charts which show the sky as it looks from the Earth.

To find your way through the maze of constellations, you can group them into smaller sections. One way to group them is by seasons. The star charts on the next pages show the constellations as they appear each season. Another grouping is to keep those constellations together which share a common story or origin. The lists which follow divide the constellations into six groups. Groups one through five contain the constellations whose stories come from the great myths and religions of Asia Minor, Egypt, Greece, and Rome. The sixth group contains all the constellations that people have added since classical times. Therefore, most of their names and shapes are from the imaginations of individuals rather than the stories of whole cultures. Most of them are also located in the skies of the southern hemisphere. What do you suppose the early inhabitants of Australia, New Zealand, South Africa, and Polynesia saw in those skies before the Europeans came?

There are several familiar groups of stars in the sky which make shapes that are easy to recognize. These groups are not separate constellations, they are parts of one or more constellation. We call them **asterisms**. Here are some asterisms you can find in the night sky.

In this next project you can start learning the names, location, and stories of the constellations.

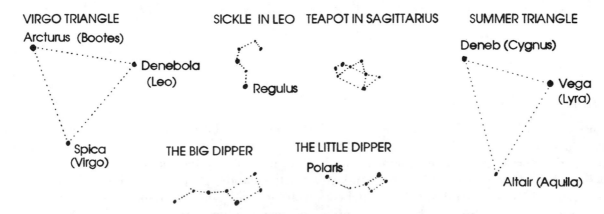

———————————— **Project 19:   Learning the Constellations** ————————————

MATERIALS

star group illustrations in this book
star chart without connecting lines (in Sky Files)
colored paper
paste or glue

sheet of black or dark blue construction paper
colored pencil (white or yellow)
scissors

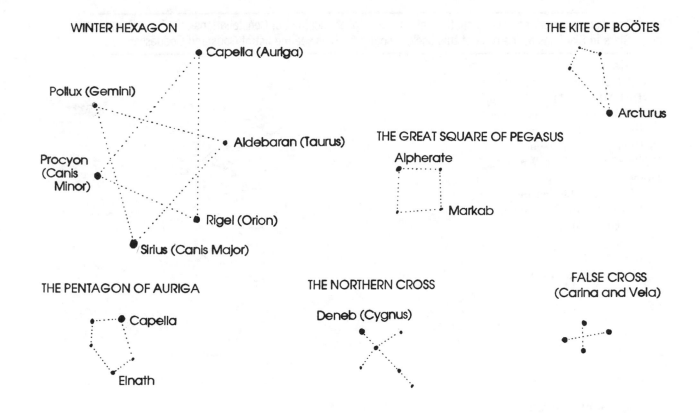

WINTER HEXAGON

Capella (Auriga)

Pollux (Gemini)

Aldebaran (Taurus)

Procyon
(Canis
Minor)

Rigel (Orion)

Sirius (Canis Major)

THE KITE OF BOÖTES

Arcturus

THE GREAT SQUARE OF PEGASUS

Alpherate

Markab

THE PENTAGON OF AURIGA

Capella

Elnath

THE NORTHERN CROSS

Deneb (Cygnus)

FALSE CROSS
(Carina and Vela)

PROCEDURE

1. Study the constellations in each of the six star groups. Try to find them in the star chart that has no connecting lines.

2. Find the asterisms listed in this chapter.

3. Choose one non-zodiac constellation from each of the six star groups which you would like to learn more about. You can learn one a day.

4. Find out each constellation's story.

5. Paste down the main stars of each constellation onto the black sheet of paper using small squares (or any other shape) cut from the colored paper. Use the lightest colors of paper. Use the other colors to finish your illustration. You could also use one color for the main stars and one color for the rest of the constellation.

6. Write the name of each constellation at the bottom of your picture using a light colored pencil.

Aquarius

OBSERVATION

Look for your constellations in the night sky and as many other constellations as you can see from your latitude.

The numbers after each constellation refer to the alphabetical list of Constellations and Their Brightest Stars in Sky Files at the back of this book. Also in Sky Files see the list of Gods and Goddesses.

1. THE ANDROMEDA GROUP
ANDROMEDA (1) Andromeda
CASSIOPEIA (16) Cassiopeia
CEPHEUS (20) Cepheus
PERSEUS (63) Perseus
PEGASUS (62) The Winged
Horse
CETUS (21) The Sea Beast
ERIDANUS (36) The River
TRIANGULUM (80) The
Triangle
ARIES (7) The Ram
PISCES (66) The Fishes

THE ANDROMEDA GROUP

2. THE OSIRIS GROUP
ORION (50) Orion
LEPUS (48) The Hare
CANIS MAJOR (14) The Great
Dog
CANIS MINOR (15) The Lesser
Dog
TAURUS (78) The Bull
AURIGA (8) The Charioteer
GEMINI (38) The Twins

THE OSIRIS GROUP

3. THE HARNESSING AND HARVESTING GROUP
LEO (46) The Lion
HYDRA (42) The Sea Serpent
CORVUS (28) The Crow
CRATER (29) The Cup
VIRGO (86) The Young Woman
BOÖTES (9) The Ploughman
URSA MAJOR (83) The Great
Bear
URSA MINOR (84) The Lesser
Bear
THE SHIP ARGO
   VELA (85) The Sail
   PUPPIS (68) The Stern
   CARINA (17) The Keel

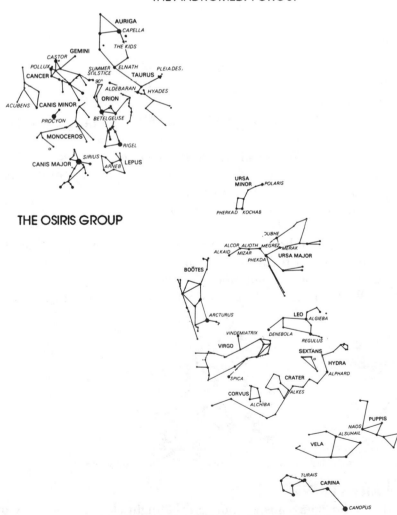

THE HARNESSING AND HARVESTING GROUP

4. THE HERO AND HEALER GROUP

OPHIUCHIUS (59) The Serpent Holder
SERPENS (76) The Serpent
SCORPIUS (73) The Scorpion
CENTAURUS (19) The Centaur
LUPUS (50) The Wolf
ARA (6) The Altar
SAGITTARIUS (72) The Archer
HERCULES (40) Hercules
DRACO (34) The Dragon
CORONA BOREALIS (27) The Northern Crown
CORONA AUSTRALIS (26) The Southern Crown
LIBRA (49) The Scales

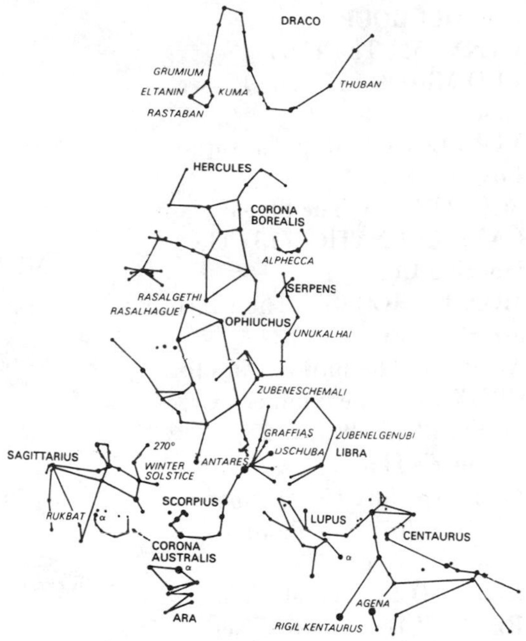

THE HERO AND HEALER GROUP

5. THE BIRDS AND SEA DWELLERS GROUP

CYGNUS (31) The Swan
AQUILLA (5) The Eagle
SAGITTA (71) The Arrow
LYRA (52) The Lyre
DELPHINUS (32) The Dolphin
PISCIS AUSTRINIS (67) The Southern Fish
AQUARIUS (4) The Watercarrier
CAPRICORNUS (16) The Sea-Goat

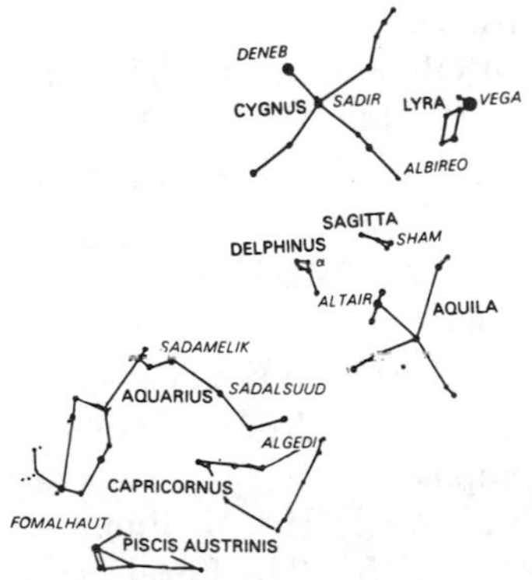

THE BIRDS AND SEA DWELLERS GROUP

6. THE MODERN AND SOUTH POLAR GROUP

LYNX (51) The Tiger
LEO MINOR (47) The Lesser
Lion
VULPECULA (88) The Little
Fox
SCUTUM (75) The Shield
CANES VENATICI (13) The
Hunting Dogs
MONOCEROS (55) The Unicorn
MUSCA (56) The Fly
APUS (3) The Bird of Paradise
CRUX (30) The Southern Cross
COMA BERENICES (25)
Berenice's Hair
OCTANS (58) The Octant
PICTOR (65) The Painter's
Easel
DORADO (33) The Goldfish
RETICULUS (70) The Net
HYDRUS (43) The Water
Monster
TUCANA (82) The Toucan
PAVO (61) The Peacock
TRIANGULUM AUSTRALE
(81) The Southern Triangle
CIRCINUS (23) The Compasses
CHAMAELEON (22) The
Chamaeleon
VOLANS (87) The Flying Fish
SEXTANS (77) The Sextant
SCULPTOR (74) The Sculptor
LACERTA (45) The Lizard
FORNAX (37) The Chemist's
Furnace
HOROLOGIUM (41) The Clock
COLUMBA (24) The Dove
CAELUM (10) The Engraving
Tool
CAMELOPARDALIS (11) The
Camel
EQUULEUS (35) The Foal
PYXIS (69) The Mariner's
Compass
ANTLIA (2) The Air Pump
NORMA (57) The Level
TELESCOPIUM (79) The
Telescope
MICROSCOPIUM (54) The
Microscope
GRUS (39) The Crane
INDUS (44) The American
Indian
PHOENIX (64) The Phoenix
MENSA (53) The Table

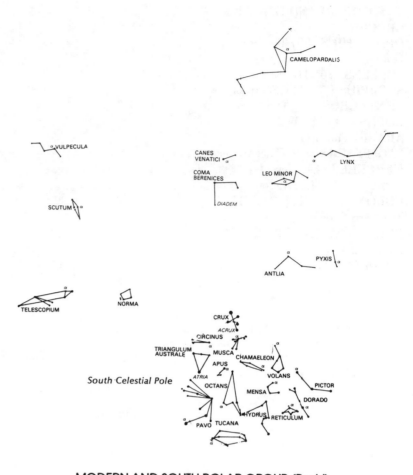

MODERN AND SOUTH POLAR GROUP (Part I)

MODERN AND SOUTH POLAR GROUP (Part II)

When he was seven years old the British astronomer **Sir Patrick Moore** set himself the task to learn one new constellation every night. He soon discovered that the task was not as hard as it may sound and that it only took a few minutes each clear evening. What the job did require was patience. As you become more familiar with the constellations they will become like old friends who come back to visit every year. You will find yourself looking forward to their arrival and the season that brings them.

In this next project you can learn how to use a star chart to help you recognize any constellation in the sky at any time of the year.

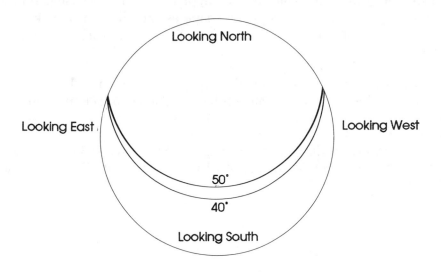

─────── Project 20: Using a Star Chart ───────

MATERIALS

Star chart for whole sky
drawing compass
sheet of plastic (the stiff kind used for
    report covers)
fine point felt-tip pen (permanent ink)
flashlight

paper bag
rubber band
tape
scissors
regular pen or pencil

PROCEDURE

1. Draw an 8 5/16 inch (21 centimeter) circle on the plastic sheet. Cut it out. Write "Looking North, South, East, and West" as shown using a permanent marking felt-tip pen. Outline the outer edge of the circle so you can see where it ends.

2. Place the center of the plastic circle on the equinox point of the star chart. Carefully mark a small " + " in the center where the vertical and horizontal lines cross on the star chart.

3. Replace the pencil in the compass with the felt-tip pen. (Tape the pen on if it doesn't fit.)

4. Put the point of the compass on the vertical line at the number of degrees in your latitude (above the celestial equator for the northern hemisphere, below it for the southern hemisphere). Put the other end of the compass (with the felt-tip pen on it) on the vertical line on the opposite side of the celestial equator at the number which is *10° more than your latitude*. Draw an arc on the plastic circle from one side of the circle to the other. This arc is your **horizon**. The plastic circle is your **viewing circle**.

USING YOUR STAR CHART

1. Go out at night and get your eyes used to the darkness.

2. Find a place to lie down, if possible—it's easier on your neck and it removes houses, trees, and cars from your view leaving only the sky.

3. Use the flashlight covered with a paper bag and rubber band to help you see your chart.

4. Place the center of the viewing circle on the celestial equator at today's date. (Each small vertical line is one day). What you see above your horizon is the sky for this night facing south. If you face north, east, or west, keep your viewing circle in place on the chart and turn them *both* around so the word for the direction you are facing appears right side up and at the bottom.

OBSERVATIONS

Locate the six star groups mentioned in this chapter. Are all the constellations easy to find? Do the constellations on the chart have the same shape as they have in the sky or do they appear stretched out or squashed on the chart? Technical assistance for setting these star charts to different latitudes provided by George Lovi.

What makes a constellation are its individual stars. Many of them have their own stories and particular qualities. In the next section you will have a chance to look at them.

READING MORE

Allen, Richard Hinkley. *Star Names: Their Lore and Meaning.* New York: Dover, 1963.

Raymo, Chet. *Starry Nights: An Introduction to Astronomy For Every Night of the Year.* Englewood Cliffs, New Jersey: Prentice-Hall, Inc., 1982.

SEPTEMBER
Sun in Virgo, September 16–October 30
Astrological Sign Libra, September 22–October 23
Night Sky March's daytime sky

OCTOBER
Sun in Libra, October 30–November 22
Astrological Sign Scorpio, October 23–November 22
Night Sky April's daytime sky

NOVEMBER
Sun in Scorpius, November 22–December 17
Astrological Sign Sagittarius, November 22–December 21
Night Sky May's daytime sky

DECEMBER
Sun in Sagittarius, December 17–January 20
Astrological Sign Capricorn, December 21–January 20
Night Sky June's daytime sky

JANUARY
Sun in Capricornus, January 20–February 16
Astrological Sign Aquarius, January 20–February 19
Night Sky July's daytime sky

FEBRUARY
Sun in Aquarius, February 16–March 11
Astrological Sign Pisces, February 19–March 20
Night Sky August's daytime sky

MARCH
Sun in Pisces, March 11–April 18
Astrological Sign Aries, March 20–April 19
Night Sky September's daytime sky

APRIL
Sun in Aries, April 18–May 13
Astrological Sign Taurus, April 19–May 20
Night Sky October's daytime sky

MAY
Sun in Taurus, May 13–June 21
Astrological Sign Gemini, May 20–June 21
Night Sky November's daytime sky

JUNE
Sun in Gemini, June 21–July 20
Astrological Sign Cancer, June 21–July 22
Night Sky December's daytime sky

JULY
Sun in Cancer, July 20–August 10
Astrological Sign Leo, July 22–August 22
Night Sky January's daytime sky

AUGUST
Sun in Leo, August 10–September 16
Astrological Sign Virgo, August 22–September 22
Night Sky February's daytime sky

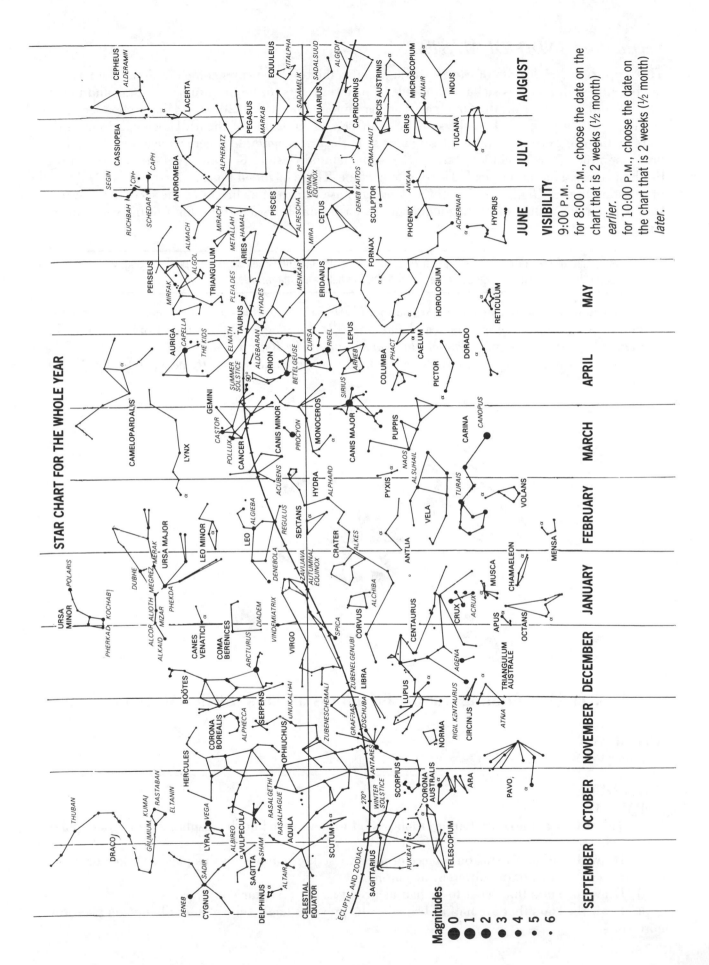

STAR CHART FOR THE WHOLE YEAR

VISIBILITY
9:00 P.M.

for 8:00 P.M., choose the date on the chart that is 2 weeks (½ month) *earlier*.

for 10:00 P.M., choose the date on the chart that is 2 weeks (½ month) *later*.

SEPTEMBER OCTOBER NOVEMBER DECEMBER JANUARY FEBRUARY MARCH APRIL MAY JUNE JULY AUGUST

Magnitudes
0
1
2
3
4
5
6

59

Section 3: INDIVIDUAL STARS

The Apparent Brightness of Stars   As night falls, the brightest stars come out first. The term for the brightness of a star is **stellar magnitude**. This term refers to the brightness of a star and not its size. This idea came from the Greek astronomer **Hipparchos** (190–120 B.C.). Hipparchos set out to catalogue the brightness of all the stars he could see (about 1,028 of them). He categorized all the stars by their brightness, calling the brightest stars the **first magnitude**. There were about 21 of these first magnitude stars, including Sirius (Canis Major) and Castor (Gemini). Stars that were half as bright as these, Hipparchos called **second magnitude**. These included Polaris (Ursa Minor) and most of the stars in the "Big Dipper" and Cassiopeia. Those stars half as bright as the second magnitude stars Hipparchos called **third magnitude** and so forth until he reached the limit of his vision at the **sixth magnitude**.

---

stellar magnitude comes from the Latin word *stella* = star, and the Greek word *(makpos)* = long, which became the Latin word *magnus* = large, and the English word *magnitude.*

The German astronomer **Friedrich Argelander** (1799–1875) and his associates used an interesting method in preparing the great star catalogue, the *B.D. Catalogue.* B.D. is the abbreviation of the German title of the catalogue, *Bonner Durchmusterung, The Bonn Catalogue.*

In this next project you can use the same method that Argelander used to measure the brightness of stars.

—— **Project 21:   Finding Out the Brightness of Stars (Stellar Magnitude)** ——

MATERIALS
   paper   pencil

PROCEDURE
   PART 1
   1. Take a look at the constellation Orion (visible to viewers on both hemispheres) or a circumpolar constellation.
   2. Draw the brightest star on a piece of paper. Use the symbols on this page as a key or make up your own to indicate the different magnitudes.
   3. Draw the stars that seem to be half as bright as the first star you drew.
   4. Draw the stars that are half as bright as the previous ones, and so on until you can't see any more stars.

PART 2

1. Go out again to observe the constellation you measured in Part 1. You are going to try a different approach which, with practice, can produce fairly accurate results (within 1/10 of a magnitude).

2. Compare the apparent brightness of a star in the constellation with two or more nearby stars whose magnitudes you already know. A star that appears somewhat fainter than a neighboring star of 2.4 magnitude and somewhat brighter than another neighboring star of 2.6 magnitude you will say has a magnitude of 2.5.

3. Make sure that:

    a. the star you are measuring and the star with the known magnitude are at about the same height above the horizon.

    b. the known magnitude stars are as close as possible to the star you are measuring.

    c. one of the known magnitude stars is somewhat brighter and the other is somewhat dimmer than the star you are measuring.

4. Check with the list after this project for the apparent magnitudes of the stars you can use to help you in determining the magnitude for other stars.

OBSERVATIONS

Do you think this method is very accurate? Check your findings with the star catalogue in Sky Files at the back of this book.

A helpful magnitude guide for people in the northern hemisphere is to use the four stars in the head of the constellation Draco (the dragon). The brightest star is first magnitude. The second brightest is second magnitude, the third brightest is third magnitude, and the fourth brightest is fourth magnitude. There are also four stars in Ursa Major which you can use in the same way. For those in the southern hemisphere, Centaurus contains stars from −0.27 to 5.

In this next project you can make a handy device to measure magnitudes just by looking at a star through it.

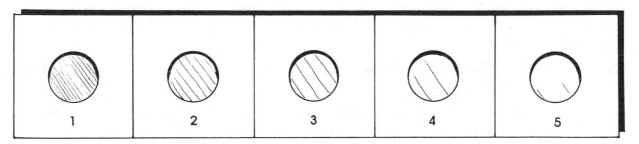

———— Project 22:   Making a Brightness Measuring Tool ————

MATERIALS

a piece of cardboard, 2 × 10 inches   glue
   (5 × 25 centimeters)   scissors
a pencil   ruler
a small coin
5 cellophane strips 1¼ inches
   (3 centimeters) wide

INSTRUCTIONS

1. Divide the cardboard into five 2 inch (5 centimeter) sections.
2. Trace a circle in the center of each section by drawing around the penny.
3. Cut out the five circles.

4. Glue a strip of cellophane onto the cardboard so that it covers all five of the holes. Be sure to keep the glue away from the cellophane where the holes are.

5. Glue the second cellophane strip onto the first strip so that it only covers four of the holes in the cardboard.

6. Glue the third cellophane strip onto the second strip so that it only covers three of the holes in the cardboard, and so on until the last strip only covers one hole in the cardboard.

7. Write the number *1* in the space on the cardboard next to the hole with the five layers of cellophane.

8. Write the number *2* in the space on the cardboard next to the hole with the four layers of cellophane, and so on until the last hole, *5*, with only one strip.

USING YOUR BRIGHTNESS MEASURING TOOL

Look at a constellation through your brightness measuring tool. If you can see a star through the hole marked *1*, that star is a first magnitude star. If you can see a star through the hole marked *2*, that star is a second magnitude star, and so on down to the fifth magnitude.

OBSERVATION

How accurate is this tool compared to the method used in Project 21, Finding Out the Brightness of Stars? This project is adapted from *The Night Sky Book* by Jamie Jobb, Boston: Little Brown and Company, 1977. Used with permission.

Many stars have their own names given to them by Arab astronomers hundreds of years ago. These names describe the position of the star in the picture of the constellation. In 1603, the Bavarian astronomer **Johann J. Bayer** published his own star catalogue in which he used the Greek alphabet to name the stars in order of brightness. The brightest star was α *(alpha)*, the next brightest was β *(beta)*, and so on. After the Greek letter came the constellation name in Latin written in the possessive or *genitive* case . The name for Sirius would be **Canis Majoris,** meaning that Sirius *belongs* to Canis Major. Star catalogues often abbreviate the names of constellations. Canis Major becomes **C Ma.** A complete listing of the genitive case endings and abbreviations for *all* constellations and a listing of the Greek letters for the stars appears in Sky Files at the back of this book.

Remember how important the star Sirius was for the Egyptians? Other stars were just as important for other peoples. Arcturus in Bootes and Aldebaran and the Pleiades' in Taurus were favorite planting time reminders.

"When the Pleiades, children of Atlas first arise, begin your harvest: when they leave the skies, plough."—Hesiod, 8th century B.C.

Some stars, including the North Star, are well known orientation markers for navigators (see Chapter 3). The catalogue, "The Constellations and Their Brightest Stars" appearing in Sky Files in the back of this book tells briefly about the names of the brighter stars.

Visibility of Stars Side vision (peripheral) can make stars visible for some people down to sixth and seventh magnitudes, but those below fourth magnitude will usually disappear when you stare directly at them. They will come back out once you look slightly away from them. This happens because of the "blind spot" in your eyes where the optic nerve connects with the inside of your eye. This spot is not sensitive to very dim light. If you want to see a dim star, don't look *at* it, look *around* it and it will pop into view.

---

peripheral comes from the Greek word περι *(peri)* = around
See Chapter 5, Section 2 for more about the eye and how you see.

You may not always be able to see even the sixth magnitude stars. When the Moon is bright your eyes will not become very dark-adapted, so you will not see these stars. Nor will you see them if there are any bright street lights nearby. A slight haze will also hamper visibility, even on a moonless night.

Starwatchers everywhere have been concerned about the "shrinking sky" made smaller and dimmer by street lamps, city lights, and smog. One famous research observatory has closed because of this. Many people are joining the efforts of starwatchers to control pollution and the amount of vision hampering light. The International Astronomical Union met in 1988 to discuss the problem and make recommendations.

On a dark, clear night, try counting the stars in a small area of the sky. If the night is really dark and clear, you have from 1,500 to 2,000 to chose from. If you had binoculars you could see many thousands. With a small telescope, almost half a million. If you took a photograph through a large professional telescope, you could find millions upon millions of stars.

See Chapter 5, Sections 2 and 3 for more about telescopes and cameras.

This next project has three parts. Do all three if you can to learn some important characteristics about the brightness of stars that will help you understand how astronomers measure distances to stars.

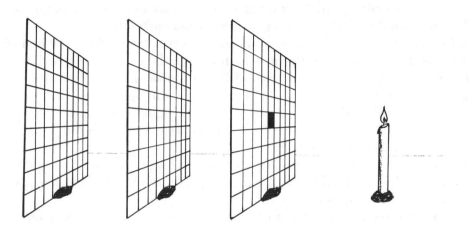

―――――――― **Project 23:   Measuring Brightness and Distance** ――――――――

MATERIALS

a sheet of glass	pencil
2 candles	ruler
2 lamps	scissors or utility knife
1 25-watt light bulb	clay
1 75-watt light bulb	matches
3 cardboard sheets, 9 × 9 inches (23 × 23 centimeters)	

PROCEDURE
PART 1

1. Move the sheet of glass slowly over a candle flame several times so that the soot collects on the glass in an even layer.

2. Light the two candles and place them next to each other on a table. From a distance of several feet, observe the two candles through the smoked glass.

3. Move one of the candles about a foot closer to you. Look at both flames through the smoked glass.

4. Place one of the candles at least halfway between you and the other candle.

OBSERVATION

By looking at both flames through the smoked glass at different distances what do you notice about their brightness compared to one another?

PART 2

1. Place a lamp with a 25-watt bulb on a table next to a lamp with a 75-watt bulb. Turn the lamps on and observe them through the smoked glass from a distance of several feet.

2. Place the 25-watt bulb closer to you so that when you look through the smoked glass both lights appear equally bright.

OBSERVATION

If you had no way of knowing the actual brightness and distance of each bulb and could see them only through the smoked glass, would you be able to tell which one was closer?

PART 3

1. Draw 81 1-inch (23 centimeter) squares (nine across and nine down) on each of the three cardboard sheets.

2. Cut out the middle square from one of the sheets of cardboard.

3. Stand up each cardboard sheet using a piece of clay as a base. Arrange the cardboard sheets so that they are exactly 6 inches (15 centimeters) from each other.

4. Light a candle and set it exactly 6 inches (15 centimeters) from the first cardboard sheet so that its flame is directly in line with the hole in the middle of the cardboard.

5. Notice how bright each square inch of light is on the first cardboard sheet. Now look at the second cardboard sheet. Notice that the light that passed through the one inch square hole has spread out on the second cardboard sheet so that it covers four squares. Compare the amount of brightness (intensity) of a square inch of light on the first cardboard sheet with the intensity of a square inch of light on the second cardboard sheet.

6. Remove the second cardboard sheet so that the light passing through the hole in the first cardboard sheet lights up the third cardboard sheet. Notice that the light has spread out even more and covers about nine squares.

7. Move the third cardboard sheet another six inches away. Upon how many squares does the intensity of the light **decrease** as you **increase** the distance of the cardboard sheet from the light?

OBSERVATIONS

If you did not know that both light sources were the same distance from you, which would seem closer? If you didn't know the brightness of each light source and could only see them through the smoked glass, would you be able to tell which was closer?   This project is adapted from *Science Experiments for the Space Age* by Sam Rosenfeld, Irvington: Harvey House, Incorporated, Publishers, 1972.

If two stars that give off different quantities of light were the same distance from the Earth, would they appear equally bright in the sky?

If two stars appear to be equally bright in the sky, does it mean that they are the same distance from the Earth?

Why does a star appear dimmer the farther away it is?

When you describe the brightness of the stars based on what you see, you are referring to its **apparent visual magnitude**. You have seen in Project 23 *Comparing Brightness and Distance* that the apparent visual magnitude does not necessarily tell you which light source is actually brighter, which one is dimmer, which one is really closer and which one only appears to be closer. In order to compare the true brightness of stars you would need to have them side by side so that when you viewed them, they would each be the same distance from you. This is what you did when you looked at the candles and the lamps. To put stars side by side you need to set up an imaginary location in space, determine that location's distance from the Earth and calculate how bright a star would be if it was shining from there. Every star whose brightness you want to measure will be measured as if it was at this one location. The distance from Earth to this location becomes the standard distance for comparing the magnitudes of all stars.

Astronomers have chosen the distance of about 190 trillion miles (306 trillion kilometers) away. They use the apparent visual magnitude of a star to calculate how bright it would be if you viewed it from this distance. The brightness of a star at that distance is its **absolute magnitude**. The apparent magnitude of the Sun is -26.8. The apparent magnitude of Sirius is -1.43, which means that to our eyes, the Sun appears to be 14 thousand million times brighter than Sirius. The absolute magnitude of the Sun is 4.8, while Sirius is 1.3. According to this measurement, the Sun is only about ⅟₂₅ as bright as Sirius. At a distance of 190 trillion miles the Sun would barely be visible to the naked eye. This means that the Sun is really 21 times dimmer than Sirius.

The distance for absolute magnitude = 10 parsecs See Chapter 7, Section 1.
The symbol for **absolute magnitude = M, apparent magnitude = m**

In the third part of the last project, you noticed that the farther the square inch of light traveled, the more it spread out and the dimmer it became in the process. On the second cardboard sheet the light covered four squares. Each square received ¼ of the light. On the third cardboard sheet (3 units of 6 inches or 23 centimeters) the light covered nine squares. Each square received ⅑ of the light. When you double the distance from the candle, the light on each square is ¼ the original amount of light; when you triple the distance, the light is ⅑. Do you see the pattern that is emerging? The bottom number in the fraction is the distance times itself. Twice as far away = 2 × 2 or 4. Each square is ¼ the original amount of light. You can see that the change in the amount of light is the opposite of the distance the light changes multiplied by itself. The way the law of distance states this is that **light varies inversely as the square of the distance**. This is the **inverse square law**.

The Color of Stars   Not all of the stars shine with the same bright white light. Stars actually glow with hues from white to yellow, blue, orange, and red. These colors depend on the star's size, temperature, and distance from us.

The colors of stars, like their apparent magnitude, will differ according to the sensitivity of your own eyes. For real stellar beauty, look for Sirius, Algol, and Arcturus. Not only are they bright and colorful, but their colors flash and glisten like sparkling gems.

The star catalogue in Sky Files lists the colors for all of the visible stars. Here is a short list of the brighter ones. See how many of these you can find in the night sky.

You can find out more about the colors and temperatures in stars in Chapter 7, Section 2.

RED Betelgeuse (α Orionis), Antares (α Scorpii)
REDDISH Aldebaran (α Tauri), μ Cephei is the reddest
ORANGE Arcturus (α Boötis), Pollux (β Geminorum)
YELLOW The Sun, Capella (α Aurigae)
YELLOWISH Procyon (α Canis Minoris)
WHITE Canopus (α Carinae)
GREENISH β Librae
BLUE-WHITE Sirius (α Canis Majoris), Vega (α Lyrae), Rigel (β Orionis), Spica (α Virginis)
BLUISH Altair (α Aquilae)
BLUE Mintaka (δ Orionis)

THE STAR

Twinkle, twinkle, little star,
How I wonder what you are!
Up above the world so high,
Like a diamond in the sky.

When the blazing sun is gone,
When she nothing shines upon,
Then you show your little light,
Twinkle, twinkle all the night.

Then the traveler in the dark
Thanks you for your tiny spark;
He could not see which way to go,
If you did not twinkle so.

In the dark blue sky you keep,
And often through my curtains peep,
For you never shut your eye
Till the sun is in the sky.

As your bright and tiny spark
Lights the traveler in the dark,
Though I know not what you are,
Twinkle, twinkle, little star.

—Ann and Jane Taylor

READING MORE

Burnham Jr., Robert. *Burnham's Celestial Handbook.* New York: Dover Publications, Inc., 1978.
Ronan, Colin. *The Practical Astronomer.* New York: MacMillan, Inc., 1981.

Section 4: THE MILKY WAY

NAGACORK'S GOODBYE

"And the old man Nagacork, the Creator, went on a long walkabout to see all the tribesmen, the birds, animals, fish, and reptiles.

And as Nagacork traveled through all the different countries of the tribes he sang:

'Allo, allo, allo, allo, allo, cha nallah, wirrit, burra burra, cubrimilla, cubrimilla. Bo bo!' This means, 'Oh well, all you people who belong to me have changed into men, animals, birds, reptiles, fish, sun, moon, and stars. I go now. I go forever. You will see me no more. But all the time I will watch about you.'

And the tribesmen say that you can see the old man Nagacork lying among the stars. His lubral (woman) is lying near him with one arm behind her head. And the tribesmen say that the stream of stars that the white man calls the Milky Way is the smoke of Nagacork's campfire drifting across the night." From *Aboriginal Myths and Legends: Age-Old Stories of the Australian Tribes.* Selected by Roland Robinson, London: Paul Hamlyn, 1969.

Seeing the **Milky Way** with its wisps of faint stars suggests far distances and the clouds of mystery between us and what lies beyond. It is not surprising that for so many centuries people have seen the Milky Way as a path or road from Earth to the heavens.

The Andromeda Galaxy (M31). *Photo courtesy of Observatoire de Haute Provence*

Our name **Milky Way** comes to us from the ancient Greeks. Their title for this band of star dust was Γαλακτικος or Γαλαξιας *(galactic or galaxy)* = milk. The Romans called it *Via Galactica* which means "Milky Way." The milk is from the breast of the goddess Hera (Juno) spilled while nursing the infant Herakles (Hercules).

According to a French tale, the stars in the Milky Way are lights held by angel spirits to show mortals the way to heaven. The native American Algonquins believed that this was the path of souls leading to the villages in the Sun. As the spirits travel along the pathway, we see their blazing campfires as bright stars.

An old Chinese tale tells of the Spinning Maiden (the star Vega in Lyra) and the Shepherd Boy (the star Altair in Aquila). The girl is free to cross the "Silver River of the Sky" by a bridge made of magpies and visit her husband only on one night of the year; the seventh day of the seventh month. Should it rain on that day the birds will seek shelter and, in the absence of a bridge, the Spinning Maiden must spend another year of separation from her husband. The people on Earth send their wishes skyward for a clear day on July 7th with festive celebrations for the star lovers.

Arabic and African traditions tell of a heavenly path strewn with straw. In Mexico, the Milky Way is the "Sister of the Rainbow."

This is our galaxy and all the stars, planets, the Sun, and the Moon dwell and move within it. In this next project you can make a glittering picture of what the Milky Way looks like from Earth.

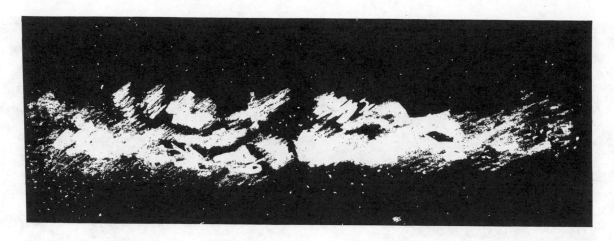

Project 24:   Creating a Picture of the Milky Way

MATERIALS

map of the Milky Way (from the star
  chart in Sky Files)

black or dark blue paper or poster board

pencil

silver glitter

glue

paper cup

PROCEDURE

1. Go out and look at the Milky Way before making a picture of it. The best times of year for this are January, July, and November.

2. Sketch the outline of the Milky Way lightly onto the black paper using a pencil and the map from Sky Files. While the exact outline of the Milky Way is unclear, its general shape is thicker in some areas and thinner and broken in others.

3. Put glue on all the areas where the stars of the Milky Way are.

4. Sprinkle silver glitter onto the glued areas being very careful to put less glitter around your outline so the stars appear to fade out around the edges of your illustration as they do in the night sky.

5. Spread the glitter around using your finger or a stick.

6. Clean up while your picture is drying. When it is completely dry, tip the paper sideways and collect the extra glitter in a paper cup so you can use it again.

OBSERVATIONS

In which part of the Milky Way do you think there are the most stars? Look at Chapter 7, Section 3 for another view of our galaxy.

Early Ideas About the Universe   When you look at the Milky Way, you see the border of our universe. We live inside it surrounded by planets and stars. What does our neighborhood look like? How is it arranged? The ideas, beliefs and theories that attempt to explain the layout of our universe come from as many places and times as the constellation stories. We call such an explanation a **cosmology**.

---

cosmology comes form the Greek word κοσμος *(cosmos)* = order, and therefore the **universe**, because of its perfect arrangement. **Cosmology** = layout, or the way the universe looks. How the perfect order of the universe came to be is the subject of **cosmogony**. **Cosmogony** = beginnings or the origin of the universe. You pronounce the "g" in cosmogony like the "g" in beginnings. In the adjective cosmological, you pronounce the "g" like a "j."

The early cosmological ideas of the universe were thought pictures, meant to create an image or impression rather than a map. Here are how some drawings based on the cosmological stories of several ancient cultures.

India   The great serpent biting its own tail surrounds the universe. Resting on the coils of the great serpent is the tortoise, symbol of force and creative power. On the back of the tortoise stand four elephants supporting the lower region, the Earth (Mt. Meru) and the upper region (shown by a triangle, symbol of creation).

China   The sky was like an upside down bowl turning around the Pole Star. The sky carried with it the other stars fixed to the inner surface of the bowl. The Earth was a cube with the four seas coming from the four cardinal directions and lapping at its sides.

Babylonia   A wall supported the dome of the sky under which all the celestial bodies lived. The oceans surrounded the flat Earth which rested on a water chamber.

Egypt   The star-covered sky goddess Nut arched over Earth to form the universe. Below lay her leaf-covered husband Geb, the Earth. Shu, the god of the air, floated in between his two parents Nut and Geb.

A later Egyptian thought picture showed the universe in the shape of a rectangular box. Egypt was at the bottom center surrounded by great mountain ranges. Four tall peaks supported the flat sky. Gods stood on top of the sky and lowered the stars through holes in the sky when it was night. Night came when the Sun, traveling on the sky river through the mountains, went behind a mountain peak.

Greece   The Greeks had the biggest collection of cosmological ideas. Astronomy was a required study for all learned people so it was a subject much on the minds and hearts of all the great thinkers. Instead of a single "Greek picture of the universe" there are many. Let's look at three of them.

  The Pythagorian Brotherhood   The Pythagorean Brotherhood followed the teachings of the great mathematician and philosopher, **Pythagoras,** who developed the theorem for measuring right triangles. The brotherhood experimented with geometrical shapes. For their experiments they chose those shapes which had equal sides and equal angles. We call these shapes **regular polygons.** They include the **triangle** (3 sides, 3 angles), the **square** (4 sides and angles), the **pentagon** (5 sides and angles), the **hexagon** (6 sides and angles) and so on.

---

polygon comes from the Greek words πολι *(poly)* = many, and γονυ *(gonu)* = the knee or angle

---

The Pythagoreans used these polygons to make regular solids in which all edges, faces and angles were equal. We call these solids **regular polyhedra.** Four triangles connected together form a pyramid called a **tetrahedron.** Τετρα *(tetra)* = 4 Six squares connected together make a cube which is a **hexahedron.** Ἑξα *(hexa)* = 6. Two tetrahedra placed together form an eight-faced figure called an **octahedron.** Ὀκτα *(octa)* = 8. The Egyptians had known about these three shapes since ancient times.

---

polyhedra comes from the Greek words πολι *(poly)* = many, and ἑδρα *(hedra)* = base

---

The Pythagorean Brotherhood had the pentagon for its symbol. By putting together five **equilateral triangles** they discovered they could construct a hollow, dome-shaped figure whose open base formed a perfect pentagon. The next step was to combine more equilateral triangles in order to make a solid. After much experimenting, the brotherhood found that they could use two of the dome-shaped figures, one for the top and one for the bottom. For the sides they constructed a band of ten equilateral triangles based on an old Babylonia pattern. It took exactly 20 triangles to construct this new regular polyhedron, so we call it an **icosahedron.** Εικοσα *(eikosa)* = 20.

In their further explorations of regular solids and pentagons, the Pythagoreans put together a flower petal form composed of a central pentagon with five others around it, one on each of the five sides. By connecting the edges of the outer pentagons, a hollow, dome-shaped form resulted. Placing this dome on top of another upside down dome produced a completely new regular polyhedron, the **dodecahedron**, made from the faces of twelve pentagons. Δωδεκα *(dodeka)* = 12.

Today there are still only five regular polyhedra: tetrahedron, hexahedron, octahedron, icosahedron, and dodecahedron. As **Lewis Carroll** (1832–1898), the author of *Alice In Wonderland* once commented, they are "provokingly few in number." To the Pythagoreans (and later to Plato) these five solids contained the building blocks of all creation: Earth, Air, Fire, and Water. The cube, which stands so firmly on its base, imitates the solidity of the Earth. The octahedron, which rotates freely when held by its two opposite ends, resembles the freely moving air. The tetrahedron, which has the smallest volume for its triangular size, is related to the tongues of fire. The almost spherical icosahedron is connected with water. The dodecahedron, with its 12 faces, mirrors so much of the cosmos (The 12 signs of the zodiac, the 12 months, etc.) that it was clearly the image of the whole universe.

The great geometer **Euclid** devoted the last 13 books of his famous work *Elements* almost entirely on these solids including proof that only five of them existed.

All five of these remarkable shapes can fit inside a sphere and inside each other. You can draw them within a circle, within themselves and each other. Many examples of these regular polyhedra appear in nature. Over the years people have called them the "Dice of the gods" and the "Platonic Solids." In this next project you can make your own models of these beautiful shapes.

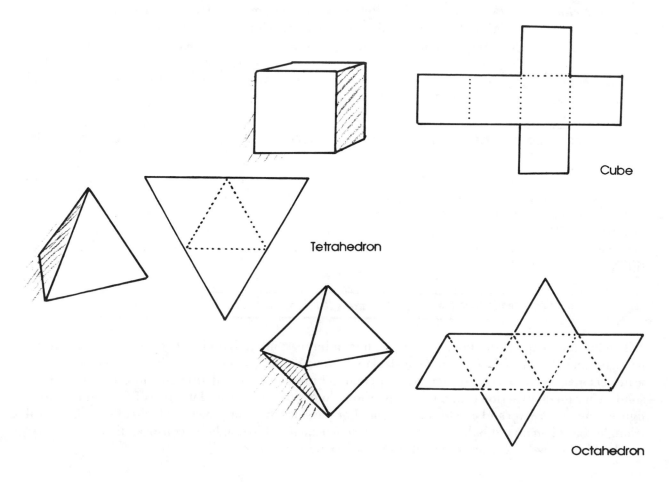

Cube

Tetrahedron

Octahedron

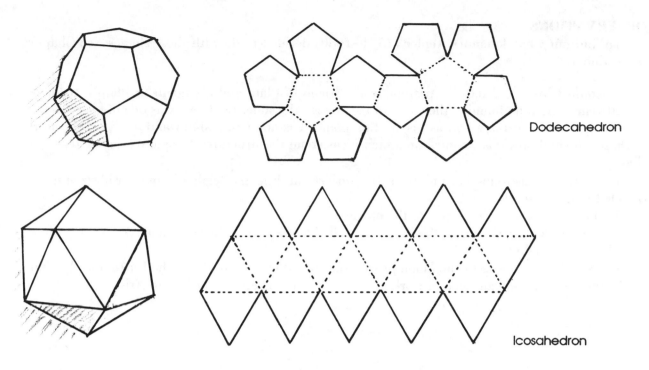

Dodecahedron

Icosahedron

———— Project 25: Making Models of the Platonic Solids ————

MATERIALS

tape
drinking straws
string
ruler
stiff paper
pencil

scissors
toothpicks or small dowels
glue or modelling clay
paint
access to a photocopier

PROCEDURE

In this project you can construct models which will let you see either the edges or the faces of each solid.

EDGES

1. Cut equal lengths of drinking straws, toothpicks, or small dowels 2 inches (5 centimeters) or longer.
2. Thread string through straws and tie them together to form 6 squares and 31 triangles. You can also make these shapes by attaching toothpicks or dowels together with glue or modelling clay.
3. Tie, attach, or glue squares together to form a cube. Use triangles to make: a tetrahedron, octahedron, and icosahedron.
4. Attach or glue toothpicks or dowels together into 12 pentagons. (You can't make a dodecahedron using straws).
5. Attach or glue pentagons together to make a dodecahedron.

FACES

1. Photocopy the drawings of the "unfolded" shapes and glue them onto stiff paper.
2. Cut out the shapes.
3. Fold as necessary along the edges of the polygons.
4. Tape the solids into place.
5. Paint your completed Platonic solids.

OBSERVATIONS

To find out what **Johannes Kepler** (1571–1630) decided to do with these shapes, see Chapter 5, Section 1.

Aristotle (384–322 B.C.)   Aristotle was a friend of Plato and a student at Plato's Academy for 20 years. Aristotle founded the Lyceum in Athens. **Alexander the Great** was one of his students.

Using the observable world as his starting point, Aristotle wrote about and analyzed the work of those who had previously contributed their ideas about the structure of the universe. He reasoned that:

1. the Earth was round because the stars appeared at different heights from your horizon if you traveled north or south.

2. the Earth was at the center of the universe.

3. the Sun was farther from the Earth than the Moon because during a solar eclipse, the Moon completely blocked the Sun.

4. the crescent phases of the Moon proved that the Moon was between the Earth and the Sun.

In this project you can make a working model of the universe according to Aristotle.

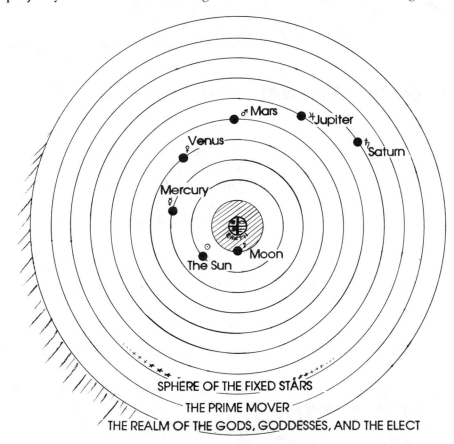

—— Project 26:   Making a Moveable Plan of the Earth-Centered Universe ——

MATERIALS

polar graph paper (from Sky Files at the back of this book)
stiff paper or posterboard
sheets of clear plastic (from report covers)
drawing and painting supplies
glue (household or contact cement)

scissors
paper fastener
large nail
ruler
access to a photocopier
almanac

PROCEDURE

1. Cut the paper or posterboard into a circle with a 12-inch (30½ centimeter) diameter. Find the center of the circle and mark it.

2. Draw seven concentric circles beginning with a 2-inch (5-centimeter) diameter, then a 3-inch (8-centimeter) diameter, and so on until 11 inches (28 centimeters).

3. Color the circles lightly following the list below:
   a. 2-inch (5-centimeter)—purple (the Moon)
   b. 3-inch (8-centimeter)—white (the Sun)
   c. 4-inch (10-centimeter)—yellow (Mercury)
   d. 5-inch (13-centimeter—green (Venus)
   e. 6-inch (15-centimeter)—red (Mars)
   f. 7-inch (18-centimeter)—orange (Jupiter)
   g. 8-inch (20-centimeter)—blue (Saturn)

4. Photocopy the polar graph paper and use it to mark 360° around the outside edge of the 8-inch (20-centimeter) circle with 0° on the top.

5. Divide the 9-inch (23-centimeter) circle into twelve 30° sections for the twelve zodiac constellations. Label each section with its zodiac symbol starting with Pisces on the right and moving counterclockwise so that Gemini is at the top and so on. You might want to draw a picture for each constellation.

6. Title the 10-inch (25½-centimeter) circle *The Fixed Stars.* Draw stars around the rest of the circle. Color the space in between the stars blue.

7. Title the 11-inch (28-centimeter) circle *The Prime Mover* and color the circle purple.

8. Title the 12-inch (30½-centimeter) circle *The Realm of the Gods* and color the circle gold.

9. Measure and cut out seven circles from the plastic sheets with the same diameters as the colored paper circles and mark the center of each plastic circle.

10. Label the outer edges of each plastic circle with their planetary symbols. Use paint or write the symbol on small pieces of paper and glue them onto the plastic circles.

11. Put the plastic circles together in order, largest on the bottom, and place them on the paper circles lining up the center marks. Make a large hole with the nail through the center of all the plastic circles and the posterboard.

12. Put a paper fastener through the hole with the head under the posterboard and the metal prongs on the plastic side. Spread the prongs out so that they lie flat but do not prevent any of the plastic circles from turning freely, especially the smallest one on the top.

13. Draw a circle 1 inch (2½ centimeters) in diameter on a separate piece of posterboard. Divide it into four with a cross in the center. In each section draw a representation of one of the four elements: Earth, Air, Fire, and Water. This circle is the Earth. Glue or tape the Earth onto the prongs of the paper fastener.

14. Illustrate or decorate the rest of your model as you see fit. It needs to be beautiful, but not cluttered. Decorate only the Earth itself and the area beyond Saturn, nowhere in between.

OBSERVATIONS

You now have a "model of a model." Arrange the daily positions of the Sun, Moon, and planets from an almanac, ephemeris, or astronomical calendar. Use your model to demonstrate the movement of the stars in one direction while the planets move in the opposite direction.

The Ptolemaic Picture **Claudius Ptolemy** (c. 90–165 A.D.) lived and worked nearly 200 years after Hipparchos. During that time there had been a serious decline in Greek astronomy. Ptolemy's first task, as Aristotle had once done, was to review the work of those who had come before him. Ptolemy lived in Alexandria long after Alexander the Great had established a great library and world center there.

Ptolemy. Relief by Giotto and Andrea Pisano on the Campanile of the Duomo in Florence, Italy.

Ptolemy's two important books were *Tetrabiblos* (on planetary influences and astrology), and *Syntaxis Mathematica* (called in Arabic *Al Majisti* or the *Almagest*, meaning "The Greatest"). In these books Ptolemy:

1. used a star-measuring instrument for accurately determining the positions of the stars, Moon, and planets.

2. extended the star catalogue of 1,022 stars, correcting older star positions to compensate for changed positions due to the precession of the equinoxes.

3. refined the epicycle theory to include 40 circles and epicycles, a mathematical model which enabled anyone to accurately predict planetary positions.

History remembers Ptolemy for the following statement and how he chose to put it into practice.

"We believe that the object which the astronomer must strive to achieve is this: to demonstrate that all the phenomena in the sky are produced by uniform and circular motions. Having set ourselves the task to prove that the apparent irregularities of the five planets, the Sun and Moon can all be represented by means of uniform circular motions because only such motions are appropriate to their divine nature, we are entitled to regard the accomplishment of this task as the ultimate aim of mathematical science based on philosophy and is to be considered a great thing, very difficult and as yet unattained in a reasonable way by anyone."—from the *Almagest*

Ptolemy's solution to the problem of how to "save the appearances" of uniform circular motion by using mathematical explanations was the generally accepted world view for the next 1,400 years.

READING MORE

Diggins, Julia E. *String, Straightedge and Shadow: The Story of Geometry.* New York: The Viking Press, 1965.

Tauber, Gerald. *Man's View of the Universe: Evolving Concepts of Astronomy from Babylonian Times to Present.* New York: Crown Publishers, Inc., 1979.

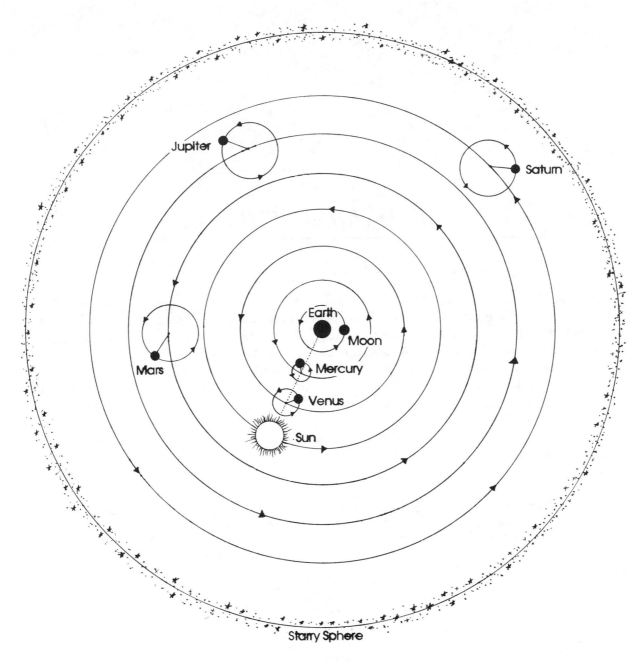

PTOLEMY'S SYSTEM

Showing the Earth in the center and the planets traveling around in circles (epicycles) on their orbits

Chapter 3:   MEASURING THE SKY

Section 1:   MAPPING THE SKY

The Celestial Sphere   When Hipparchos and Ptolemy compiled their star catalogues, they had several ways of telling other watchers of the stars exactly where each star in the catalogue was in a sky full of millions of stars. One way was to say how far a star was above the horizon and how far it was from a fixed position somewhere in the sky. If they wanted to point out a planet in the sky, they could say where it was on the ecliptic. The catalogue readers could also locate a star at some particular distance from one of the two poles of the celestial sphere. To find the star or planet, you would need to know how far it was from the poles and how far along the celestial equator. Finding exact positions was simply a matter of finding where the imaginary lines of the measurement of up and down crossed those which measured the distances sideways. When two roads cross each other, we call the crossing point an **intersection**. On maps, these intersecting lines of measurement are **coordinates**.

---

intersection comes from the Latin words *inter* = between and *sector* = one who cuts
Coordinates comes from the Latin words *co* = together with and *ordo* = a row or line

---

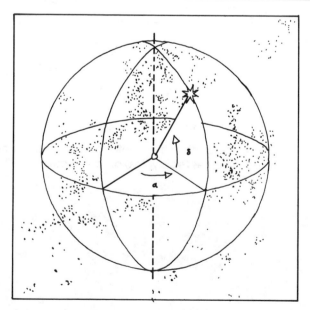

    Coordinates form a grid on which you can pinpoint the object you are trying to locate. In the next project you can make a model of the celestial sphere which will help you see how the ancients imagined the universe.

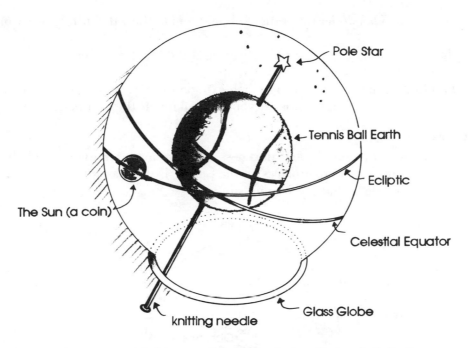

Pole Star

Tennis Ball Earth

Ecliptic

Celestial Equator

The Sun (a coin)

Glass Globe

knitting needle

─────── **Project 27: Making a Model of the Celestial Sphere** ───────

MATERIALS

clear glass globe (from a light fixture)
tennis ball
knitting needle
3 rubber bands
colored felt-tip pens (of various colors,
    particularly orange and blue)
grease pencil
protractor

lamp
scissors
gummed stars
modeling clay
thick cardboard (from a grocery box)
tape
small coin

PROCEDURE

1. Draw a map of the Earth on the tennis ball, using felt-tip pens and paints.
2. Put a rubber band around the middle for the equator. Color it blue with a felt-tip pen.
3. Push the knitting needle through the north and south poles of the tennis ball *Earth*.
4. Cut a piece of thick cardboard the same size as the opening on the glass globe.
5. Mark the top center of the glass globe with the china marking (grease) pencil. Put the protractor inside the globe and mark the outside of the globe at a point 23½° below the top mark. Glue a star on this spot. This is the *pole star*.
6. Reach inside the globe and place a small ball of modelling clay where the star is.
7. Put a rubber band around the globe from the top to the bottom. Use this rubber band and protractor to find and mark 23½° near the bottom of the globe. Place another rubber band on the outside of the globe 90° below the top mark. Color this rubber band orange with a colored marking pen. This is the *ecliptic*.
8. Mark the solstice and equinox points and indicate the month names for each.
9. Move the rubber band on the outside of the glass globe so that it lines up with the rubber band on the tennis ball. Color this rubber band blue just like the one on the tennis ball. This is the *celestial equator.*
10. Remove the tennis ball Earth. Push the knitting needle through the thick cardboard circle so that the needle stays lined up with the 23½° line. Tape the cardboard in place.
11. Mark the circumpolar stars using the grease pencil.

12. Place a coin (the *Sun*) under the orange rubber band to show the different seasonal positions of the Sun.

13. Shine the light through the celestial sphere onto the Earth from each solstice and equinox position.

14. Turn the knitting needle so that the Earth experiences day and night: clockwise if you are looking at the North Star, counterclockwise if you are looking at the Southern Cross.

OBSERVATIONS

How does the amount of sunlight and darkness compare at different times of the year where you live? How does it compare at other places on the Earth? Is there anyplace that receives sunlight all the time? Is there any place that receives no sunlight?

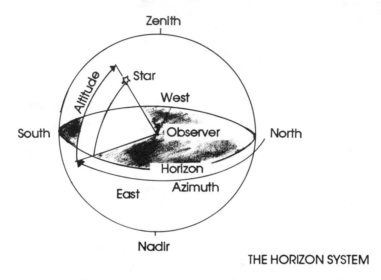

THE HORIZON SYSTEM

The Horizon System   Start with the horizon. Find your meridian. The point on the meridian directly overhead (90° above the horizon) is the **zenith**. The point directly below you on the other side of the world is the **nadir**.

---

zenith comes from the Middle English spelling *senyth* of the Arabic word *samt* = direction above the head
nadir comes from the Arabic word *nazir* = opposite

To find the coordinates of a star, first measure the star's height above or below the horizon. Use the meridian or another vertical circle like it drawn around the celestial sphere, crossing through the zenith and nadir and passing through the star you are measuring. The height of the star on this vertical line in degrees above or below the horizon is the **altitude**. Since the altitude of the zenith is 90° above the horizon, 90° minus the altitude of a star will give you the number of degrees from the star to the zenith.

---

altitude comes from the Latin word *altitudo* = height or elevation

---

When it comes to finding coordinates using just your eyes, it is easier to come up with an estimate of the altitude and azimuth than it is to use the other coordinate systems. In this next project you can make a simple degree-measuring device.

The other coordinate is the distance from the north point on the horizon eastward (clockwise) along the horizon to the vertical circle which passes through the star. You measure this in degrees from 0° to 360°. This is the **azimuth**.

---

azimuth comes from the Arabic word *as-sumut* = the way, direction

---

Project 28: Measuring Degrees Between the Stars (Star Bow)

MATERIALS

yard or meter stick
twine
dowel, ¾ inch (2 centimeters) x 2 feet
  (61 centimeters)

saw
hammer
nail

PROCEDURE

1. Cut the yardstick down to 2 feet or the meterstick down to 61 centimeters.
2. Nail the dowel to the center of the measuring stick.
3. Tie both ends of the measuring stick with twine to form a bow. The string of the bow should be 2 inches (5 centimeters) from the center of the measuring stick.

USING YOUR STARBOW

Put the end of the dowel on your cheek bone and beside your nose, just below your eye. Look down the dowel at the measuring stick and aim at a group of stars. Line two stars up with the marks on the measuring stick. Read how far apart the stars appear on the stick, then divide that number by 2 to find how many degrees apart the stars are.

OBSERVATION

Your Starbow can work for planets, the moon, and objects on Earth. *Never use it to look at the Sun!*

The Ecliptic System   The ecliptic system uses the path of the Sun or the ecliptic as its starting point for measuring. Imagine each of the 360° around the ecliptic as a point where a huge circle around the celestial sphere crosses the ecliptic. 0° on the ecliptic is the circle which passes through the **First Point of Aries**, the place where the vernal equinox occurs. This is also the place where the ecliptic crosses the celestial equator. This place is 0° **celestial longitude**. Celestial longitude tells you how far away east or west an object is from 0°. **Celestial latitude** tells you how far above or below the ecliptic an object is.

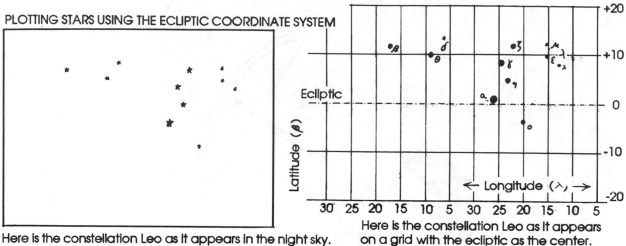

PLOTTING STARS USING THE ECLIPTIC COORDINATE SYSTEM

Here is the constellation Leo as it appears in the night sky.

Here is the constellation Leo as it appears on a grid with the ecliptic as the center.

To indicate celestial latitude above the ecliptic you write the word North (N) or a plus sign (+). To indicate celestial latitude below the ecliptic you use the word South (S) or a minus sign (−). To write parallels of longitude you use the Greek letter λ in front of them. They start with 0° at the First Point of Aries and move eastward along the ecliptic forming twelve groups of 30° each. Parallels of latitude have the Greek letter β in front of them starting with 0° at the ecliptic.

Using the grid showing the constellation of Leo, fill in the coordinates for the stars listed on the chart below.

Star	λ	β
α		
β		
γ		
δ		
ε		
ζ		
η		
θ		
λ		
μ		
ο		

The λ which stands for latitude is the Greek letter for *l* in our word *l*ongitude.

Ptolemy and those before him most frequently used the ecliptic system.

The Equatorial System   The equatorial system uses the celestial equator as its reference point. It is the 0° marker like the ecliptic was in the ecliptic system. In the equatorial system you measure positions above and below the celestial equator in degrees up to 90° which is the celestial pole. This distance is the **declination**. You measure declination north of the celestial equator from 0° to N 90° (+90°). South of the equator you measure declination from 0° to S 90° (−90°). Declination resembles the celestial latitude in the ecliptic system.

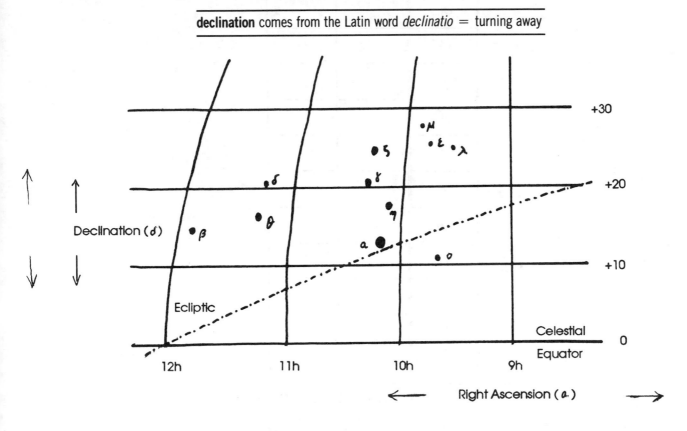

declination comes from the Latin word *declinatio* = turning away

The east-west coordinate in the equatorial system that is similar to celestial longitude is the **right ascension**. You measure it along the celestial equator in degrees or time eastward from the vernal equinox. There are 24 major divisions in the 360° of right ascension. Each division is equal to 15° and is also equal to one hour of time. This is how far (space) the sky moves as it turns in one hour (time). You found this out when you measured the star trails in Chapter 1. As you noticed from your measurement of sidereal time, 1° of arc is equal to 4 minutes of time. 90° minus the declination of a star gives its distance to the celestial pole. A star changes its altitude or its distance from the horizon. It does not change its declination. Its distance above the celestial equator always stays the same.

As a result of the precession of the equinoxes the position of the vernal equinox moves slightly every year. Since this is the starting point for the equatorial system, the precession means that over the years declinations and right ascensions of all the stars will shift gradually. The stars stay in their same places in the sky. The grid we use to map them changes. As a result, approximately every 50 years astronomers must adjust their star charts to keep them precise. They calculate new right ascensions and declinations positions which are accurate for a particular year or epoch. This book uses the epoch 2000 for its star charts, which means the star positions are accurate for the year 2000. The last remeasuring occurred for the year 1950.

epoch comes from the Greek word ἐποχη (epoche) = fixed point in time

Parallels of *Right Ascension* or hour angles have the Greek letter α or the abbreviation **R.A.** in front of them. Parallels of Declination have the Greek letter δ or the abbreviation **Dec.** in front of them.

Fill in the coordinates of right ascension and declination.

Star	α	δ
α		
β		
γ		
δ		
ε		
ζ		
η		
θ		
λ		
μ		
ο		

EQUATORIAL SYSTEM COORDINATES

The letter α which stands for right ascension is the Greek letter alpha, the first letter of the Greek alphabet. It stands for the *a* in our word right *a*scension. The letter δ is delta, the Greek letter for *d* in our word *d*eclination.

How do these coordinate measurements compare with those using the ecliptic coordinate system? In the next project you can do what many astronomers have done and plot your own star chart.

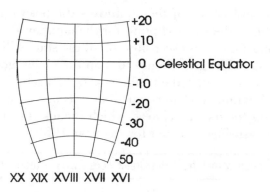

+20
+10
0 Celestial Equator
-10
-20
-30
-40
-50

XX XIX XVIII XVII XVI

Project 29: Mapping Stars (Equatorial Coordinate System)

MATERIALS
star chart grid   pen or pencil

PROCEDURE
1. Plot a star map using the star chart grid and the coordinates given in the list below. Your map should accurately show:

a. The positions of all stars listed, including their Greek letter names,

b. The names of the constellations,

c. The location of the ecliptic and the positions of the Sun on it, showing the dates for each position.

STAR POSITIONS

#	STAR	α		δ		#	STAR	α		δ	
1	α Sct	18	35	−8	14	18	η Sgr	18	17	−36	45
2	β Sct	18	47	−4	44	19	λ Sgr	18	27	−25	25
3	γ Sct	18	29	−14	33	20	σ Sgr	18	55	−26	17
4	δ Sct	18	42	−9	03	21	τ Sgr	19	06	−27	40
5	α Ser	15	44	+6	25	22	α Cr A	19	09	−37	54
6	δ Ser	15	34	+10	32	23	δ Cr A	19	08	−40	29
7	η Ser	18	21	−2	53	24	ξ Cr A	18	33	−42	18
8	χ Ser	17	37	−15	23	25	η Cr A	18	48	−43	40
9	α Oph	17	34	+12	33	26	α Sco	16	29	−26	25
10	β Oph	17	43	+4	34	27	β Sco	16	05	−19	48
11	ζ Oph	16	37	−10	34	28	δ Sco	16	00	−22	37
12	η Oph	17	10	−15	43	29	ε Sco	16	50	−34	17
13	κ Oph	16	57	+9	22	30	ξ Sco	17	37	−42	59
14	γ Sgr	18	05	−30	25	31	κ Sco	17	42	−39	01
15	δ Sgr	18	20	−29	49	32	λ Sco	17	33	−37	06
16	ε Sgr	18	24	−34	23	33	π Sco	15	58	−26	06
17	ζ Sgr	19	02	−29	52						

SUN POSITIONS

DATE	α		δ	
Nov.7	14	46	−16	02
Nov.17	15	27	−18	47
Nov.27	16	09	−20	58
Dec.7	16	52	−22	31
Dec.17	17	36	−23	19
Dec.27	18	20	−23	22
Jan.6	19	04	−22	37
Jan.16	19	48	−21	08
Jan.26	20	30	−18	58

OBSERVATIONS

How does this system compare with the others for accuracy and your ability to read it?

The Chinese astronomer-priests practiced a pole-oriented astronomy. In this book you will be using the equatorial system since it is the one which people generally use in astronomy today.

The Galactic System If you want to locate an object on or beyond the Milky Way, you can use the galactic system of coordinates. It is similar in some ways to the equatorial system. Instead of the equator of the celestial sphere, the galactic system uses the line that marks the middle of the Milky Way or the "equator" of the galaxy. The "equator" of the galaxy is the **galactic plane** or **galactic circle**. It is 90° above and below the galactic poles. You measure **galactic longitudes** eastward along the galactic plane from the point where it crosses the celestial equator. This occurs at 18 hours 44 minutes according to the equatorial system. You measure galactic latitudes North (+) or South (−) of the galactic plane toward the galactic poles. The galactic plane is inclined 62° from the celestial equator. The north pole of the galaxy is in the constellation Coma Berenices, the south pole is in the constellation Sculptor. People use galactic coordinates only in the three-dimensional study of the universe. You can look into this kind of measurement further in Chapter 7, Section 3.

Locating Positions and Measuring Degrees Since you can't see any of the coordinate grids that are in the sky, you need to find ways to help you locate positions and measure degrees.

LOCATING THE CELESTIAL EQUATOR

The following stars are on the celestial equator:

SPRING	γ Vir	α Sex	ι Hyd	δ Mon
	η Vir	β Sex		
	ζ Vir			
SUMMER	α Aqr			
	ζ Aqr			
AUTUMN	λ Psc	α Aqr		
	κ Psc	ζ Aqr		
		η Aqr		

LOCATING THE ECLIPTIC

The following stars are on or near the ecliptic:

SPRING	β Vir	α (Spica) It is not as close to the ecliptic as the other stars in Virgo, but it is easier to find.
	η Vir	
	λ Vir	
SUMMER	β Sco	θ Cap
	π Sgr	
AUTUMN	λ Aqr	ε Psc
		ζ Psc
WINTER	δ Gem	δ Can (between the Pleiades and Hyades in Taurus)
	η Gem	α Leo
	μ Gem	

MEASURING DEGREES WITH YOUR HAND

Hold your hand out at arm's length.

These measurements are approximate and depend on the size of your hand. Compare them with the measurement of the Moon whose disk is ½°.

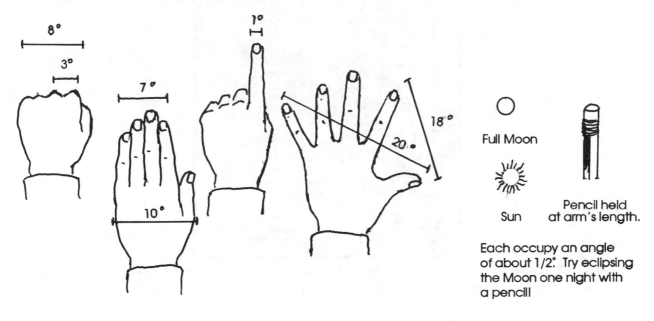

Full Moon

Sun

Pencil held at arm's length.

Each occupy an angle of about 1/2°. Try eclipsing the Moon one night with a pencil!

NightStar   The newest and most practical kind of star map is NightStar, an invention of **Bruce King**, an engineer and guitar-maker from New Zealand. When Bruce was twelve years old, a friend pointed out the star Alpha Centauri. Twenty years later King decided to make a star map that looked and acted like the sky dome. It took fifteen years to realize his dream. NightStar is a soft, moveable star map which you can easily adjust to match what the sky looks like for any place and any time in the world without distorting any of the constellations.

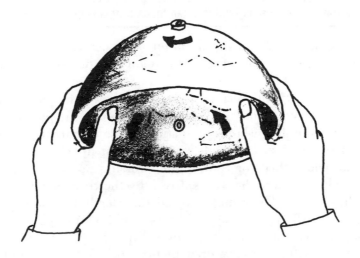

Nightstar, a new kind of star map.

READING MORE

Hirsch, S., Carl. *The Globe for the Space Age.* New York: The Viking Press, 1963.
Rand McNally. *The Rand McNally New Concise Atlas of the Universe.* Chicago: Rand McNally, 1974.

The Jewish astronomer Masha Allah from the Eighth Century measures a globe. *Etching by Albrecht Durer, De Scientia Motus Orbis, From Space Time Infinity by Charles Phillips, c Smithsonian Institution.*

Section 2: *MAPPING THE EARTH*

Map Coordinates   You have seen how people charted the sky using coordinate systems. Since the Earth is round like the celestial sphere, some of the same problems and solutions exist when you try to map it.

The words **map** and **chart** describe the materials people first used to make them. **Map** comes from the Latin word *mappa* = cloth. **Chart** comes from the Latin word *charta* = paper. Throughout history people have drawn maps on birch bark, blocks of wood, animal skins, iron, and clay. Today we usually use the word map when we are showing positions on the land (like a roadmap). Charts usually show positions in the sea or sky (like "charting the seven seas" and the star charts in this book).

Maps usually begin with a small area with your location as the central point. On some maps there is an arrow which points out "You are here." That is the main task of a map: to indicate where you are and to show others how to get there.

Different civilizations have come up with their own versions of how to map their particular country. To map their country of many tiny Islands, the Polynesians mapped the patterns of waves around the islands. The natives of the Marshall Islands used sticks made of narrow strips from the center ribs of palm leaves. They tied these sticks together with coconut fiber cords. To show where the islands were, the natives attached shells or coral at the crossing points of the sticks. The sticks themselves represented the places where the waves driven by the trade winds met the wave crests formed by breakers near the shore. These maps helped the Marshall Islanders find islands they couldn't see. To feel the effect of the waves, the navigators would lie down in their canoes, pointing their boats toward the more active waves which led toward the shore.

For their maps, the native North American drew pictures of what you would see on your way from one place to another.

Because the Nile River flooded every year, washing away most of the boundary markers, the ancient Egyptians had to resurvey their land every year.

The ancient Greeks gave us the first map of the entire world that we know of. It was the work of Anaximander (c. 600 B.C.) Through the work of another Greek, we have the first accurate measurement of the size of the Earth.

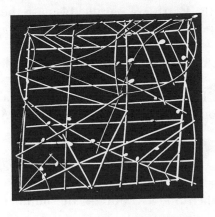

A stick chart from the Marshall Islands.　　　A Babylonian world map on a clay tablet.

Geography in Greek means "Earth writers or (describers)" from the Greek worlds γεο (geo) = earth, and γραφος (graphos) = to write. Today **Earth Science** includes the parts of geography that have to do with what the surface and interior of the Earth are made of. You can find out more about the structure of the Earth in Chapter 4.

Eratosthenes (276–192 B.C.) was a geometer, geographer, mapmaker, and chief librarian at the museum in Alexandria, Egypt. He knew that at noon every year on June 21st in the town of Syene the Sun's rays shone right to the bottom of a deep well without casting any shadows. Eratosthenes also knew that on the same day in his city of Alexandria, the Sun cast a slight shadow from the tall gnomon outside the library where he worked. Eratosthenes figured that since the Earth was a sphere and the two towns were 5000 stadia apart, the well and the gnomon would appear like this:

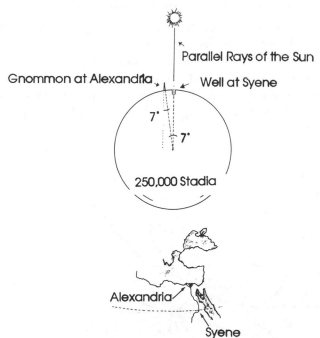

Eratosthenes set up a geometry problem using what information he had:

1. He imagined the tall gnomon in Alexandria and the deep well at Syene both to be pointing to the center of the Earth.

2. He assumed that Alexandria and Syene were on the same meridian circle (Syene is actually 3° east of Alexandria).

3. He knew that Syene was 5,000 stadia or 500 miles (800 kilometers) south of Alexandria. He assumed that Syene was in the tropics (it was actually 37 miles or 63 kilometers north of being exactly under the Sun in the tropics).

4. He assumed that the rays of the Sun which reach the Earth are parallel because the Sun is so far away. (Sunlight shining through pinholes in a curtain or through dust in the air appears as parallel rays).

5. The shadow cast from the gnomon indicated that the Sun's rays formed a 7° angle with the top of the gnomon.

6. He also knew from geometry that when a straight line cuts across two parallel straight lines, it makes equal angles with both of them, so the 7° angle could also be the distance between Alexandria and Syene.

7. A circle has 360°.

8. $360°/7$ will tell you what part of a complete circle the distance from Alexandria to Syene is. It is $\frac{1}{50}$ of a circle. $7°/5000$ stadia is $360°$/the circumference.

9. If $\frac{1}{50}$ of the circle of the Earth is 5,000 stadia, then $50 \times 5,000 =$ the number of stadia completely around the Earth. It is 250,000 stadia.

10. Most people agree that 1 stadia = close to 500 feet (158 meters). Since 1 mile = close to 5,000 feet and 1 kilometer = 1000 meters.

   1 stadia = 500 feet/5000 feet (0.10 mile) or 158/1000 meters (0.16 kilometer)

   250,000 stadia × 0.10 mile = 25,000 miles

   250,000 stadia × 0.16 kilometer = 40,000

Therefore, according to Eratosthenes 2,200 years ago the Earth is 25,000 miles or 40,000 kilometers around. The current figure given for the circumference of the Earth is 24,902 miles or 40,075 kilometers. Not Bad.

According to the Chaldeans, if a person walked at a steady pace of 30 stadia an hour (about 3 miles or 5 kilometers), it would take a year to go completely around the Earth. This would make the circumference of the Earth 263,000 stadia—a figure very close to the 250,000 stadia calculated by Eratosthenes.

Using the formula $C = 2\pi r$ or $C = \pi d$, what is the diameter of the Earth based on Eratosthenes' value for the circumference? Use 3.14159 for the value of π.

The ultimate authority in map-making and astronomy from Greek times to the Age of Exploration was another Greek, Ptolemy, who wrote the first known world atlas in history. The two main coordinates in making maps of the Earth are **latitude** and **longitude**. In this next experiment you can make a clay model of the Earth showing the lines of latitude and longitude.

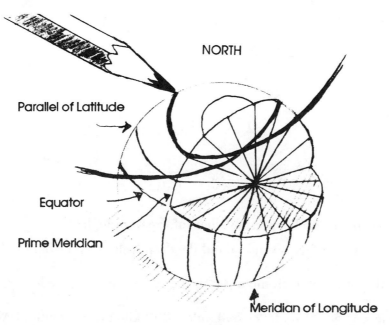

NORTH

Parallel of Latitude

Equator

Prime Meridian

Meridian of Longitude

SOUTH

Project 30: Demonstrating Latitude and Longitude

MATERIALS
modeling clay

string

knife

protractor

drawing compass

pencil

file card (index card)

scissors

ruler

PROCEDURE
1. Make a ball of clay about 3 inches (8 centimeters) in diameter.
2. Cut out a quarter section from the clay ball.
3. Draw a circle on the file card (using the compass), with the same diameter as the ball.
4. Divide the circle (using the protractor) into thirty-six 10° sections, drawing lines through the center of the circle for each section.
5. Cut out the circle and fold it in half along one of the lines and fit it into the cut out portion of the clay ball.
6. Continue the lines from the file card onto the clay ball using the string and pencil.

OBSERVATIONS
Lines of **latitude** are really circles around the Earth parallel to the equator. Their measurements come from the angles they make from the center of the Earth to a point above (north) or below (south) the equator. The equator itself is 0° latitude.

Lines of **longitude** are circles around the Earth which all pass through the north and the south pole. Their measurements also come from the angles they make from the center of the Earth to a point east or west of the prime meridian. The prime meridian is 0°. In Ptolemy's day, the prime meridian passed through The Canary Islands. Today it passes through **Greenwich, England**.

When you combine latitude and longitude lines, they form a grid. You can use this grid to find any place on the Earth.

Before Ptolemy, the Egyptians had the reputation of the greatest land-measurers. As early as 2800 B.C. using precise astronomical observations they:
1. could measure latitude to within a few hundred feet,
2. could measure longitude almost as accurately,
3. knew the length of the circumference of the Earth very precisely,
4. knew the length of their country almost to the cubit (about 1 yard or 1 meter).

Maps of a Sphere   How do you make a map of a sphere? One way is to make a sphere and put the map on it like you did when you made your tennis ball sky dome (Project 3, Making a Tennis Ball Sky Dome) and the model of the celestial sphere (Project 27, Making a Model of the Celestial Sphere). **Martin Beheim** (1459–1509) of Nurnberg, made the first globe of the Earth to survive to the present. It was 20 inches in diameter and made of wood. Martin Beheim called his globe the **Erdapfel**. He divided it into 12 spear-head-shaped sections of 30° each called **gores**. To make his globe, Beheim arranged his 12 gores like an unravelled orange peel, as if he had peeled away the skin of the Earth.

---

erdapfel comes from the German words *Erd* = Earth and *Apfel* = apple
gore comes from the Old English *gara* = spear. A gore is a garment maker's term for part of a pattern.

You can do what Martin Beheim did and make a globe map from gores in the next project.

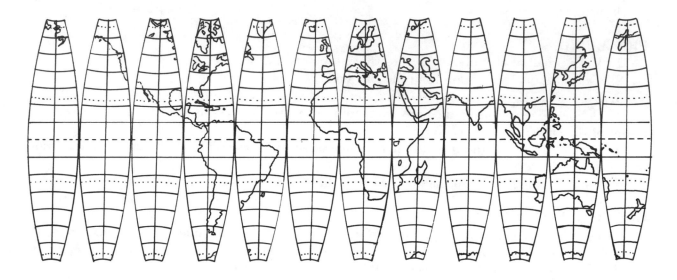

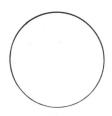

─────── **Project 31: Assembling a Global Map** ───────

MATERIALS

gores from book	scissors
glass globe (from light fixture)	tape
paints, colored pencils, or felt-tip pens	paper glue

PROCEDURE

1. Enlarge the gores so that the length of the equator is the same as the circumference as the glass globe.

2. Color in each section of the map using paints, colored pencils, or felt-tip pens.

3. Cut out the gores and the two blank circles for the north and south poles. Keep all the gores attached in the middle.

4. Glue each gore down one at a time using the glass globe as a mold.

5. Glue the two polar circles on, cutting and folding as necessary to fit. When they have dried, fill in the areas that connect with the land on the gores.

6. Set the finished globe on a stand made of a section cut from an empty paper towel roll (which you have painted gold, silver, or brown).

OBSERVATIONS

In this project you have started with a flat map and turned it into a sphere. Cover your "erdapfel" as carefully as you can with a large sheet of tracing paper. Trace the continents with a felt-tip pen. Unwrap and smooth out the tracing paper. Use the felt-tip pen to join the lines that aren't connected. What happened? The individual coast lines may be quite accurate, but your map does not resemble the whole Earth.

Martin Waldseemuler made a world map in 1507. His maps were the first to use the name *America*. Waldseemuler suggested the name America for the New World in honor or his colleague, Amerigo Vespucci, who explored and named the Venezuelan coast in 1499.

America, like Europa and Asia end in an "a," making them names of women, the common practice in naming countries.

Every flat map of the round Earth distorts the true picture of the world. One-eighth of the globe is about as much as you can show flat without distortion. Distortion can be a serious problem for a navigator who depends on maps to give an accurate picture of size, shape, distance, and direction of land and water areas. No flat map can show all four of these accurately. A big step in making a flat map of the spherical Earth came about through the work of **Gerhart Kramer** (1512–1594) whose name in Latin was **Gerardus Mercator.** In his time Mercator was the most honored mapmaker in Europe. He called his collection of maps an **atlas** and people have used that word ever since to describe a book of maps.

Atlas is the name of the Greek hero who had to hold the world on his shoulders.

Mercator used the idea of projecting an image of the Earth's sphere onto a flat surface as if the Earth was transparent and a light was inside it. Mercator invented two map projections: The **Mercator** and the **Conic.** Today people use the projection named after him for nearly all sea charts. Depending on where the light is inside the globe of the Earth, you will get a different projection.

When you try to show large areas of the Earth you have to imagine that you are projecting the image of these areas onto a shape other than a sphere which can be more easily "unpeeled" and opened out flat. Three popular shapes are the cylinder, the cone and the flat plane.

A **cylinder** touches the globe around the equator so cylindrical projection maps are most accurate for areas around the equator. They are not very accurate for showing size or distance. Mercator's map is a variation of the cylindrical projection.

A **cone** touches the globe at 40° latitude. This latitude passes through the United States. Conic projection maps are most accurate for the Northern Hemisphere and the United States. They are not very accurate for direction. Ptolemy's map is a variation of the conical map.

A flat plane can touch the globe at any one point. Because maps made from flat plane projections are accurate in one area we call them **azimuthal projections**. Mapmakers often use azimuthal projections in maps of the north or south poles. They are very accurate at showing direction.

In the next project, you can see for yourself how to create different projections.

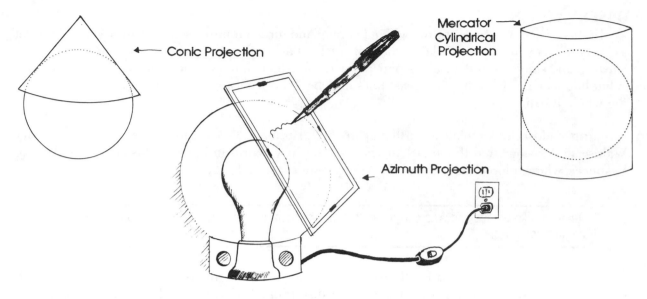

---------------- **Project 32: Drawing Map Projections** ----------------

MATERIALS

glass globe (or map from Project 29)   plastic sheet
lamp socket   felt-tip pen
15 watt bulb   stapler
15 inch (38 centimeter) strip of strong   masking tape
   cardboard   sheet of plexiglass or glass

PROCEDURE

1. Cut holes in the cardboard strip; staple both ends together to make a ring.
2. Place the cardboard ring over socket and bulb. Set globe on top of ring.
3. Tape tracing paper or wax paper onto the plexiglass. This is your *screen*.
4. Shine the light through the globe and place the screen next to it to receive the map's projected image.
5. Draw the Earth placing the plastic sheet flat, as a cone and as a cylinder to create the different projections.

OBSERVATIONS

Which projection shows the least distortion? Which is easiest to read?

Triangulation   **Gemma Frisius Regnier** (1508–1542), a German surveyor, perfected a system for measuring far distances. The system uses the observer's knowledge of triangles from trigonometry, so we call it **triangulation.** Gemma Frisius did not invent triangulation. It probably came from ancient Egypt.

A triangle has six parts: three sides and three angles. If you know the sizes of three parts of a triangle, one of which must be one of the sides, then you can figure out each of the three other parts.

Jacques Cassini (1678–1756) of the French Academy used the method of triangulation to measure and map all of France. His son, Cesar Francois and his cousin, Maraldi, assisted him in this massive undertaking. They completed their measurements and in 1744, published a map based on them. In triangulation you make triangles out of the distances you are going to measure. Then you find out the angles and lengths that you can measure and calculate the distances that are too far to measure just as you would with any triangle.

This method also works when you want to measure the distance to stars, see Project 83, Surveying with Triangles (Triangulation) in Chapter 7, Section 1).

Topographic Maps   Some maps actually show both the height of various points on the map compared to other features around these points, and the elevation or the height of a feature above sea level. These measurements are **contours** and the kind of map that shows them is a **topographic** map. Topographic maps give you a very good idea of the shape of the land and where the high and low spots are. In this next project you can see how people prepare topographic maps by making a mountain of your own and mapping it.

Part of Cassini's triangulation map of France, 1744.

---

topographic comes from the Greek word τοπος *(topos)* = place or spot, and γραφος *(graphos)* = to write

---

Benjamin Banneker (1731–1806) was an American mathematician, surveyor, and astronomer. In 1790, Thomas Jefferson appointed him to survey the team that was to lay out the plans for Washington, D.C. When the chief architect and city planner left the project, they took their detailed maps with them. Banneker was able to redraw the plan from memory. He later published an astronomical almanac.

93

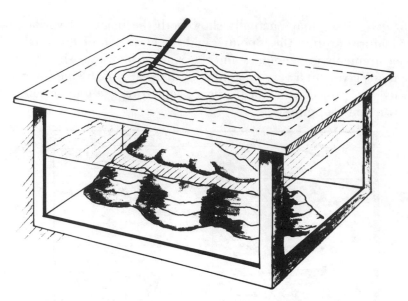

Project 33: Mapping Elevations (Topographic Map)

MATERIALS

a long, flat watertight pan with high
   sides (an aquarium is perfect)

modeling clay

water

nail, wire, paper clip, or pencil

sheet of glass or heavy plastic that will
   cover the top of the pan

ruler

grease pencil

PROCEDURE

1. Make a model of a mountain range inside the pan. Have at least one peak in the range almost as tall as the aquarium.

2. Place the ruler in the tank so that it stands upright.

3. Pour enough water into the tank to fill it up to the ½ inch (1 centimeter) level of the ruler.

4. Use the nail to mark the clay where the top of the water touches it.

5. Add more water, filling the pan to the 1-inch (2-centimeter) level and again mark the water level on the clay.

6. Repeat this procedure, adding ½ inch (1 centimeter) of water each time until you cover the mountain with water.

7. Pour off the water carefully.

8. Place the glass sheet on top of the tank.

9. Look straight down into the tank and use the grease pencil to trace patterns of the nail scratches you see in the clay, onto the glass.

10. Remove the glass and look at it, comparing what you have drawn to the actual shape of the mountain.

OBSERVATIONS

Does your map give you an accurate picture of the mountain's shape? Lines on a topographic map are contour lines. They connect all points of equal elevation. On your map, each contour line is ½ inch (1 centimeter) above the one below it. If each mark equals 500 feet (115 meters), how high is your clay mountain?

READING MORE

Dicks, Brian, consultant editor. *The Children's World Atlas.* Milbrae, California: Celestial Arts, 1981.

Kjellstrom, Bjorn. *Be an Expert with Map and Compass.* New York: Charles Scribner's Sons, 1976.

The Pleiades (M45). *Photo courtesy of Observatoire de Haute Provence*

Section 3: *CELESTIAL NAVIGATION*

Star Positions and Degrees in Between   Knowing how to read the map of the sky can help you get around on the Earth. Explorers, adventurers and sailors all over the world have known this for thousands of years. Even with all of the technology available to them, navigators still carry star-reading tools and charts on board. They never break down.

    To travel on the Earth using the sky as your guide you need to know the altitude of several important stars, when they will cross the meridian and what time they rise and set. You also need to know exactly where they are. In the sixteenth century, Tycho Brahe and others used an instrument to help answer these questions. Because this instrument was in the shape of a quarter circle these astronomers called them **quadrants**. In this next project you can build the same instrument.

---

quadrant comes from the Latin word *quatuor* = four

95

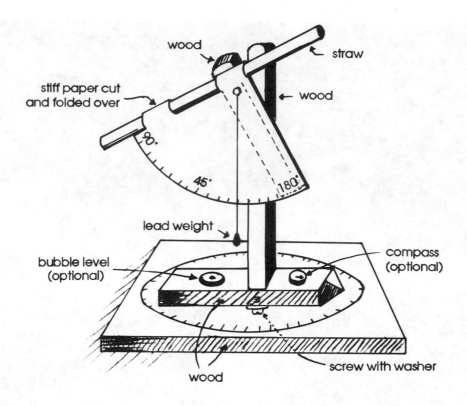

—— Project 34: Making a Quadrant and Azimuth Measuring Instrument ——

MATERIALS

drinking straw
bolt with wing nut and washer
wood   *base:* 12 × 12 × ¾ inches
    (30 × 30 × 2 centimeters)
   supports: 1 × 1 inch
    (2½ × 2½ centimeters)
   pointer: 1 × ½ inches
    (2½ × 12 millimeters)
red thread

small lead weight (fishing sinker)
flat head screw with washer
quadrant and Azimuth drawing from this
  page
sheet of stiff paper
bubble level
compass
access to a photocopier

PROCEDURE

1. Cut the wood pieces as they appear in the drawings
2. Photocopy the quadrant and azimuth circles.
3. Assemble as shown in the drawing.

USING YOUR COMBINED QUADRANT & AZIMUTH MEASURING INSTRUMENT

1. Sight Polaris through the straw. Line up the base so it reads 0° at the north pointer.

2. Keep the base stationary and move the sighting instrument to find a star. The pointer on the instrument will point to a number on the circle on the base. This is the **azimuth** of the star. See Section 1 of this chapter for an explanation of the azimuth as part of the horizon coordinate system. The weighted string will indicate the **altitude** of the star on the protractor.

OBSERVATIONS

You can remove the quadrant and use it by itself to find altitudes. The altitude and azimuth measurements depend on your local horizon. Measurements of the same star made from another location may be different.

Using the backstaff, 1681.　　　　　　A backstaff.　　　　　　Using the cross-staff, 1681.

The Sun and the North Star are the two most reliable sources with which to determine direction and location. In 1607, John Davis published a description of his astronomical device which he called the **backstaff**. It was a version of another astronomical instrument that was popular for a long time, the **cross-staff**. The cross-staff used the line of the horizon and the position of the Sun. To use it meant that you had to look right at the Sun. You also had to look at both ends of the crosspiece at the same time while one end touched the horizon and the other the Sun. The backstaff placed the back of the observer to the Sun, sighting along the staff at the line of the horizon. At the end of the staff was a small screen, the observer moved the crosspiece until its top cast a shadow on the bottom of the screen. The crosspiece now lined up with a number on the staff which gave the altitude angle between the horizon and whatever you were observing in the sky.

In this next project you can build a model of the cross-staff designed for measuring degrees in the night sky. *Do not use it to look at the Sun.*

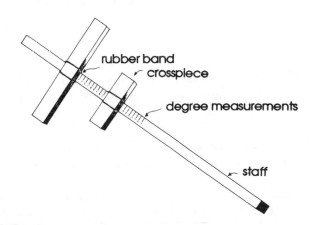

rubber band

crosspiece

degree measurements

staff

───────── **Project 35: Making a Cross-Staff** ─────────

MATERIALS

wood:　*staff* 1 × 1 × 30 inches
　　　　(2½ × 2½ × 76
　　　　centimeters)
　　　　crosspieces
　　　　1½ × ½ × 12 inches
　　　　(3¾ × 1¼ × 30
　　　　centimeters)
　　　　1½ × ½ × 6 inches
　　　　(3¾ × 1¼ × 15
　　　　centimeters)

flat black paint
dark brown stain or paint
protractor
white pencil
ruler
rubber band
small piece of cloth

PROCEDURE

1. Cut out all the pieces of wood.
2. Paint the staff flat black, and stain or paint the crosspieces brown.
3. Draw a line on the crosspieces using the white colored pencil to mark the middle of each crosspiece.
4. Lay the large crosspiece on top of the staff. Loop one end of the rubber band around one end of the crosspiece, pass the rubber band under the staff, and loop it around the other end of the crosspiece.
5. Adjust the crosspiece so that the staff is under the exact middle mark of the crosspiece. If you have difficulty sliding the crosspiece up and down the staff, wrap the rubber band with the small piece of cloth.
6. Hold the end of the staff on your cheek and against the side of your nose, next to your eye. Slide the large crosspiece (also called a transversal) until it fits in between your horizon and a star whose altitude you already know (e.g., Polaris). Let's say that distance is 38°. Using the white colored pencil and the ruler, carefully mark a line and the number 38° on the staff right where the side of the crosspiece nearest you crosses the staff.
7. Use the stars and their degree measurements listed at the end of the first section of this chapter (and the protractor if necessary) to mark more lines and degrees on your staff.
8. Replace the large crosspiece with the shorter one for smaller distances, and sight with the opposite end of the staff. Make your marks for the shorter crosspiece on the other side of the staff.

USING YOUR CROSS-STAFF

To measure the degrees between two stars, hold the end of the staff on your cheek and against the side of your nose, next to your eye. Slide the crosspiece along the staff until the ends of the crosspiece fit in between the stars. Look at the staff and see what line and degree number the crosspiece is near. This will tell you how many degrees apart the two stars are.

OBSERVATIONS

You can measure distances above the horizon, distances between stars and the changing position between planets and stars. Some cross-staffs had four crosspieces with scales on each side of the staff.

Around 170 B.C. Hipparchos developed a way to draw the celestial sphere onto a flat surface: the stereoscopic projection. Using this projection he invented a device called the **astrolabe.**

---

astrolabe comes from the Greek words $\dot{\alpha}\sigma\tau\eta\rho$ (aster) = star and $\lambda\alpha\beta\omega$ (labo) = to take hold of

---

With this instrument you could "take hold of the stars" for surveying, time keeping, charting the skies, and casting horoscopes. Its use developed and spread during the Islamic Empire. It was a way to find out the correct date from the stars so you could celebrate the required religious festivals. Every citizen who could afford one owned an astrolabe. It helped them know the correct time to pray and the direction of the city of Mecca towards which they were to pray.

The Moors reintroduced the astrolabe to Europe when they conquered Spain in the Middle Ages. European instrument makers produced astrolabes for scholars, noblemen, freemasons, and astronomers. In the fourteenth century, the English poet **Chaucer** (c.1342–1400) called it the "Noble Instrument." He wanted to teach his ten-year-old son how to use the "Noble Instrument." The only texts on the astrolabe were in Latin, so Chaucer translated a Latin instruction text into English. The instructions for building an astrolabe in this next project are also in English.

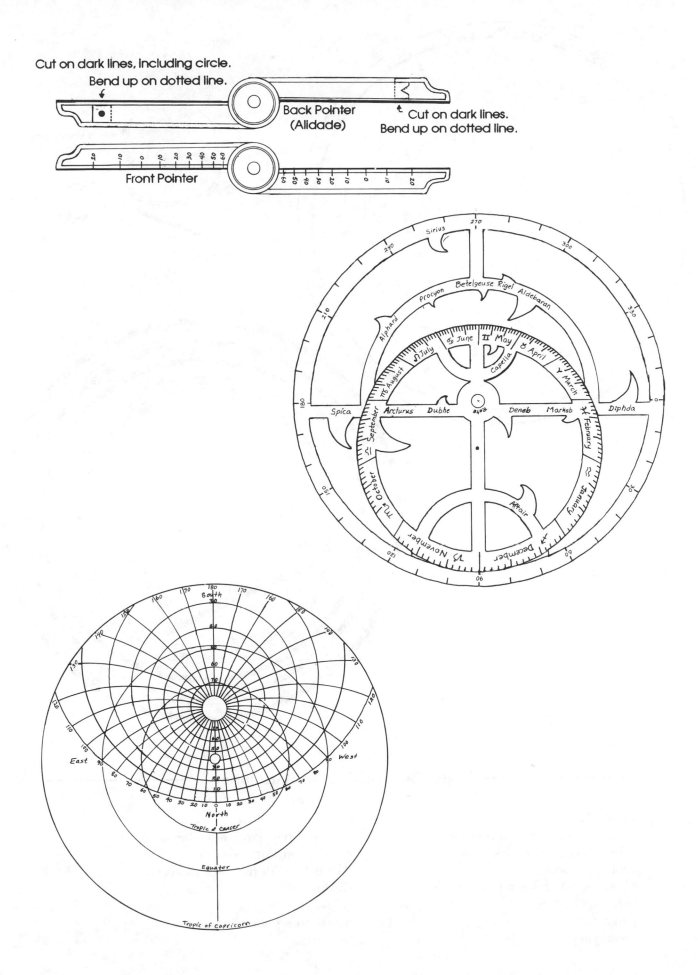

Cut on dark lines, Including circle.

Bend up on dotted line.

Back Pointer
(Alidade)

Cut on dark lines.
Bend up on dotted line.

Front Pointer

99

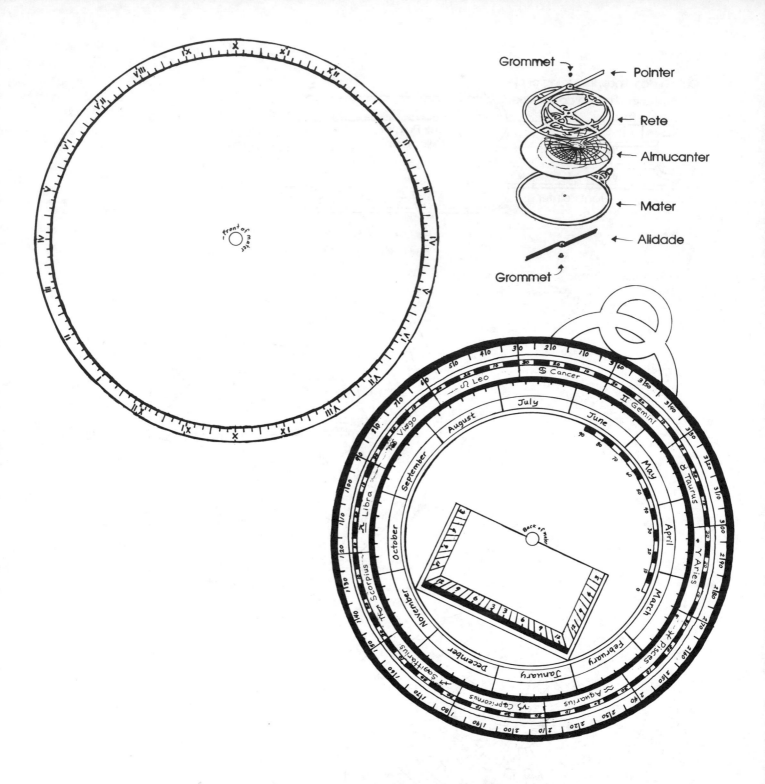

Project 36: Making an Astrolabe

MATERIALS

astrolabe plans and computer
   instructions from Sky Files
rubber cement
plastic sheet (from report covers)
stiff paper
paper fastener
metal ring

gummed paper reinforcements
colored yarn or rope
flashlight with paper bag covering
cardboard
scissors
access to a photocopier

PROCEDURE
1. Photocopy the astrolabe sheets and glue them onto a piece of cardboard.
2. Use computer program to determine the measurements for your particular latitude
3. Cut out the parts
4. Assemble as shown.

FINDING THE ALTITUDE AND AZIMUTH OF A STAR

Hold the astrolabe by the ring on the top and sight a star through the two viewing holes in the alidade (on the back of the astrolabe), moving the alidade as needed. The alidade will now be pointing to a number on the rim of the mater. This is the altitude angle of the star above the horizon. Use the flashlight to read this angle or go inside to complete your calculations.

If the star you are sighting is Arcturus, for example, and you find it to be 30° above the eastern horizon, you turn the rete until the tip of the Arcturus star finder on it lines up with the almucantar (declination circle) which shows an altitude of 30° above the eastern horizon.

You can now check the position of the rete to find the azimuth of Arcturus as well as the altitude and azimuth of the other stars which have pointers on the rete (as long as they are above the horizon).

You can also find the azimuth by holding the astrolabe sideways so that the mater is horizontal. The 0° marker on the top of the back of the mater must point to the north.

Calculating Star Positions, 1533. *Engraving by Petrus Apianus, Instrument Buch, 1533*
from Space Time Infinity *by Charles Phillips, c. Smithsonian Institution*

FINDING THE RISING AND SETTING TIMES OF A STAR

You can tell the hour when a star will rise, cross the meridian or set for any time of the year. Locate the star finder in the rete for the star whose rising time you want to know. Set the tip of the star finder to the eastern horizon (meridian), for crossing or western horizon (for setting). Line up the pointer with the Sun's position on the correct date as shown in the ecliptic circle. The rule now points to a time on the rim of the mater which is the rising, crossing or setting time of the star.

FINDING THE RISING AND SETTING TIMES OF THE SUN

Set the rete so that the Sun's position on the ecliptic for the date you want touches the eastern horizon (for sunrise) or the western horizon (sunset). Set the pointer to line up with this point. The pointer points to the hour on the rim of the mater.

FINDING THE TIME USING THE STARS

Using the steps described in *Finding the Altitude and Azimuth of a Star*, locate the position of a star visible in the sky at some unknown time at night. Set the pointer to line up with the First Point of Aries, marked on the ecliptic circle. The end of the pointer will point to the hour of star time on the rim of the mater. You may or may not need to add 12 to this hour, depending on how many degrees the First Point of Aries is from the meridian.

FINDING THE TIME USING THE SUN

Look on the back of the astrolabe for the circle of months and the circle of the zodiac. Line up the alidade with the correct date on the circle of months and find where it points on the circle of the zodiac. This is the position of the Sun on the eclipic for that day. The rete needs to be set up as described in Finding the Altitude and Azimuth of a Star, above. Turn the astrolabe over. Set the rule to line up with the correct Sun position on the ecliptic circle that you just found out. The end of the rule will point to the hour of Solar time on the rim of the mater.

You can also find time from the altitude of the Sun. Using the alidade, find the altitude of the Sun. The position of the Sun on a particular date as shown on the ecliptic circle is the "Sun Pointer" for that day. Turn the rete until the "Sun Pointer" lines up with the correct almucantor. Set the rule to line up with the First Point of Aries marked on the ecliptic circle. The end of the rule will point to the hour on the rim of the mater.

OBSERVATIONS

You can also use the astrolabe to locate positions of the Moon and the planets. Both the cross-staff and the backstaff were far more practical on board ship than the astrolabe proved to be. An astrolabe needed to be held in a level position. Such conditions were rare at sea. However, if you knew how to use it, an astrolabe was like having an observatory on board. The computer program in Sky Files which allows you to construct your astrolabe to be accurate in your latitude was programmed especially for this book by David Schaefer.

The invention of the printing press in 1454 by **Johann Gutenberg** (c.1398–1468) was a major event in history. For mapmakers it meant the possibility of producing many copies of maps for a wide audience. Artistic skill blossomed forth in both charting and decorating maps of the sky, seas, and Earth. Librarians no longer needed to have scribes recopy these highly detailed documents. Printed copies as accurate as the originals were available. Navigators used the new presses to print up their own charts and tables with which to calculate star positions. These calculations were far more accurate then those their astrolabes could offer.

Navigators soon altered the appearance of the astrolabe. They added mirrors and later telescopes to the alidade and the mater so they could sight the Sun, a star or the Moon and the horizon at the same time, much like a backstaff. With each change in the astrolabe, there was a change in its name.

In 1669, **Jean Picard** (1620–1682) added a telescope to the sighting portion of the staff of the quadrant. By 1678, Hooke, Hevelius, and Halley had all tried the same idea. Halley's improvement was to add to the telescope a piece of glass, half mirror and half clear with which to both view the horizon (with the clear part) and to reflect the light of the Sun (the mirror part). You could move the reflected light to line up with the horizon. Sometime before his death in 1727, **Sir Isaac Newton** (1643–1727) had worked on variations of the quadrant using mirrors. In 1730, two men working independently developed a variation of the quadrant that relied on 1/6 of a full circle, for their measurements. They called their instruments **sextants**.

---

sextant comes from the Latin word *sex* = six

Both **John Hadley** from England and **Thomas Godfrey** of the United States designed a sextant with two mirrors. The sextant makes use of the principle that the angle which a ray of light makes when it reflects off two mirrors in a row is two times as big as the angle between the two mirrors. In this next project you can make sextant very much like the ones used by Hadley and Godfrey.

As you pursue your study of astronomy, you will find a number of examples of discoveries made by two people at about the same time who didn't even know who the other person was or what he or she was doing. In some cases, after their discoveries, they met.

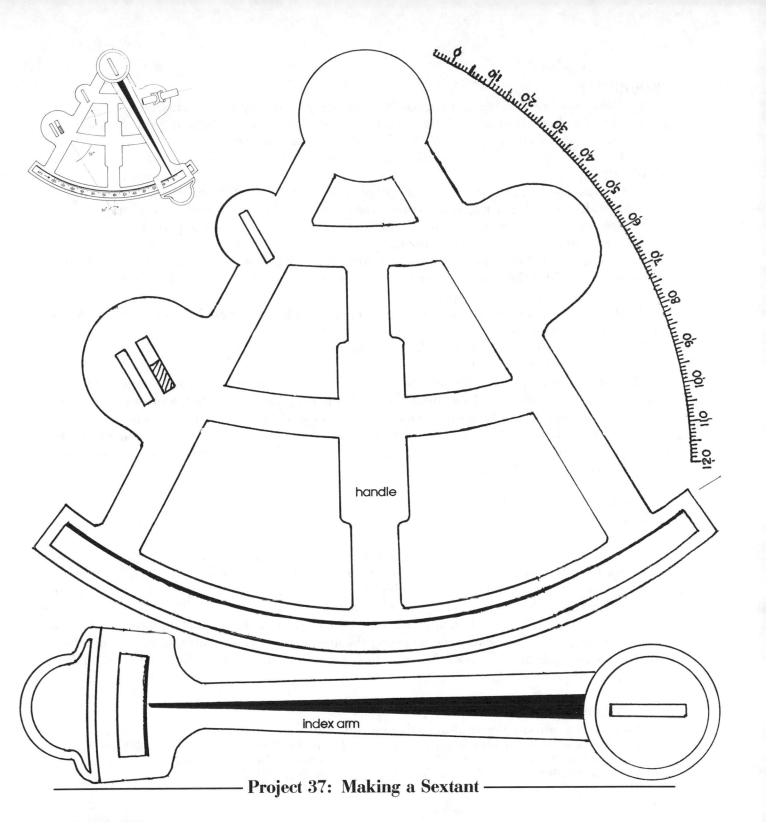

handle

index arm

Project 37: Making a Sextant

MATERIALS

2 small mirrors, 1½ × 1⅜ inches
  (4 × 3 centimeters)
l sheet of thick posterboard
rubber cement or strong glue
stiff paper
paper fastener
razor blade
scissors

2 pairs of sunglasses (one to wear and
  one to take apart)
clear fingernail polish
1 × 6 inch (2½ × 15 centimeter) piece
  of corregated cardboard (from a
  grocery box)
access to a photocopier, one with
  enlarging capability

103

PROCEDURE

1. Photocopy the drawing and cut out (vernier) scale. You may wish to enlarge it.
2. Glue the drawing of the index arm and frame onto thick posterboard and cut them out.
3. Cut the index arm circle out of the piece of corregated cardboard.
4. Take measurements of mirror and shade (sunglass) holders and telescope tube and cut them out of stiff paper.
5. Prepare horizon glass by scraping off half the silver backing of one of the mirrors with a razor blade. Keep the line straight in between the clear part of the glass and the mirror.
6. Remove lenses from an old pair of sunglasses and use them for shade glasses.
7. Attach index arm with paper fastener.
8. Use the razor blade to scrape out a space for the head of the paper fastener under the cardboard circle. Glue the cardboard circle onto the index arm. Make sure that the arm moves freely and the cardboard circle stays in place.
9. Mount mirrors and shade glasses using stiff paper holders in the exact positions shown. Make sure they are perpendicular to the frame and index arm.
10. Glue the piece of wood on back for the handle.
11. Install the telescope tube.
12. Set up two lighted candles side by side, 2½ inches (6 centimeters) apart. Stand 50 feet (15 meters) from the candles and look through the tube, holding the sextant flat. Move the index arm slowly until the two flames blend into one. Make a mark at the place on the limb where the index arm is pointing. This is where the zero point on the arc should be. Line up the zero point on the vernier scale with the zero point on the arc and glue the scale into place. When the index arm is at zero, all mirrors should be parallel.

USING YOUR SEXTANT

First check to see that frame, index mirror, and horizon glass are perpendicular and that when the index is at 0, all mirrors are parallel.

When sighting, always keep both eyes opened and *wear sunglasses*! **Never** look directly at the Sun. Look for a level horizon with no hills in the distance. A lake or the ocean is best. Your task is to observe the Sun as it climbs towards its highest point in the sky, then stops and descends again so you can measure the angle of its highest elevation.

Just before noon, sight the horizon through the telescope tube. Bring the Sun into your field of view by moving the index arm. Keep adjusting the arm as the Sun ascends toward the meridian. When the Sun stops climbing, read the angle on the arc. Record the angle, the exact time, and the date of your observation.

OBSERVATION

The sextant is an instrument that navigators still prize and use today.

This project is adapted from plans which first appeared in EVERYBODY'S GUIDE TO ASTRONOMY, prepared by the editorial staff of "Popular Science Monthly," New York: Popular Science Publishing Company, Inc., 1934, and later in the SEA EXPLORER MANUAL, New Brunswick: Boy Scouts of America, 1954.

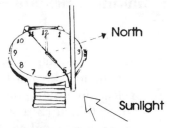

Locating North with Your Watch   Hold your watch level or lay it on the ground and stand a thin stick straight up beside it. Turn the watch until the shadow of the stick falls across the hour hand in a straight line to the time on the opposite side. Half-way between the shadow and the number 12 on the watch is the direction of north.

To Find Your Latitude First subtract your observed angle from 90°. You may need to consult a table of the Sun's declination to correct for the Sun's declination on that date. Add or subtract the number of degrees from the chart with the degrees of your observation. The result is your latitude. For people in the northern hemisphere, the altitude of the North Star is the same as your latitude.

To Find Your Longitude Clocks have teamed up with navigators in other ways to help find directions and locations. The most significant combined effort has been in determining longitude.

People have generally measured time from the transit of the Sun across the meridian (see Chapter 1, Section 3). The upper transit occurs at noon, the lower transit at midnight. Since 1925, the lower transit has been the standard measuring point. This means that a new day starts at midnight. When we map the Earth with a global grid we find that the Sun transits the various meridians at different times. This means that you can measure the differences between any two places on the Earth both in distance and in time.

It is inconvenient, however, to have people in the same town using different times just because they live at different meridians. One way to solve this problem is to divide the world into time zones and pretend that, for the sake of convenience in telling time, all the meridians within a particular time zone are compressed into one. Each of these zones is more or less 15° wide and runs from east to west across the globe. These zones have irregular shapes to conform to national boundaries.

If you compare the Sun's crossing of your local meridian with its crossing of your standard time zone meridian it probably won't be exactly at 12:00 noon. You will have to add or subtract a few minutes on your observation time. The additional minutes you added or the difference between the two times will give you the number of degrees longitude you need to adjust your standard time meridian. The way to figure your calculations is to remember that the Sun travels a distance of 15° for every hour of time or 1° every 4 minutes. If the Sun crosses this meridian before noon, you need to add the degrees eastward from your standard time meridian. If the Sun crossed your local meridian after noon, you measure the difference in longitude west from your standard time meridian.

To measure time and longitude, you need a starting point that everyone agrees to use. Hipparchos had chosen Rhodes as his Prime Meridian or zero point. For Ptolemy, it was the "Fortunate Isles" (the Canary Islands) which was the western boundary of the then-known world. Other astronomers and mapmakers have chosen some city in their native land.

In 1634, **Cardinal Richelieu** (1585–1642) called together mathematicians and astronomers in Paris to decide on a Prime Meridian. They based their decision on Ptolemy's suggestion and chose the island farthest west in the Canary Islands, called Ferro or Isle de Fer. In the 1700s many people had been using the meridian passing through the Royal Observatory outside London in the suburb of Greenwich (pronounced *Gren-itch*). At that time the two most important observatories for navigators in Europe were the one in Paris and the one in Greenwich.

A geographic conference in 1884 chose Greenwich. At this same conference, the members made the decision to begin the day at midnight on the Prime Meridian instead of noon. It wasn't until 1924 that all the nations (except parts of Saudi Arabia) accepted the recommendations for the Prime Meridian midnight starting time and worldwide time zones all based on the meridian at Greenwich.

In one hour the Sun moves 1/24 of a complete circle around the Earth travelling west. Since there are 360° in a circle, 1/24 would be 15°. If the Sun starts in Greenwich which is 0°, in one hour the Sun will be over the meridian that is 15° west of the Prime Meridian. When this happens and it is noon at 15°W, it is 1 P.M. at Greenwich. If you are sailing west and it is noon at Greenwich and the time where you are is 3:30, you are 3 and 1/2 times 15° or 52° 30' west. How are you going to know what time it is in Greenwich? People asked this question at a point in history when sundials, sand clocks and huge, unreliable timepieces were the only ways of keeping time. The other problem was that, as you saw in Chapter 1, Sun time and clock time are not always the same. On November 2nd, the Sun passes the meridian around 11:42 A.M., Local Mean Time while on February 9th, it passes at 12:13 P.M. The Equation of Time corrects this difference between the real Sun time (apparent) and the Local time (mean). Tables showing these corrections were carried on board ship.

In 1530 Gemma Frisius said that you should be able to carry an accurate clock with you to sea, keeping it set so that it always told you the time at port from which you left. You could find your local time from the Sun. With this information you could change the difference in the time between two places into the difference longitude between them.

In 1714 the British Parliament offered a prize of £20,000 "for providing a Publick Reward for such Person or Persons as shall discover the Longitude at Sea." As you can see from the amount of the prize money this was a difficult contest. To win you had to try out your method on a voyage to the West Indies and back with a total error of less than 30' or two minutes of time. Up until that date, people kept time on board with a sand clock measuring half-hour intervals. The job of keeping track of the sand clock also included writing down the intervals and ringing a bell each half-hour in eight hour shifts. This is the origin of telling time at sea by bells: one for the first half hour, two for the first hour, two close together, a pause, and then a single one for the third half an hour, and so on. When the bell tolled, someone else had the task of marking the ships position with a peg on a huge board. The board had holes in it at various points along the ships course at half-hour intervals.

The two most common ways of finding longitude were by observing eclipses and occultations of the planets by the Moon's disc, then comparing differences in local apparent time and converting to longitude.

John Harrison (1693–1776), a carpenter from Yorkshire, England won the contest by building the first accurate, sea-going clock. Altogether it took him 43 years and six different versions to perfect his timepiece. The final version was about the size of a large stopwatch. People called this unique clock a **chronometer** to show that it was different from a regular clock.

John Harrison was born in Yorkshire England. His father had been a carpenter and John was to be one, too. John caught smallpox when he was six and had to spend quite a bit of time recuperating. A friend gave him a watch to play with to keep him occupied while he was getting better. From that day on, he was fascinated with all kinds of timepieces. As a hobby, he built and repaired clocks, building an entire grandfather clock by himself.

John Harrison's chronometer, final version, 1759. *Photo courtesy of National Maritime Museum, England*

In 1767, the **Reverend Nevil Maskelyne,** the Astronomer Royal of England, compiled the first **Nautical Almanac**. In it were all the charts and tables, the locations of the 57 stars used for navigation, in fact, the fruits of all the labors of astronomers since their science first began. Using the Nautical Almanac, the sextant and the chronometer, sailors and sea captains greatly expanded their knowledge of celestial navigation and our knowledge of the world.

The Naval Observatory in Washington D.C. also publishes an American version of the Nautical Almanac. In 1842 **Matthew Fontaine Maury** (1806–1873) started this work. A young naval lieutenant, Maury had broken his leg in a stagecoach accident. Assigned to a land-based job at the Navy's Bureau of Navigation in Washington D.C. at age 36 because he could no longer carry out sea duty, Maury set out to make the best use of his situation. Maury was in charge of the Depot of Charts and Instruments. He published a book for sea pilots, listing wind and sea currents based on the vast amount of records and logbooks stored at the depot. He established the Naval Observatory and the Hydrographic Office. Maury was the first head of the Naval Observatory. He also started the Weather Bureau, suggested building the Panama Canal and the port of Norfolk, Virginia, recommended the use of steamer lanes at sea 25 miles (40 kilometers) apart, called for lighthouses on the Gulf Coast, recommended close observation of the rise and fall of the waters of the Mississippi River, and encouraged the use of circle sailing and the reclaiming of drowned lands. He was decorated and honored by many countries for the international usefulness of many of his ideas.

The Naval Observatory, like the one in England, told time for its nation and tested and corrected all nautical instruments used by the Navy. Both observatories once used a bright red ball on a long shaft sitting on top of the observatory where ships at sea could easily spot it. At noon, the ball would be dropped down from the top of the spire. When it reached the bottom of the shaft (like the ball in Times Square on New Year's Eve), it would be precisely 12 noon. Ship captains would adjust their clocks and set sail. Both observatories have transit sighting telescopes and very sophisticated time-keeping devices. They both continue to publish Nautical Almanacs and other useful documents.

Another important document that came out earlier in 1569, was Mercator's World Map. In it he tried to make a chart which could locate places by their longitude and latitude and in which the straight traveling line between any two places would be represented as a straight line whose angle from every meridian would be the same. If a person in London and another person on the 180th meridian were to both point to the north, to an observer on the celestial sphere above the Earth's north pole, both people would be pointing in the same direction. The same would be true if both people pointed south. If, however, they pointed east, to the observer on the celestial sphere, they would be pointing in opposite directions. The same would be true if they pointed west.

If you and a friend could walk to the north pole from two different places on the Earth, you both would always be heading north. Both of you would meet at the north pole. Once you got there, if you kept walking, you would pass each other and would be heading south. Now, suppose both you and your friend are standing together right at the north pole. Which direction is east? What about north and west?

Suppose you and your friend start your journeys from the same points where you began but instead of venturing north, you head slightly south and a little east of north. As you both travel stick to your north-east course, crossing each meridian you come to at the same angle. What will happen? What you will see from the celestial sphere point of view is two people walking in an ever-tightening spiral around the globe until they meet at the north pole. Anytime you travel on the globe in any other direction other than the 4 cardinal points—north, south, east, west—you will be traveling in a spiral. This pattern is a **loxodromic curve.** It is also called a **rhumb line.**

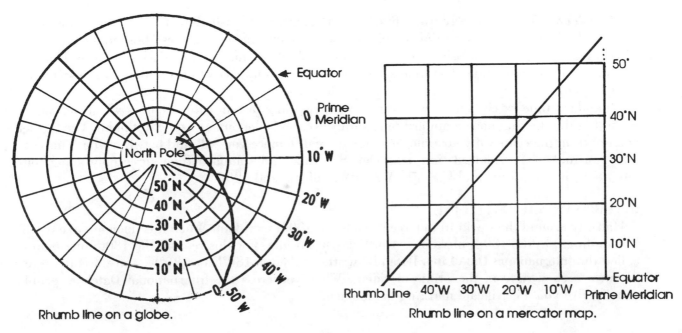

Rhumb line on a globe.

Rhumb line on a mercator map.

107

The straight traveling line or rhumb line is the direction you would sail without altering your course and without being thrown off course by any causes. On a globe map, rumb lines are not straight. They tend to spiral gradually. Mercator's map shows the rumb lines as straight which makes it much easier to plot your course on a flat map and to stay on it at sea.

---

loxodromic curve comes from the Greek words λοχος *(loxos)* = slanting, crosswise, and δρομος *(dromos)* = a course. **Rhumb** comes from the Old Spanish word *rumb* = room, space, hold of a ship, and the Greek word ρομβος *(rombos)* = anything that may be spun or whirled around

---

Great Circle Maps   Look at a flat map of the world and plan the shortest possible voyage from San Francisco to Yokahama, Japan. Now do the same planning using a globe. Would you pick the same route that you did with the flat map? On a globe, the shortest distance between two points is a line cut out on the globe by a plane intersecting the Earth's center. This line is called a **great circle**. Airplane pilots know about the great circles and use them often. They have maps based on the **gnomonic projection**. In this projection, great circles appear as straight lines. The captain looks at his gnomonic chart, plots his course, and transfers it to a Mercator chart which he will use.

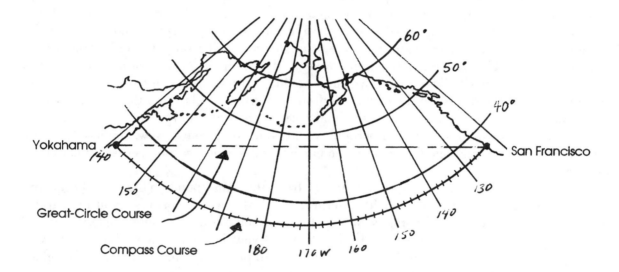

U.S. Time Zones   In 1918, the United States Congress established the four standard time zones used in the U.S. today. Before that time, there were many smaller zones established locally which caused travelers much confusion. While the time zones have uneven boundaries, each on is about as wide as 15° of longitude. The time zones have uneven boundaries because they follow state and river borders.

Standard time rarely agrees with Sun time. According to Sun time, noon is when the Sun is highest in the sky. But noon standard time hardly ever finds the Sun at its highest point. The farther you are from the center of your time zone, the more difference you will find between what Sun time tells you and what standard time tells you. Sun time and standard time agree only along four longitudes in the continental U.S. (75°W, 90°W, 105°W, and 120°W).

INTERNATIONAL DATE LINE

Halfway around the world from Greenwich is the 180th meridian. When it is noon at Greenwich, it is midnight at the 180th meridian. A new day has begun. For this reason, the 180th meridian is called the **International Date Line.** It can be written either as 180°E or 180°W, since it is the same distance each way from the prime meridian. When you cross the International Dateline, people usually give you a certificate marking the moment.

108

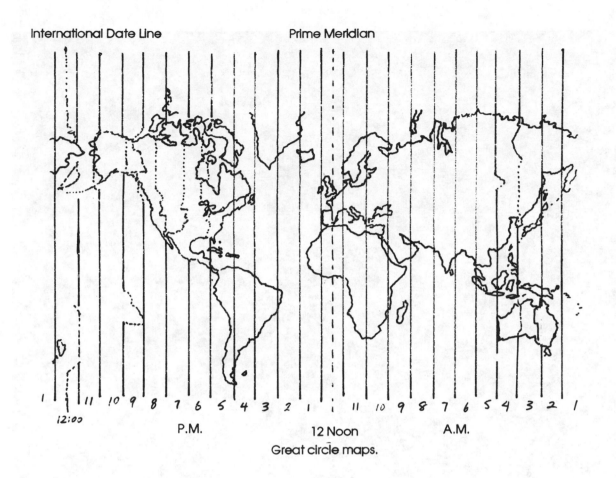

International Date Line   Prime Meridian

12:00

P.M.   12 Noon   A.M.

Great circle maps.

MAPS OF THE EARTH

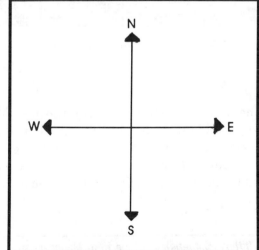

Looking Down onto the Earth
⟵ Sunlight and time move in this direction.

MAPS OF THE SKY

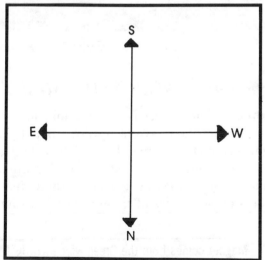

Looking Up into the Sky
Stars and planets move in this direction. ⟶

READING MORE

Bauer, Commander Bruce A. USN (retired). *The Sextant Handbook: Adjustment, Repair, Use and History.* Annapolis: Azimuth Press, 1986.

Hale, John R. and the editors of Time-Life Books. *Great Ages of Man: Age of Exploration.* New York: Time Incorporated, 1966.

Hirsch, S. Carl. *On Course! Navigating in Sea, Air and Space.* New York: The Viking Press, 1967.

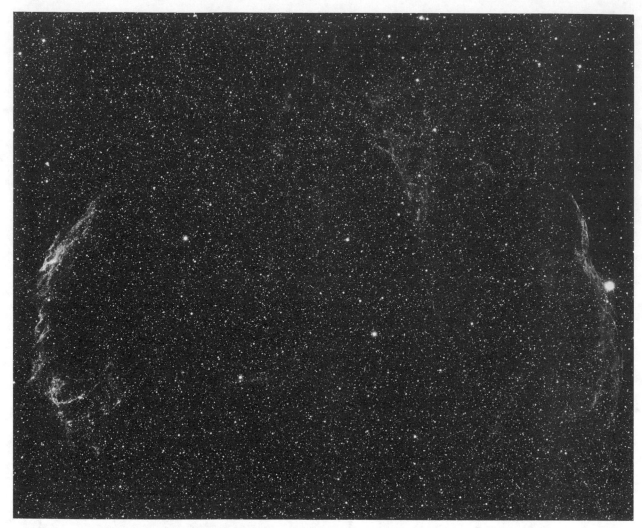

Veil Nebula (NGC 6990-92-95). *Photo courtesy of Observatoire de Haute Provence*

Section 4: *POLES AND MAGNETISM*

Magnets   You are used to seeing magnets and watching how they "stick" to certain metals. Most of the magnets you have seen were probably flat pieces of metal in the shape of a bar or a horseshoe. Magnets come from minerals which have had many names down through the ages: magnes, magnetis, heraclion, sideritis, and lodestone. The minerals are naturally occurring iron ore which we call **magnetite**. Most researchers seem to think that the ancient Chinese were the first to notice the unusual features or properties of these minerals around 3000 B.C.

Magnet comes from the Greek words λιθος Μαγνητις *(lithos magnetis)* = stone from Magnesia an ancient city in Asia Minor, near the Ural Mountains. There was a huge stone near this ancient city which used to "pull" at the iron tips of shepherds' staffs and the nails in their boots.

If you placed a piece of iron next to the magnetic mineral, the mineral would somehow "pull" the iron toward it and "hold" on to it. The piece of iron would then hold on to another piece of iron placed on it. The same thing would happen if you put two magnets near each other. However, if you turned one of them around, the two would "push" each other apart. Imagine what an impression such a stone would make on the first people to observe it. Clearly the stone was magic. In this next project you can take a closer look at some of the magic happening around a magnet.

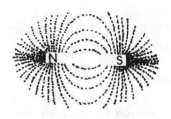
"one magnet"

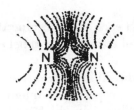
two magnets—same ends

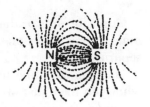
two magnets— opposite ends

Project 38: Investigating Magnetic Forces

MATERIALS
2 bar magnets
iron filings
paper

colored pencils
strings

PROCEDURE
PART 1
1. Place one of the bar magnets under a sheet of paper.
2. Sprinkle iron filings on top of the paper and spread them until they make a pattern.
3. Draw on another sheet of paper the pattern that the iron filings make.
4. Title your drawing: "One Magnet."

PART 2
1. Place 2 magnets under the sheet of paper with opposite ends about ¼ inches to ½ inches (or about 1 centimeter) apart.
2. Spread the iron filings until they make a pattern.
3. Draw the pattern that the iron filings made on another sheet of paper.
4. Title this drawing: "Two Magnets, Opposite Ends."

PART 3
1. Place two magnets under the sheet of paper with the same ends about ¼ inches to ½ inches or about 1 centimeter apart.
2. Spread the iron filings until they make a pattern.
3. Draw the pattern that the iron filings made on another sheet of paper.
4. Title this last drawing: "Two Magnets, Same Ends."

PART 4
1. Tie a piece of string to one of the magnets and let the magnet hang suspended in the air while you hold the other end of the string.
2. Have someone else take the other magnet far enough away from you so that the two magnets don't affect each other.
3. Now bring the magnets together, first the opposite ends.
4. Now bring the same ends together.

OBSERVATIONS
What did you notice happening in each case? The iron filings have given you an opportunity to see what lives around a magnet. The curved lines shown in the pattern of iron filings are made by lines of magnetic force coming from the magnet. These force lines are more concentrated at the ends of the magnet as you can see by the amount of iron filings which collects there.

What do you notice about how the two magnets behave when they have stopped moving? Try standing in different places.

Opposite ends of the magnets attract each other joining their lines of force or force fields together making one larger magnet. Like ends of the magnets repel each other, keeping their own force fields separate.

Magnets also line up in a certain direction with one end always pointing the same way. From what you have just observed about the properties of magnets, why do you suppose they always line up and point in a certain direction? What is it which with they are lining up and to what are they pointing?

The ends of a magnet are the **north seeking end** and the **south seeking end.** These ends are also called **poles.** Opposite poles attract each other, similar poles repel each other because magnetized pieces always take up a position of minimum blockage to the flow of the magnetic field. The north seeking end of a magnet is really the magnet's south pole. Because it is the opposite of Earth's north pole, the two magnet ends attract one another, causing the magnet's south pole to seek the north pole of the Earth.

Long ago someone discovered this curious relationship between the Earth and magnets. The piece of magnetite that people used as a magnet pointed north to the Earth's pole and thus to the Pole Star. The pole star was called the **lodestar.**

---

lodestar comes from the Anglo-Saxon word *lad-steorra* = leading star, so the mineral that pointed to it was named **lodestone** or leading stone

---

The ancient Chinese used magnets to line up people's graves to help them enter the after life. By 900 B.C. people began using magnets to tell directions. Soon people were navigating, led by the forces of the leading stone.

"By means of this instrument you will be able to direct your steps to cities, islands, and to any places whatever in the world, wherever you may be on land or sea."—Petrus Perigrinus, 1269

When people dug up the pirate loot of Captain Kidd in the year 1699, the list of buried treasure included "one large lodestone." For many years, a lodestone remained one of the most important items aboard a sailing vessel, kept under lock and key in the captain's quarters. In this next project you can use a piece of lodestone to make a copy of the first **compass.**

---

compass comes from Middle English word *compas* and the Middle French word *compasser* = to go around, measure or divide

---

——————— **Project 39: Making a Water Compass (Stella Maris)** ———————

MATERIALS

a sliver of lodestone or magnetized needle

drinking straw or piece of cork

bowl

water

PROCEDURE
1. Fill the bowl with water.
2. Place the sliver of lodestone through the straw at right angles to it to form a "+."
3. Float the straw and the lodestone gently on the surface of the water.

OBSERVATIONS
One end of the lodestone will point to the north, the other to the south. The two ends of the straw point to the east and west. The Stella Maris is the ancestor of the compass. The early sagas of the Faroe Islands mentions the use of a Stella Maris, so do other sources concerning the Norsemen, Italians, Persians, and Arabs.

Stella Maris = "Star of the Sea" in Latin. It served as an all-weather, day and night guide.

When people found out that they could magnetize a thin piece of metal or a needle by rubbing it in one direction against a magnet, they decided to replace the floating lodestone in the Stella Maris. In time, people also removed the water in the Stella Maris, put a small dent under the center of the magnetized needle and set it on a pivot. The needle was now free to float, balanced on the pivot, and to point out the north-south directions even on board a rocking ship. The needle and pivot were mounted on a card which had the cardinal directions written on it. Later still, people again placed the disk and needle in a container filled with water. The card floated on the water. The water cushioned the movement of the tossing ship like shock absorbers in a car. The container also had a cover to keep the water from spilling out. The name for the container was "the box" and in some parts of the Mediterranean, people still call a compass is "the box" (bussola) rather than "the needle."

Another improvement was to replace the needle itself. Instead, the compass maker glued magnetized wires under the compass disk and pivoted the whole card. The compass card is also known as the **wind rose** because the points on it show the directions from which the winds blow and because the pattern of the card resembles the petals of the rose. The rose pattern also resembles the pattern of a star.

The stellar rose pattern appears in a variety of places in nature, particularly in members of the rose family: rose hips, hawthorn, apples, strawberries, raspberries, meadow sweet, acrimony, blackberries.

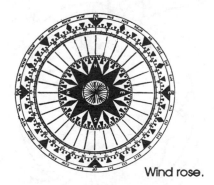

Wind rose.

In the early days of sailing, navigators spoke of direction at sea in terms of following a certain wind, "from Crete to Carpathus is 60 miles with the wind Favorius (the west wind)."

> Remember, remember the circle of the sky
> The stars and the brown eagle
> The supernatural winds
> Breathing night and day
> from the four directions . . .
> —from the Pawnee, Osage Omaha

113

Why does a magnet hanging by a string point in a certain direction? To find the answer, **William Gilbert** (1544–1603), the first great researcher in the field of magnetism, put together his observations with an experiment to try out an idea he had. Gilbert thought that the Earth itself was a giant magnet. Like a magnet, the Earth had a great concentration of its magnetic fields at its two poles. The Earth's magnet attracted other magnets and compasses, lining them up with the north-south magnetic field of the Earth, where there is the minimum blockage of the flow. To pursue his idea, Gilbert worked with a piece of lodestone, which he shaped into a globe-like magnetic ball. He called this ball the **Terrella** (Little Earth).

The Terrella had a north and south pole, with a magnetic field lining up along the meridians. It also had an equator which actually indicated the natural division between the two poles. At the equator, the compass needle pointed horizontally; at the poles it pointed vertically. Gilbert published the results and methods of his experiments in his book *De Magnete: On the Magnet, Magnetick Bodies Also and on the Great Magnet the Earth; A New Philosophy Demonstrated By Many Arguments and Experiments.* This was the earliest and most comprehensive work on magnetism. The first section was about the lodestone and the properties of magnets, the second section was about navigation and the third about astronomy.

The open seas now became less of a threat. You could leave the security of the familiar Mediterranean and head out westward. **Columbus** (1451–1506) relied heavily on the truth of this possibility. He wanted to do what seemed perfectly believable on a globe—to reach the east by travelling west.

Don Christobal de Colon (Columbus' full name in Spanish, not Latin) of Genoa Italy "sailed the ocean blue in 1492" and "found " America. The voyage of Columbus was an important one for the development of geography and astronomy.

Columbus also learned some important characteristics about compasses. One was that the compass points to the Earth's North **Magnetic** Pole, not the geographical north pole. The two aren't the same. The focal point of the Earth's magnetic field moves every year. The point on the globe 90° above the equator doesn't. As you might imagine, this could cause some real problems for navigators. The difference between compass (magnetic) directions and true (geographic) directions is known as **variation.** From his experiences with the compass at sea, Columbus came to the conclusion that the variation was different in different parts of the globe.

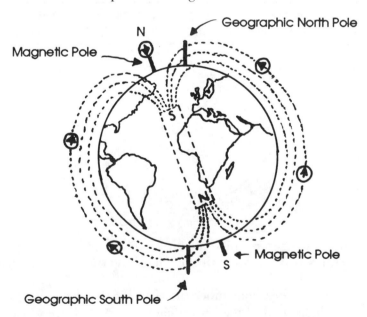

The angle of magnetic variation is also called the **magnetic declination.** It can vary from zero to a full 180°. Compasses always show north as an arrowhead. Magnetic north is only a half an arrowhead. Only when both the magnetic pole and the geographic north pole are in line on a meridian will the compass needle point to true north.

The lines on this map represent lines of equal magnetic declination. They are called **isogonic lines.**

---
isogonic comes from the Greek words ισο *(iso)* = equal and γωνια *(gonia)* = angle

---

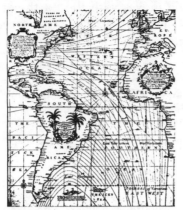

Map by Edmond Halley showing Isogonic lines.

The lines of magnetic force enter and leave the Earth at various points and at specific angles. These angles are called **magnetic inclination.** The lines on this map show these points of equal magnetic inclination. The lines are called **isoclinic lines.**

---
isoclinic comes from the Greek words ισο *(iso)* = equal and κλινω *(klino)* = incline

---

If you hang a compass needle straight up and down, it will come to rest parallel with the lines of magnetic force surrounding it and passing through it. We call this instrument a **dip needle** and we use it to measure magnetic inclination. At the magnetic equator, the dip needle shows no dip. It is parallel to the surface of the Earth. At either magnetic pole, the needle follows the lines of force and points straight up and down, perpendicular to the surface of the Earth.

In this next project you can make a model of Gilbert's Terrella and use a dip needle to check the magnetic variations on the Earth.

←Geographic North Pole

Geographic South Pole↗

—————— **Project 40: Making a Model of the Magnetic Earth (Terrella)** ——————

MATERIALS

alnico magnet (regular bar magnet)   rubber band
tennis ball   X-acto knife
compass
dip needle (follow the plans in this
   project to make one)

PROCEDURE

1. Put a hole in the tennis ball with the X-acto knife and place the magnet inside to act as the Earth's north and south magnetic poles.
2. Use a compass to check for magnetic declination.
3. Use the dip needle to check for magnetic inclination.
4. Use a rubber band to indicate the magnetic equator.

OBSERVATION

This model, like Gilbert's Terrella, comes close to explaining how the Earth acts as a magnet. The current theory (see Chapter 4, Section 2) is that the center or core of the Earth is a hot and partly molten mass of iron. This fluid moves with the Earth generating electric currents which in turn produce the magnetic fields around the Earth. As the strength and direction of the magnetic fields change, so do the Earth's magnetic poles. It is thought that the Earth's magnetic poles reverse every 500,000 years.

Television personality **Hugh Downes** has been involved in physically moving a marker at the South Pole to indicate its exact magnetic position after it has changed.

Keeping up with the shifting magnetic fields is part of the responsibility of map makers and those who use the maps, the navigators.

READING MORE

Ley, Willy, and the editors of Life. *The Poles* (Life Nature Library), New York: Time, Inc., 1962.

Trifid Nebula (Sagittarius). *Photo courtesy of Observatoire de Haute Province*

Chapter 4: EXPLORING THE EARTH

Section 1: LIFE ON EARTH

"In the beginning . . ."   With these three words cultures from all over the world have told the story of the Creation. It is a basic part of being human to want to know where we came from and where we are going. We also want to know how the universe began and how the planets, especially the Earth, came to be. In this chapter, you can look at many creation stories. They come from ancient Babylonia, Scandanavia, Mexico, Japan, New Zealand, and Greece, as well as nineteenth and twentieth century science. As you read these stories you can listen to people speaking across the ages about the most human of all questions. Perhaps the answers we have today will seem strange to a future generation with answers of its own.

Babylonia   There was only Apsu (Sweet-Water), Tiamat (Salt-Water), and their son, Mummu (the Mist). From the mingling of these waters came the gods. Tiamat was angry at the gods, who were restless inside her and sent monsters to destroy them once they were born. Filled with fear, the gods were unable to defend themselves, except for the brave Marduk, son of Ea. He killed Tiamat with his arrow and created the heavens and Earth from her body. A mountain towered upwards from her head, from her eyes flowed the Tigris and Euphrates rivers, Marduk changed the monsters into statues to hold up the gates where the Sun rises and sets. Marduk became the supreme god. He set up the zodiac, determined the length of the year, assigned three constellations for each of the twelve months, caused the Moon to shine with her different phases to measure the days and months, and created the first people to live on the Earth.

Scandinavia (the Norsemen)   There was nothing but a huge gulf, Ginnangagap. This Yawning Void stretched from Niflheim, the northern realm of ice, darkness, and mist to Muspelheim, the southern realm of fire. Deep down within Ginnungagap lay Hvergelmir, the well of Life whose waters flowed into the Yawning Void. These waters joined those the fire and icy mist had made as they came together. The cold of Niflheim turned the waters into blocks of ice, the fires of Muspelheim turned them into masses of ice and slush. This half-frozen water filled in the once empty gulf. As more warmth came up from Muspelheim, the blocks of ice began to melt. This first trickle of water was the ancestor of everything that lives, because the drops formed the body of the first giant, Ymir. Ymir was soon joined by Audhumla, the cow. From Audhumla's udders flowed four rivers of milk with which to nourish Ymir. For her food, Audhumla licked the ice around her and found in it the Salt of Life, from the Well of Life. On the first day she licked the ice, the warm drops made by her tongue on the ice formed the hair of a man. On the second day, the head took shape and on the third day, the whole man was there. His name was Buri. Buri created a son, Bor, who married the giantess Bestla, one of Ymir's descendants. Bor and Bestla were the parents of the great Aesir gods Odin, Vili, and Ve. Ymir fathered a race of giants which constantly fought against the Aesir.

The sons of Bor killed Ymir and set to work to form the world from his body. From the blood of Ymir, the gods made the seas. From his body, which they threw into the gap, the gods made the

Earth. From his bones, they made the mountains, from his hair, the forests and plants. His teeth became the gravel and stones. His brains became the clouds. The ice-blue skull of the giant became the dome of the heavens. From his eyebrows the gods made Midgard (middle Earth) the land between Niflheim and Muspelheim. Gathering the sparks that constantly flew out from Muspelheim, the Aesir placed stars into the sky and set their course.

They also brought molten gold from Muspelheim and made a glowing Sun chariot. The horses Early-Waker and All-Strong drew the chariot with the goddess Sol controlling the reins. Before her went the Moon chariot drawn by the horse All-Swift. In the chariot was the boy Mani. In this way, night came first, followed by day, and Aesir caused time to exist. Odin created the first man from the ash tree, calling him Ask and created the first woman Embla from an elder tree. These people and their descendants lived in Midgard, protected from the giants by the wall of mountains made by Ymir's bones. The world of humans was connected to Asgard, the world of the gods, by the Bifrost Ridge, made from the rainbow.

Mexico (the Toltecs)   The world lay in darkness. All things were orderless and water covered the slime and ooze that the world was then. When the waters parted, land, forests, and mountains appeared. Tloque Nahuaque, the Lord of All Existence created the universe. He made the first man and woman. After 676, on the date 4 Tiger, this first Earth was destroyed. The Sun disappeared. Tigers ate the people. Another Sun followed. After 364 years on the date 4 Wind, the Sun disappeared. Mighty winds swept the people away. Another Sun followed. After 312 years on the date 4 Fire-Rain, the Sun disappeared. Fire rained down on the people. Another Sun followed. After 676 years on the date 4 Water, the Sun disappeared. A flood destroyed the world and only one man and one woman survived. Another Sun followed. This is our Sun. In time, earthquakes will destroy our world.

Marduk.

Tonatiuh, one of the Aztec Suns.

Japan   There appeared above the great swirling ocean mass a pair of gods, Izanagi and Izanami. They stood on the Rainbow Bridge of Heaven and Izangi thrust his jeweled spear into the ocean mass. Water dripping from its tip thickened and formed an island. This island became the Earth. Izanagi and Izanami came down to Earth where they married and became the parents of the world, including islands, seas, rivers, herbs, trees, mountains, and the wind.

After his wife's death, Izanagi gave birth to the Sun goddess Amaterasu (Heaven-Illumining Lady) from his left eye. From his right eye, he gave birth to the stars and Tsuki-yami-no Mikoto (the Moon). From Izanagi's nostrils came the storm god Susanowo (the Impetuous Male) who dwelt in the seas.

The Sun goddess and the storm god often quarreled. Once Susanowo ruined his sister's fields and frightened her so much that she accidentally cut herself while weaving. Extremely angry and ashamed, Amaterasu left the sky and hid herself in a cave. There was darkness on the Earth. The gods assembled and discussed how they might persuade the Sun to come out from her hiding place and bring her light to Earth. The gods welded stars together to form a mirror and hung it in front of the cave with jewels and other offerings. Night birds sang at the entrance to Amaterasu's cave. The goddess of laughter, Ama-no-uzume (Heaven-Alarming Female) put on a headdress, stood on top of an upturned tub, and danced to please the gods. They roared with laughter. Curious, Amaterasu peeked out from the cave. She was so fascinated by her reflection in the mirror made by the gods that she came out of the cave. Normal day and night returned to the Earth.

New Zealand (the Maori)   There was Rangi (Heaven) and Papa (Earth). Although Rangi and Papa had created many human beings, the gods had never seen them because Rangi and Papa clung tightly to each other keeping the humans and all the light from view. The gods met to plan a way to separate their parents, Rangi and Papa. Tane-mahuta, the god and father of forests, birds, and insects decided that Papa should remain below as their mother and that Rangi should be pushed far above. It was Tane-mahuta who was able to put his head on Papa and with his feet push Rangi away. Now there was darkness *and* light. People lived on the Earth below and the sky was above.

Greece   There was Chaos (Space). From Chaos came Gaea (Earth) and Eros (Love). Next came Erebus (Darkness) and Nyx (Night). Erebus and Nyx brought forth Aether (Light) and Hemera (Day). Gaea gave birth to Ouranos (the Starry Heavens) as a covering for herself. Next Gaea brought forth the mountains, fields, plains, the sea, plants, and animals. Then she gave birth to Pontus (the Deep Waters which surround the Earth). Eros brought Ouranos and Gaea together. They became the parents of the twelve Titans. Ouranos banished three of his children. Gaea pleaded with her other children to help rescue their brother. Cronos (Time), the youngest Titan, responded and with his sharp sickle, seriously wounded Ouranos.

Cronos now reigned as lord of Heaven and Earth with his wife Rhea. Cronos did not free his brothers as he promised, so his mother, Gaea, vowed that he would know the fate that befell his father. To prevent one of his own children from rising up against him, Cronos swallowed each of them as they were born. Rhea decided to save her sixth child, Zeus, so she went to Crete where Zeus was born and raised him in secrecy. In Zeus' place, Rhea brought Cronos a stone wrapped in swaddling clothes, which he ate. When Zeus came of age, he gave Cronos a potion which caused him to vomit up the children he had swallowed. Zeus and his brothers and sisters went to Mount Olympus after defeating Cronos. Out of the eastern side of the world rose Eos (Dawn), Helios (Sun), and Selene (Moon). Each had a place which they left each day to ride in their chariots bringing day and night to the world of mortals.

"And God saw everything that He had made, and behold, it was very good."—*Genesis*

NEBULAR HYPOTHESIS

Nebular Hypothesis (1796, Immanuel Kant and Pierre Simon La Place)   The protosun contracted to form a huge rotating gas cloud (primeval solar nebula). As the gas cloud cooled it contracted even more and the size of the Sun became smaller. The decrease in size caused an increase in the speed at which the Sun was turning, and thus increased the accelerating forces coming from the Sun. When the accelerating force from inside the Sun became stronger than the Sun's forces of attraction, a ring separated from the main body of the Sun. As the Sun continued to contract and cool, more rings of matter, like ripples in a pool of water, moved out from the Sun. These gaseous rings gradually condensed into spheres which became the planets.

Tidal Theory (1785, Georges Louis de Button)   A passing star raised a great tide on the Sun and released the gas which later formed the planets due to forces of acceleration.

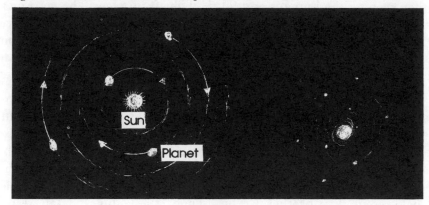

PLANETESIMAL

Planetesimal Theory (1900, Forrest R. Moulton and Thomas C. Chamberlain)   The tidal action of a passing star released matter from the Sun. This matter cooled and by the forces of acceleration large enough to overcome the gravitational pull of the Sun, formed small particles (planetesimals). These grew in size by picking up scattered material nearby and formed the planets.

BIG BANG THEORY Explosion, formation, and expansion of galaxies.

The Big Bang (1930s, Abbe Georges Lemaitre; 1967, Robert Wagoner and William Fowler)   There was a vast fireball, the **primeval atom** or primeval cosmic egg. This contained all the material of the universe in the form of radiation. There was nothing outside the fireball—it *was* the entire universe. There was tremendous temperature and enormous pressure on this dense cloud of burning gas. Ten or fifteen billion (thousand million) years ago, the fireball exploded, breaking into billions of pieces and ejecting them into space at tremendous speeds. These pieces also broke into smaller pieces. When the fireball exploded, it exploded to everywhere from everywhere. The exploding material created the space in which it expanded. No one knows how or why the primeval fireball came to be or even what happened before it exploded.

As the primeval fireball expanded, its temperature dropped from the original 100 billion degrees. More and more of the radiation became matter, mostly hydrogen, about 25% helium, and a trace of deuterium. Three seconds after the explosion, the temperature fell from 1 trillion degrees to about 5 million. After three minutes, the temperature cooled to about a billion degrees. After about one million years, the temperature fell to about 5000° absolute, and there was more matter than radiation in the universe. The width of the universe then was less then 1/1000 of its present size. For the next few hundred thousand years, the fireball was like the inside of a star.

Large concentrations of matter developed and grew by attraction and collecting more material as they moved through space. This broke the universe up into large masses of gas. About one million years after the big bang, galaxies began to form from these clouds of gas. Thermonuclear reactions began taking place in certain gas clouds, and stars were born. Our Sun was one of those stars. From within the gas cloud where the Sun was born, a smaller gas cloud flattened and its dust and gas condensed into the planets. One of these became the Earth. The material of our bodies comes from material in the fireball.

Arno A. Penzias and **Robert Wilson** received the Nobel prize in 1978 for detecting and identifying the hum of the cosmic background radiation left over from the big bang explosion. The universe will last more than ten billion years.

Steady State (1950s, Hermann Bondi, Thomas Gold, and Fred Hoyle) The universe had no beginning and it will have no end. The way it appears now is the way it has always appeared and will always appear no matter where in the universe you are looking. Its condition (state) remains steady. There are always the same number of galaxies. As some galaxies move away into the distance, new ones move in to take their place. Aging stars give off the materials (gases, dust, and energy) needed to produce new stars, as old trees in the forest give material to produce new trees. As it is needed, hydrogen comes into existence through continuous creation.

Oscillating Universe At some point in the future after the big bang, the gravitational force exerted by the combined masses of the galaxies will stop the universe from expanding. The universe will then reach its maximum possible size and begin to contract bringing back all the material to the original fireball. This is the "big crunch" (a term which John A. Wheeler made up). When the universe reaches its maximum possible density level, a second big bang will occur and the universe will start to expand. The universe will continue to expand and contract, almost like breathing (oscillation).

Combination/Accumulation Protoplanet Hypothesis (1950 G. P. Kuiper) The protosun formed at the center of the protosolar nebula. Rotation supported this nebula as it collapsed. Dust grains flew through the nebula and collected into a thin disk of material. Gravitational instability caused the disk to break up into small particles (planetesimals). Over time, the planetesimals formed the planets. Near the Sun, only the rocklike materials could survive the high temperatures; farther away from the Sun, the icy material could condense. For this reason, the inner planets are small, heavy, and rocky, while the outer planets are large, light, and icy. The thin disk of material from the collapsed nebula caused the orbits of all the planets to lie in a flat plane around the equator of the Sun and all the planets except Venus and Uranus to rotate in the same direction.

The accumulation theory predicts that the moons around a planet should resemble a solar system in miniature. They should all lie within the equatorial plane of the planet, have circular orbits, and revolve and spin in the same direction.

In this next project you can make a simple model which can show you the various ways people think the universe might be expanding.

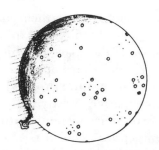

Project 41: Making a Model of the Expanding Universe

MATERIALS

a round balloon
paper
rubber cement
felt-tip pen

pencil and paper
ruler
hole punch

PROCEDURE

1. Punch holes in the paper and save the small paper circles. Glue the paper circles all over the balloon at different distances apart using the rubber cement. These circles represent the **galaxies.** The balloon represents the size of the universe.

2. Measure and write down the distances between several pairs of galaxies. Mark the paper circles that you measured with a letter or number. Refer to these letters or numbers in your record keeping.

THE BIG BANG UNIVERSE

3. Blow up the balloon without knotting it and notice what happens to the galaxies when you keep the balloon inflated.

4. Measure the distances between the marked galaxies.

THE STEADY STATE UNIVERSE

5. Make several very small dots with the felt-tip pen in between the paper galaxies on the slightly inflated balloon. Try to make the dots so small that you can't see them when the balloon is completely deflated. Each dot in between is new matter forming to take the place of the old.

THE OSCILLATING UNIVERSE

6. Blow up the balloon, stop, then slowly let the air out until the balloon is empty. Blow the balloon up again, stop, then slowly let the air out until the balloon is empty, and so on.

OBSERVATIONS

In *The Big Bang Universe* did any new galaxies appear? Did the galaxies themselves grow larger? Was the universe any more dense after it expanded? What happened to the speed at which the galaxies moved the farther apart they were from one another? Did two galaxies which were twice as far apart as two others move away from each other twice as fast? Check your results again. In *The Steady State Universe* did everything stay the same at all times? Did the *Oscillating Universe* "breathe"?

Your balloon project is a model of how the universe appears to be expanding. Many current creation stories describe an expanding universe. Right now astronomers are trying to find out how much mass there is in the universe. This will help them figure out how big the universe is and whether it is opened or closed (continually expanding or not). One of the biggest events in this research occurred in 1920 in the form of a debate between **Harlow Shapley** and **H. D. Curtis** held at the National Academy of Sciences.

Plants and Animals   All of the ancient creation stories tell of the variety of life on Earth. There are 1.7 million known species of plants and animals and another 5 to 30 million we don't know. The smallest group of organisms includes the 4.4 billion animals we use for food and work. Humans are the next largest group with 5 billion. Following us in size are the 580,000 billion water animals, and the 1,667,000 billion wild animals. Then come the worms and termites, the insects, the protozoa and algae, the land plants and lastly, bacteria. The numbers in these groups range from 92,428,683,600,000,000,000 billion (worms and termites) to 2,165,105,198,325,000,000,000 billion (bacteria).

All of these different plants and animals (**organisms**) have managed to live and work together wherever they are within an **ecosystem.** The living beings within an ecosystem may gather together in **populations** (groups of individuals of any one kind of organism) or **communities** (all of the populations living in one place). Where an organism lives is its **habitat.** This is its address. What the organism "does for a living" is its **ecological niche.**

---

ecosystem, ecological, ecology and even the word **economics** all come from the Greek word οικος *(oikos)* = home

---

You can easily tell a forest from a desert, a swamp from a meadow just by looking at the plants that grow there. Each of these plant communities forms the habitat for other plants as well as different kinds of animals. The names of these communities comes from the name of the main kind of vegetation that is there, (forest, desert, etc.), but it includes all plants and animals that live in such a community. We call these communities **biomes** and usually divide them into groups which occur all over the Earth:

1. Tundra and Ice Deserts
2. Mountain Vegetation
3. Coniferous Forest
   (Taiga: Russian name)
4. Deciduous Forest
5. Temperate Grassland and Steppe
6. Chaparral
7. Desert

8. Tropical Grassland & Savanna
9. Tropical Forest & Rain Desert
10. Tidepools
11. Running Fresh Water
12. Still Water
13. Oceans

Each of these biomes occupies a particular place on the Earth. Each has its own unique climate, soil or water conditions, plants, animals, and people. Life within a biome is a matter of sharing the available resources, including the chemicals in the air. Animals and people breathe in oxygen and breath out carbon dioxide. In 1782 the Swiss botanist **Jean Senebier** (1742–1809) proved that plants absorb carbon dioxide from the air and turn it back into oxygen. In this next project you can see for yourself what Senebe discovered.

———— **Project 42: Testing for Oxygen Production in Plants** ————

MATERIALS

glass bowl
vinegar
baking soda

water plant (elodea/anacris or water
   weed)
water

PROCEDURE
1. Fill half the glass bowl with water.
2. Add a little baking soda and a few drops of vinegar.
3. Place the water plant in the bowl.
4. Place the bowl and plants in the sunlight for a few days.

OBSERVATION
If bubbles appear in the water, oxygen is coming out of the plant. Why did you use the baking soda and vinegar?

Rhythms   Several rhythms or cycles in nature bring about changes which occur regularly within the plant and animal communities.

1. *Daily rhythms* of day and night and the temperature changes which this brings about.

2. *Seasonal rhythms* of the different lengths of day and night, the temperature and amount of rainfall. In some cases, early and late spring and early and late summer are as different from each other as autumn and winter.

3. *Lunar rhythms* during which time the ocean level rises and falls. The high and low ocean levels are called tides and their rhythm is 12½ hours from one high tide to the next. This means in most places, high tides occur twice daily, 50 minutes later each day. Approximately every two weeks, unusually high tides and unusually low tides occur. See Chapter 6, Section 2 for more detail on the tides.

The Nereis worm on the Atlantic coast of North America spawns twice each lunar month during the summer. This worm normally lives in burrows on the bottom of the sea and swim out in huge numbers at the full moon and again at the quarter moon.

4. *Internal rhythms* which tell an organism when to sleep or wake up, etc.

5. *Community rhythms* that occur within a specific group of plants or animals.

Water Life   The Earth, like our bodies, is ¾ water. The most intensive study of the oceans began in 1872, with the voyage of the HMS *Challenger*, one of the first ships to be specifically equipped to study the sea. The study of the physical, chemical, geological, and biological parts of the sea is **oceanography.**

Location   (There is really only one ocean, but we have given it different names for different places on the Earth)
1. Pacific—between the Americas, Asia, and Australia
2. Atlantic—between the Americas and Europe/Africa
3. Indian—between Africa and Australia
4. Arctic—above Canada and U.S.S.R., around the Arctic Circle
5. Southern—below the Pacific, Atlantic, and Indian Oceans, around Antarctica

Climate   (The ocean is in continual circulation so the temperature range is small)
1. **Warm** currents flow especially in the Indian and in those parts of the Atlantic and Pacific around the equator from the Americas to Africa and across to Asia.
2. **Cold** currents flow in the Arctic and Southern oceans.

Composition   Life extends to all depths of the ocean. There is more life in the oceans than in all the land and fresh water combined. During the year, there is almost a continual stirring up of the waters due to wind and weather. This brings minerals up from below providing food for the plants above. Ocean water is 3.5% salt. 27/1000 of the salt is sodium chloride and the rest is mostly magnesium calcium and potassium salts.

Plants   algae, seaweed, kelp, grasses, and phytoplankton. Phytoplankton are simple plants without roots, stems, or leaves such as bacteria, fungi, and algae, most of which you need a microscope to see. These microplants attract whole communities of microscopic or near-microscopic animals. The free-floating plants and the free swimming animals feeding on them drift with the water currents.

---

phytoplankton comes from the Greek words $\phi\upsilon\tau o$ *(phyto)* = that which has grown: a plant, and $\pi\lambda\alpha\nu\kappa\text{-}\tau o\varsigma$ *(planktos)* = to wander or drift. This is from the same word from which we get the word **planet,** for the heavenly bodies which wander about in the night sky.

Animals   zooplankton, jellyfish, shrimp, crustaceans, worms, sponges, molluscs, fish, sharks, whales, marine birds, seals, sea turtles, corals, squid—similar increase and decrease brought about by feeding during spring and fall blooms.

In 1845, **Johannes Muller Regiomontanus,** (1436–1476) used fine-meshed silk nets to catch very young starfish to help him study the life cycle of this sea animal. He was excited to find all kinds of sea life captured in his nets which no one had really noticed before. He told the biologist **Ernst Haeckel** (1834–1919) about his find. Haekel, Muller, and other biologists began to use similar nets and study what they found in them. In this way, they all became pioneer students of the places and ways people, plants, and animals live together. Haekel himself made up the word **ecology** 24 years later in 1869. In this next project you can study the ecology of your own biome.

———— Project 43: Setting Up Life in a Jar (Terrarium) ————

MATERIALS

large clear commercial-size jar with a lid   small stones
(a huge mayonnaise jar would be   soil
ideal)   small plants
sand   water

PROCEDURE

1. Clean and rinse the jar and lid thoroughly.
2. Lay the jar on its side.
3. Put about a 1 inch (2½ centimeters) layer of sand and small stones inside the jar.
4. Cover the sand and stones mixture with a 1½ inch (4 centimeters) layer of soil. If possible, use soil that came from the same place the plants did.
5. Moisten the soil with water, but don't flood it.
6. Place the plants in the soil leaving them enough room to grow. Be careful not to disturb the roots as you plant them.
7. Press the soil gently around the plants.
8. Cover the jar with the lid or with plastic wrap and a rubber band.

OBSERVATIONS

How can the plants survive without additional air and water?

We're All in This Together

The Biosphere   Life on Earth extends only a few feet below and above the Earth's surface. This includes the thin outer shell of the Earth, the oceans, and the atmosphere. Only ⅕ of the Earth's total land surface, or less than 40 million square miles (64 million square kilometers) can support a permanent standing crop of some kind of vegetation. This is home for all the people on Earth, and an even larger number of species of plants and animals. Here chemical and physical changes occur though the interaction of the Sun, air, water, soil. These changes help make it possible for organisms to exist. We call this "realm of life" the Earth's **biosphere.** In the biosphere all life is interrelated. For this reason, it is essential that we come to know who we are sharing life with on the Earth and how we can live together.

THE FOOD WEB OR CHAIN

Humans eat from all parts of the pyramid.

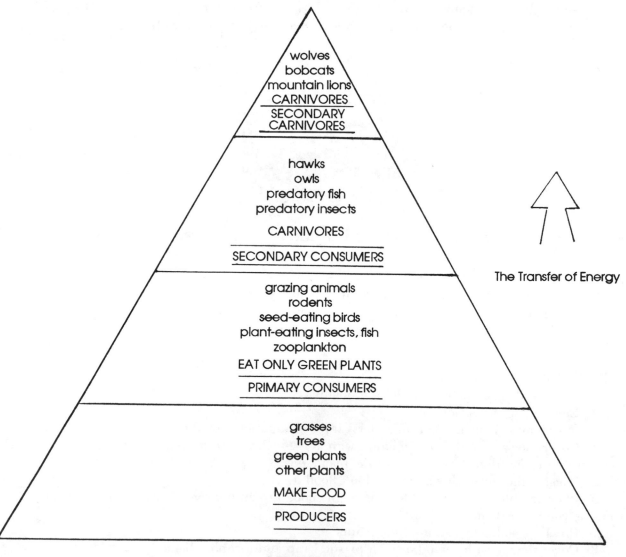

The Transfer of Energy

βιος *(bios)* = life, and σφαιρα *(sphaira)* = ball, globe

The Earth's natural landscapes and life forms are the result of processes that have been occurring for billions of years. If left alone, the same processes would continue indefinitely to shape and to reshape the land, the plants, and the animals. When human beings arrived, we gradually put ever greater demands and stresses upon the rest of creation. Humans change the landscape by farming, mining, building, etc. We grow food and we use energy. Sometimes the energy we use to power our cars and to manufacture things in our factories causes pollution. Because of our presence, some animals no longer exist. They have become **extinct.** Also because of our presence, some desert areas are now rich in vegetation. They have become **fertile.**

One way to help is to use other forms of energy which don't pollute or use up natural resources. We call these **renewable resources.**

"Go to Nature's School—the one true University."—John Muir

Energy Sources and Resources

Sunlight and wind are renewable resources. To make electricity we can use turbines and generators. Concentrated sunlight can boil water.

Oil, Natural Gas, and Coal are fossil fuels and nonrenewable resources. Two-thirds of the coal mined is used to make electricity. The largest coal reserves in the world are in the United States.

Biomass is a renewable resource to make electricity. You can burn things to make steam to drive turbines and generators.

Hydroelectric is renewable. The force of falling water turns the blades of turbine, which in turn runs a generator and makes electricity.

Nuclear fusion/fission are controlled reactions to make electricity indirectly. Nuclear energy boils water to make steam. Steam turns the blades of a turbine.

Geothermal is renewable and will not run out. Turbine operates a generator.

Electricity is a secondary energy source which we get from other energies: oil, gas, water, atoms, wind.

Ocean Thermal Energy Conversion (OTEC) is renewable. Surface water from tropical oceans is warm enough to boil liquid ammonia. Steam produced from boiling ammonia spins the blades of a turbine. The turbine runs a generator which makes electricity. Cold ocean water cools the steam, which condenses back into liquid ammonia. You can then reuse the liquid.

Hot Dry Rock Energy is renewable and comes from volcanoes. It is a form of geothermal energy. In 1960, a scientist named Robert Potter got the idea while he was reading a science fiction book, *At the Earth's Core* by Edgar Rice Burroughs (the author of *Tarzan*). Potter's idea developed into the hot dry rock energy process which people are trying out at an experimental plant in Tenton Hill, New Mexico. Engineers drilled deep pipelines into the hot rock below ground. They pump water into the pipe which travels through the hot rock. The hot rock heats the water far above its boiling point. When the heated water returns to the surface through another pipe, steam from the boiling water spins the blades of a turbine which operates a generator to produce electricity.

Generators turn large loops of wire. When the wire moves near a magnet, electricity flows in the wire. Power lines carry this electricity to wherever it is needed.

In this next project you can try your hand at heating water with the Sun instead of using gas, oil, or electricity.

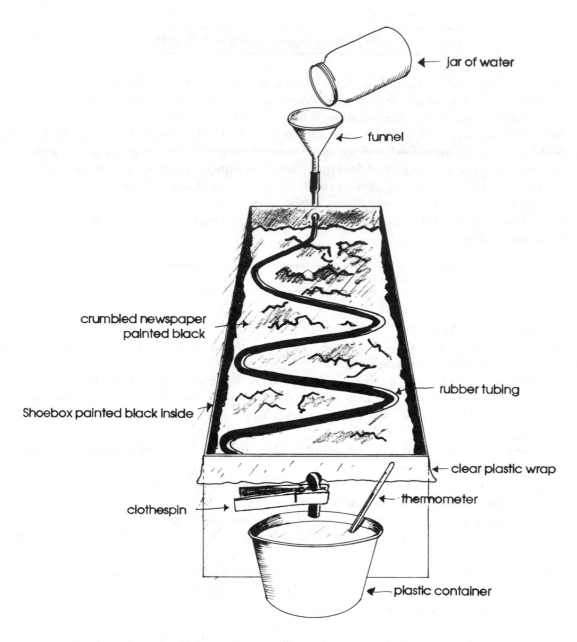

jar of water

funnel

crumbled newspaper
painted black

rubber tubing

Shoebox painted black inside

clear plastic wrap

thermometer

clothespin

plastic container

—— **Project 44: Testing an Alternative Energy Source (Solar Collector)** ——

MATERIALS

shoe box
flat black paint
newspaper
knife
¼ × 36 inches (6 centimeters × 1
   meter) rubber or plastic tubing
funnel to fit into tubing
masking tape

paperback book (like this one)
medium-size jar
plastic food container
clothespin
plastic wrap
thermometer
water
paper & pencil

PROCEDURE

1. Paint the inside of the shoe box and several sheets of newspaper black.
2. Fill the shoebox half way with crumpled black sheets of newspaper.
3. Cut holes the width of the tubing at each end of the shoe box.

4. Arrange the tubing as shown and tape it in place.

5. Cover the box tightly with plastic wrap.

6. Fill a jar with water and measure and record its temperature.

7. Place the shoebox in direct sunlight. Put a paperback book under one end. Face the opposite end towards the south.

8. Clamp the clothespin on the tube at the south facing end. Put an empty container under the tube.

9. Place the funnel into the tube at the north end and pour water into it. Open the clothespin and allow the water to flow through the tubing until it starts to come out at the other end. Then clamp hose closed with clothespin.

10. Let water sit in the tube for 15 minutes. Open clothespin and let water flow into the empty container.

11. Measure and record the temperature of the water.

OBSERVATIONS

How did your solar collector affect the water temperature? What would happen if you left the water in the tube longer? This project is adapted from *Heath Physical Science* by Louise Mary Nolan and Wallace Tucker, Lexington: D. C. Heath and Company, 1984. Used with permission.

Nuclear Winter Of all of humanity's many inventions, nuclear weapons are the most useless and destructive. One of these weapons is too many, but we have tens of thousands. We are in the unfortunate predicament of having made something before we really knew what we were getting into. As research into nuclear weapons continues we find ourselves up against the biggest challenge ever to face the human race. We have the power to destroy all life on this planet. We can make the human race extinct.

No one wants to do this. For this reason, many people would like to believe that it is not possible. In 1971, research began on the planet Mars using the Mariner 9 spacecraft (see Chapter 6, Section 4). The huge dust storms which raged frequently on the planet blew into the upper atmosphere blocking most of the light from the Sun. The planet received very little light and warmth because of this blockage. As a result, the surface of Mars became a "chilly desert." A research team looked into what would happen to the Earth's atmosphere during a nuclear war. They came to the startling realization that the smoke and dust caused by fires and explosions set off by only 5% of the world's nuclear weapons would create a Mars-like condition in the Earth's atmosphere. Light and warmth would not reach the Earth. Winds would carry these dark clouds to places where the weapons hadn't even been. In a matter of months, the Earth would begin to resemble the frozen lifeless surface of Mars. Ecological systems and food webs and chains would break, causing many plant and animal species to become extinct. Radioactive fallout, lack of food, dramatic temperature changes, poisonous fumes, and ultraviolet rays in this "nuclear winter" would combine to eliminate the possibility of anyone surviving—anywhere.

Fortunately there are many people all over the world who are determined to keep this from happening. We all realize how important it is, now more than ever, to see the world as it really is: Home For All Life. When we see our home from space, it becomes so clear, so obvious that we are all in this together.

> "Think of it. We are traveling on a planet, revolving around the Sun, in almost perfect symmetry. We are blessed with technology that would be indescribable to our forefathers. We have the wherewithal, the know-it-all, to feed everybody, clothe everybody, give every human on Earth a chance. We dwell instead on petty things. We kill each other. We build monuments to ourselves. What a waste of time. . . . Think of it. What a chance we have. . . . " —Buckminster Fuller

In this next project there are many suggestions of things you can do to take care of the Earth and her resources.

Project 45: Looking After the Earth

MATERIALS

a little thoughtfulness

PROCEDURE

Try as many of these ideas as you can. In a friendly way, mention some of them to others.

1. Turn the lights, radio, and TV off when no one is in the room.
2. Recycle cans, glass, and paper in your home and school.
3. Don't accept junk mail—tell your post office or have mail returned to sender.
4. Bring your own shopping bags to stores, especially grocery stores.
5. Put a brick in the tank of your toilet—it raises the water level and lowers the amount of water you use.
6. Put a water-saving shower head on your shower. (Showers use less water than baths.)
7. Use paper bags instead of plastic ones for garbage.
8. Eat lower on the food chain (more vegetables, less beef, more poultry).
9. Walk, bicycle, or use public transportation instead of cars.
10. Close closet doors so there is less space to heat or cool.
11. Pick up trash—even if it's not yours.
12. Don't throw trash on the ground or out of the car window.
13. Throw metal soft-drink tabs and plastic can carriers in the trash.
14. Dry your clothes on the line whenever possible instead of using the dryer.
15. Wait until your dishwasher or washing machine is full before you use it. Use shortest cycle and air-dry dishes. Wash clothes with cold water.
16. Plant trees to shade your house in summer and to protect against wind in winter.
17. Don't play your radios and tapes loudly outside (or at all in scenic places).
18. Replace mechanized recreation (motorcycles, dunebuggies, snowmobiles, power boats, trail bikes, and jeeps) with quieter, nonpolluting, less destructive alternatives (bicycles, skates, skiis, canoes, windsurfers, surf boards, sail boats, etc.)
19. Use a living, potted Christmas tree.
20. Consider giving gifts that encourage creativity and increase concern for the environment: gardening sets; tool kits; art and craft materials; cooking equipment; camping equipment; cameras; sports equipment; books (especially about nature); subscriptions to nature magazines; new games; pets; "rain checks" for trips to the beach, zoo, or mountains; contributions to nature and environmental organizations.
21. Become a volunteer at a wildlife protection agency.
22. Insulate the attic and walls of your house including hot water heater and pipes.
23. Examine and compare the efficiency ratios of several similar appliances before you buy.

24. Keep a record of everything your family consumes in one week (food, water, electricity, gasoline, etc.). Use meters to check electricity and water. Also keep a record of how much garbage your family throws away in one week. Consider yours an average family and multiply your consumption and garbage by the population of your town or country to get an idea of your impact on the environment.

25. Fix leaky faucets.
26. Lower the temperature on your hot-water heater.
27. Open and close the refrigerator as little as necessary.
28. Use a microwave or toaster oven.
29. Use the lowest possible setting on the stove.
30. Don't preheat the oven for more than 10 minutes.
31. Clean furnace and air conditioner filters once a month.
32. Dress warmer in the house and turn the heat down.
33. Keep the damper closed when you're not using the fireplace.
34. Light the places where you are working (your desk, etc.) instead of the whole room.
35. Keep the coils under refrigerator clean.
36. Air or towel dry your hair.
37. Install storm windows and doors and weatherstrip windows and doors.
38. Turn the thermostat down at night.
39. Walk, bicycle, carpool, or take the bus to save gas.
40. Close the curtains and shades at night to save heat.

READING MORE

Diagram Group, The. *A Science Digest Book: Spaceship Earth Its Voyage Through Time.* New York: Hearst Books, 1980.
Kyselka, Will and Ray Lanterman. *North Star to Southern Cross.* Honolulu: The University Press of Hawaii, 1976.
Nickelsburg, Janet. *Ecology: Habitats, Niches, and Food Chains.* Philadelphia: J. B. Lippincott Co., 1969.

Section 2:   FROM CORE TO MANTLE

Inside the Earth How far down into the Earth do you think people have explored? Tens or hundreds of miles or kilometers? The answer is a surprising 10 miles (16 kilometers), which is about twice as high as Mount Everest. No one has been to the center of the Earth. When I was very little, I would see a construction crew digging a hole and I would wonder, are they going to dig down as far as hell? When I got a little older I wondered, are Chinese people going to come out of the hole? When I got even bigger I wondered, are they going to make a hole right through the Earth so you can see the sky on the other side? A favorite question when I was in college was, if you did manage to dig a hole through the Earth and you dropped something into it, where would it go?

The French writer, **Jules Verne** (1828–1905) had his own answers to these questions. He wrote a great adventure story entitled *Journey to the Center of the Earth.* At the center of the Earth, in Jules Verne's world were vast caves and oceans. Jules Verne's description of the center of the Earth sounds a bit like that of the Roman writer **Seneca** (c. 4 B.C.–65 A.D.) who said:

"Be assured that there exists below, everything that you see above. There are vast caverns, immense recesses and vacant spaces with mountains overhanging on either hand. There are yawning gulfs, stretching down into the abyss, which have often swallowed up cities that have fallen into them. These retreats are filled with air, for nowhere is there a vacuum in nature; through their ample spaces stretch marshes over which darkness ever broods. Animals are also produced in them but they are slow-paced and shapeless."

From our study of earthquake waves we have put together our own picture of the interior of the Earth. The Earth has three main spheres. The word sphere means a ball but it can also mean an area of activity or influence. In the case of the Earth's spheres, it means both. There is a sphere for each of the three forms of matter: **solid, liquid,** and **gas.**

Lithosphere   The solid part of the Earth, that part upon which we live, is mostly rock and soil, so we call it the **lithosphere.** The lithosphere encloses the 4-layered interior of the Earth: the **inner core,** the **outer core,** the **mantle,** and the **crust.** As you move towards the center of the Earth from the crust the temperature increases 1°C per 100 feet, 96° F per mile, or 30° C per kilometer.

---

lithosphere comes from the Greek words λιθος *(lithos)* = stone and σφαιρα *(sphaira)* = globe or ball

---

The Inner Core   The pressure is so great in the inner core (close to 9 million pounds per square inch or 4 million kilograms per square centimeter) that it compresses the nickel-iron material, raising its boiling point which keeps it solid. Still, the temperature at the center of the Earth is estimated to be about 9,000° F (5,500° C).

The Outer Core   Surrounding the inner core is an outer layer of liquid iron. This liquid metal is believed to circulate at 0.008 inches (0.02 centimeters) per second. This motion sets up electric currents which create the Earth's magnetic field.

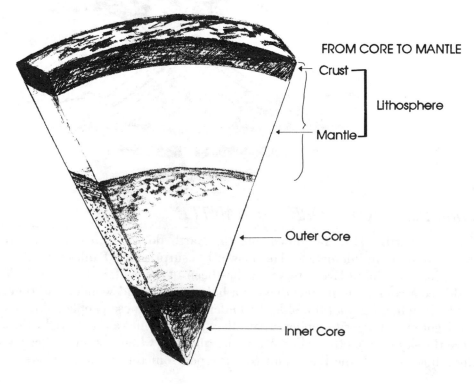

FROM CORE TO MANTLE

Crust
Lithosphere
Mantle

Outer Core

Inner Core

The Mantle   The mantle is a semi-molten layer which wraps itself around the outer and inner core of the Earth. We have never seen the mantle, even though it lies only a few tens of miles or kilometers beneath our feet. Most of what we know about what the mantle is made of has literally come up to us from it by way of deep volcanoes. This material is made of dense, solid rocks. These rocks are rich in iron and minerals made of oxygen, silicon, magnesium, iron, and calcium. The part of the mantle closest to the core we sometimes call the **mesosphere** because it is between the center and the surface of the Earth.

---

mantle comes from the Latin word *mantele* = a towel, napkin, or covering
meso comes from the Greek word μεσος *(mesos)* = middle

The upper part of the mantle is a soft layer of nearly molten rock about the consistency of asphalt. This is the **asthenosphere** = without strength. The study of waves coming from quakes on the Earth or any planet we call **seismology.** People have charted the boundary between the next layer, the crust and the mantle based on seismology. The speed of a wave depends on how dense the material is that it is traveling through. The speed of these waves increases as the density of the material increases. *Primary waves* (P waves) can travel through both solid and liquid materials. *Secondary waves* (S waves) can only travel through solid material. If a layer of one material with a particular density and compostition lies above another layer whose density and composition are different, the direction of the earthquake waves will change sharply as they pass from one material to another.

By careful studies of seismograms, you can locate the depths at which these abrupt changes occur. This is what **Andrija Mohorovicic,** a Yugoslavian, did in 1909. He detected a sharp change in the path of earthquake waves at a depth of 25 miles or 40 kilometers below the continents. At this level he noticed that the waves met a zone of increased density. In this zone, they could travel 25% faster than they could above it. Their travel path had changed or discontinued their previous wave pattern. The waves had entered the mantle. To this dividing line at 25 miles (40 kilometers) below the Earth's surface which marks the end of the crust and the beginning of the mantle we have given the name **Mohorovicic discontinuity** or simply, the **Moho.** Earthquakes can occur at depths of no more than 700 kilometers within the mantle.

---

asthenosphere comes from the Greek word ασθενος *(asthenos)* = without strength
The lithosphere technically includes all of the crust and part of the upper mantle above the asthenosphere.

In this next project you can put all of this information together in a model of what the Earth looks like inside.

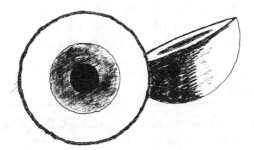

——————— **Project 46: Making a Model of the Inside of the Earth** ———————

MATERIALS

4 different colors of modelling clay   paper
thin wire   colored pencils (4 different colors)
string   glue

133

PROCEDURE

1. Make a ball of the first color of modelling clay. This is the inner core.

2. Flatten out a piece of the second color of modelling clay 1½ times as large as the inner core. This is the outer core.

3. Flatten out a piece of the third color of modelling clay twice as large as the inner core. This is the mantle. Roll it around the other two layers without losing the shape of the sphere or thinning out the modelling clay.

4. Flatten out a very thin piece of the fourth color of modelling clay. This is the crust. Cover the sphere keeping it round and without thinning out the modelling clay.

5. Take the thin wire and carefully cut the sphere in half. Write the names of each part of the Earth's interior on a small piece of paper using the same color of pencils as the parts of the Earth. Connect each name to the model using string with one end stuck into the modelling clay and the other end glued onto the paper.

OBSERVATIONS

Use your model while you reread about the inside of the Earth. Does it help you get a better picture of the different parts? You may want to add the asthenosphere and the Moho.

The Crust   This is the layer we know the best. Under the continents, it is about 30 miles or 48 kilometers thick, under the oceans only about 3 miles or 5 kilometers. Overall, the ocean floor sinks farther below sea level than the continents rise above sea level. The average depth of the oceans is about 2½ miles (4 kilometers) below sea level, whereas the average height of the continents is about ½ mile (0.8 kilometer) above sea level. In some places, such as the Marianas Trench in the Pacific, the ocean is almost 7 miles (11 kilometers) deep. By comparison, the highest mountain on the land, Mt. Everest, is only a little more than 5½ miles (9 kilometers) high. Compared to the entire Earth, the thickness of the crust is like the thickness of the skin of an apple. Its wrinkled surface even resembles the skin of an old apple. These wrinkles (which create the mountains, valleys, and flatlands) are due to the activity of the crust whose several segments are always on the move. We call the segments of the Earth's crust **plates**. There are about 10 large plates and several small ones, each only about 30 miles (50 kilometers) thick.

Sir Francis Bacon (1561–1626) and others after him, suggested that the continents had drifted apart. Rock samples from both continents were of similar type and age and in the same order in layers at those places where the continents would have been joined. Fossil remains showed similar plant and animal life. Mountains lined up with each other.

In 1869, **Antonio Snyder Pellegrini,** a meteorologist (a person who studies the weather) helped develop the idea of **continental drift.** In 1912, in his book *The Origin of Continents and Oceans*, **Alfred Wegener** (1880–1930), a German geologist, meteorologist and explorer presented as much evidence as he could to present the theory of continental drift. People considered him to be the founder of this theory, although the idea did not originate with him.

Alfred Wegener began his scholarly career as an historian of astronomy, studying the thirteenth century Alfonsine tables of planetary motions.

In 1965, **J. Tuzo Wilson** took the theory of continental drift, the concepts of magnetic studies and sea-floor spreading and combined them into one theory, the **theory of plate tectonics**. According to this theory, seven major plates and several smaller plates make up the Earth's surface.

If Earth's plates are moving, then where they are now is not where they have always been. Under the Earth's hard crust there is a general temperature increase about 1°F for every 60 feet (18 meters) you go down toward the center (or 10° C for every 98 feet or 30 meters). While not hot enough to melt the rock under the crust, this heat flow does make the material under the crust slightly soft. This slightly soft layer is the asthenosphere. From within the asthenosphere (60–120 miles or 100–200 kilometers deep) over time the material "flows" in currents like the oil in the next project,

EARTH'S PLATES AND THE DIRECTION OF THEIR MOVEMENT

Project 47, Making a Model of the Earth's Changing Surface (Plate Tectonics). The hard plates of the Earth's crust which "float" on top of the soft rock are carried around the surface of the Earth by the movement going on underneath. The speed which the plates travel is a few inches or centimeters per year. The continents which are attached to a certain plate, move whenever the plate moves.

When one plate meets another, there is no empty space in which to move, so they jam into each other and burrow under each other, sliding right into the mantle. The places where this happens are called **trenches**. A good example of a trench is the Japan Trench along the coast of that country. The process of pushing underneath to form trenches is called **subduction**. The continents, however, don't usually get shoved under. Instead they crash head on into each other and either join together or force the land to push upwards at the boundaries to form mountain ranges. Mt. Everest and the Himalaya Mountains came about when India joined Asia. Sometimes plates collide with each other without sliding underneath. Then they buckle up to form mountains just as continents do. These are called **ridges.** The MidAtlantic Ridge upon which Iceland sits is an example of this activity.

---

subduction comes from the Latin words *sub* = under, and *duct* = to lead

---

The boundaries of plates look like cracks in the surface of the Earth. A good way to imagine them is to look at a crack in a rock or a mountain. The cracks in the Earth's crust are **faults.** A famous fault line in the United States is the San Andreas Fault from the west of San Francisco in the north to the Gulf of California in the South. The fault line or boundary between two plates is also a place where new material for the crust can flow up from the mantle. The material may come gradually or be thrust out from volcanoes in the form of lava. The new material joins on to the edge of the

135

plate and in this way, the Earth replenishes its surface. Knowing where the greatest amount of volcanic activity is occurring can help you locate the boundaries of the plates.

If Sir Francis Bacon and Alfred Wegener were right, the continents were once joined together. What would that have looked like? Wegener made up the name **Pangaea** for this land mass.

---

pangaea comes from the Greek words $\pi\alpha\nu$ *(pan)* = all, and $\gamma\alpha\hat{\iota}\alpha$ *(gaia)* = Earth

---

According to Wegener's theory in the first separation of the lands, Pangaea divided into two large areas, almost along the equator. To the north was **Laurasia** which was to become North America, Europe, and Asia. To the south was **Gondwanaland** which included present day India, Australia, Africa, South America, and Antarctica.

Laurasia = combination of North America, Europe, and Asia
Gondwanaland = a province of India of geological interest

Laurasia and Gondwanaland

Pangaea

Approaching the present position.

THE DRIFTING CONTINENTS

The Earth's crust is rich in rock and mineral deposits. New material is constantly working its way up from the Earth's interior. New Hampshire farmers will tell you that their first crop of the season is always rocks. Residents of Rockland County, New York make a similar boast. Most of these "crops" consist of silicate—rich granitic rock types. The rocks below the oceans and mountains are mostly basaltic rock, volcanic in origin. 46.6% of the crust is composed of oxygen, with 27.7% silicon, 8.1% aluminum, 5.0% iron, 3.6% calcium, 2.8% sodium, 2.6% potassium, and 2.1% magnesium. "Soil" is usually not more than 20 feet (6 meters) deep. We also call soil "earth." Sometimes we call it dirt. Our idea of "dirty" or "earthy" being unclean probably comes from Aristotle's picture of the planet Earth as that place farthest from the gods.

In this next project, you can get a very good idea of the movement of the Earth's plates.

— Project 47: Making a Model of Earth's Changing Surface (Plate Tectonics) —

MATERIALS

    long, flat cooking dish   stove or burner
    cooking oil   light
    flour

PROCEDURE

    1. Pour enough cooking oil into the cooking dish for the oil to be 1–2 inches (about 5 centimeters) deep.

    2. Place the dish over low heat.

    3. Place a bright light above the dish.

OBSERVATIONS

Notice how the convection currents carry the heat to the surface of the oil. Watch how the heat divides the surface of the oil into different areas. These areas are like the Earth's plates.

4. Sprinkle a little flour onto the surface of the oil so that it forms a light skin. This skin is like the continents on the Earth's plates.

OBSERVATIONS

What did you see? Observe the movement of the plates and the continents. Watch for examples of continental drift and plate collisions, unions, and separation.   This project is adapted from *Astronomy: The Cosmic Journey* by William K. Hartmann, Belmont: Wadsworth Publishing Company, 1978. Used with permission.

Water on the Earth   The oceans contain 97% of all the water on Earth. The largest of these is the Pacific Ocean whose surface area is greater than that of all the continents put together. The Atlantic Ocean is the next largest ocean, followed by the Indian Ocean and the Arctic Ocean.

There are many lakes, streams, rivers, ponds, and creeks. The water in these places usually comes from melted snow in mountain peaks and is **fresh.** The water in the oceans and some seas is **salty.** We sometimes call it **brine.** The fresh water bodies hold less than 1% of the Earth's water. The remaining 2% of the total is frozen into ice in glaciers and around the north and south poles.

Salts lower the freezing point of water. The deeper the water, the greater the pressure, and this prevents freezing too. The Sun warms the water on the surface. At the poles it is usually colder than 0°. (In the middle latitudes, the temperature changes with the seasons. Near the equator, surface water can be as warm as 85°F or 30°C.) Sunlight only reaches about 330 feet (100 meters) into the water. Plants need energy from the Sun so ocean plants live inside or just below this layer.

Water seeks to take the shape of a sphere. When moving, it creates spirals and curled shapes. In the crest of a wave or the wavy-lined shape of river banks, we see the signature of the forces of form and movement. In this next project you can see these shapes yourself as you make the signature of form and movement visible in water.

──────── Project 48: Interpreting Patterns of Movement in Water ────────

MATERIALS

container (long, flat cooking dish)   fine powder (lycopodium)
ink or food coloring   pencil
eyedropper   water
glycerine   camera with ASA 400 film

PROCEDURE

1. Fill the cooking dish with water.
2. Fill the eyedropper with ink or food coloring.
3. Squirt the ink into the water from one end of the cooking dish with the eyedropper under water. Squirt slowly at first, then faster. Observe the patterns the ink makes in the water.
4. Empty the container and refill it with water.
5. Add enough glycerine to make the water thicker.
6. Sprinkle the surface of the water with the fine powder.
7. Hold the pencil straight up and down in the water at one end of the cooking dish.
8. Move the pencil straight across the water. Photograph what you see.
9. Move the pencil faster across the water. Photograph what you see.
10. Move the pencil twice through the water. Photograph what you see.
11. Repeat steps #8 and #9 with your thumb. Photograph what you see.

OBSERVATIONS

Where in nature have you seen these forms before? Compare your photographs with photographs of the surfaces of Jupiter and Saturn.   This project is adapted from the work of Theodor Schwenk appearing in his book *Sensitive Chaos: The Creation of Flowing Forms in Water and Air*, London: Rudolf Steiner Press, 1965.

READING MORE

Beiser, Arthur and the Editors of Time-Life Books. *The Earth.* New York: Time-Life Books, 1970.
Clayton, Keith. *The Crust of Earth: The Story of Geology.* Garden City: The Natural History Press, 1967.

THE ORION NEBULA *From* The Story of the Heavens *by Sir Robert S. Ball, London:* Cassell and Co., Ltd. 1886

Section 3: *FROM ATMOSPHERE TO EXOSPHERE*

The Air Around the Earth   When you look up at the blue sky you are looking at a blanket of air which surrounds and protects our Earth. This blanket filters out the harmful ultraviolet rays from the Sun and helps balance out extremes in temperature. We call this protective air blanket the **atmosphere.** The atmosphere contains five layers: the **troposphere,** the **stratosphere,** the **mesosphere,** the **thermosphere,** and the **exosphere.**

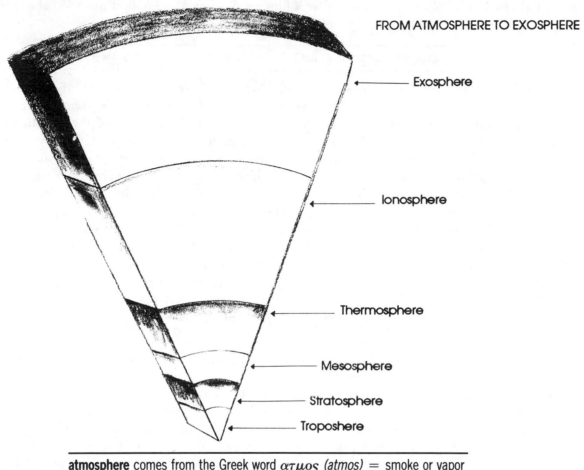

Exosphere

Ionosphere

Thermosphere

Mesosphere

Stratosphere

Troposhere

---
atmosphere comes from the Greek word $\alpha\tau\mu o\varsigma$ *(atmos)* = smoke or vapor
---

The Troposphere   The **troposphere** contains about 9/10 of the atmosphere's total mass and all the constantly changing elements that cause the weather: water vapor, dust, smoke, clouds, and winds. All of our weather occurs within this sphere. The air currents sweep up and down causing winds, storms, clouds, snow, and rain.

---
troposphere comes from the Greek word $\tau\rho o\pi o\sigma$ *tropos* = a turn, direction, or way
---

If you move upward through the troposphere, the temperature of the air decreases steadily at a rate of 1°F for every 300 feet (90 meters). When you reach the top of the troposphere, the temperature begins to rise again. The temperature at the top of the troposphere is warmest just above the Earth's poles where the air is almost always 50° below zero. Here the troposphere extends to a height of about 5 miles (8 kilometers). Above the equator where the troposphere layer reaches the highest, about 11 miles (18 kilometers), the temperature at the top of the troposphere normally remains near 100°F or 38°C. The average height of the troposphere is 10 miles (16 kilometers), about twice the height of Mount Everest. Practically all of the moisture in the atmosphere is in the troposphere. About 90% of all the gas in the atmosphere is also within the troposphere. The air you breathe is 78% nitrogen, 21% oxygen, and 1% argon, with traces of water (as a gas), carbon dioxide, and other gases. The boundary between the troposphere and the stratosphere is the **tropopause.**

The Stratosphere   Above the ever changing troposphere is the **stratosphere**. Here the air is calm, and almost completely free from water vapor, dust, and gases. A few thin clouds sometimes appear here but there is no turbulence. The air currents flow in horizontal layers rather than in vertical columns as in the troposphere. For all of these reasons, airline pilots prefer to fly their large jets in the stratosphere. Since the air outside the plane is too "thin" to support life, the plane must supply air for people to breathe. Temperatures in the 25 miles (40 kilometers) of the stratosphere remain constant from 70°F to −45°F (21°C to −43°C) in the lower half to about −30°F (−35°C) in the upper half. In 1942, V2 rockets launched at White Sands, New Mexico, first recorded above freezing temperatures in this region.

---

stratosphere comes from the Latin word *stratum* = covering or layer

---

Within the stratosphere layer are winds which blow usually from west to east at speeds of up to 300 miles (480 kilometers) per hour. This narrow band which seems to follow roughly the southern edge of the large cold air mass that covers much of the northern parts of the North American continent. We call it the **jet stream.** During the winter when this air mass is large, the North American jet stream passes directly over the center of the United States. U.S. pilots in 1944 discovered the jet stream when they attempted to fly westward above the troposphere. They met the jet stream head on, blowing from the opposite direction with such a force that the planes, the largest and highest flying aircraft ever built at that time, could hardly move.

The boundary between the stratosphere and the mesosphere is the **stratopause**.

The Mesosphere   The stratopause marks the beginning of a sharp increase in the temperature of the air, within the 25 miles (40 kilometers) of the **mesosphere**. In the lower levels of the mesosphere, temperatures climb to +170°F (77°C). At the upper limit of the mesosphere, the temperature plunges to −150°F (−101°C). The lowest temperatures in the atmosphere occur here.

---

mesosphere comes from the Greek word $\mu\varepsilon\sigma o$ *(meso)* = middle

---

The boundary between the mesosphere and the thermosphere and ionosphere is the **mesopause**.

The Thermosphere and the Ionosphere   When you reach beyond the mesosphere you encounter four layers of gases whose names come from the chief elements that they contain: the **nitrogen layer** (about 70 miles or 112 kilometers thick), the **oxygen layer** (almost 575 miles or 925 kilometers thick), the **helium layer** (about 150 miles or 240 kilometers thick) and the hydrogen layer (about 20,000 miles or 32,000 kilometers thick). The air in this sphere is very hot because of the energy from the Sun which collects here. For this reason, we call this sphere the **thermosphere**. The air is also very thin in this sphere.

---

thermosphere comes from the Greek word $\theta\varepsilon\rho\mu o\varsigma$ *(thermos)* = warm or hot

---

Overlapping the mesosphere and the thermosphere are several layers of electrically charged particles. The Sun seems to be responsible for creating these charged particles from material in the air. The particles are **ions**. The ionosphere reflects radio waves. These waves do not follow the curved shape of the Earth but follow straight lines. (For more information about radio waves, see Chapter 5, Section 4.) Since some of the waves are reflected back, we can send them around the world. **Guglielmo Marconi** (1874–1937) recognized this possibility on December 12, 1901 when he sent the code letter "S" using radio waves from Cornwall, England, across the Atlantic to St. John's on the coast of Newfoundland. His Nobel Prize–winning work led to the discovery and further use of the layers of ionized particles in the upper atmosphere.

Working apart but at the same time, an Englishman named **Arthur Edwin Kennelly** (1861–1939) and an English electrical engineer named **Oliver Heaviside** (1850–1925) concluded that there must be an electrical reflecting layer high in the atmosphere which reflected certain radio waves back to the Earth while letting others pass through. We call this "radio roof" the **Kennelly-Heaviside layer** after its discoverers. Auroras occur here. Here too is where meteoroids burn up and produce meteors.

The Exosphere Above the ionosphere, 300 miles (480 kilometers) above the Earth's surface, the air is very, very thin. This final layer of the Earth's atmosphere reaches right out into space. For that reason we call it the **exosphere**.

The atmosphere protects us from the Sun's full energy by absorbing the ultraviolet rays while letting some of the light and warmth ray down on us. The atmosphere also provides us with two unique and beautiful features of living on Earth: blue skies and sunsets. How? The next project based on the work of the German poet and scientist, **Goethe** (1749–1832), will help you answer this question.

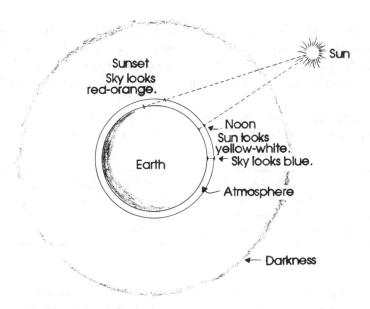

——— Project 49: Demonstrating How the Colors of the Sky Are Made ———

MATERIALS

an aquarium or large, clear container   liquid detergent or milk
slide projector   water

PROCEDURE

1. Fill the tank with water. Add enough liquid detergent to the water so that it is semi-transparent.
2. Shine the projector on the *side* of the tank. Look through the front of the tank. What color is the water?
3. Shine the projector on the *back* of the tank. Look though the front of the tank at the light behind it. What color is the water?

OBSERVATIONS

The presence of an atmosphere around the Earth creates a "dusty" layer of material through which light must pass: air, tiny droplets of water, and dust particles. The bluing and reddening of the sky is due to the spreading out of the sunlight through this dusty layer. We call it **diffusion**. The blue light reaches us from all directions, while the red is more focused.

The moist particles of dust and smoke in the atmosphere act as tiny mirrors sending the reflection of light back to the Earth. This happens before sunrise when the Sun's light is reflected and after sunset, thus providing additional daylight and daytime. City lights at night often light up the sky. You can look at light and the effects the atmosphere has on it in more detail in Chapter 5, Section 2.

Weather

Whether the weather is cold
or whether the weather is hot,
We'll weather the weather
whatever the weather
whether we like it or not!

Climate is the average yearly and seasonal pattern of weather conditions which you find in any location. Climate limits the growing season and restricts the crops that you can grow. Because of its effects on the soil, the climate is responsible for how fertile the land will be. This helps explain why people are spread so unevenly over the Earth. They're looking for places where the climate will let them grow food.

Weather is how we describe what is happening to the air and the water in it at a specific time and in a specific place. It is what the climate is right here, right now.

---

climate comes from the Greek word κλιμα (klima) = inclination or slope of the Earth toward the pole, in ancient geography. A climate was one of seven astrological belts or zones on the Earth. Each of the seven planets had a zone which it looked after.
weather comes from the Middle English word weder = weather

Air is constantly moving where there are differences in temperature and therefore pressure. The greater the differences in pressure, the stronger the winds will blow. In an effort toward balance, hot air is sent toward the poles, cold air toward the tropics. When each reaches its goal, the temperature it meets changes the temperature of the air causing it to move again.

We call the cool air traveling toward the tropics and the breeze it makes the **trade winds.** These are the steadiest winds we know of. Columbus relied on them to get his ships to the New World. The trade winds from the northern hemisphere meet the trade winds from the Southern Hemisphere at the equator where they both stop. Underneath them hot air from the tropics is rising, creating a band of low pressure. The continual upward movement of warm air is very slow. This means the air is usually calm—no breezes. This area is called the **doldrums** (a word which means nothing is happening—boring!)

A similarly nonbreezy mass of air occurs at 30° N and 30° S where hot air from the equator moves toward the poles. By the time it has reached 30° it has cooled and descends forming a high pressure belt known as **horse latitudes**. Early sailors traveling on the seas in this hot, unhealthy area panicked at the lack of wind to move their ships. Legend has it that they threw their horses overboard to lighten their load.

From about 30° to 55° the air from the horse latitudes makes its way toward the pole traveling from the west. Because the winds this movement creates come from the west, we call them the **westerlies.**

Winds are named according to the direction from which they are coming.

In 1680, the British Astronomer-Royal, **Sir Edmund Halley** (1656–1742) published a paper in which he made the first attempt to show that the flow of cold, dense, air toward regions of warmer, lighter air caused the different wind patterns around the globe. The body of air that the prevailing winds carries as it moves is an **air mass**. These air masses are large and their entire mass has the same amount of moisture and the same temperature. Each air mass forms in a different location. If it forms near the north or south pole it is a *polar air mass* (P). If it forms over land, it is a **continental air mass** (C). If it forms over an ocean, it is a *maritime air mass* (M). If the air mass forms near the tropic of Cancer or the tropic of Capricorn, it is a *tropical air mass* (T). These types of air masses can join together to form combinations like continental polar (cP), maritime tropical (mT), etc.

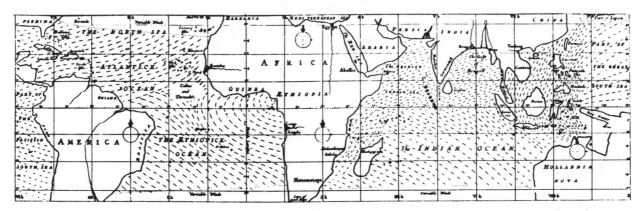

Edmond Halley's chart of the trade winds, 1686.

The place where a mass of cold air meets a mass of warm air is a moving boundary. The movement depends on which air mass is pushing the other air mass ahead of it. If the colder air is pushing the warmer air, this boundary is called a **cold front**, because of the moving cold air mass and the back of the retreating warm air mass. If the warm air pushes the cold air, the boundary is called a **warm front**.

How can you tell whether the air pressure is high or low? In 1643, a student of Galileo named **Evangelista Torricelli** (1608–1647) invented an instrument to do just that. He called his instrument a **barometer**. When Torricelli made his barometer he used liquid mercury in a thin glass tube standing above a glass dish. The column of mercury stopped moving down the glass tube and into the dish when the pressure due to its weight was balanced by the pressure of the air pushing down on the mercury in the dish. The level of mercury in the tube in this balanced position was 30 inches (76 centimeters) above the surface of the mercury in the dish. When the air pressure gets heavier, it pushes down on the surface of the mercury in the dish, sending the mercury higher up in the column. Thus you can actually see the pressure rising. A pressure of 30 inches (76 centimeters) is equal to 1,016 millibars, the unit of measurement which the Weather Bureau prefers to use.

To change from inches to millibars, multiply the pressure in inches by 33.87.

In this next project you can make your own barometer just as Torricelli did. Instead of liquid mercury, your barometer uses air and a thinly stretched balloon.

---

barometer comes from the Greek words $\beta\alpha\rho o\sigma$ (baros) = weight or pressure, and $\mu\epsilon\tau\rho o\nu$ (metron) = to measure

---

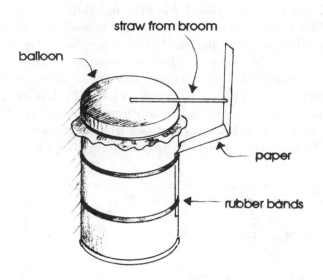

straw from broom

balloon

paper

rubber bands

Project 50: Making an Air Pressure Measurer (Barometer)

MATERIALS

a straw from a broom
small juice can or glass jar
balloon
3 rubber bands
1 × 5 inch (2½ × 13 centimeter)
   strip of stiff paper
rubber cement

pencil
ice
bowl
candle
telephone number of the
   local weather bureau

PROCEDURE

1. Stretch a balloon tightly over one end of an empty tin can. Use a rubber band to hold the balloon onto the can.

2. Glue the straw from a broom onto the center of the balloon with rubber cement. This is the pointer.

3. Fold and attach the strip of stiff paper to the side of the can with two rubber bands. This is the scale. Make sure the pointer touches the scale.

4. Draw a line on the scale where the pointer touches it. Call the weather bureau to find out what the air pressure is and write that number where your mark is.

5. Hold the finished barometer about 6 inches (15 centimeters) above a lit candle. Draw a line on the scale where the pointer touches it. Mark it "warmest."

6. Set your barometer in a bowl full of ice. Mark where the pointer touches the scale, and mark it "coldest."

7. Paint or cover the outside of the can. Don't paint the balloon.

8. Set your barometer indoors where you can check its readings daily. It should be in a place where you won't have to move it and where the temperature stays pretty much the same.

OBSERVATIONS

Warm air is lighter and cold air is heavier. When you hear the expression "the barometer is falling," it means that the pressure is below 30 inches (76 centimeters). Keep checking with the weather bureau to add new marks to your barometer. "When the glass falls low prepare for a blow, when it rises high let all your kites fly."

"We live submerged at the bottom of an ocean of the element air."—Evangelista Torricelli, 1644

In 1843, **Lucien Vidie,** a French scientist invented a barometer that was less expensive, smaller, lightweight, and portable. He removed the air from a tiny accordion-like box. Changes in air pressure caused the little box to collapse or expand slightly. These changes were indicated by a needle and a dial on the box. Because this barometer had no liquid in it, we call it an **aneroid barometer**.

---

aneroid comes from the Greek word α (a) = without, and νηρον (neron) = liquid

---

In 1612, Galileo constructed an instrument to measure the temperature of the air. He called his instrument a **thermometer**.

---

thermometer comes from the Greek word θερμος (thermos) = warm, and μετρον (metron) = to measure

---

COMPARING FAHRENHEIT, CELSIUS, AND KELVIN TEMPERATURES

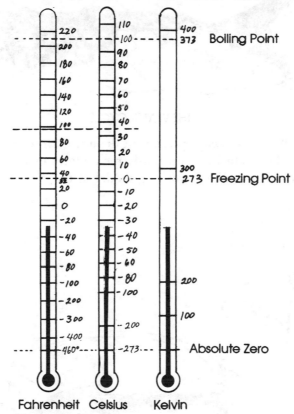

Moisture   The amount of moisture in the air contributes to its pressure. There is dry, hot air in low pressure areas. Wet, cold air is in high pressure areas. This moisture is what you hear people complain about when they say, "It's not just the heat, it's the **humidity**."

---

humidity comes from the Latin word *humidus* = moist, damp

In 1783, the Swiss geologist **Horace Benedict de Saussure** invented a method to measure the moisture or humidity in the air. He called his invention the **hair hygrometer**. de Saussure used strands of human hair attached to a dial. When the air was moist, the hair stretched. When the air was dry, the hair shrank. A dial showed the change.

---

hygrometer comes from the Greek word ύγρος (hygros) = wet, moist

---

In 1714, **Gabriel Daniel Fahrenheit** (1686–1736), a German scientist invented the familiar **Fahrenheit** scale. On his scale, the boiling point of water is 212° and the freezing point of water is 32°. In 1742, **Anders Celsius** (1701–1744), a Swedish astronomer, invented the **Centigrade** scale. On this scale, the boiling point of water is 100 and the freezing point of water is 0°. In 1850, the English scientist William Thomson (**Lord Kelvin**, 1824–1907) developed the **Kelvin** or **Absolute** scale. In this scale, absolute zero is the lowest possible temperature.

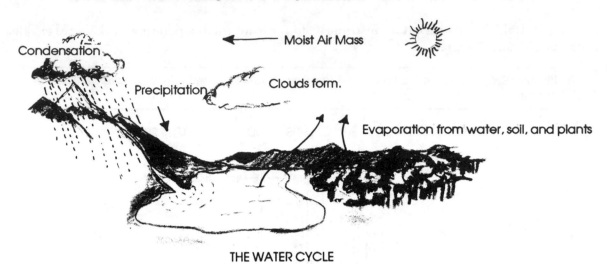

THE WATER CYCLE

The Water Cycle   Water is always present in the air, even in the desert. About 9/10 of it is in the air above the Earth. This moisture constantly recirculates in what we call the **water cycle**.

In this next project you can make a working model of the complete water cycle that will fit on top of a table.

———————— **Project 51: Making a Model of the Water Cycle** ————————

MATERIALS

bright lamp

modelling clay

plastic wrap

water

ice (crushed)

clear plastic take-out food
container with tight-fitting lid

grease pencil

razor blade or knife

masking tape

146

PROCEDURE

1. Build a model of a mountain, valley, and shoreline to fit inside the plastic container. The mountain should be slightly higher than halfway from the bottom of the container.

2. Pour water over the mountain so that it flows down the valley and into the lake. Make sure no water is left on the sides or behind the mountain.

3. Snap the lid tightly on the top of the container.

4. Draw a circle on the lid with the grease pencil that is slightly more than half the diameter of the mountain. Cut the circle out with a knife or razor blade.

5. Cover the hole in the lid with a sheet of plastic wrap. Push the plastic wrap down so it is about ½ inch (1¼ centimeters) above the top of the mountain and tape it to the lid. Fill the plastic wrap with crushed ice, making sure that it does not touch the mountain.

6. Shine a bright light through the lakeside end of the plastic container and onto the water in the lake.

OBSERVATIONS

Can you see any water forming on the top of the container? Is it raining on the mountain? If so, where does the rain water go?

From the clouds come rain and snow, returning moisture to the Earth. In order for this to happen, a cloud must contain water droplets and ice crystals. Water vapor gathers into clouds by collecting onto tiny particles of dust, dirt, and salt spray in the air. The cloud droplets around these dust particles are about 1/2500 inch or 0.0010 of a centimeter in diameter. They contain water or ice crystals or both. Water forms around the ice crystals making them heavier. When they are too heavy to float in the air, they fall. If they pass through a warm sky, the ice crystals melt and fall as **rain.** If the air is cold, the crystals fall to the Earth as **snow.** If the ice crystal passes back and forth in a large thunderstorm cloud between freezing and nonfreezing air levels, onion-like layers of ice gradually fall as **hailstones** at about 7 miles (11 kilometers) per hour.

Raindrops range in size from about 1/100 to ¼ inch or ¼ to 6 millimeters or less in diameter. They start round but end up flat at the bottom and round at the top, like a mushroom. No two snowflakes are alike, but they all have six sides. The largest hailstone found was more than 5 inches (13 centimeters) across.

Thunderstorms occur when warm rain is pulled straight up into cold skies where it condenses into a cloud. Because of the heat of the day, more and more air is pulled upward and heated. The cloud grows taller and taller as more moist air is pulled into it. Droplets of water form at the top of the cloud where it meets the very cold air of high altitudes. The raindrops that fall carry positively charged particles with them, leaving the cloud overly full of negatively charged particles. These negatively charged particles are attracted to the positive ones wherever they can be found in another part of the same cloud, in another cloud, a tree, a house, a living creature. The negatively charged particles make a great leap through the air to get to the positively charged particles. The air in their path crackles and glows as it expands violently from the heat of the charged particles passing by. The sounds of this violent expansion are thunder and the glow is **lightning,** traveling 20,000 miles or 32,000 kilometers a second.

About 2,200 thunderstorms are going on almost constantly all over the Earth.
Lightning strikes the Earth about 100 times per second which adds up to about 3.15 billion times a year. Lightning is about 54,032°F (30,000°C) which is more than five times the temperature of the Sun's surface.

There are three conditions needed for water vapor to condense into a cloud:
1. Warm moisture
2. Dust particles on which the water vapor can condense
3. Drop in pressure at the same time that the moisture cools

You can combine all three of these to make your own clouds in this next project.

Project 52: Forming Clouds

MATERIALS

glass jar or jug   warm water
chalk dust

PROCEDURE

1. Moisten the glass jar with warm water, and leave a small amount of water in the bottom.
2. Sprinkle chalk dust into jar.
3. Blow air into the jar several times, then stop suddenly, letting outside air enter the jar.
4. Repeat as often as you need to until you form a cloud inside the jar.

OBSERVATIONS

What happens to the cloud when pressure is increased compared to when it is decreased?

Hurricanes (also called **typhoons** in the Western Pacific or **cyclones** in the Indian Ocean or **Willy Willys** in Australia) occur when a very warm mass of air over the southern part of tropical oceans filled with water meets a cold air mass. There is no front. The cold air is warmed as it sits over the ocean and lifts both masses higher into the southern skies. The warm air on top meets the cool air high in the southern skies and wants to come back down again. The pushing and pulling that follows sends out rain from a whirlpool-shaped mass of air 10 miles above the sea. The winds are moving at about 200 miles or 320 kilometers an hour in a circle about 500 miles (800 kilometers) across, heading north. The center or "eye" of the hurricane is calm. There is no rain and almost no wind in the area of low pressure and humidity but high temperatures. A hurricane may last for several weeks.

> **hurricane** comes from the Spanish word *huracan* = winds

Tornadoes (or **twisters**) come about much like hurricanes do. They may last only eight minutes but they are highly destructive. The twisting effect caused by the Earth's spinning creates funnels made of sets powerful whirling masses of warm and cold air.

Predicting the weather is tricky—and very important. When will it rain? Is a hurricane coming?

meteorology, the study of weather, comes from the Greek word μετεωρολογοσ *(meteorologos)* = talking or treating of the heavenly bodies

Weather forecasters rely on information provided by nearly 3,000 weather stations throughout the world on land, on ships at sea, and satellites circling the Earth. Four times a day these stations send information to the national weather bureau which makes a map of the information. Meteorologists read these maps and predict what may happen in a certain location. Usually weather travels from west to east at about 15 miles (24 kilometers) per hour in the summer and about 25 miles (40 kilometers) per hour in the winter. In the summer, today's weather for people 400–500 miles or 650–800 kilometers west of you will probably be your weather tomorrow. In the winter, today's weather 700 miles (1,125 kilometers) west of you is likely to be your weather tomorrow. If there is warm air behind cool air, there is usually rain 500 miles or 800 kilometers ahead. Still, with all the charts, maps, and satellite pictures available, predicting what the weather will actually do is not always easy or accurate.

READING MORE

Donnan, John A., and Marcia Donnan. *Rain Dance to Research.* New York: David McKay Company, Inc., 1977.
Milgrom, Harry. *Understanding Weather.* London: Crowell-Collier Press, 1970.

Photo courtesy of NASA.

Section 4: THE EARTH IN SPACE

The Moving Earth   "Once a photograph of the Earth, taken from the outside, is available . . . a new idea as powerful as any in history will let loose."—Sir Fred Hoyle, 1948

Such a photograph *is* available. It is the one on page 149. When it first appeared in 1969, it startled many people. Imagine looking at the Earth and not being on it! It certainly changes your perspectives about the Earth, the people on it, and our relationship to each other when you can see the whole world in a glance.

Mapmakers often have relied on brass or wooden globes to represent the Earth. Globes of the sky showed the Earth in the center giving you an "extraterrestrial" point of view, looking down through the celestial sphere. The constellations appear backwards seen from this view point.

---

extraterrestrial comes from the Latin words *extra* = outside, and *terra* = the Earth

---

Point of view makes a big difference. In the middle ages, when people were trying to understand the stars and planets and their relationship to the Earth and the Sun, they had a point of view which they considered "acceptable." This was the view that your own eyes could prove: the Earth stood still in the center of the Universe, while everything else, including the Sun, the Moon, the planets, and stars, circled around it. This was the view that your own feelings could prove: the Earth was the home of people, the peak of creation, where else but in the center of the universe would God place it? This was the view that the most reliable and knowledgeable scholars could prove: Aristotle, Ptolemy, and Thomas Aquinas had all written about it in great detail. With your common sense, religious conviction, and scientific thoroughness you had formed a standpoint.

In 1506, a young Polish priest Nicojak Koppernigk (**Nicolaus Copernicus** in Latin, 1473–1543) looked over the same ideas. As an astronomy and mathematics teacher, he was looking for ways to explain things better and more simply both to himself and his students. He found the ideas of Ptolemy fascinating but cluttered up with all the cycles and epicycles, equants, eccentrics, deferrents, etc., which he used to explain the motions of the planets. On paper, the priest worked out a much simpler way of showing how the planets moved. He still used epicycles and deferrents etc., but far less.

The Copernican System.
From the original copy of de Revolutionibus

Nicolaus Copernicus

The way Copernicus managed to unclutter the dance of the heavens was to have two of the dancers change places. Where one had been in the very center of the dance, that one was now among those dancing around the center. This was the planet Earth. The dance and the other dancers stayed the same. Copernicus had seen that by trying to make everything work with the Earth in the center, the whole arrangement got terribly complicated. If instead you placed the Sun in the center you could much more easily account for the movement of everything. Another step was to have the Earth join in the dance by moving around the Sun like the other planets did. A further step was to have the Earth turning around itself while it circled around the Sun.

150

The young teacher circulated descriptions of his ideas to his friends. They encouraged him to publish his work so that others could read it and think about it. He was not very excited about doing this. The more he thought about the idea, the more Copernicus realized what problems it was creating inside him and what problems it would surely create inside others. It is not surprising, then, that the first published copy of this work entitled *De Revolutionibus Orbium Coelestium* (Concerning the Revolutions of the Heavenly Spheres) was handed to its author in 1543 as he lay dying.

Copernicus is the father of the **Scientific Revolution** (from the title of his book). He had turned the Earth into a planet and made his own picture of the Earth available which let loose a new idea as powerful as any in history. This idea is the basis of our own picture of the universe today. In it we place the Sun at the center of what we call the **solar system**. We have stopped the celestial sphere from turning. The Earth turns, not the starry sky. The Earth turns, the Sun doesn't rise and set. The planets circle around the Sun—so do we. Nothing but the Moon circles around the Earth.

We have all grown up with these ideas. Imagine, however, hearing them for the first time maybe as one of the students in Copernicus's class. How would you feel? How would you feel about yourself and your place in the universe? If you carefully consider these feelings then you will be able to understand why it was that people fought so hard not to believe or accept Copernicus's ideas.

In the model that Copernicus suggested, the Earth moves as one of the planets around the Sun which is in the center. For this reason, we call his model the **heliocentric** system. In the system represented by Ptolemy and the ancients before him the Earth is at the center. We call this arrangement the **geocentric** system.

---

heliocentric comes from the Greek word ἥλιος *(helios)* = Sun, and κεντρυμ *(kentrum)* = center
geocentric comes from the Greek word γεω *(geo)* = Earth and κεντρυμ *(kentrum)* = center

---

Our present concept of a heliocentric system is quite different from that of Copernicus'; yet the two seem very similar. Copernicus did not disprove the geocentric system, he simply replaced it with another system that was simpler and more accurate.

In the geocentric system, the Earth is motionless. It sits at the center of the universe while the entire heavens parade in front of it. In the heliocentric system, the Earth is active. It participates in a complex combination of at least six motions.

1. *It rotates about its axis once a day.*

The Earth spins counterclockwise about its axis, making one complete turn, or rotation in about 1,000 miles or 1,600 kilometers per hour or about 1,500 feet or 450 kilometers per second.

2. *It revolves around the Sun once a year.*

The Earth travels in a counterclockwise orbit around the Sun.

3. *The axis of the Earth precesses.*

The Earth's axis is not perpendicular to its orbit, but makes an angle of 23°27'. It is this tilt which causes the seasons. As it revolves around the Sun and spins about its axis, the pole of the Earth traces a small circle in the sky. It takes 25,800 years to trace the complete circle. In the process of making this circle, the north pole of the Earth points to different stars making them the North Star.

4. *The axis of the Earth nutates.*

The curve which the Earth's axis traces is not a smooth circle. It has small waves due to the "nodding" of the Earth's axis from its average position of 23°27'. The period of one complete wave is 19 years, causing a nod of 9 seconds of an angle from the 23°27' angle. The main cause of Earth's nutation is the gravitational pull of the Moon.

5. *The solar system moves.*

The Sun, with the Earth and the other planets, speeds through the local cluster of stars at a speed of 12 miles or 19 kilometers per second.

6. *The galaxy moves.*

The local cluster of stars takes part in the rotation around the center of our galaxy at a speed of hundreds of miles or kilometers per second.

In this next project you will be doing an experiment invented in 1851 by the French physicist, **J. B. L. Focault** to prove that the Earth rotates.

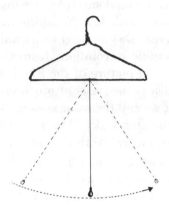

———————— Project 53: Proving the Rotation of the Earth ————————

MATERIALS
PART 1
  lead weight (e.g., a fishing sinker)   wire coat hanger
  string

PART 2
  pen or pencil   record player
  paper

PART 3
  suspension wire   chalk
  bearings   scissors
  string   lead weight

PART 1
PROCEDURE
  1. Make a pendulum by attaching the weight to the string and tying the other end to the wire coat hanger.
  2. Aim the wire hanger at an object on the wall.
  3. Pull the weight back and let it swing in the same direction that the wire hanger is aimed.
  4. While the pendulum is swinging, slowly turn the hanger away from the object on the wall.

OBSERVATIONS
  Does the pendulum change its direction? Suppose the object on the wall was a star. What would happen if the star was moving? What would it mean if the star wasn't moving but was fixed in space?

PART 2
PROCEDURE
  1. Draw a circle on the piece of paper and write the four directions on it. This circle will be the *Earth.*
  2. Put the Earth on top of a record player, lazy susan, piano stool, or anything that can turn.
  3. Hang the end of the pendulum above the Earth and start it swinging in a north-south direction. Turn the Earth in a counterclockwise direction.

OBSERVATIONS

Does the pendulum still swing in a north-south line? To an observer on Earth, in the Northern Hemisphere, in what direction does the pendulum appear to be changing, clockwise or counter-clockwise? How about to an observer in the Southern Hemisphere?

Focault performed his experiment in the Pantheon in Paris with a 200 foot (60 meter) length of suspension wire. Pendulums will continue to swing in whatever direction you start them until they come to a rest.

PART 3
PROCEDURE

1. Attach the suspension wire to the bearings so the wire can move freely.
2. Attach the bearings to the ceiling.
3. Place the lead weight at the end of the wire. Tie one end of some string to the weighted end of the wire and pull it to one side. Tie the string to a stationary object. When the weighted wire has stopped moving, cut the string to start the pendulum swinging.
4. With chalk, mark a line on the ground showing the path made by the swinging weight.

OBSERVATIONS

Notice the path of the weight a half hour later. What do you see? What do you think happened? To obtain a complete circle in 24 hours, you would have to perform the experiment at the Earth's north pole.

Proofs of the Rotation of the Earth   Another proof of the Earth's rotation came from a discovery of **James Bradley** (1693–1762). In 1725, Bradley found that starlight moves over or shifts from the position it actually holds in the sky. If it didn't, it would travel down from the sky in a straight line and directly into the tube of a telescope. What happens instead is that you have to tilt the telescope to receive the light in much the same way as you have to tilt an umbrella while walking in the rain, no matter how vertical the rainfall is. You have to tip the umbrella because you are moving and thus meeting the raindrops as though they were coming at a slant. You have to tip the telescope because the Earth is moving and thus you are meeting the starlight as if it was coming at a slant, or from a place other than where it actually started. This apparent shift of the light from a star is the **abberation of starlight.** The tilt changes to the opposite direction every 6 months.

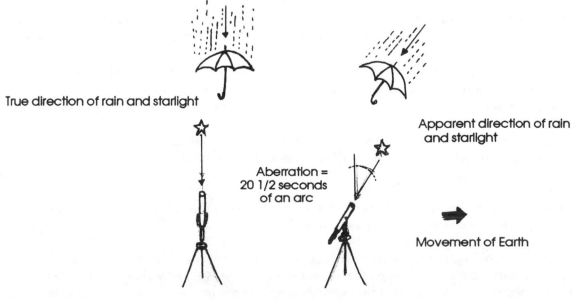

True direction of rain and starlight

Apparent direction of rain and starlight

Aberration = 20 1/2 seconds of an arc

Movement of Earth

THE ABERRATION OF STARLIGHT

153

Focault carried out yet another proof of the Earth's rotation in 1852 using a gyroscope. The axis of the gyroscope usually remains in its original direction. As the Earth rotates, the gyroscope swings into a north-south line over the Earth's axis, a proof of the Earth's rotation.

The spinning Earth causes:

day and night—the Earth turns into the Sun bringing day
the direction of Earth's axis—the Earth axis continues to point to the North Star
flattening of the Earth at the poles—probably caused while the Earth's surface was in a more liquid form

Because the Earth is spinning, its roundness gets slightly distorted. The Earth bulges slightly in the middle and flattens slightly at the poles. At the equator, the Earth is about 27 miles or 44 kilometers larger than it is at the poles.

In this project you can see for yourself what spinning does to the shape of the Earth.

Project 54: Demonstrating the Bulging of the Earth

MATERIALS

pencil with an eraser
thumb tack
paper

tape
hole punch

PROCEDURE

1. Cut two strips of paper about 1 inch (2½ centimeters) × 11 inches (27½ centimeters). Overlap the ends and tape them together to form a round loop about 20 inches (50 centimeters) long.
2. Punch a hole in the bottom of the loop. The hole should be slightly larger than the diameter of the pencil so that the paper can move freely around the pencil.
3. Push the eraser end of the pencil through the hole until the eraser touches the inside of the top of the loop.
4. Fasten the top of the paper loop to the eraser using the thumb tack.
5. Twist the pencil quickly between your hands and observe the shape of the loop.

OBSERVATIONS

What happens to the shape of the loop? Where is the widest diameter? What happens to the size of the bulge when you make the loop turn faster?

We call Earth's rapid spinning its **rotation.** The whole Earth turns at once, but because it is a sphere parts of it turn faster than others. Places on the equator travel faster than those closer to the poles. The distance around the Earth at the equator is bigger so it has farther to travel. As the Earth turns at different speeds from west to east, the air which was traveling from the equator to the pole in a straight line, gets "bent." Its path curves almost as much as 90° as it moves from the swifter rotating equator to the slower rotating poles. Everything in the Northern Hemisphere is deflected to the right, including sea currents and water. Water going down a drain enters on the right and moves in a counterclockwise spiral. In the Southern Hemisphere, everything is deflected to the left, including water. Water going down a drain enters on the left and moves in a clockwise spiral.

rotation comes from the Latin word *rotare* = to turn

Gaspar de Coriolis, a French mathematician first explained this deflection of freely moving objects in 1835. We call this deflection the **Coriolis effect** after him. The Coriolis effect is strongest at the poles and weakest at the equator. The faster the wind, the stronger the Coriolis effect. George Halley of England also suggested this idea—a hundred years earlier.

Swirls of clouds on the photograph of the Earth from space show some of the Coriolis effect. The Earth's atmosphere appears as a thin blue layer wrapped around the Earth. In this next project you can create your own Coriolis effect.

— Project 55: Showing the Effects of the Earth's Spinning (Coriolis Effect) —

MATERIALS
PART 1

    merry-go-round or piano stool   a partner
    ball

PART 2

    globe or basketball   chalk

PART 1
PROCEDURE
1. Stand or sit in the middle of a merry-go-round.
2. Have someone stand or sit in the outer edge of the merry-go-round.
3. Turn the merry-go-round counterclockwise.
4. Throw a ball to that person.

OBSERVATION
What happened to the path of the ball?

PART 2
PROCEDURE
1. Rotate the globe counterclockwise.
2. Draw a line on the globe while it is moving, right down from the north pole to the equator.
3. Draw a line on the globe while it is moving, straight up from the south pole to the equator.

OBSERVATIONS
What happened when you drew the two lines?

Part One of this project is adapted from *Everybody's Guide to Astronomy* prepared by the editorial staff of "Popular Science Monthly," New York: Popular Science Publishing Company, 1934.

Proof that the Earth is Round   You can prove that the Earth is round in a number of ways:

As a ship sails out to sea, we see the body of the ship disappearing first and the top last.
The edge of the shadow of the Earth on the Moon during an eclipse is always an arc of a circle.
Northern Stars are higher as you travel north and lower if you travel south.

For each 69 miles or 110 kilometers you travel north, the North Star appears one degree higher above the horizon. For each 69 miles or 110 kilometers you travel south, the North Star appears one degree lower above the horizon.

A level line that surveyors make is not straight but arched.
Photographs taken from great heights above the Earth show the horizon to be curved.
Navigators calculate their positions as if they were on a sphere.

These calculations have also successfully located positions of ships on the Earth.

Many people have traveled around the globe in the same direction and have returned to their starting points.

The Earth has a gentle curve. In 10 miles (16 kilometers) the curve only drops 67 feet (20 meters).

The Magnetosphere   The **magnetosphere** is a blanket of particles surrounding the Earth. It extends about 4,000 miles or 6,500 kilometers out from the Earth. Radiation from the Sun, also invisible, sweeps out into space with the force of an air current. For this reason we call the Sun's radiation the **solar wind**. When the solar wind hits the Earth's magnetosphere, it pushes the magnetosphere in at one side while stretching it out on the other.

In 1958, the U.S. satellites, The Explorer 1 and in 1959, Pioneer III and later Explorer III, Explorer IV, and Pioneer I included radiation detecting instruments designed by **James A. Van Allen,** a physicist at the State University of Iowa. The satellites detected two belts of very strong radiation within the magnetosphere. These belts had a shape like two doughnuts , a small one inside a large one. We call these belts **Van Allen Belts,** after their discoverer.

As Others See Us   What do you suppose life on Earth looks like to visitors from another planet? If a team of scientists came to Earth from another planet, how would they describe what they found? In this next project you can take the part of a visiting team from another planet and see what you find on the blue planet Earth.

——— Project 56: Filing an Extraterrestrial Report on the Planet Earth ———

MATERIALS

paper

pencil

photographs from magazines

drawing supplies

PROCEDURE

Imagine you are on a scout team from another planet. Your team's mission is to land one "manned" spacecraft on Earth and file a report after carrying out the following experiments. Use photographs from magazines or create drawings of your own. Prepare a written description to go with your photographs, or use the descriptions without photographs.

IMAGES OF EARTH AND LANDING SITE AREA
1. Photographs of Earth from Space
2. Photographs approaching landing site areas from different locations in space
3. Photograph of landing area taken on the ground

NATURE OF AREA IMMEDIATELY AROUND LANDING SITE
1. Vegetation
2. Air
3. Rocks, hills, water
4. Temperature
5. Visibility

RETRIEVING SAMPLES
1. Describe natural surroundings of area where you removed the sample material
2. Describe process of removing sample
3. Describe experiments performed on sample

CONTACT WITH EARTH LIFE
1. Description of life forms
2. What tests did you perform to indicate the presence of life?
3. Description of communication ability of life form
   a. How was it able to communicate?
   b. How would you describe the mood or intent of this communication?

LANDING SITES
Team 1: in the desert

Team 2: your neighborhood

Team 3: downtown in any large city anytime

Team 4: on a farm anytime

Other possible sites: at the Olympic Games, Antarctica, the Dead Sea, New Orleans at Mardi Gras, the Alps

OBSERVATIONS

Do you think the teams got a very accurate picture of what it is like on Earth from their visit? To see how people from Earth responded when they sent probes to other planets, see Chapter 7, Section 4 and parts of Chapter 6.

READING MORE

Feldman, Anthony. *Space.* New York: Facts on File, Inc., 1980.

Sagan, Carl, F.D. Drake, Ann Druyan, Timothy Ferris, Jon Lomberg, Linda Salzman Sagan. *Murmurs of Earth: The Voyager Interstellar Record.* New York: Random House, 1978.

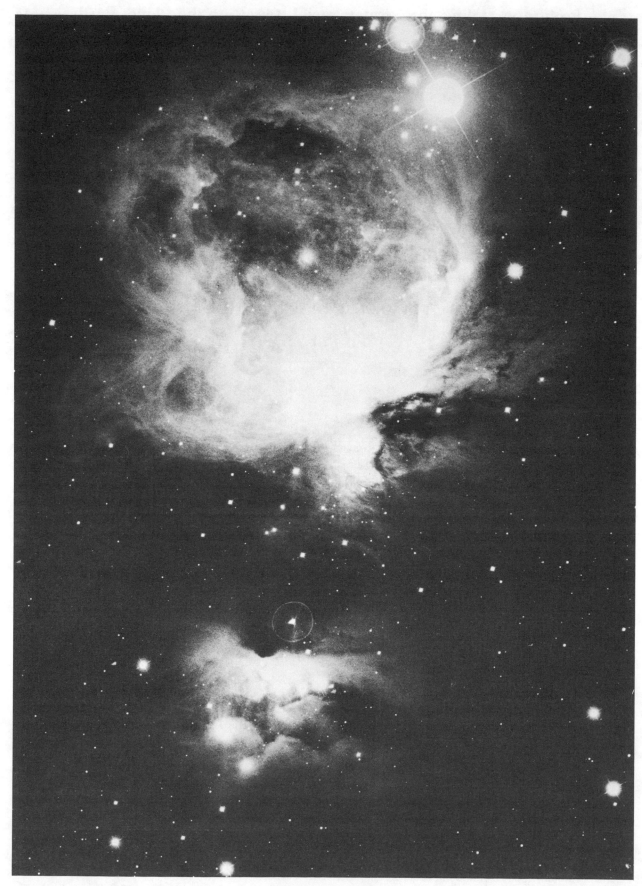

The Orion Nebula.

Chapter 5: SKY-GATHERING TOOLS

Section 1: A NEW LOOK AT THE PLANETS

The Solar System   As recently as the 1500s, the geocentric system was the accepted view of the order of the heavens. To practically everyone on Earth, this picture made sense. The Sun rose, moved across the sky, and set. The stars changed seasonally. The Sun, Moon, and planets moved in front of the zodiac constellations in predictable rhythms. The variety of life on Earth and the ever-unfolding mental powers of the human being proved that the inhabitants of the Earth were unique. The gods and goddesses of every religion visited or cared for these inhabitants, entrusting them with enormous responsibilities. Clearly the Earth was the center of some great plan and those living on it were destined to carry out this plan.

Copernicus   Copernicus had set out to simplify this geocentric system of Ptolemy's because it did not succeed in showing uniform motion. To do this, Copernicus used 34 or more epicycles and placed the Sun rather than the Earth in the center. All orbits were perfect circles. He said that the sky doesn't move overhead, nor does the Sun rise and set. These motions only *seem* to occur. What is really happening is that the Earth is moving.

Copernicus arrived at his conclusions by using mathematics and rational thought and far less accurate observing equipment than Ptolemy had. In fact, Copernicus only made 27 recorded observations.

"So the Sun sits as upon a royal throne ruling his children, the
planets, which circle around him."—Copernicus

Copernicus waited 36 years to publish his six-volume work which he patterned after Ptolemy's *Almagest*. Pythagoras had waited 9 years before fully presenting his ideas.

Tycho Brahe (December 14, 1546–October 24, 1601)   "It is something divine that men could know the motions of the stars so accurately that they were able a long time beforehand to predict their places and relative motions."—Tycho Brahe

When he was 14, Tycho saw a partial eclipse of the Sun from his native Denmark. He was so struck by this sight that from then on he devoted his life to making and recording accurate observations of the heavens. His relatives weren't thrilled with his decision, so Tycho had to struggle to finally achieve his goal without hiding what he was doing. Eventually, he became quite a well-known and respected astronomer.

Tycho was also quite a flashy character. He lost the tip of his nose in a duel and replaced it with one he made out of gold and silver. He was given an island in Denmark with a castle, which he turned into an observatory. Tycho called his castle Uraniborg. There he lived and worked like a king for 20 years with an amazing collection of observing instruments and assistants to help him use them. Among these instruments were a seven-foot metal quadrant and a wall quadrant that he could sit in while someone measured the degrees. His favorite was a sextant. Tycho named Uraniborg after Urania, the Greek muse of astronomy.

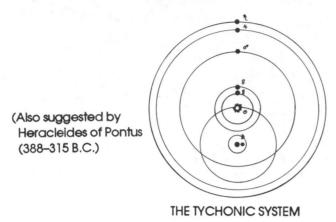

(Also suggested by Heracleides of Pontus (388–315 B.C.)

THE TYCHONIC SYSTEM

Tycho Brahe

Tycho observed supernova and several comets. He made thousands of extremely accurate observations of the positions of planets, the stars, and the Sun over a period of many years. Tycho developed a system which combined the systems of Ptolemy and Copernicus.

Johannes Kepler (December 27, 1571–November 15, 1630)   Like Copernicus, Kepler was a successful astrologer and teacher. Like Tycho he saw a supernova. Kepler also worked with Tycho for one year.

After Tycho died, Kepler used the records of Tycho's observations to do further studies. Kepler was skinny, sickly, and suffered from multiple vision and nearsightedness, which made it impossible for him to carry out any astronomical observations. Using the ideas of the Platonic solids from Pythagoras, Kepler imagined the five Platonic solids stacked one inside the other, with a sphere in between each one. Each sphere was the orbit of a different planet. The spaces between the spheres would determine the distance between the orbits of the planets they represented. This idea impressed Tycho and made him write Kepler to come and work with him. Kepler planned to spend eight days on his assignment from Tycho which was to figure out the orbit of Mars. It took him close to eight years.

Johannes Kepler

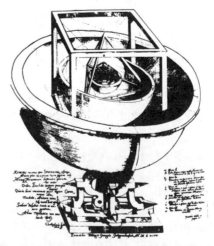

Kepler's model of the Platonic Solids showing the distances between planetary orbits.

"The earth is the sphere, the measure of all; round it describe a dodecahedron; the sphere including this will be Mars. Round Mars describe a tetrahedron; the sphere including this will be Jupiter. Describe a cube round Jupiter; the sphere including this will be Saturn. Now inscribe in the earth an icosehedron, the sphere inscribed in it will be Venus; inscribe an octahedron in Venus; the circle inscribed in it will be Mercury." —*Mysterium Cosmographicum*

Kepler wrote three laws about the orbits of planets which removed all circular motion and epicycles.

1. Each planet moves in an orbit that is an **ellipse** with the Sun at one focus.
2. The line between the Sun and each orbiting planet sweeps over equal areas in equal amounts of time.
3. The square of the speed of each planet's orbit is proportional to the cube of its average distance from the Sun.

An **ellipse** is like an oval. Aristotle, Ptolemy, and Copernicus and everyone before them had insisted that the planets traveled in orbits that were in the shape of a perfect circle. Ellipses have two points inside them as their focal point instead of one as in a circle. Each point is the **focus.** The plural of focus is foci. The distance between the two foci determines the shape of an ellipse. As this distance increases, the shape of the ellipse becomes more elongated. When the two foci meet at the center, you have a circle.

In this next project, you can draw ellipses for the orbits of each of the planets to demonstrate Kepler's laws.

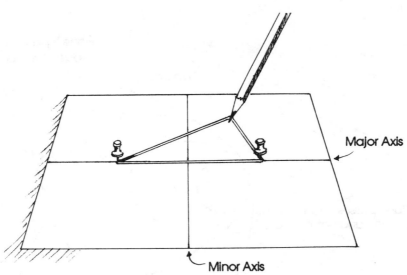

Major Axis

Minor Axis

Project 57: Drawing Planetary Orbits (Ellipses)

MATERIALS
2 pushpins   pencil
piece of wood   paper
string

PROCEDURE
1. Fold paper to create major and minor axis. (Always place pins at equal distances from the center point.) Place the paper on the piece of wood.
2. Stick one pin near the center of paper on the major axis fold. Label it the Sun.
3. Stick the second pin on the same fold as the focus of a planet.
4. Double the string and tie a knot 3⅞ inches (9.9 centimeters) from the end. This will give you a loop about 3⅞ (9.9 centimeters).
5. Do the same for each of the planets using the measurements below. 1 inch = 83 million miles, 1 centimeter = 33 million kilometers. The first measurement is in inches, the second is in centimeters.

PLANET	DISTANCE BETWEEN PINS	SIZE OF LOOP
Mars	1¹⁄₁₆ (1.7)	7⅞ (19.9)
Earth	³⁄₃₂ (0.2)	4¾ (12.1)
Venus	¹⁄₃₂ (0.1)	3⁷⁄₁₆ (8.8)
Mercury	⅜ (1.0)	2⁹⁄₁₆ (6.5)

OBSERVATIONS

Which planet's orbit is closest to being a circle?

Which planet's orbit is least like a circle?

Which two planets could come the closest together as they travel in their orbits?

Which two planets have orbits of nearly the same shape?

The ellipse belongs to a family of curves which come from taking a cut or a section out of a cone. For this reason we call them **conic sections.** In 225 B.C. **Appolonius** wrote *Conic Sections* in which he described how you can form the ellipse, parabola, and hyperbola by passing a plane through a cone at various angles. In this next project you can make models of these sections by actually cutting them out of cones.

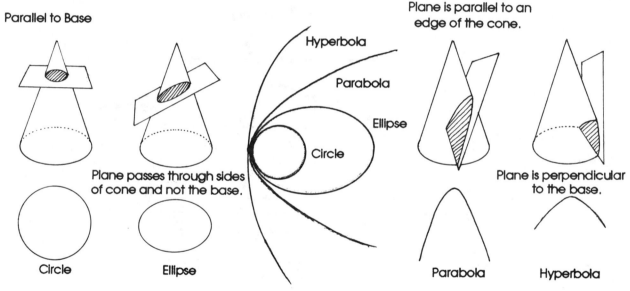

Project 58: Making Models of Conic Sections

MATERIALS

modelling clay in two contrasting colors
thin wire

PROCEDURE

1. Mold a cone from the lighter color of modelling clay. Be sure the bottom of the cone is a perfect circle. Using the darker color modelling clay make a thin "coat" about ³⁄₁₆ inch (5 millimeters) to go around the cone. Place the coat carefully onto the cone so that it completely covers it.

2. Pull the wire so that it is straight and tight like a cheese slicer, so you can use it to slice through the modelling clay easily.

3. Cut out a slice from the top, side, etc., without bending the cone or the removed slice. The darker colored modelling clay will be in the shape of a circle, ellipse, parabola, and hyperbola.

OBSERVATIONS

Does it matter how tall and thin or short and thick the cones are?

Galileo Galilei (February 15, 1564–January 8, 1642) Galileo enrolled at the University of Pisa (where the leaning tower is) at age 16 to study medicine. His nickname in college was "The Wrangler" because he refused to accept statements that were supposed to be true simply because some famous person long ago said they were.

"In questions of science, the authority of a thousand is not worth the humble reasoning of a single individual."—Galileo

Galileo felt that you needed to back up what you said with proof, experiments, evidence. He spent most of his life experimenting and writing. The invention of the telescope (see Chapter 5, Section 2) gave the Wrangler a tool with which he could prove or disprove statements and observations.

Galileo Galilei

Isaac Newton

Isaac Newton (1643–1727) According to the Julian calendar, Isaac Newton was born less than a year after Galileo died on Christmas Day, 1642. According to the Gregorian calendar, he was born on January 4, 1643. When he died on March 20, 1727, people used only the Gregorian calendar. Newton was so small as an infant that he could fit in a cooking pot. For awhile, he slept in a drawer. Like Kepler, he was nearsighted. Also, like Kepler, he wanted to know how planets moved in space. Newton changed the way people thought about the tides, mathematics (he coinvented the calculus), gravity and motion and light. So great and long lasting were Newton's discoveries that the poet Alexander Pope wrote:

"Nature and Nature's Laws lay hid in Night:
God said, Let Newton be! and All was Light."

Newton felt that his contributions were only possible thanks to the work of the Greek scientists and Copernicus, Tycho Brahe, Kepler, and Galileo.

"If I have seen further than other men, it is because I have
stood on the shoulders of giants."—Sir Isaac Newton

Planetary Motion Galileo said that the movement of the planets is a natural condition. His experiments showed that it is just as natural for an object to be in motion as it is for an object to be at rest.

Sir Isaac Newton put Galileo's thought this way in his *First Law of Motion:*

An object at rest tends to remain at rest, and an object in motion tends to remain in motion. This tendency is **inertia.**

---

inertia comes from the Latin word *inertia* = lack of skill, inactivity

---

Inertia is what makes it so hard to move something when it has been standing still. Once the object is in motion, it is easier to keep it moving. Once it's moving, it is also harder to stop it. In 1687, Newton published his *Laws of Gravitation.* In this book Newton stated that two quantities that are related so that one increases when the other increases are said to be in direct relation or in **direct proportion.** If one quantity decreases when another increases, they are said to be in **inverse proportion.**

The Law of Universal Gravitation Every particle of matter attracts every other particle of matter with a force of attraction that is directly proportional to the product of their masses and inversely proportional to the square of the distance between them.

The greater the masses of two objects, the greater the gravitational force between them. Gravitational attraction is greater when objects are close together.

CHARACTERISTICS OF MATTER

Gravitation = the universal attraction which all objects have for all other objects.

Gravity = Earth's gravitational force. We state this in units of acceleration. The farther you are from the center of the Earth, the less the amount of gravitational force. The amount of force is inversely related to the distance to the center. You weigh less on a mountain top and even less in an airplane. Astronauts get so far away from the strength of Earth's gravitational pull that they find themselves floating in the air as if they were weightless.

DISTANCE FROM THE CENTER OF THE EARTH		YOUR WEIGHT	
16,000 miles	(25,750 kilometers)	9 pounds	(4 kilograms)
12,000 miles	(19,300 kilometers)	16 pounds	(7 kilograms)
8,000 miles	(12,900 kilometers)	36 pounds	(16 kilograms)
4,000 miles	(6,435 kilometers)	144 pounds	(65 kilograms)

Volume = the amount of space an object occupied.

Mass = the quantity of matter present. No matter where you are, your mass remains the same.

Density = the quantity of matter or the weight per unit volume of matter in terms of pounds per cubic foot or grams per cubic centimeter.

Weight = the measure of the force of gravitational attraction between two objects. We state this in units of weight such as pounds or grams. It is the acceleration of gravity (g) multiplied by the mass (m).

weight = m × g Weight depends upon location.

Specific gravity = the density of object compared with the density of water

Look at marble and a steel ball, both the same size. Do they both have the same volume? Do they weigh the same? Which has the greater density? Do they have the same mass?

How much do you weigh on other planets? With a pencil, paper, and the planetary information chart from Sky Files, look at the column on the planetary chart marked **Surface Gravity.** This number tells you how much heavier or lighter you would feel on other planets. Simply take each number and multiply by your weight on Earth to find how much you would weigh. On which planet would you weigh the most? The least? About the same?

"Gravity is the mutual bodily tendency between material bodies toward contact; two stones for example would come together, after the manner of magnetic bodies, each approaching the other in proportion to the other's mass."—Kepler, *New Astronomy*

The **centripetal** force needed to keep an object moving in a circular path increases as the speed of the object increases. If you keep the speed the same, you need less centripetal force to make the circle larger. There are other effects from applying centripetal force. Have you noticed how a runner or a bicycle racer leans inward (banks) on turns? Pilots also bank their airplanes to make turns. Banking provides centripetal force to keep you, your bicycle, or your airplane or car from skidding off into a straight line. The centripetal force needed to keep planets moving in their orbits is different for each planet. It depends upon their speed and their distance from the Sun. The Sun's gravitational force is the "attraction" which pulls the planets into their nearly circular orbits. The centripetal force is just equal to this gravitational force. The centripetal force prevents the planets from flying off into a straight line.

In this next project, you make a model of the Sun which will hold a planet traveling around it in an orbit by using centripetal force. In this project the centripetal force comes from a magnet, much like Kepler's idea that the Sun acted like a huge magnet carrying the planets around, and the planets were also like magnets.

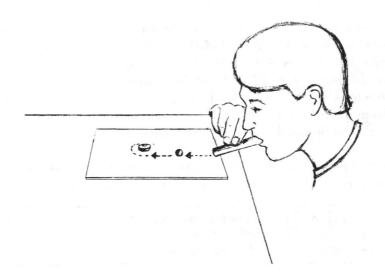

——— **Project 59: Demonstrating Planetary Orbits (Centripetal Force)** ———

MATERIALS

piece of paper
ball bearing
sheet of glass

candle
matches
round or square magnet

PROCEDURE

1. Roll the paper into a tube the size of the ball bearing. The ball bearing should fit loosely inside.

2. Move the sheet of glass over a candle flame several times so that soot collects on the glass in an even layer. Place the glass, smoked side up, on a level surface.

3. Place the magnet on the smoked glass.

4. Use the paper tube as a blowgun to launch the ball bearing. It should roll gently across the smoked glass, curving around the magnet, leaving a trail in the soot on the glass.

5. Vary the force with which you launch the ball bearing so you can produce ellipses, parabolas, and hyperbolas, similar to the orbits of the planets and comets around the Sun.

OBSERVATIONS

Notice that the ball bearing would travel in a straight path if it weren't for the force of the magnet (Sun) acting on it. This is why the planets don't go flying out of their orbits into space or one another.   This project is adapted from *Everybody's Guide to Astronomy* prepared by the editorial staff of "Popular Science Monthly," New York: Popular Science Publishing Company, Inc., 1934.

The Solar System   Why are the distances between the planets the way they are? Is there some pattern to them? Kepler thought the pattern might be based on fitting the Platonic solids in between the orbits. In 1772, **Johan Daniel Titius** translated the French book *Contemplating Nature* by Charles Bonnet into German. In his translation, Titius included some of his own ideas about the distances of the planets from the Sun. **Johan Elert Bode** also published a book that year, the second edition of his book *Introduction to the Study of the Starry Sky*. Bode included as footnotes in his book the comments he had read about planetary distances by Titius in his translation of *Comtemplation of Nature*. These comments became known as the **Titius-Bode Law,** even though only Titius invented them and they weren't a law. Bode later gave credit to Titius for coming up with the idea.

Titius had suggested a mathematical pattern for the planets' distances in which you add 0, 3, 6, 12, 24, etc., (doubling the previous number to 4 for each planet). Taking the distance from the Sun to Saturn as 100 units:

Mercury's distance from the Sun is $4 + 0 = 4$ of these units
Venus' distance from the Sun is $4 + 3 = 7$ of these units
Earth's distance from the Sun is $4 + 6 = 10$ of these units
Mars' distance from the Sun is $4 + 12 = 16$ of these units
? distance from the Sun is $4 + 24 = 28$ of these units
Jupiter's distance from the Sun is $4 + 48 = 52$ of these units
Saturn's distance from the Sun is $4 + 96 = 100$ of these units

By moving the decimal point one place to the left you have the number of **Astronomical Units** each planet is from the Sun. One astronomical Unit = the distance from the Earth to the Sun.

In 1781, **William Herschel** (1738-1822) discovered the planet Uranus at 192 units or 19.2 Astronomical Units. In 1891, **Giuseppi Piazzi** (1746-1826) discovered the first asteroid in the empty space between Mars and Jupiter. See Chapter 6, Section 4 for more details.

By the time of Newton's death in 1727, the picture people had of the solar system was very much as you see it today (except that it didn't include the three trans-Saturnian planets Uranus, Neptune, and Pluto).The members of our Solar System are:

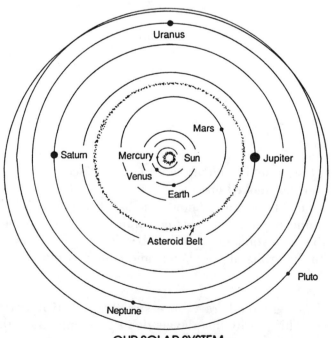

OUR SOLAR SYSTEM
From Teaching With Nightstar by Richard Moeschl

The Sun
The Planets and their satellites (in order from the Sun)

Mercury	Saturn
Venus	Uranus
Earth	Neptune
Mars	Pluto
Jupiter	

The minor planets (asteroids) are in between the orbits of Mars and Jupiter. If there are any more planets orbiting around the Sun, they will be considered part of our solar system. Comets, meteors, stars, nebulae, pulsars, quasars, galaxies, and black holes are beyond our solar system and in most cases, outside our Milky Way Galaxy. You can find out about these other members of our solar system in Chapter 7.

READING MORE

Ronin, Colin. *Man Probes the Universe.* Garden City: The Natural History Press, 1964.
Sullivan, Navin. *Pioneer Astronomers.* New York: Atheneum, 1967.

Percival Lowell. *Photo courtesy of Lowell Observatory*

Section 2: TELESCOPES

Light, the Eye, and Lenses   Most of our information about the universe comes to us in the form of radiation. Much of this radiation is the kind we are most familiar with, light which the human eye can see. Visible light is only one small form of radiation. You can find out about the other forms of radiation in Section 4 of this chapter. Light is a form of energy. You can describe its speed, wavelength, frequency, and intensity. Light also has to do with how we see. da Vinci thought that light moved in waves, much like sound does. Newton thought of light as a stream of particles.

The Eye   Light travels in a straight line from what you see (the object) to your eye, passing through these five parts:

1. The **cornea,** a tough, transparent layer covering the front of the eye. It helps focus the light and protect the eye.

2. The **aqueous humor,** a watery fluid between the cornea and the lens. It helps focus the light and nourishes the eye.

3. The **pupil,** a small round hole in the center of the colored **iris.** The iris controls the amount of light that enters the eye by widening or contracting which makes the pupil larger or smaller.

4. The **lens,** a transparent, layered tissue. It helps focus light on the retina by becoming thinner or thicker.

5. The **vitreous humor,** a clear jelly filling the inside of the main portion of the eye behind the lens. It helps focus light on the retina. It also helps the eye keep its proper shape.

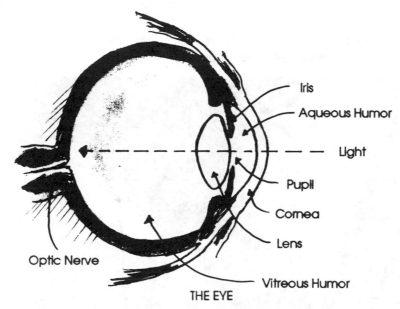

THE EYE

The light then shines onto the **retina** which lines about 2/3 of the inside of your eye. An image of the object you are looking at appears on the retina. The image is upside down and backwards because the lens in your eye is a convex lens and that's how the world looks through a convex lens. Your **optic nerve** and brain work together to help you see the object as it actually is and not how it appears in the retina.

> The size of your pupil depends upon the amount of light your eye needs to let in so you can form a clear image on your retina—and see. When it is dark outside, your eyes need more light so your pupils open wider (about 1/4 inch or 7 millimeters). When it is bright outside, your eyes need less light, so your pupils close together (about 3/32 inch or 2 millimeters). Check it yourself. Look at a friend's pupils in a normal light, have your friend close his or her eyes and keep them closed for awhile, then open them. What did the pupils do?

Refraction   In addition to traveling in a straight line, light can also be reflected from a smooth surface such as water or polished metals such as bronze or silver. Water and glass can carry light from one place to another through themselves.

Light will continue to travel through the air, water, or glass in a straight line if what it is passing through has the same conditions all through it. A change in temperature or thickness will break the path of the light. This change in the light's straight path is **refraction.** The different densities of the Earth's atmosphere affect any light that passes through it just as the different densities of the Earth's interior affected the path of Earthquake waves. See Chapter 4, Section 3. When a beam of light from a star passes through the atmosphere at an angle, it bends or refracts.

The least amount of refraction occurs when light travels in a line that is perpendicular to the places where there are changing conditions. Light from a star directly overhead goes right through the atmosphere in a straight line. The layer of different temperatures in the atmosphere are horizontal so the starlight is not refracted. When a star is low on the horizon, its light comes through the Earth's atmosphere at an angle. As it passes through the layers of our Earth's atmosphere, the light curves downward slightly. This makes the star seem higher in the sky than it actually is.

Have you ever noticed how the Sun seems to flatten when it sets? The part of the Sun closest to the horizon has its light refracted upward. The refraction at the bottom of the Sun is greater than at the top which makes the Sun look fatter and flatter.

Lenses   By using the laws of refraction, lens-makers can design lenses that bend (refract) light rays so that they can redirect the path of the light. The two main forms of lenses are **convex** and **concave.**
Convex lenses are thick in the middle and thin around the edges. They bring the rays of light closer together by refracting the light toward the center.
Concave lenses are thin in the middle and thick around the edges. They spread out the rays of light by refracting the light away from the center.

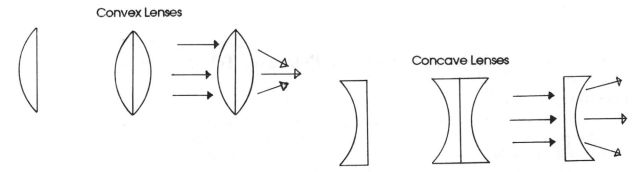

Convex Lenses

Concave Lenses

Two convex lenses back-to-back or one curved on both sides resemble the shape of a lentil. The Latin word for lentil is **lens.**

People have known about lenses and magnification for a long time, maybe as far back as 2000 B.C. In England, **Roger Bacon** (1220–1292) used lenses to help him with reading. Soon afterwards, eyeglasses came into use in Italy. The country most noted for the manufacture of lenses was the Netherlands.

The Telescope   Several people claim to have invented the telescope. According to a story, **Hans Lippershey** (c. 1570–c. 1619), a glasses-maker in the Netherlands was the first. He found his apprentice playing with two lenses, a strong concave and a weak convex. The apprentice put the concave lens near his eye and the convex lens further and was looking out of the window. He noticed that a weathervane on top of a distant house appeared to be much larger and closer. Lippershey placed the two lenses in a metal tube and called his invention a "looker." The name changed to "optic tube," "optic glass," and "Dutch perspectives."

Galileo called his device an "instrumentum" (instrument), a "perspicillum" (lens) or "occhiali" (eyeglass). In 1611, a Greek mathematician, **Ioannes Demisiani** suggested the word **telescope,** which comes from the Greek words τῆλε *(tele)* = far, and σκοπος *(skopos)* = to see. By 1650, telescope became the accepted word.

In 1609, Galileo built his own telescope based on Lippershey's model. Galileo's first telescope, which used two lenses and a lead pipe, made objects appear three times their actual size. Galileo figured the magnification by cutting out different sized circles. He compared the sizes the circles appeared through the telescope with their actual sizes. Galileo's later model telescope had a wooden tube and made objects appear 30 times larger. In this next project, you can make a similar telescope.

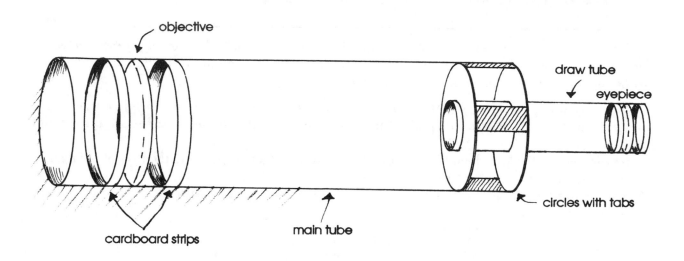

Project 60: Making a Refracting Telescope

MATERIALS

two cardboard tubes or rolled sheets of stiff paper:

one cardboard tube:
3¼ inch diameter x 31 inches (8 1/4 x 79 centimeters)

one cardboard tube:
1¼ inch diameter x 10 inches (3 x 25 centimeters)

flat black paint

3¼ inch (8¼ centimeter) lens (achromatic coated, 30–40 inch focal length, f number = 12.3)

½ inch (13 millimeter) focal length lens (coated , if possible, 40 degrees apparent field of view)

cardboard strips

glue

black paper

scissors

pen or pencil

ruler

Look for lenses at surplus stores, secondhand shops, optometrists, and science supply stores. The lenses mentioned here will give you the exact power of Galileo's second telescope. You can use whatever lenses you can find to make your telescope. Find out the focal lengths and make the necessary changes to the size of your telescope.

PROCEDURE

1. Paint the inside of the two tubes flat black.

2. Cut out cardboard rings to hold lenses in place.

3. Draw a line around the inside of the objective end of the tube, 2 inches (5 centimeters) from the end.

4. Glue one of the cardboard strips for the objective so that it sits just behind the 2 inch (5 centimeter) line inside the tube. Place the lens in front of the strip and glue the other strip in front of the lens.

5. Repeat step #4 for the eyepiece lens, but do not set the lens back 2 inches (5 centimeters).

6. Cut out two cardboard circles with 1¼ inch (3 centimeter) holes in the center and tabs around the edges. Fold the tabs over and glue them together. When they are dry, put glue on the tabs and insert the circles in the eyepiece end of the large tube.

7. Insert the eyepiece tube into the cardboard circles.

8. Cut a ring of black paper and place it over the outer edge of the objective lens, leaving the center of the lens uncovered. Experiment with various sizes to overcome the color fringes in your view.

OBSERVATIONS

Does your telescope show you anything that you can't see at all without it? Use your telescope to demonstrate what a telescope can do as you read about it in this chapter.

Color fringes are due to the colors of light not all meeting at the same point. We call this **chromatic abberation.** Achromatic lenses help correct this problem.

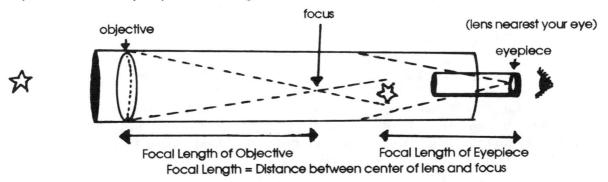

(lens nearest the object you are viewing)

objective

focus

(lens nearest your eye)

eyepiece

Focal Length of Objective   Focal Length of Eyepiece

Focal Length = Distance between center of lens and focus

How Telescopes Work   Since Galileo's telescope used a convex and a concave lens, the image he saw appeared right side up and the right way around. Your telescope uses an arrangement of lenses designed by Kepler in 1611. This arrangement uses two convex lenses instead of a convex and a concave lens. **Christian Huygens** (1629–1695) used Kepler's lens design in his tubeless telescope which he built in 1659. With this telescope, Huygens discovered the rings of Saturn.

"O, telescope, instrument of much knowledge, more precious than any scepter! Is not he who holds you in his hand made king and lord of the works of god?"—Kepler

The image that resulted in Huygen's telescope and the one you built is similar to the image that appears on your retina. It is upside down and backwards. That is the price you pay for greater magnification. Astronomers are used to looking at the Moon, the stars, and planets upside down and backwards. If they wanted to view things as they really were, astronomers would have to add an extra lens. However, with the addition of more glass and more bending of the light, the image would become dimmer and less clear. It is more important to astronomers that their images be bright and clear than right side up.

171

How does the telescope help you see objects brighter, clearer, and bigger? A telescope gathers the light from an *object* . . . in one lens, the **objective,** and sends an image of the image as close to your eye as possible. The place in the telescope where the objective sends the image is the **focus.** The lens in the **eyepiece** magnifies the image formed at the focus and sends this larger image to your *eye*.

---

focus comes from the Latin word *focus* = fireplace. The fireplace was the center of the house where the family often "focused" its attention. To get a picture of the focus and focal length, hold a convex lens (like the one in a magnifying glass) up to direct sunlight. Sprinkle some chalk dust (or other white powder) into the air on the side of the lens opposite the sun. If the background is dark enough you will see particles of powder show how the magnifying glass causes the sun's rays to come together at the focus and then spread out again.

The telescope does three important things:

1. Increases the apparent brightness of a distant object. This is its **Light-Gathering Power**. The greater the light gathering power, the brighter an object appears.

2. Brings out detail on a distant object that cannot be seen with the unaided eye. This is its **Resolving Power**. The greater the resolving, the clearer the detail appears.

3. Enlarges the apparent size of a distant object. This is its **Magnifying Power**. The greater the magnifying power, the bigger or closer an object appears.

Light-Gathering Power   The objects you will want to look at in the heavens are very far away and often quite dim. It is important that your telescope gather as much light as possible from the object. What the telescope does is to take all the rays of light that the objective lens collects and concentrate them into a space the size of the eyepiece. The result of this concentration of light is that the object appears much brighter.

The light gathering power depends on the diameter of the objective. The diameter of the objective is the **aperture**. This diameter usually tells you the size of the telescope. A 200-inch telescope has a lens that is 200 inches across.

---

aperture comes from the Latin *apertura* = to open, uncover

To make dim objects seem brighter you want the light coming from your telescope to fill as much of the pupil of your eye as possible. Your pupil at night is about ¼ inch (6–8 millimeters) in diameter. To find the diameter of the concentrated rays of light coming from the eyepiece of your telescope divide the aperture by the magnification:

$$\text{diameter of light from eyepiece} = \frac{\text{aperture}}{\text{magnification}}$$

To find out how much more light your telescope can gather (light-gathering power) compared with your eye, multiply the square of the diameter of the objective by the number of times it is larger than the size of the pupil.

$$\text{light-gathering power of a telescope} = (\text{number of times the diameter of the objective is larger than the pupil})^2$$

A telescope with a 2 inch (5 centimeter) diameter objective is eight times larger than the pupil. That means that 8^2 or 64 is how much more light gathering power the telescope has compared to the human eye. With this telecope you can see stars 64 times dimmer than a star visible to your eye without a telescope.

The amount of light-gathering power of an objective is its focal ratio or **f number**. To find the f number of an objective divide its focal length by its diameter:

$$\text{f number (or focal ratio)} = \frac{\text{focal length}}{\text{aperture}}$$

To get the most light-gathering power you should have a telescope with a fairly short focus and low magnifying power. The more efficiently a lens collects light, the smaller its f number. An objective 6 inches (15¼ centimeters) in diameter has a focal length of 48 inches (122 centimeters). Its f number is 48/6 = 8. Focal ratios like these will make it possible for you to see fainter nebulae and star clusters.

Resolving Power   The human eye can only see as separate, two objects no closer than 6 minutes of an angle apart. The eye will see objects less than 6 minutes of an angle apart as one object. A telescope makes it possible for you to see two stars which are very close together as two separate images even if the angle between them is less than 6 minutes. This is the separating or **resolving power** of a telescope and it depends on the diameter of the objective (aperture).

$$\text{Resolving Power (in seconds of a degree)} = \frac{5}{\text{aperture (in inches)}}$$

For example, what would be the resolving power of a telescope with a 2 inch objective?

$$\text{Resolving power} = \frac{5}{2 \text{ inches}} = 2.5 \text{ inches}$$

That means that you can see two stars whose distance apart is an angle of 2.5 seconds. An angle of two seconds of an arc is the same angular size a small coin would have if you saw it without a telescope at a distance of 2 miles or 3 kilometers. Telescopes with a longer focus give you larger images and better magnification for looking at objects such as the Moon, the planets, and double stars. There is always a limit to the amount of detail that a telescope can show you. This depends on the quality of the lens, the effects of Earth's atmosphere, and the nature of light.

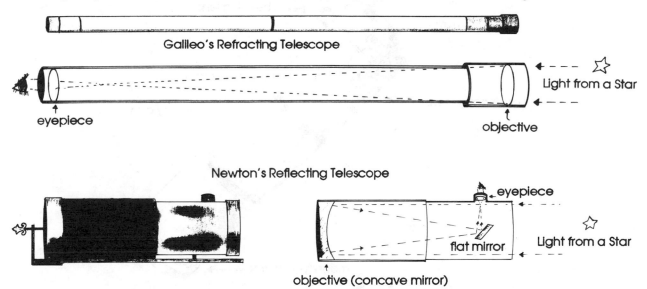

Galileo's Refracting Telescope

eyepiece   objective   Light from a Star

Newton's Reflecting Telescope

eyepiece

flat mirror

Light from a Star

objective (concave mirror)

REFRACTING AND REFLECTING TELESCOPES

Magnifying Power   The magnifying power of a telescope increases or modifies how much space an object appears to take up measured in degrees. We call this **angular modification** and it makes the object seem bigger and therefore closer. The angular modification of a telescope depends on the focal lengths of both the objective and the eyepiece.

$$\text{Angular modification} = \frac{\text{focal length of eyepiece}}{\text{focal length of objective}}$$

To get the most magnification from a telescope, the objective should have as long a focal length as possible and the eyepiece as short a focal length as possible. There is a limit to how much you can enlarge any image. You reach this limit when the magnification is about 50 times the size of the aperture. A 2-inch objective can usually magnify an object about 100 times (2 × 50 = 100).

The bigger a telescope makes an object appear:

1. the less clear and distinct the object appears. Stars twinkle more.

2. the less bright the object appears since you are spreading the same amount of light over a larger area.

3. the less you see of the object since it fills up more of the view in the telescope. This is the **field of view** or how many degrees of an arc you can see.

Check the side effects of magnification by looking at something under a magnifying glass or with your telescope and see what happens to clearness, brightness, and amount of object you can see.

Reflecting   There are several styles of telescopes, but they all use one of two ways of collecting light: **refracting** and **reflecting**.

Isaac Newton decided to improve on the design of the telescope and built the first reflecting telescope in 1668. It was about 6 inches (15 centimeters) long. In 1721, **John Hadley** (1682–1744) built the first professional quality reflecting telescope.

In a reflecting telescope, the top is open, light enters and goes to the bottom of the telescope where it is concentrated by a concave mirror. The light is then reflected back up the tube of the telescope to a flat mirror which reflects the light into the lens of the eyepiece. The concave mirror eliminates two major defects lenses often have; chromatic and spherical abberation.

In the next project you can make a reflecting telescope much like the kind in use in observatories around the world.

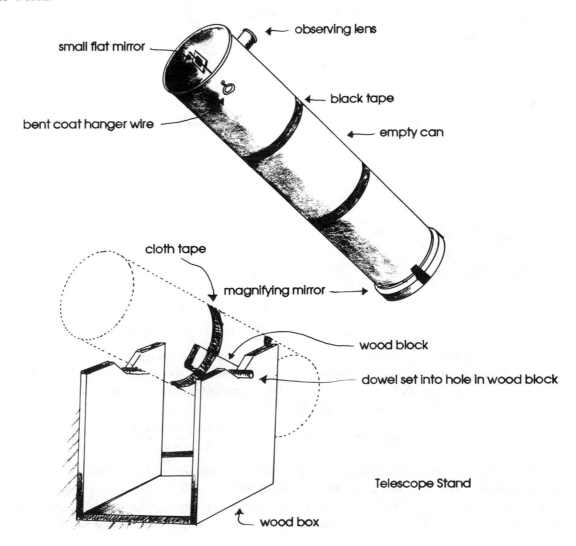

small flat mirror

observing lens

bent coat hanger wire

black tape

empty can

cloth tape

magnifying mirror

wood block

dowel set into hole in wood block

Telescope Stand

wood box

Project 61: Making a Reflecting Telescope

MATERIALS

three large cardboard or metal cans or
  tubes
  (from juice, oatmeal, etc.)
flat black paint
observing lens (eye loupe from a
  hardware store)
small flat mirror
coat hanger wire

electrical tape or other black tape
rubber band
ruler
nail
scissors
stiff paper tube
piece of paper

PROCEDURE

1. Measure the distance from the mirror to where the Sun's rays focus on a piece of paper. This is the focal length of the mirror.

2. Remove both ends of three large cans. Paint the insides of the cans flat black. Tape them together with electrical tape.

3. Tape the mirror to one end of the cans. Put the rubber band around the opposite end. Mark on the outside of the cans the point which is 4¾ inches (7 centimeters) shorter than the focal length of the mirror, and roll the rubber band to this point. Measure from the rubber band to the edge of the top can to be sure it is the same distance all the way around.

4. Punch a hole with a nail at opposite sides of the top can where the rubber band is.

5. Cut a ¾ inch (2 centimeter) hole overlapping the rubber band and in between the two punched holes. Remove the rubber band.

6. Push the coat hanger through the two punched holes. Bend the ends of the coat hanger into handles and remove the remaining length of the wire.

7. Tape a ¾ inch (2 centimeter) square piece of mirror onto the coat hanger.

8. Insert a paper tube into hole on side of can. Tape the observing lens to the outer end of tube.

9. Turn the mirror so that light is reflected out of the hole cut into the side of the top can. Look at the mirror through the magnifying glass. Aim the top of the telescope at a distant object. *Never look at the sun!*

OBSERVATIONS

Why do you think most large observatories use reflecting telescopes like this one? This project is adapted from Exploring Earth Science by Walter A. Thurber, Robert E. Kilburn, and Peter S. Howell, Newton: Allyn and Bacon, 1976. Used with permission.

Kinds of Reflecting Telescopes:

Gregorian was designed in 1663, but not built until later. The design of this telescope inspired Newton.

Newtonian **Isaac Newton** designed it in 1668. There is a 98 inch (2.5 meter) Newtonian telescope at La Palma Observatory, Canary Islands.

Cassegrain Small convex mirror instead of flat one. Designed by **Sieur Guillaume Cassegrain** in 1672. The 200 inch (5 meter) Hale telescope on Palomar Mountain, California is a Cassegrain. To observe, you sit in the telescope and move with it.

Prime Focus invented by **Maurice Lowey** (1833–1907) Austrian-French astronomer in 1894 as an adaptation of the Newtonian and Cassegrain. Hale telescope (see above).

Coude Focus 24 inch in California. This type of telescope requires many mirrors. The focus does not move, only the telescope does. You can set up large observing equipment without attaching them to the telescope. The focus is in another room.

coude comes from the French word *coude* = elbow

Schmidt **Bernhard Schmidt** (1879–1935) invented the Schmidt telescope in 1931. "The rapid coma-free mirror system described here offers great advantages in regard to the light-gathering power and aberration-free imagery." The size of the Schmidt telescope is the diameter of the correcting lens which is usually ⅔ of the aperture of the objective. The 48-inch Schmidt telescope, Palomar Mountain Observatory, has a 48-inch correcting lens and a 72-inch (1.83 meter) objective.

Schmidt Photographic used for wide angle astrophotography. Makesutov, Wright, and others changed it. It has extremely fast speeds and large fields of view. 48-inches (122 centimeters), Schmidt at Siding Spring Observatory, Australia.

Uranus was the first planet to be discovered with a telescope.

Buying a Telescope Telescopes have added so much to our understanding of the sky that many people automatically think of telescopes whenever you mention the word astronomy. As you have seen, a tremendous amount of what we know about the Earth, the Sun, Moon, planets, and stars we learned over the centuries *without* the aid of a telescope. There is still much you can learn with your own eyes aided only by clear thinking and your imagination.

There does come a moment when you might think about owning your own telescope. They certainly are fun and highly educational. But, *before* you buy a telescope:

1. Read and learn all you can about astronomy.
2. Learn the names and locations of the constellations and the brightest stars.
3. Use binoculars and other people's telescopes to become familiar with what these instruments can and can't do.
4. Join an astronomy club or subscribe to a good astronomy magazine. *Then* when you are ready to buy a telescope, the following suggestions should help.

Cost around $200

Type the best telescope for serious amateurs is a *reflecting telescope.* It gives the greatest aperture for the lowest price. There are no distracting colors around the edges of the image. First choice is a six-inch reflector or a three-inch refractor and a second choice is a four-inch reflector.

Objective the object lens or mirror of the telescope has a limit to its ability to show two very close stars as separate. The name of this limit is the **Dawes limit** after **William Dawes** (1799–1868).

Diameter of Objective		*Separation*
inches	millimeters	seconds arc
3	75	1.52
4	100	1.14
5	125	0.91
6	150	0.76
8	200	0.57

Most telescopes will enable you to see stars to about 12th magnitude.

Eyepieces Remember that to calculate magnifying power you divide the focal length of the objective by the focal length of the eyepiece. This will help you know what the magnification of an eyepiece will be when you use it on your telescope. Often on the side of an eyepiece you will see a number with an X after it. This is the focal length of the eyepiece, not its magnifying power. You should have three eyepieces, one each for low, medium, and high power.

Eyepiece	*You can see*
Low power	Moons of Jupiter at 15X, rings of Saturn at 30 X, comets and nebulae
Medium power	Entire Moon at 60X
High power	Double stars as separate at 120 X

176

Barlow lens is a handy device to have also. When you put it in front of any eyepiece, it doubles the power of the eyepiece.

Drive

This is a motor attached to your telescope that automatically moves the telescope as fast as the Earth is moving. This makes it possible to keep an image in view without having to adjust the telescope. A drive is especially useful when you want to take a long photograph without having trails.

Stand and Mount

The stand should be sturdy and not shaky. The best would be a well-made **altazimuth** stand. This kind of stand uses a fork as a mount to hold the telescope. The fork rotates on a horizontal axis. You can direct and rotate the telescope to any altitude from horizontal to zenith and any azimuth from 0° to 360°.

Comfort

Your telescope should be easy to carry, set up, and use. The control knobs should be big enough for you to find and turn easily.

Build it Yourself

Consider building a reflector. You can grind your own mirror and buy good eyepieces. It costs less than half what it would cost to build a refractor with the same size objective.

Binoculars

A binocular is a magnifier with two objectives and two eyepieces. It's like having two small refractor telescopes, one for each eye.

---

binocular comes from the Latin words *bi* = two, and *oculus* = eye

---

Binoculars use prisms to fold and shift the path of light within a small space to keep the size of the instrument small. The prisms also show you the image the way it appears normally, not upside down and backwards like a telescope sees it. Since there are two sets of telescopes in a pair of binoculars, what you see has the kind of depth and three-dimensional feeling that a single telescope can't provide. Binoculars usually cost much less than a telescope. They are small, easy to carry and very easy to use. They are good to use before buying a telescope. You can see all the planets (except Pluto) with a good pair of binoculars. You can also see the phases of Venus, the moons of Jupiter, the asteroids, comets, lunar surface features, and eclipses.

Buying Binoculars

The ideal size to buy is a 7×50. The $7 \times$ is the magnifying power. The 50 is the diameter of the objective lens in millimeters. The second choice would be 10×50 or 7×35. Be sure you are buying true prismatic binoculars and not opera or field glasses or glasses made to look like binoculars. Remember that just as with a telescope, the larger the aperture, the smaller the field of view and the more noticeable your unsteady hand will be. Take your time, be picky and be sure you can return the binoculars if you have problems.

READING MORE

Kals, W. S. *The Stargazer's Bible.* Garden City: Doubleday and Company, Inc., 1980.
Maloney, Terry. *Telescopes: How to Chose and Use Them.* New York: Sterling Publishing Co., Inc., 1968.

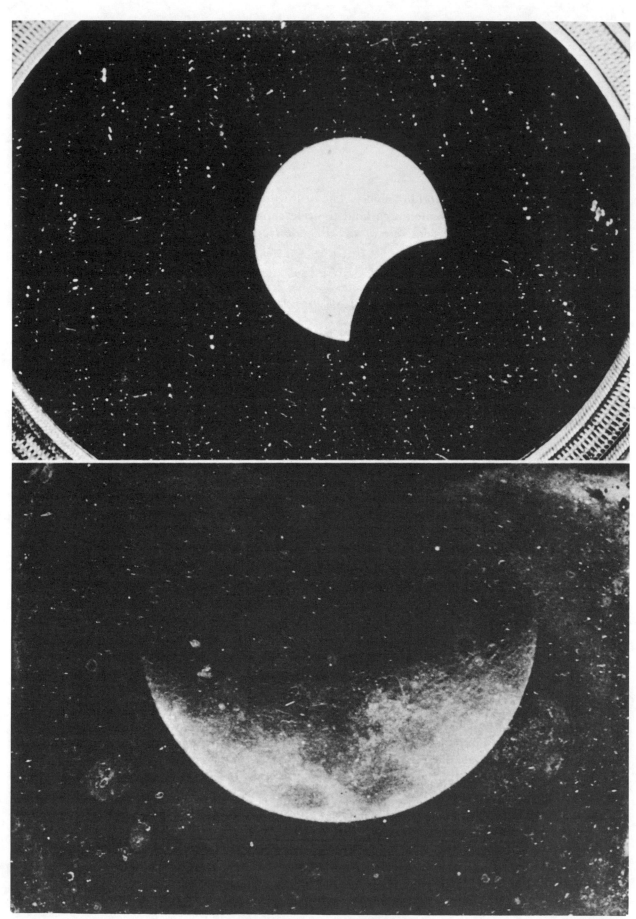

The First Photographs of the Moon.

Section 3: CAMERAS

Photography From the 1500s, alchemists knew that sunlight turned silver compounds like silver chloride black. Chemical experiments in the eighteenth century showed that it was light and not heat that caused the blackening. In 1822, the French artist, **Joseph Niepie** (1765–1833) made a copy of an engraving using the "photographic process" of combining chemicals and the Sun. Four years later, Niepie used the same process to take the world's first photograph, a view from his window. The list of firsts continued:

First photograph of a living subject 1839 by John William Draper (1811–1882)
First photograph of the Moon 1840 by John William Draper
First photograph of a star (Vega) 1850 by William Cranch Bond (1789–1859) and John Whipple.
First photographs of stars too dim for the human eye to see 1864 by George Bond (1825–1865)

"On a fine night the amount of work which can be accomplished with entire exception from the trouble, vexation and fatigue that seldom fail to attend upon ordinary observations, is astonishing. The plates, once secured, can be laid by for future study by daylight and at leisure. The record is there, with no room for doubts or mistakes as to its fidelity."—George Bond

---

photography comes from the Greek words $\phi\omega\tau o\varsigma$ *(photos)* = light, and $\gamma\rho\alpha\phi o\varsigma$ *(graphos)* = to write, paint, record
The German astronomer, **J. H. Madler** (1791–1874) invented the word **photography** a few days before John Herschel (1792–1871) did. Herschel, also an astronomer invented the words **positive, negative,** and **snapshot** to describe photographs.

First attempt to use photography to assist the study of an astronomical object (Moon) 1865 by Warren de la Rue (1815–1889)
First photograph of a double star (Alcor and Mizar) which helped measure distance between stars and determine stellar magnitude 1857 by Whipple
First astronomical discovery made with photography (photograph of a total solar eclipse showed prominences and flares were attached to the Sun, not to the Moon as people had thought) 1860 de la Rue and Pietro Angelo Secchi (1818–1878)
First planet discovered with photographs (Pluto) 1939 by Clyde Tombaugh

Since astronomers have begun using photography to help them in their work, they have discovered asteroids, satellites, and rings around planets as well as studying the surfaces of planets. What began as a visual art became a scientific tool. Photographs of objects in the night sky remain a source of incredible beauty as well as information. In this next project, you can make a simple camera and take some photographs yourself.

"A small aperture in a window shutter project or the inner wall of the room an image of the bodies which are beyond the aperture"—Leonardo da Vinci's description of a pin-hole camera

—————————— **Project 62: Making a Pinhole Camera** ——————————

MATERIALS

shoebox with lid	wax paper
aluminum foil	scissors or razor blade
thick cardboard	photographic corners
pin	ruler
photographic paper (5 × 7 sheets)—try	scissors
blueprint paper and sun picture paper	flat black paint
black electrical tape	

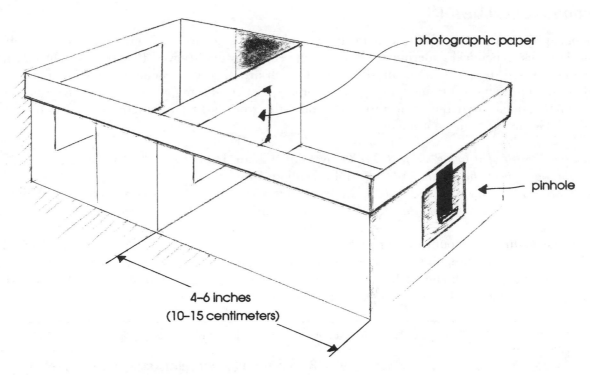

photographic paper

pinhole

4–6 inches
(10–15 centimeters)

PROCEDURE

1. Cut out a 1 inch (2.5 centimeter) square from the center of one of the ends of the shoe box. Tape a square of aluminum (1 × 1 inch or 4 × 4 centimeter) foil over the opening. Punch a tiny hole through the center of a aluminum foil with the pin.

2. Cut out a rectangle 5 × 7 inches (12.7 × 17.7 centimeters) from the center of the other end of the box. Keep the rectangle in one piece, you will need it later. Tape a piece of wax paper over the opening.

3. Cut the thick piece of cardboard to fit inside the shoebox with a 2 inch (5 centimeter) overlap on each side in the center of the cardboard.

4. Cover the shoebox with a lid and take it outside.

USING YOUR PINHOLE CAMERA

Aim the pinhole at a person, or some object. You will see whatever you are aiming at on the wax paper exactly as it appears in a camera and in your eye—upside down. To take a photograph:

1. Cover the wax paper section with the rectangle that you cut out. Tape all around it with black tape. Tape it so you can remove this section and look at the images on the wax paper later if you want to.

2. Cover the pinhole with a 2 inch (5 centimeter) piece of black tape whose last ½ inch (1 centimeter) you have folded over leaving a flap so you can easily lift the tape off the pin hole and stick it down again.

3. Go to a dark room and open one of the envelopes containing the photographic paper. Cut one of the sheets in half. Tape it inside the box on top of the wax paper. The shiny side of the photographic paper should be facing the pinhole. Cover the box tightly.

4. Take your pinhole camera outside, aim at whatever you want to photograph, open the tape from the pinhole for a few minutes, then cover it again. You must hold your camera *very* still when the tape is off the pin hole so that your picture doesn't blur. You may want to put your camera on a stool or table to hold it steady while you are photographing. The smaller the pinhole, the clearer the photograph and the longer you must expose your film.

5. Return to a dark room, remove your photographic paper and place it back in its black envelope. When you have taken a few photographs, develop them.

OBSERVATIONS

How were your photographs? Try leaving the tape off for longer periods to see what that does to the quality of your photographs.

There are many advantages to using photography to help you study the sky.

1. Photographs can record the images of stars which are far dimmer than the eye or the telescope can see. Light from the star keeps darkening the chemicals on the plate the longer you expose it. The retina in your eye takes in all the light it can all at once.

2. Photographs don't depend on the condition of your eye for you to make them.

3. You can enlarge photographs to show more detail.

4. The image on a photograph is permanent. You can study it at any time, night or day, clear or cloudy. You can examine photographs over the years to look for any changes (that's how Clyde Tombaugh discovered Pluto).

5. You can make copies of photographs and send them to other people so that they can all see the same view.

In the next project, you can take some photographs of the sky and see for yourself what a useful tool photography is.

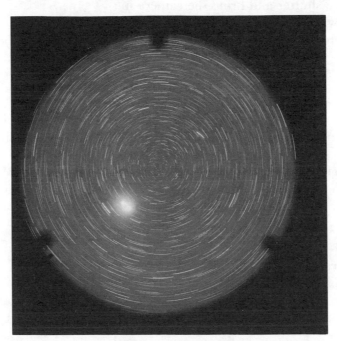

Star Trails. *Photo courtesy of Observatoire de Haute Provence*

—————— Project 63: Photographing Stars and Planets ——————

MATERIALS

camera whose shutter can be left open
tripod or stool
fast film (black and white: Tri-X—ASA 400 or Plus LX—ASA 125, color: Ektachrome 400 or Kodachrome 64—ASA 64. This is slide film and only Kodak can process it. It may take awhile to get it back. It works well for astronomical photographs)

cable release
pencil and paper
watch or clock

PROCEDURE

Before you start:

1. Be patient and be prepared to shoot one roll of black and white and one roll of color (12 or 24 exposures each) as a practice. You need to experiment with f stop settings and exposure times with black and white and color. Then when a great scene takes place in the sky, you'll be ready. Take practice photographs of all the subjects described here.

2. Keep track of all of your photographs, practice or final shots in a log. Make one of your own or copy the one in this book.

STAR TRAILS (LIKE YOU DREW IN CHAPTER 1)

1. Put the camera on the tripod pointing toward Polaris (in the northern hemisphere) or σ Octanis (in the southern hemisphere).

2. Focus camera at infinity or as far away as it will go.

3. Set the aperture (f stop) at its maximum opening.

4. Set the shutter for a time exposure.

5. Attach the cable release and open the shutter for one hour. Tightly screw the cable on, leave and return in an hour.

6. Move to the next frame and open the shutter. Leave the camera for as long as you can. Before you go to bed, close the shutter and bring the camera in.

7. Write down how long you left the shutter open (exposure time).

8. Take other photographs of star trails by pointing your camera to the east, west, south, and north.

CONSTELLATIONS

1. Put the camera on the tripod pointing toward a constellation. Choose a time when the constellation is high in the sky to avoid distortion from the atmosphere. (Check for dates and times in the constellation list in Sky Files.)

2. Use the same settings (focus, aperture, and shutter speed) as in #2, 3, 4 above.

3. Attach the cable release and experiment with shutter speeds. If you leave the camera open for a long time beyond a few seconds, you will begin to have star trails.

THE MOON

1. Make allowances for the brightness of the Moon.

2. Take photographs of different phases and colors (when close to horizon).

3. Photograph the Moon both in the daytime and at night.

THE PLANETS

1. Take photographs of the planets over a period of time to show their movement. Always include a few stars as reference points.

2. If you are using color film, try to show the red of Mars and the yellow of Saturn compared with the white of Venus. You can do the same with the colors of stars.

THROUGH A TELESCOPE

1. Take photographs using the clock drive on the telescope to allow you to make a longer exposure without trails.

2. Photograph the same constellations as you did before to see how many dimmer stars you can brighten.

3. Take photographs of nebulae and galaxies.

4. Photograph the Moon's craters.

5. Take photographs of Saturn's rings, Jupiter's bands and moons, and the phases of Venus.

OBSERVATIONS

What f stops, exposure times and film type gave you the best results? Were more stars visible on your photographs than you were able to see with your eyes?

The photoelectric effect   Albert Einstein explained the photoelectric effect in 1905 and won the Nobel Peace Prize for Physics in 1921 because of it.

---

photoelectric comes from the Greek words $\phi\omega\tau\circ\varsigma$ (photos) = light, and $\eta\lambda\epsilon\kappa\tau\omega\rho$ (elector) = the beaming Sun; $\dot{\eta}\lambda\epsilon\kappa\tau\rho\omega\nu$ (electron) = metallic substance produced from amber by friction

---

Electrically charged particles can blacken photographic plates. They can also generate an electrical current. The photocell is a simple light-sensitive detector in which light falls on a surface called the **photocathode.** This causes electrons to be ejected from the photocathode. The electrons then travel to a collecting electrode which causes an electric current. The current can then be used to power a motor to open doors automatically for you in a store. Look for the light by the door. It is focused on a photoelectric cell. As long as the light can reach the cell, there is enough electricity to keep the door closed. If you walk in front of the light, you interrupt the flow of electricity and the door opens.

In the Spring of 1933, a beam of light from Arcturus (α Boötis) opened the Chicago World's Fair. The "Century of Progress" Exposition aimed its telescopes at the bright star and focused the gathered light onto photoelectric cells. These cells generated enough electricity from the starlight to turn on the switch that controlled the floodlights at the exposition grounds. The exposition planners chose Arcturus because they calculated that the light reaching the Fair had left Arcturus forty years earlier in 1893. At that time, Chicago was celebrating another fair, the "Columbian Exposition" honoring Columbus who had arrived in America four hundred years earlier.

In 1924, astronomers began using photocells timed at a bright star to guide their telescopes and keep the star in view, like a drive. The photoelectric effect also takes place in a video camera. Light enters the camera and releases electrically charged particles. The tube in your television has an electron beam which scans all the charged particles sent to it by the camera and translates these particles back into the original image that entered the camera. In the 1950s, people aimed television cameras at the sky much as Galileo first aimed the telescope heavenward in the 1600s.

The most recent kind of image-making tube uses a phosphor screen. Electrons set the phosphor screen aglow much like a television screen. It only takes one electron to do this which makes the phosphor screen much more sensitive than a photographic plate. The image on the screen is actually brighter than the image formed by the original light. Once collected, you can photograph the image, send it to another place by way of fiber optics or feed it to a computer. The computer can remove any extra light around the image that you don't want, so you have a clear view of what you want to look at. You don't have to sit at your telescope out in the cold, straining your eye. Now you can control everything from a distance sitting comfortably in a room watching the results on your TV screen.

Because electronic methods can reveal very dim objects with a short exposure time (about 2/100 of a second) these methods are fast replacing photography in astronomical research.

Computers   The spectacular views brought back from the cameras of the astronauts are photographs. The pictures which we receive from spacecraft such as the *Voyager* did not come from photographic film. They came from television cameras with selenium-sulfur vidicom image tubes, 1 inch (2½ centimeters) in diameter. The tubes change the light entering them into electronic impulses. Radio transmitters on the spacecraft send these impulses back to Earth as black and white digital computer data in the form of a series of 1s and 0s. There are billions of these 1s and 0s or binary bits arriving on Earth from the spacecraft. Computers and their operators process this information so that an image results.

Voyager could transmit 115,200 bits per second to produce a single image which would end up containing 5,120,000 bits.

Voyager 2 Space Probe. *Photo courtesy of Jet Propulsion Laboratory*

The image on the computer screen appears as a large grid. Each square in the grid stands for part of the object which the television camera in space recorded. These squares are *pic*ture *elements* or **pixels** for short.

In the *Voyager* images, there were 640,000 pixels arranged in a grid of 800 × 800 squares. Each pixel had an 8-digit binary number signal code.

As the computer processes the information it gives a number value for light or darkness and color to each pixel. This is **digital image processing.**

What image does the computer process? On the *Voyager*, there are two television cameras, one with a wide angle lens, the other with a narrow angle. The narrow-angle camera has a 60 inch (1,500 millimeter) focal length and a 0.4° field of view. It also has 7.5 times the resolving power of the wide angle camera. The wide angle camera can see an area 56 times larger than the narrow angle camera. It has a 7 inch (200 millimeter) focal length and a 3° field of view. Each camera has a rotating filter wheel to select the color of light the camera will see. There is also a filter to focus on wavelengths of sodium and methane. Usually the cameras take three images of the same subject, once each through the blue, green, and orange filters.

Back on Earth at your computer you can combine the images which appear on the screen to get any result you want. You can make the image have nearly the exact colors of the object the cameras looked at. The human eye is much more sensitive to colors than the lens of a camera, so your image won't be exact. You can deliberately exaggerate the brightness levels of each pixel if you want to make it easier to see certain parts of the image, especially the details. In this way, you are enhancing the contrast. You can also use false color to emphasize slight differences in color due to changes in temperature, chemicals, and land formation.

In the next project, you can sit at your computer or TV set and enhance some images of your own.

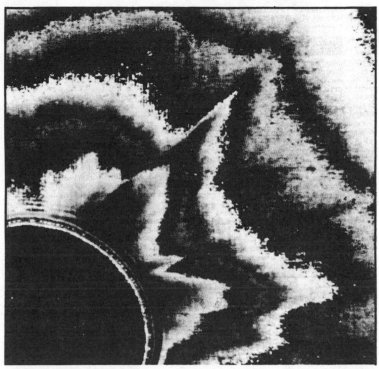

Digital image of the Sun's corona. *Photo courtesy of Nasa*

———————— Project 64: Creating Images with a Computer ————————

MATERIALS

computer with graphics capability
painting, drawing, or graphics software
pencil and paper

photograph of Digital Image of the Sun's
corona (above)
color printer (or camera with color film)

PROCEDURE

1. Load the graphics program into computer.
2. Copy the photograph onto the screen using following key:
   a. outer edges and particles = magenta
   b. next layer = blue
   c. next layer = green
   d. next layer = yellow
   e. next layer = orange
3. Change the colors so that the image is the natural color of the object.
4. Change the image to black and white to resemble the photograph.

OBSERVATIONS

What advantages do you think there are in using computers to record images from space instead of photographs? What disadvantages are there? If you don't have a computer, use your TV set. Change the contrast, brightness, color, and tint to bring out or hide certain details of an image on the screen.

READING MORE

Burgess, E. *Celestial Basic.* Sybex, 1982.
Kals, W. S. *The Stargazer's Bible.* New York, Doubleday and Company, Inc., 1980.
Paul, Henry E. *Outer Space Photography.* New York: Amphoto, 1976.

Deep Space Network Antennae, Australia.
Photo courtesy of Jet Propulsion Laboratory

Section 4: *SPECTROSCOPES AND RADIO RECEIVERS*

The Color of Light   Have you ever seen a rainbow inside your house made by a crystal or a prism near your window? It's not raining, so why is there a rainbow? For centuries, people asked the same question. They figured that light from the Sun was pure and when it went through the crystal or prism, the impurities in the glass colored the light.

". . . in the beginning of the year 1666 (at which time, I applied myself to the grinding of Optick glasses of other figures than *Spherical*), I procured me a Triangular glass—Prisme, to try therewith the celebrated *Phaenomena of Colours.* And in order thereto having darkened my chamber, and made a small hole in my window-sheets, to let in a convenient quantity of the Sun's light, I placed my Prisme at his entrance, that it might be thereby refracted to the opposite wall. It was at first a very pleasing divertisement, to view the vivid and intense colours produced thereby . . ."
    —Sir Isaac Newton in the *Philosophical Transactions* of the Royal Society in London, 1672

The beam of light bent as it passed through Newton's prism and created a rainbow on his wall. The prism bent each color at a particular angle: violet refracted the most, then indigo, then blue, then green; yellow and orange with red refracted the least. Newton named the rainbow pattern of colors the **spectrum.**

---

spectrum comes from the Latin word *spectrum* = an image or an appearance

---

Why was the light colored? Newton tried different sized holes in the window shutter, different sized prized prisms, different placements of the prism, including outside the window. No change. To get only one color, he made a small hole in the screen on which the spectrum was shining right where the red light appeared. He took another prism and placed it on the other side of the screen into the path of the red light. The red light passed through the second prism, and came out refracted with the same angle and red. Newton tried this with each of the other colors and had the same result. He then passed the light from the first prism through a second prism held upside down, thinking all the colors would spread out even more. Instead, the colors joined together and came out as a shaft of pure light, casting a spot of white light on the screen.

These experiments convinced Newton that white light was made up of all seven colors of the rainbow. In order to see these colors, you need a prism, glass, water or rain to help separate the light into it's parts. We call the separation of light into the spectrum **dispersion.**

dispersion comes from the Latin word *dispersus* = to scatter, to spread abroad

In this project, you can repeat some of Newton's experiments plus a few of your own.

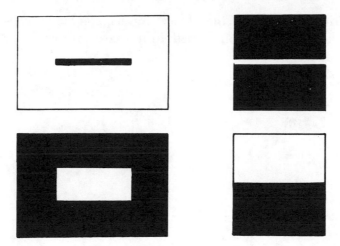

Project 65: Experimenting with Prisms and Light

MATERIALS

two prisms
white paper
straight pin

colored pencils or water color paint
tape
black construction paper

PROCEDURE

1. Put a small pin hole through a sheet of paper. Tape the paper to a window through which the Sun is shining.

2. Hold one prism up to the light shining through the pin hole and move it until rainbow colors appear on the opposite wall. Tape a piece of white paper on the wall where these colors appear. Notice the order of the colors.

3. Place the other prism in between the first prism and the wall where the colors appeared. Notice what happened to the colors.

4. Hold one prism up to the light and look through it at the edges of people and furniture in the room.

5. Set up four arrangements of black and white as shown below using the black and white paper:
   a. black on top, white on the bottom,
   b. black on the bottom, white in the center,
   c. white strip made from two black pieces on top of white,
   d. black strip made from two white pieces on top of black.

6. Observe each arrangement through the prism and draw or paint what you see.

OBSERVATIONS

The prism has the ability to break (refract) white light into the spectrum of purple, blue, green, yellow and red, the "rainbow" colors. What happened to the orders of these colors when you used the black and white arrangements?

In the late 1800s **Michael Faraday** and **Hans Christian Oersted** showed the close connection between electricity and magnetism. **James Clark Maxwell** pointed out that light is also related to electricity and magnetism and that light, electricity, and magnetism are all related to electromagnetic waves. Included in the electromagnetic spectrum are three forms of light:

1. *very long wavelengths*   infrared (invisible)
2. *visible light*   makes up only a small fraction of the electromagnetic spectrum
3. *very short wavelengths*   ultraviolet, X-rays, gamma rays (invisible)

Sir William Herschel, the discoverer of the planet Uranus, conducted experiments to find how much heat each color of the Sun's spectrum carried. In this next project, you can do the same kind of experiment.

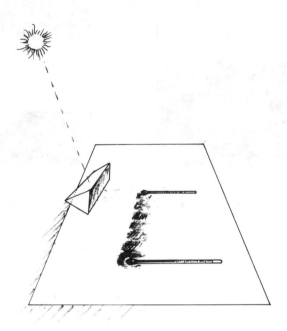

———— Project 66: Measuring the Temperatures of Infrared Rays ————

MATERIALS
prism

two thermometers

white piece of paper

flat black paint

PROCEDURE
1. Paint the bulbs of the two thermometers black.
2. Place the white paper on a flat surface on to which the Sun is shining. Place a thermometer on the paper and record the temperature after three minutes.
3. Place a prism in the path of the Sun. Place the thermometer in any color on the blue violet end of the spectrum and record the temperature after three minutes.
4. Place the thermometer in the deep red and record the temperature after three minutes.
5. Record the temperature just beyond the red and just beyond the blue.

OBSERVATIONS
Which wavelength has greater heating effect? How far do the rays extend beyond the visible end? Herschel named the invisible radiation beyond the red end of the spectrum **infrared.**

---

infrared comes from the Latin word *infra* = below

Newton separated the visible light from the Sun into the spectrum. You can also separate the light coming from the stars or passing through gases of different elements. To do this you need an instrument to split up the light and spread it out into a band of colored lines representing the spectrum. **Robert Bunsen** (1811–1899), the inventor of the bunsen burner invented the **spectroscope** to create and view the spectra of stars. You can make photographic studies with a spectroscope using a spectrograph, studying the spectra of stars and light passing through gases is called spectral analysis and it is an important part of astronomy.

In 1802, **William Wollaston** (1766–1828) from England, while observing the Sun's spectrum noticed thin dark lines among the bands of color. He thought these lines were the natural boundaries between the colors. In 1817, **Joseph von Fraunhofer** (1787–1826) saw between 600 and 750 lines and assigned letters to the strongest lines starting with "A" in the red band. A help in figuring out what the black lines were came when people realized that they could reproduce these black spectral lines in the laboratory. When you pass a beam of white light through a cloud of gas, the Fraunhofer lines appear in the spectrum. The spectra of light emitted from certain glowing gases also showed several separate bright lines. Each gas displayed its own pattern of spectral lines and colors. Von Fraunhofer invented the diffraction grating which you will be using in the next project.

In 1859, **Gustav Kirchoff** (1824–1887) of Germany offered the following explanation for the lines and separate colors. Any source could both emit or absorb radiation: the temperature determined which took place. When light passes through a gas that is cooler than the light source, the spectrum that results has thin dark lines crossing it. These lines represent missing colors that the gas took out of the light, or absorbed. Each chemical element in the gas selects a certain grouping of colors to absorb that no other element chooses, thus producing its own characteristic pattern of dark lines on the spectrum. It's as though each element puts it fingerprint on the light as it passes through.

When you burn an element and examine its spectral pattern against a dark background, only certain colors appear in narrow lines. Each element produces or emits its own pattern of colors. These emission lines of an element show up in the same places on the spectrum as the dark absorption lines for that element. A gas at high pressure, a liquid, or a solid, if heated to incandescence, will glow with a **continuous spectrum.** A hot gas under low pressure will produce only certain colors called bright **emission lines.** A cool gas at low pressure, if placed between the observer and a hot continuum source, absorbs certain colors, causing dark **absorption lines** in the observed spectrum.

The study of the spectra of celestial objects (spectroscopy) is the most powerful tool an astronomer has to find out information about the Universe. So critical is spectroscopy, that many astronomers devote their entire careers to it. Using Kirchoff's laws, physicists returned to the solar spectrum. Examining it carefully, they found tens of thousands of Fraunhofer lines. In their laboratories, using bunsen burners (gas flames) or electric arcs as light sources, the physicists shone this light through gases of various compositions. They burned metal salts and examined the spectra of their flames, all in an effort to reproduce the lines in the solar spectrum. The hope was to find what elements were responsible for the Faunhofer lines. This would reveal what the Sun and the stars were made of.

In this next project you can do your own spectrum studying using a spectroscope which you can make yourself.

—— Project 67: Making a Spectrum Analyzing Instrument (Spectroscope) ——

MATERIALS

spectroscope plan from book (see index)
diffraction grating
scissors
rubber cement
ruler
tape
paper clip

a nail
3 × 5 inch (7½ × 12½ centimeter) file
   card
X-acto knife
access to a photocopier, one with
   enlarging capabilities

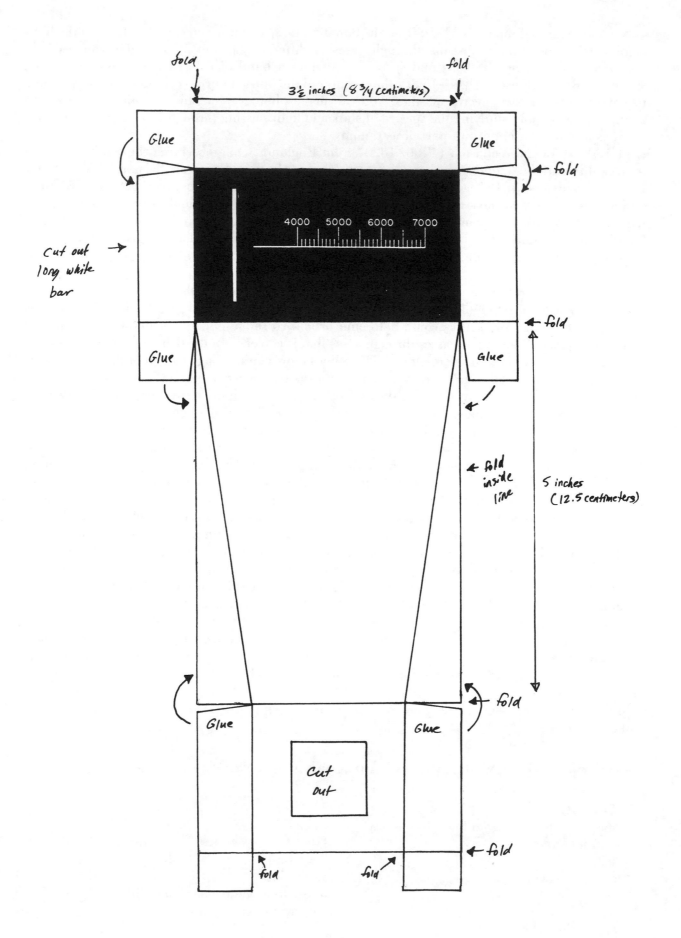

fold

fold

3½ inches (8¾ centimeters)

Glue

Glue

fold

4000   5000   6000   7000

Cut out
long white
bar

Glue

Glue

fold

fold
inside
line

5 inches
(12.5 centimeters)

Glue

Glue

Cut
out

fold

fold

fold

fold

190

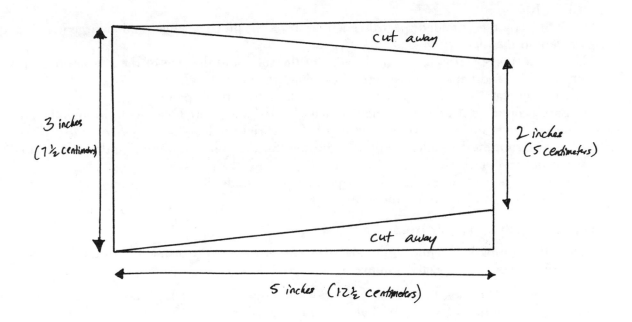

3 inches
(7 ½ centimeters)

2 inches
(5 centimeters)

cut away

cut away

5 inches (12 ½ centimeters)

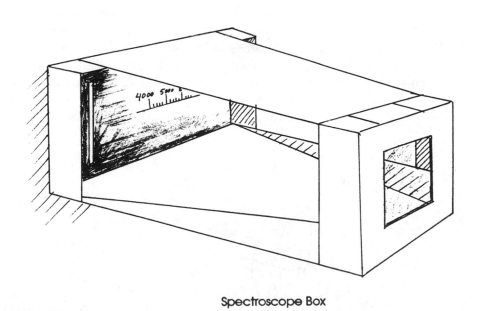

4000 5000

Spectroscope Box

PROCEDURE

1. Photocopy the unfolded spectroscope plan from the previous pages and enlarge it so it is the size written on the plan.

2. Cut out the spectroscope. Use the edge of the ruler and the side of the scissors to help you fold up the sides and flaps of the spectroscope along the lines.

3. Glue the flaps as shown *under* the spaces where the arrows point.

4. Paper clip the diffraction grating into place behind the square hole. Look through the grating while aiming the scale end of your spectroscope at a bright indoor light *(Not the Sun)*. If you do not see a spectrum on the scale, remove the grating, turn it ¼ of the way around to the next edge, and put it back in place.

5. Cut the file card to the size and shape shown. Glue the file card on top of the spectroscope and glue the flaps in place above the grating.

USING YOUR SPECTROSCOPE

Look through the hole while aiming the scale end of your spectroscope at a bright light (*not the sun*). If you do not see a spectrum above the scale:

a. Remove the grating, turn it ¼ of the way around to the next edge, and put it back in place. If it works, remove the paper clip and glue the grating down.

b. Move the razor blades so their edges are in a straight line and are closer or nearer to each other.

Look at regular incandescent lights, fluorescent lights, street lamps, neon signs, and at the reflected light of the Sun on a piece of white paper. *Do Not Look at the Sun*. You might try taping the diffraction grating in front of your camera lens and photographing various light sources with color slide film. Write down what each source is. Project your slides onto the wall or a screen and use a meter stick to measure the wavelength.

OBSERVATIONS

One way of being certain that you are reading the correct fingerprint of an element as it appears on the spectrum is to measure the width of its wavelengths. A wavelength is just what the name says, the length in between the tops of two waves. This distance is extremely tiny so we use special numbers to measure it. A man named **Anders Jonas Ångstrom** (1817–1874), a Swedish astronomer working in the 1860s developed a wavelength measuring scale based on unit equal to 1/10,000,000,000 of a meter. He called this unit "10th metre," but people preferred to call it an Ångstrom unit (or Å for short) after its inventor. We now use the term **nanometer** which is equal to 10 Angstroms or 10. Using Ångstroms, wavelengths of violet light are about 4,000 Å, wavelengths of red light are about 7,000 Å. What would these be in nanometers?   This project is adapted from *Modern Astronomy: An Activities Approach* by R. Robert Robbins and Mary Kay Hemenway, Austin: University of Texas Press, 1982. Used with permission.

A RADIO TELESCOPE RECEIVING RADIO WAVES

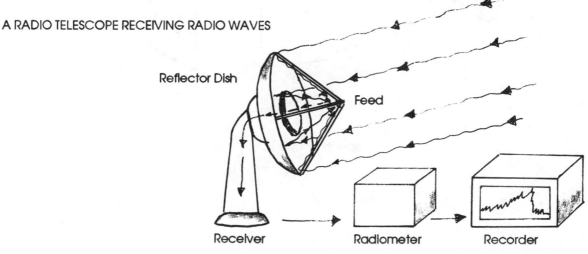

192

Radio Astronomy *"the unseen universe"*   American **Thomas Alva Edison** (1847–1931) and English physicist **Joseph Lodge** (1851–1940) both suggested that there might be radio waves coming from the Sun. No one could check up on their idea. The electromagnetic spectrum is vast. The visible portion of it is very small by comparison. Most of astronomy up until 1931 has focused on understanding the universe through studies of its visible light.

In 1937, an electrical engineer named **Karl Jansky** (1905–1950) was working for the telephone company trying to figure out why there was so much static on the phones from conversations sent by radio between New York and London. The usual causes such as thunderstorms were only making part of the static. A hissing sound remained. Jansky built an antenna made of wires stretched on wooden frames. Jansky made the world's first radio telescope out of eight large metal rectangular hoops attached to a wooden frame shaped like a long rectangle. The telescope rotated slowly on a set of Model T Ford wheels. This antenna found that the hissing noise came from a point in space where 14 years before **Harlow Shapley** (1885–1972) had said was the center of the galaxy. Jansky had discovered radio waves from space. He reported his findings in 1932. Astronomers did not follow up on Jansky's discovery until almost 15 years later.

Grote Reber (b. 1911) an amateur astronomer living in Illinois decided to listen in on these radio waves. In 1936, he built a 31 foot dish antenna to collect the radio waves the way reflector telescope mirrors collected light. Since radio waves can go through clouds, fog, and mist and light can't, Reber could use his dish anytime and in any weather. Using his **radio telescope,** Reber listened to the sky and made a contour map of the radio sky which he published in 1944. People considered this map the first and best of its kind for the next 15 years.

Radio Interferometry   If you place two radio dishes some distance apart and have both observe the same source at the same time, one dish will receive the radio wave slightly before the other. By measuring the time lag in between, you can figure out the direction of the source. The further apart the distance (base line) between the two dishes, the more accurately you can locate the direction of the source. *Very long baseline interferometry* (VLBI) is possible by using one telescope in one part of the world (e.g., California) and another telescope in another part of the world far distant from the first (e.g., Australia).

Radio Telescopes   The only device sensitive to radio waves is an antenna, which is simply a wire which allows electrically charged particles to move freely along it. When electromagnetic radio waves reach the **antenna,** they come in contact with the electronically charged particles on the antenna and cause them to change the direction they are moving.

The **receiver** detects any change in the current of the antenna. The receiver operator can select or amplify the frequency of the current just like you do with a radio. He or she sends the signal to the **recorder** which prints out a chart of these changes. The recorder uses a pen that writes across a moving roll of paper. If you connected the receiver to a loudspeaker instead of a pen, you would hear the "cosmic hiss" that Jansky heard. When strong radio waves come across the antenna, it would sound like the radio in your car when you drive under a power line. To build up a "picture" of the source, the telescope scans back and forth across it so that it can measure its brightness and every point. The telescopic computer stores the measurements and builds up a "map" of the source. The map is usually like a contour map (see Chapter 3, Section 2) with the most intense source in the center surrounded by rings of lessening levels of intensity.

A radio telescope is really a highly sensitive version of a regular radio. Radio waves come to your radio at home from a variety of radio stations. Each of these radio stations has permission to use a certain wavelength on which to send their broadcasts. The wavelength is the station's number on the radio dial. If it is AM, the wavelength is measured by *Amplitude Modulation* from 530 to 1600 kilohertz. FM is *Frequency Modulation* from 880 to 1080 Megahertz. When our radio receives the broadcast it does the opposite of what the transmitter at the radio station did, it changes radio waves back into music and voices. Radio telescopes change radio waves into images of their sources. The maps can also appear on a TV screen as a "radio photograph." In this way, using image intensifiers, false color, and computer enhancing techniques, you can build up a more detailed picture of the source. A radio telescope view of a typical radio station broadcast would show the shapes of the radio station's broadcasting antennas. Radio telescopes have their own radio dial numbers which no one else may use, especially radio stations.

In this next project you can hear how radio signals sound when you receive them using an antenna.

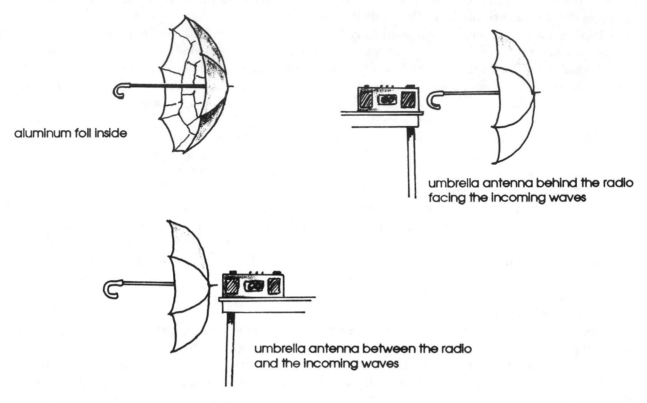

aluminum foil inside

umbrella antenna behind the radio
facing the incoming waves

umbrella antenna between the radio
and the incoming waves

Project 68: Receiving Radio Signals

MATERIALS

portable radio
umbrella
heavy duty aluminum foil

masking tape
pencil
paper

PROCEDURE

1. Place the radio on a table. Turn the dial all the way to the left and begin to search for stations you can barely hear. Write down the dial number of five of these stations whose signals are so weak you can't tune them in clearly.

2. Open the umbrella and tape the inside of it with the aluminum foil.

3. Turn the radio to one of the five weak stations, turning the radio around until you get the best reception you can.

4. Hold the umbrella behind the radio so that the aluminum foil faces the waves going past the radio.

5. Move the umbrella slowly toward the radio or farther from it until you find the position that best improves the reception.

6. Repeat steps #3–#5 for the other four weak stations. Mark each station on your list whose reception the umbrella improved.

7. Chose a station that comes in clearly. Place the umbrella in front of the radio and the incoming radio waves.

OBSERVATIONS

Your umbrella strengthened the radio waves before they reached the radio. Where did these waves come from? What happened when you put the umbrella in front of the radio with a clear station tuned in?   This project is adapted from *Scott, Foresman Earth Science* by Jay M. Pasachoff, Naomi Pasachoff and Timothy M. Cooney, Glenview: Scott, Foresman and Company, 1983. Used with permission.

Radar Astronomy is the technique of sending radio waves to an object waiting for them to bounce back to the Earth and measuring how long the round-trip took. By using the speed of light, you can figure how far away the object is. The birth of radar astronomy was in 1946, when Hungarian physicist **Zoltan Lajos Bay** sent out a beam of microwaves to the Moon and detected the return echo. Since radio waves can go through clouds, radar astronomy gave us our first views of the cloud-covered surface of Venus in 1961.

---

radar = *ra*dio *d*etection *an*d *r*anging (determination of distance)

Microwaves are the shortest waves in the electromagnet spectrum between radio and infrared and overlapping radar. Microwaves are the source of radio waves in radar. Microwave reflection has provided startling information about: Venus (its rotational period and its retrograde motion), Mercury (its rotational period), Asteroids, meteors, Mars, Jupiter, and Saturn. Water absorbs microwave radiation. If you put anything moist (like meat, soup, cake batter) in a microwave oven, the moist substance will absorb the radiation and become hot very quickly. This heat comes from within the food itself rather than from the coils in the oven. That is why you can cook things very quickly in a microwave oven. You need to be careful to keep the radiation inside the oven since it can damage living tissue.

---

microwave comes from the Greek word μικρος *(micros)* = small

---

Infrared

Infrared astronomy is like heat sensitive photography. In infrared photographs, the red stars (like Antares and Betelgeuse) show the brightest and the blue stars (like Rigel) are dimmest. This would make Betelgeuse the brightest star in the sky. You can feel the infrared radiation from the Sun. Remember the temperature of infrared rays in Project 66, Measuring the Temperatures of Infrared Rays? Water vapor and carbon dioxide in the Earth's atmosphere absorb large amounts of infrared rays making the infrared sky practically invisible. High-flying aircraft, balloons, and specially equipped telescopes that pass through the Earth's atmosphere can detect infrared radiation coming from the planets and stars. As a result, we have photographed a complete survey of the infrared sky. Many infrared sources are clouds of dust around very young or very old stars, warmed by the heat of the nearby star.

X-rays

Wilhelm Konrad Rontgen (1845–1923) discovered and named **X-rays** in 1895. In 1970, international scientists launched the first orbiting X-ray observatory from Kenya. The name of the observatory was *Uhuru.*

Uhuru comes from the Swahili word *uhuru* = freedom

For three years *Uhuru* scanned the sky for X-ray sources and charted more than 200. The name of these sources comes from the constellation where we find them (like Cygnus X-l, Hercules X-l).

Other X-ray observatories in space include the *High Energy Astrophysics Observatory* (HEAD), the Einstein Observatory, *Exostat* and *Rostat* (named for Rontgen). X-rays are able to penetrate most materials except lead.

Optical telescopes and radio telescopes each provide an important view of the sky. Recently there has been an increasing use of radio astronomy, partly because of the many advantages it has over optical observing. You can use a radio telescope day or night, in any weather. With it you can see farther into space with no interfering background. A radio telescope is less expensive to build, with crude materials and you are not limited to any size. With an optical telescope you need clear skies. This is not a problem for radio telescopes.

The radio window has truly opened an unseen universe for astronomers and made us continually revise our picture of what is "out there."

READING MORE

Freeman, Ira M. *Light and Radiation.* New York: Van Nostrand Reinhold Company, 1981.
Learner, Richard. *Astronomy Through the Telescope.* New York: Van Nostrand Reinhold Company, 1981.

Chapter 6:   THE SUN-CENTERED SKY

Section 1:   THE SUN

The "two great lights" the Sun and the Moon are closely intertwined with the Earth. The Sun is the major source of life and light for our planet. It also gives us an idea of the size and power of a star seen closer up. The Moon gives us reflected sunlight and a constant reminder of our place in space. To see its cratered surface with the naked eye offers us a closer view of another heavenly body, a glimpse at what a planet might look like.

Pepin: What's the Sun?
Alcuin: The splendour of the universe, the beauty of the sky, the glory of the day, the divider of the hours.
—the monk Alcuin, teaching Pepin, the son of Charlemagne

Helios, the Greek Sun God. *From a Greek vase in the British Museum*

Names   People have always held the Sun in high esteem. Many cultures saw in the Sun, the god of life. They watched this god's daily, monthly, and yearly movements with great care. To the Greeks, the god of the Sun was **Helios** or **Sol** and thus we have the words **helicentric** and **solar.** The Greeks also called the Sun Apollo. The Egyptians worshipped the Sun as Ra.

Early Observations   Some cultures planned and built large cities on the basis of the Sun's movements. Such a city was Tenochtitlan, capital of the Aztec Empire. It had more people in it, was larger and better planned than many cities in Europe.

Sunrise between the towers of Temple Mayor, Tenochtitlan, Mexico.

Four large avenues divided the city into four sections. These four sections point to the four cardinal directions. Near the center of the city was Temple Mayor, a double temple, more than 270 feet (82 meters) wide at its base and about 90 feet (27 meters) tall. At sunrise on the equinoxes, the Sun would appear between the two towers at the top.

Sun observatories appear throughout the world. Chapter 1 describes some of them. Some are oriented toward the winter solstice as in the shrine at Burro Flats, Los Angeles and the Tipai Indian shelter in Baja, California.

At the temple of Ramses II in Abu Simbel in Egypt is a row of baboons carved from stone. The baboon was a symbol of Thoth, god of wisdom. Baboons also have a connection with sunrise. Like roosters and birds, baboons chatter at dawn. In Abu Simbel, the first light of dawn falls upon this row of stone baboons who chatter silently to greet the day.

The View From Earth   The Sun looks huge in the sky. How big is it anyway? This next project will help you find out.

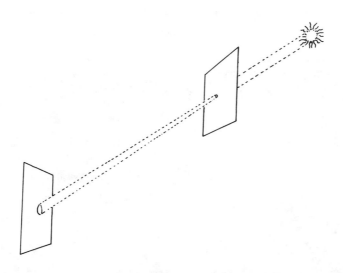

─────────────── **Project 69: Measuring the Sun** ───────────────

MATERIALS
ruler   nail
2 sheets of white cardboard or stiff paper

PROCEDURE
1. Poke a hole with the nail through the center of one of the sheets of cardboard about the size of a dime or smaller.
2. Place this piece of cardboard at a point above you so that the Sun shines directly on it.
3. Direct the light through the hole in the cardboard onto the other piece of cardboard.
4. The Sun's image will appear on the second sheet of cardboard.

5. Measure:
   a) the diameter of the Sun's image
   b) the distance between the two sheets of cardboard

6. Divide the distance by the diameter. The distance is just about 109 times bigger than the size of the Sun's image. To solve for the diameter of the Sun, diameter=distance/109. To solve for the distance to the Sun, distance = 109 × diameter.

Diameter of Sun's image/Diameter of Sun = Distance from 1 cardboard to the other/Distance to Sun

Distance from 1 cardboard to the other/Diameter of Sun's image = Diameter of Sun/Distance to Sun. Use 93,000,000 miles or 150,000,000 kilometers for the distance to the Sun.

7. Move the pieces of cardboard much farther apart and repeat the two measurements.

8. Move the pieces of cardboard even farther apart and repeat the measurements.

OBSERVATIONS

What have you noticed about the results when you divided distance/diameter? Try using a smaller image of the Sun and a longer distance between sheets of paper. Do you still find the same diameter for the Sun?

The Sun gives you day and night. This means that as the Earth turns counterclockwise on its axis, it turns toward or away from the light of the Sun. As it turns, dawn comes to people living on the Earth and with it, the day. This dawn is preannounced by the singing of birds, a beautiful sound known as the "dawn chorus." The coming of the dawn chorus and the sunrise which it announces move across the face of the Earth from East to West sweeping away the darkness and bringing light to all those on the north-south line of dawn. Again humanity has the opportunity to participate in a shared experience. Those people living in a line north and south of you experience dawn at the same time that you do. They hear the dawn chorus when you do. The Sun rises and sets for them when it does for you.

Composition   Like the Earth, the Sun has a core, and grows outward from the core in layers, the final one, being the atmosphere which reaches out into space connecting with the rest of the universe.

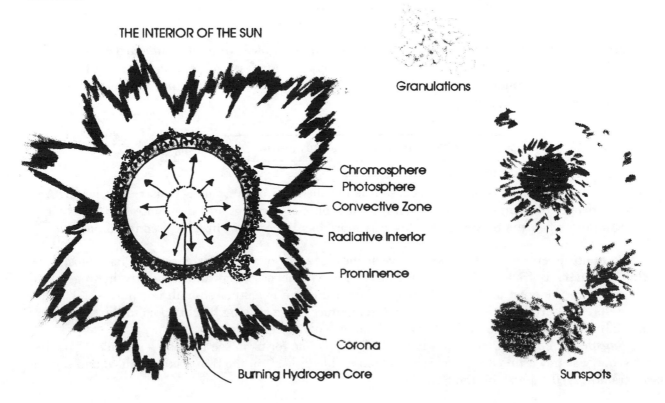

THE INTERIOR OF THE SUN

Granulations

Chromosphere
Photosphere
Convective Zone
Radiative Interior
Prominence
Corona
Burning Hydrogen Core

Sunspots

The Core   The core is the source of most of the Sun's energy. This energy moves to the surface by both radiation and convection. Radiation carries the energy like a heater heats a room by sending it out, warming the air in front of it. As the energy travels, the air closest to the heat source remains the hottest, while the temperature drops in the air farthest away from the source. This cooling zone within the Sun meets a zone made of currents of hot turbulent gases. This convecting zone carries hot gases to the Sun's surface and sends cooler gases back down to the core. This is similar to the way heating pipes work in a house. They carry hot water to warm a room and send the cooler water back to the furnace to be reheated and recirculated.

Temperatures within the core of the Sun are as high as 25,000,000°F (15,000,000°C), the average being around 11,000°F or 6,000°C. With temperatures this high, the pressure inside the Sun would have to be the same as the pressure of the gases surrounding it, otherwise the Sun would collapse. The great pressure at the Sun's core produces tremendous heat and matter that is exceptionally dense, as much as 100 times denser than water.

The Sun gets its energy from hydrogen particles joining (fusing) together in a process called **nuclear fusion.** Some of the fused hydrogen produces helium. The rest of the hydrogen changes into energy. The amount of energy produced is equal to about 500 sextillion horsepower, or as **Hermann von Helmholtz** calculated in 1871, it is the same as having coal burning on every square foot or ⅓ meter of the Sun at the rate of 1,500 pounds or 680 kilograms of coal an hour. This massive energy output has kept the Sun burning for at least 4½ billion years and will keep it burning at least another 4½ billion years.

In 1868, the French astronomer **Pierre Janssen** (1824–1907) and the English astronomers **Norman Lockyer** (1836–1920) and **Sir Edward Frankland** (1825–1899) working independently discovered a new element on the Sun. They were observing the spectrum of the Sun's chromosphere during an eclipse and found spectral lines which indicated the presence of the unknown element. Because he first found this element on the Sun, Frankland named it helium. In 1882, **helium** showed up in the flame spectrum of Mt. Vesuvius. In 1895, **William Ramsay** (1852–1916) isolated and identified helium in the laboratory and with it started a new column of gasses made from liquid air in the Periodic Table of Elements.

---

helium comes from the Greek word $\acute{\eta}\lambda\iota o\varsigma$ *(helios)* = Sun

---

The Sun's Surface   The energy carried to the Sun's surface stimulates the particles of matter it finds there. These stimulated particles give off energy in the form of heat, light, and other forms of electromagnetic radiation. This is the **photosphere,** the part of the Sun that we can see and the place that sends us sunlight.

---

photosphere comes from the Greek words $\phi\omega\tau o\varsigma$ *(photos)* = light

---

"They say that the Sun is not hot because it is not the color of fire, but is whiter and clearer. And to these people one can reply that when melted bronze is very hot and it is more like the color of the Sun, and when the bronze is less hot it is more like the color of fire." —Leonardo da Vinci

The photosphere is the boundary between the last layer of the Sun's gases and its atmosphere. This boundary is from 100–250 miles (160–400 kilometers) deep and is mostly hydrogen and helium. Like the crust of the Earth, the "skin" of the Sun is neither smooth nor inactive. The hot gases that the corrective zone sends up can sometimes cause bulging bright spots in the photsphere that have a pebbly, rough grained texture. These spots are granules.

Sunspots   Powerful telescopes have made it possible for us to see the Sun's granules. The first telescope was powerful enough to reveal the first "blemishes" on the Sun's skin. Galileo and several others observed "spots" on the Sun.

Sunspots are likely to be cooler than the rest of the photosphere (about 8,132°F or 4,500°C). That is why they appear dark against the Sun. If you could put sunspots out into space they would shine brightly, like stars. The very dark central part of a sunspot is the **umbra.**

The lighter part around the umbra is the **penumbra.** In 1908, astronomer **George Ellery Hale (1868–1938)** came to the conclusion that sunspots were areas of intensely powerful magnetic forces thousands of times more powerful than the magnetic field of the Earth or the Sun. Sunspots vary in size from 2,000 miles (3,200 kilometers) across to more than 90,000 miles (144,000 kilometers) across. Most of them are bigger than the Earth.

In this next project, you can look at sunspots, the safe way, and see what the early Chinese observers and Galileo saw.

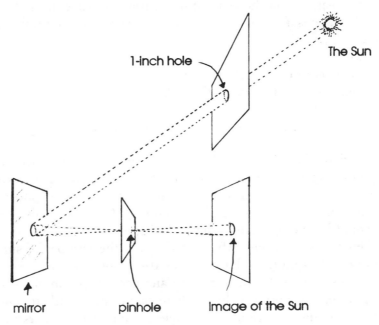

The Sun

1-inch hole

mirror   pinhole   Image of the Sun

Project 70: Examining Sunspots

MATERIALS

3 pieces of stiff, white paper   tape
scissors   newspaper
mirror   pencil
pin   paper
aluminum foil

PROCEDURE

1. Tape a sheet of white paper on the wall in a darkened room below a window through which the Sun is shining. Cover the window with newspaper except for one small section. Cover this section with a piece of paper that has a 1 inch (2½ centimeter) hole cut into the center.

2. Place a mirror on the opposite wall so that the sun hits it and is reflected onto the paper below the window.

3. Cut a square out of the center of another piece of stiff white paper. Tape a piece of aluminum foil onto the paper covering the square. Punch a tiny hole into the center of the aluminum foil no bigger than the diameter of the pin.

4. Put the piece of paper with the hole in it between the mirror and the paper on the wall focusing the image.

OBSERVATIONS

Check on the positions of the sunspots every day and sketch them noting the date of your observations. Do your findings indicate that the Sun is rotating?

The Sunspot Cycle   Around 1816, the German astronomer **S. H. Schwabe** (1789–1875) began observing sunspots as a hobby. After keeping track of his observations for 27 years, Schwabe announced in 1843 that every 10 years, the number of sunspots reaches its maximum. There may be months in between where there may be no spots. Further research has shown that this cycle is closer to 11 years than 10. In 1851, Schwabe said that there was also a greater sunspot cycle of 22 years. The following year people discovered that compass variations on the Earth follow the same 22 year cycle.

The 11 year sunspot cycle shows itself in a variety of ways in the life of the Earth. According to certain research, there is a definite 11-year pattern in nature that follows the 11-year sunspot cycle:
earthquakes,
changes in weather,
number of icebergs in the North Atlantic,
number of famines in India due to the lack of rain,
rings of growth in trees,
fosilized layers of sand and clay formed in glacial zones.

During the period when there are the least amount of sunspots, the spots group around 10° from the Sun's equator. When a new sunspot cycle begins, groups of new spots appear about 30° from the sun's equator. Sunspots often appear in pairs. The eastern spot in each northern hemisphere pair has a magnetic polarity, north for example. The polarity of the sunspots in the Southern hemisphere would be the opposite—south. The spots move across the Sun, lasting for about four days or less before disappearing. After a few years, the number of sunspots reaches a maximum, clustering around 20° from the solar equator. After about 11 years, the spots appear mostly around 10° from the Sun's equator again beginning another sunspot minimum cycle. This time, however, the eastern spots in the northern hemisphere pairs have south magnetic poles and those in the southern hemisphere have north magnetic poles. In another 11 years, when the poles reverse again, the Sun will have completed a full 22-year sunspot cycle and the magnetic charge of its poles will be the way they were 22 years ago.

Since all of the sunspots move in the same direction and become visible and invisible at regular times, Galileo and others felt that the Sun moved, not the sunspots.

"Having made repeated observations I am at last convinced that the spots are objects close to the surface of the solar globe where they are continually being produced and then dissolved, some quickly and some slowly, also that they are carried around the Sun by its rotation . . ."—Galileo

Based on the slight curve of the path which the sunspots follow, observers think that the Sun is tilted 7° 10' on its axis. In March, the Sun's north pole tilts away from the Earth; in September it tilts toward the Earth.

In the next project, you can figure out the sunspot cycle yourself in much the same way as S. H. Schwabe did.

Year	Number of Sunspots
1. 1711	0
2. 1716	70
3. 1722	15
4. 1725	40
5. 1728	135
6. 1732	7
7. 1739	125
8. 1741	28
9. 1743	6
10. 1750	90
11. 1752	55
12. 1754	50
13. 1756	15
14. 1758	50
15. 1761	80
16. 1766	20
17. 1770	130
18. 1771	40
19. 1773	35
20. 1775	5
21. 1778	165
22. 1784	18
23. 1788	140
24. 1797	6

Project 71: Calculating the Period of the Sunspot Cycle

MATERIALS

sunspot cycle chart
pencil
graph paper (photocopy from Sky Files)

colored pencils
access to a photocopier

PROCEDURE

1. Plot the sunspot numbers and dates from the chart (Sunspot Numbers for 86 Years, 1711–1797) onto a graph using a pencil and the graph paper.

2. Notice when the greatest number of spots occurs and the number of years in between. Also notice when the least amount of spots occurs and the number of years in between. Mark these with a colored pencil.

OBSERVATIONS

What is the average number of years in between the times when there are the most and the least number of spots? Can you see the 22-year cycle?

The Chromosphere   The lower atmosphere of the Sun is about 1,500 miles (2,500 kilometers) thick and about 110,000° Kelvin. The lower atmosphere takes light from the photosphere and sends it off in a rose-colored glow that you can only see during an eclipse or with a telescope specially adjusted to block out the light from the photosphere. We call the lower atmosphere the **chromosphere** because of its rose color. The chromosphere gets its red color from the bright hydrogen alpha line in the Sun's spectrum.

"During an eclipse, the Moon moves across the face of the Sun at some 200 miles per second; this means that the most interesting portion of the chromosphere, its lower 600 miles, shows for only 3 or 4 seconds. The upper chromosphere, which can extend for as little as 1,000 miles to as much as 10,000 miles above the photosphere, is seen for less than a minute. In the span of a century, the lower chromosphere is visible for a total of less than 10 minutes. An astronomer who observes 10 eclipses—far more than the average—may expect to observe this region of the chromosphere for no more than a minute in his lifetime, and that only if he (or she) is luckier than any other astronomer ever born."—p. 89 *The Solar Chromosphere* by E. Grant Athay, February 1962 from *Readings From Scientific American: Frontiers in Astronomy* San Francisco: W.H. Freeman and Co. 1970.

chromosphere comes from the Greek words χρωμα *(chroma)* = color

When you look at the chromosphere, what you are seeing is about half a million jets of burning gases shooting out from the Sun's surface all at different times. These jets look like spikes of iron filings standing up on a magnet. For this reason their name is **spicules.**

---

spicules comes from the Latin word *spiculum* = spear

Spicules shoot out at a speed of about 72,000 miles (115,200 kilometers) per hour. Each spicule lasts for about 2–15 minutes and can get as high as 8,000–10,000 miles (12,8000–16,000 kilometers). Spicules are about 500 miles (800 kilometers) in diameter (the width of the state of Colorado). The spicules send matter into the Sun's upper atmosphere. Intense ultraviolet radiation travels out from the chromosphere and becomes the source of the Earth's electrically charged ionosphere.

The Corona   You also can only see the Sun's upper atmosphere during an eclipse or by using special photographic equipment. People like Plutarch and Kepler who have seen it describe it as "pearly-white." The English amateur astronomer **Francis Baily** first used the word **corona** to describe what he saw that looked like the Sun's crown around the Sun during a total solar eclipse on July 8, 1842 .

---

corona comes from the Latin word *corona* = crown

The corona marks the boundary between the Sun and its magnetic field which extends out into space through the entire solar system as the **solar wind.** The solar wind is a stream of magnetized particles that projects out into space from sunspots and cooler places in the corona. The corona itself is millions of miles long and millions of degrees Kelvin hot. It looks like a filmy white halo around the Sun.

The **chronograph** is a photograph which you take through a telescope that has a disk covering the Sun from view just as it would be during an eclipse. This makes it so you can see the corona. Using this technique, people were able to spend 8½ months observing the corona aboard skylab in 1973 and 1974. Before the invention of the chronograph, the total time people were able to make photgraphic observations of the corona from 1839 to 1974 was less than 80 hours!

Flares   The dark ribbon you see around the edge of the Sun is the limb. Sometimes the Sun ejects hugh pieces of burning gas from the chromosphere into the corona. These erruptions of energy are **flares.** Electrically charged particles from solar flares disturb the corona and reach theh Earth's ionosphere within a few hours or days. They can disturb radio, television, telephones and electricity. They also produce the aurora borealis (northern lights) and the aurora australis (the southern lights).

Prominences   Sometimes large sheets of gas fly out from the Sun twisting themselves into high arched bridges of fire before they fall back into the Sun. These are **solar prominences.** They probably happen because of the Sun's changing magnetic charge. Solar prominences may be less warm than the chromosphere or about 15,000° Kelvin which is 2,240 ° F or 1,227° C.

During the solar eclipse of 1842 an observer who saw the corona and solar prominences exclaimed, "From the black rim of the Moon there suddenly shot forth three gigantic, purple-red tongues of flame. They paused motionless, like jagged mountain peaks in an alpine sunset. . . It was as if the Sun, behind the Moon, was flaring up in monstrous volcanic explosions."—from a journalistic account quoted in Rudolf Thiel's *And There Was Light: The Discovery of the Universe.* New York: Knopf, 1957.

READING MORE

Adams, Florence. *Catch a Sunbeam: A Book of Solar Study and Experiments.* New York: Harcourt Brace Jovanovich, 1978.

The Smithsonian Institution. *Fire of Life: The Smithsonian Book of the Sun.* New York: W. W. Norton and Co., 1981.

The Earth seen from the Moon. *Photo courtesy of NASA*

Section 2:   THE MOON

"Here men from the planet Earth first set foot on the Moon, July 1969 A.D. We came in peace for all mankind."—the plaque on the Eagle's landing stage.

In Scotland, France and England, stone circles have been found which line the viewer up with rising and setting positions of the Moon. These lunar observatories also recorded the 18.6 year eclipse cycle.

Names   In ancient Greece, the Moon, like the Sun, had two aspects. One was the actual moon itself as a sphere in the sky. The other was the character of the Moon and its relationship to life on Earth, particularly to nature during the night. The goddess of the sphere of the Moon in the heavens was **Selene** or **Luna.** We get most of our words about the Moon from these names. We call the "geography" of the Moon **selenography.** Things having to do with the moon are called **lunar.**

The goddess who best represents the influences of the Moon on the Earth is **Artemis** or **Diana.** Her brother is Apollo, the other Sun god. People in Greece observed that their vegetation flourished and spread the most during the cool nights with their heavy dew. The Greeks and others knew that more dew fell when the Moon was shining in a clear sky.

People said that Diana roamed by night through woods and groves, over hills and valleys accompanied by the nymphs of the fountains. People could feel her presence beside rivers, fountains, and marshes.

The Babylonians connected **Ishtar,** their Moon goddess, with springs and dew calling her the All-Dewy One. The great Summerian city of Ur, in lower Mesopotamia was especially devoted to the worship of the Moon as a male under the name of **Nanna** or **Nannor,** the father of the Sun god Shamash. The Akkadians called the Moon-god, **Sin,** "the lamp of heaven and Earth," "the lamp of all gods," "the Divine Cresent."

> "If the Moon rises pale, expect rain;
> if it rises clear, expect fair."

Some Native Americans would not go hunting if the horns of the Cresent Moon pointed upward. That meant dry weather and the hunter needed moist ground where tracks would show the best.

In 1932, the International Astronomical Union standardized the naming of lunar features. There is a crater on the Moon named after the American Astronomer **Maria Mitchell.** It is below Mare Frigoris and next to Aristoteles Crater at $+50°$ $+21°$.

Early Observations   There is an old song called "By the Light of the Silvery Moon." For many people, the Moon's light is silvery. The Peruvian Indians said that the Moon gave mankind the gift of silver from its tears. For the alchemist, silver was the metal associated with the Moon. The ancient Greeks discovered that the Moon shines from the reflected light of the Sun. In some ways the "silvery" Moon acts like a mirror which also is silvery. Similarly, the process of photography involves capturing the light reflected back to the camera from an object. The developing and printing process in the dark room uses silver to make the photographic image visible.

The View From Earth   As you know from your own experience watching the Moon, there are times when the whole face of the Moon is illumined. There are times when just a half of the Moon appears—and there are times when only a tiny part of the moon shines back down to us. At other times, the Moon is not visible at all.

There are many stories that tell why the whole Moon doesn't shine all the time. An old African folktale tells of the keeper of the great shining stone who would gradually cover the box containing the stone when the sky people got tired of bringing him food. When fresh supplies came, he opened the box again and the stone sent its light down to Earth.

To the ancient Babylonians, Ishtar (the Moon) is following Marduk's command always to shine less when in the presence of the Sun. The closer the Sun and Moon get to each other, the dimmer the Moon appears until it no longer shines. When the Sun is farthest away from the Moon, then Ishtar shines in her fullest glory as queen of the night.

As the Moon travels around us, making its way around the Sun, we observe changes in the amount of sunlight reflected back to us. We call these changes the **phases** of the Moon. A phase is part of a process. Each phase lasts for about a week, so all four phases equal about a month.

Phases of the Moon.

The Native Americans called the complete cycle of phases a **moon,** "see you in four moons" meant "see you in four months."

---

phase comes from the Greek word $\phi\alpha\iota\nu\omega$ *(phaino)* = to appear, to bring to light

---

In this next project you can show yourself how the Moon's phases occur and what they will look like.

—————— Project 72: Showing How the Moon's Phases Occur ——————

MATERIALS

 golf ball or some other light-colored ball planesphere (chart from project 18)
  with a dull finish   modeling clay

PART 1
PROCEDURE

 1. Stand facing *(but not looking directly at)* the Sun. Hold the ball in one hand at arm's length in front of you while pointing toward the Sun with your other hand.

 2. Move the ball through all of the phases on the chart. Keep looking at the ball and moving your body as necessary while keeping your other hand pointing toward the Sun.

 3. Stop when you get to the Full Moon. Your body should be facing sideways from the Sun, arms outstretched. Turn and face exactly the opposite direction, put the ball in the hand farthest from the Sun and point to the Sun with the hand nearest to it.

 4. Continue to move the ball through all of the phases until you return to the New Moon position.

207

OBSERVATIONS

Does the changing shape of the lightest part of the ball look like the changing face of the Moon during its phases? Do the dimples in the golf ball cast shadows like Moon craters?

PART 2
PROCEDURE

1. Make a small ball out of one color of modelling clay to be the *Sun*.
2. Make a small ball out of one color of modelling clay to be the *Moon*.
3. Place the Sun and the Moon in position in the plastic circle of the planesphere to help you answer these questions.

 a. Will the last quarter Moon on Midsummer's Day (June 21, Sun in Gemini) be high, medium, or low above the horizon?

 b. In what constellation will the first quarter Moon be in October (Sun in Libra) and at what time will it rise?

 c. In which season does the Full Moon appear highest in the sky?

OBSERVATIONS

Make up some questions of your own. Check your accuracy by setting up your planesphere for today and finding where the Moon should be.

Suppose you see the Moon some day or night. What phase would it be? What angle would be forming between the Sun, the Earth, and the Moon?

---

crescent comes from the Latin word *cresco* = to grow
waxing comes from the German word *wachsen* = to grow
waning comes from the Middle English word *wanien* or *wanen* = to lessen
gibbous comes from the Latin word *gibbus* = hump on the back

---

How can you remember which quarter moon is which, what side is lit and which side is dark? If you speak French, you can use the words for first and last to help you. *Premier* is the word for first and if you draw a line down from the first quarter Moon, (**P**) it forms the letter P (the first letter of the word premier). *Dernier* is the word for *last* and if you draw a line up from the last quarter Moon (**d**) it forms the letter d, the first letter in the word dernier.

You never see more than half the sphere of the Moon. When the half that you see is lit up, it is a full moon instead of a half moon because the full disk (not sphere) that you see is completely lit. The quarters refer to the moments when the Moon has completed a fraction of its journey around the Earth—either ¼ or ¾ of the way. It just so happens, that to your eyes on Earth, the Moon really is only one-fourth lit. The word **crescent** more accurately describes the growing time after the new moon and not the shape. **Waxing** and **waning** are clearer terms.

The horns or cusps of the Moon always point away from the Sun, like the curve of a bow whose arrow is aimed at the Sun.

Go outside and look at the Moon. What quarter is it? if it is the first quarter Moon, you are looking back along the path of the Earth's orbit to the place where the Earth was 3½ hours ago.

The Moon's Distance We had to know how far away the Moon was before we could send someone there. How did people figure it out?

The ancient Greeks used the angle the Moon's disk appears in the sky (½°), the diameter of the Earth's shadow compared to the Moon's (during eclipses), geometry and trigonometry to calculate the Moon's distance.

Anaximander (c. 611–546 B.C.) was the first to write about the subject of sizes and distances of planets, including the Moon. Anaximander suggested that the radius of the orbit of the Moon was 18 times the radius of the Earth. **Aristarchos** (c. 300–250 B.C.) suggested it was 9½ times the

The first photograph of the Earth and Moon seen together (*Voyager 1*, September 18, 1977). *Photo courtesy of Jet Propulsion Laboratory.*

diameter of the Earth. Hipparchos suggested the distance was 33⅔ times the diameter of the Earth. Ptolemy suggested it was 29½ times the Earth's diameter. Our current measurements put the distance of the Moon at 30.2 times the Earth's diameter?

In 1946, when **Zoltan Bay** sent a radar beam to the Moon some of the radio waves bounced back to the Earth. Radio waves travel at the speed of light. Half the time between when the radio waves are transmitted and received back is how long it takes the beam to travel. This figure multiplied by the speed of light tells you how far the beam travelled and that will give you the distance to the Moon.

The Moon's Orbit The Moon travels around the Earth. Since the Earth is traveling around the Sun, the Moon joins in the orbit around the Sun.

---

orbit comes from the Latin word *orbis* = circular path

The Moon's Diameter Once you know the Moon's distance, you can figure out its diameter. Another interesting way is to do the same experiment you did to find the diameter of the Sun in Project 69, Measuring the Sun.

Mapping the Moon In 1609, Galileo made the first sketch of the Moon from the telescope. In 1647, **Johannes Hevelius** (1611–1681) made the first accurate lunar map in his *Selenographia*. In 1840, various people provided us with the first detailed photographs of the Moon. In October 1959, a Soviet lunar probe sent back the first photograph of the "dark side of the moon." In 1651, Hevelius' friend **G. B. Riccioli** (1598–1671) published a two-volume work assisted by **Father Grimaldi** (1618–1663). Riccioli set the pattern for naming lunar features after great scientists, historic and political figures. In 1791, **J. H. Schroeter** (1745–1818) published the first volume of lunar studies. He discovered "rills" or "clefts"—long narrow valleys in the Moon's surface. In 1879, Nasmyth and Carpenter published a beautiful book of Moon maps. In their book the authors had made models from their drawings of the Moon which they photographed in sunlight to represent the Moon's surface as accurately as possible.

FEATURES ON THE MOON

Name of Feature	East(E)/West(W)	North(N)/South(S)
1. Albategnius	0	S21
2. Aliacensis	E4	S40
3. Alphonsus	W7	S22
4. Alpine Valley	0	N46
5. Alps Mountains	W3	N45
6. Apennine Mountains	W5	N18
7. Archimedes	W8	N28
8. Ariadaeus Rille	E14	N2
9. Aristarchus	W47	N24
10. Aristillus	W2	N32
11. Aristoteles	E11	N48
12. Arzachel	W7	S28
13. Atlas	E31	N46
14. Autolycus	W2	N29
15. Caucasus Mountains	E6	N33
16. Clavius	W11	S60
17. Copernicus	W26	N6
18. Delambre	E18	S9
19. Endymion	E47	N53
20. Eratosthenes	W17	N11
21. Eudoxus	E12	N42
22. Gassendi	W45	S25
23. Grimaldi	W62	S7
24. Hercules	E20	N44
25. Herodotus	W39	N24
26. Herschel	W8	S12
27. Herschel, Caroline	W31	N34
28. Herschel, John	W28	N51
29. Hipparchus	E3	S13
30. Horrocks	E4	S12
31. Julius Caesar	E15	N5
32. Kepler	W44	N4
33. Lacus Mortis (Lake of Death)	E18	N44
34. Lacus Somniorum (Lake of Dreams)	E25	N36
35. Langrenus	E59	S12
36. Macrobius	E44	N21
37. Maginus	W8	S55
38. Manilius	E8	N10
39. Mare Crisium (Sea of Crises)	E55	N16
40. Mare Foecunditatis (Sea of Fertility)	E50	S10
41. Mare Frigoris (Sea of Cold)	W15–E25	N53
42. Mare Humboldtianum (Humboldt's Sea)	E37	N58
43. Mare Humorum (Sea of Moisture)	W41	S32
44. Mare Imbrium (Sea of Rains)	W40–E5	N30
45. Mare Nectarius (Sea of Nectar)	E35	S25

FEATURES ON THE MOON

Name of Feature	East(E)/West(W)	North(N)/South(S)
46. Mare Nubium (Sea of Clouds)	W17	S29
47. Mare Serenitatis (Sea of Serenity)	E2–E29	N25
48. Mare Smythii (Smyth's Sea)	E69	0
49. Mare Spumans (Foaming Sea)	E61	0
50. Mare Tranquillitatis (Sea of Tranquility)	E30	N5
51. Mare Undarum (Sea of Waves)	E62	N7
52. Mare Vaporum (Sea of Vapors)	E1	N10
53. Maurolycus	E12	S48
54. Mitchell	E13	N48
55. Oceanus Procellarum (Ocean of Storms)	W50	N30–S20
56. Palus Putridenis (Marsh of Decay)	W3	N25
57. Pallus	W13	N1
58. Piccolomini	E30	S37
59. Pico Mountain	W10	N45
60. Piton Mountain	W4	N40
61. Posidonius	E27	N31
62. Ptolemaeus	W8	S16
63. Pyrenees Mountains	E40	S22
64. Rheita Valley	E39	S45
65. Ricciolli	W1	S2
66. Sinus Aestum (Seething Bay)	W14	N8
67. Sinus Iridium (Bay of Rainbows)	W27	N45
68. Sinus Medii (Central Bay)	W5	S5
69. Sinus Roris (Bay of Dew)	W4	N43
70. Straight Range	W18	N47
71. Straight Wall	W13	S31
72. Theophilus	E28	S18
73. Timocharis	W17	N25
74. Tycho	W13	S51

FEATURES ON THE MOON

Tides   We call the high and low ocean levels **tides** and their rhythm is 12½ hours from one high tide to the next. This means in most places high tides occur two times a day, fifty minutes later each day. Approximately every two weeks, unusually high and low tides occur. These are the **spring tides**. The word spring has nothing to do with the spring season.

In between this 14-day period, the difference in size between high and low tides is the smallest. These are the **neap tides**.

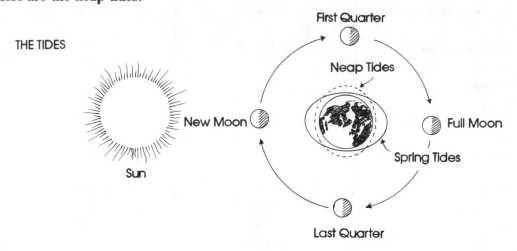

THE TIDES

First Quarter

Neap Tides

New Moon

Sun

Full Moon

Spring Tides

Last Quarter

Sir Isaac Newton researched the tides and their relationship to the Sun and the Moon. It was his feeling that the Moon (and the Sun a little bit also) tugged at the Earth at different places depending on how the Sun, Moon, and the Earth lined up with each other. The water on the Earth responded to the tug. As the Moon orbited the Earth its pull was strongest when the Sun, Earth, and the Moon were in a straight line. This happens twice a month. One of these times the Earth is in between the Sun and the Full Moon, and the other time the Earth is in between the Sun and the New Moon. The water on the side of the Earth nearest the Moon feels the greatest pull and swells outward in a **high tide.** The water on the other side of the Earth feels the least attraction so that it flows away from the Moon to produce another high tide. The high tides make the water level on the remaining parts of the Earth shallower, causing **low tides.**

Many people share Newton's tide theory. Others feel that the Moon's position and the tides are related but not caused by each other. No matter what opinion you share, you can demonstrate what the bulging of the waters on the Earth look like by doing this next project.

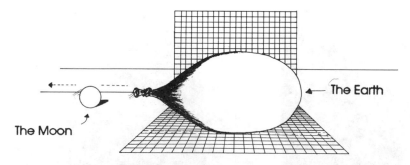

The Moon

The Earth

─────────── **Project 73: Showing How the Tides Occur** ───────────

MATERIALS

large balloon

water

stiff paper (photocopy from Sky Files)

twine

table

graph paper

books

felt-tip pen

access to a photocopier

PROCEDURE

1. Fill a balloon with water and draw a rough outline of the world and oceans on it, with the opening of the balloon on one of the sides. Tie a piece of twine about 1 inch (2.5 centimeters) onto the end of the balloon. Set the balloon on a piece of graph paper. The balloon is the *Earth.*

2. Stand another piece of graph paper behind the balloon. Hold it up with a stack of books.

3. Draw a little picture of the Moon about 2 inches (5 centimeters) in diameter on the stiff paper, leaving enough paper below it so you can fold it and make a stand for the Moon.

4. Place the Moon about 6 inches (15 centimeters) from the Earth with the twine behind it.

5. Pull quickly on the twine. The twine is the *pull* on the Earth from the Moon.

OBSERVATIONS

The side you pull on and the side opposite will bulge and the top will go down. Mark on the graph paper sheets how far the balloon bulged and flattened.

Eclipses   The Earth is four times the size of the Moon but farther from the Sun. The Sun is 390 times larger than the Moon. It is also 390 times farther from us than the Moon. Because of this relationship, both the Sun and the Moon appear to us as being the same size in the sky. If the Moon passes directly in front of the Sun, it can cover the sun's disk leaving the Earth in darkness. If the Earth passes directly in between the Moon and the Sun, it blocks the Sun's light from reaching the Moon and casts the Moon into darkness. In both cases, the light from the Sun has left the sky for a brief but startling moment, taking with it the essence of all life. We call this moment an **eclipse.**

---

eclipse comes from the Greek word ἐκκλειψις *(ekkleipsis)* = abandonment

---

Eclipses can also happen in other parts of the solar system. When we on Earth are experiencing a total lunar eclipse, what would the view be like from the Moon?

Lunar Eclipse   When the Moon is full, if the alignment of the Sun, Earth, and Moon is perfectly straight, the sunlight will hit the Earth and not the Moon. The view of the Moon from the Earth will show the unlit part of the Moon as a black shadow. This is a **lunar eclipse,** and because only part of the moon is eclipsed, it is a **partial lunar eclipse.** The Earth's shadow is circular. This led the Pythagoreans in Greece to conclude that the Earth is a sphere. Because the Earth and the Moon are traveling in their orbits around the Sun, the shadow of the eclipse on the Moon will be moving at a speed of about 2,000 miles or 3,200 kilometers an hour.

When the Earth completely blocks the path of the sunlight from the Moon, the eclipse is **total.** Instead of a black, unillumined Moon, we have a coppery-red Moon that looks like a gooseberry. The light from the Sun is refracted by the Earth's atmosphere which acts like a lens, bending the light and focusing it on the Moon. The atmosphere absorbs some of the blue and violet in the Sun's spectrum so that the light that reaches the Moon and is reflected back to us is the orange/coppery-red part of the spectrum.

The Moon's diameter is 2,160 miles (3,476 kilometers) and the Earth blocks out the sunlight for an area of about 5,700 miles (9,173 kilometers). If the Moon passed straight through the area of darkness, how long would the eclipse last?

Only about 1/6 of the lineups of the Sun, Earth, and Moon produce eclipses.

Why don't we have a lunar eclipse at every Full Moon? If the Sun, Earth, and Moon were always in a straight line with each other, we would. The Sun stays at one end of the line while the Earth and Moon take turns being in the middle and on the other end. The Moon as it travels around the Earth has its own orbit. The path of this orbit takes the Moon above and below the path of the Earth traveling around the Sun. At one point on the journey, the Moons's path is 5.2° above the Earth's path for half a month. At another, it is 5.2° below for the other half of the month. The Moon's path crosses the Earth's path (the ecliptic) twice. When it is level with the Earth's path and is about to cross it, we call that point the **node.** If the Moon above the path, it crosses the **ascending node.** If the Moon is heading below the path, it crosses the **descending node.** When you draw a line between the two nodes you have the **Nodal Line.**

---

node comes from the Latin word *nodus* = knot

In order for there to be a lunar eclipse:

a. the Moon must be in its full position at one end of the line, with the Earth in the center and the Sun at the other end. This occurs every 29.53059 days.

b. The Moon must be at one of the two nodes which occurs every 13½ days.

c. The nodal Line must point to the Sun. This occurs once every 346.6 days.

d. The full Moon cycle and the eclipse year must coincide. This occurs 223 lunar months (29.53059 days) equal 6,585.321 days; 19 eclipse years (346.6200 days) equal 6,585.781 days.

Every 18 years and 11 days a cycle of eclipses can occur. This period is the **saros cycle.** Babylonian astronomer-priests discovered and named the saros period around 2000 B.C. The saros period is a geographic cycle which charts the regular appearance of eclipses in the same places on the Earth.

The Moon's orbit moves just like the Earth's. In Chapter 1, you found that the Sun traveling on the ecliptic doesn't return to its exact starting point. It actually falls short of reaching this point by one degree every 72 years. The vernal equinox or the point on the zodiac where the Sun's path crosses the celestial equator giving us spring, moves a little each year. We call this the precision of the equinoxes. The Moon nodes also move backward along the ecliptic, taking 18.61 years to complete one rotation. Once every 346.6201 days (18.6 days short of a full year) the nodal lines point to the Sun. We call this 346.6 day period the **eclipse year.**

---

saros is a Greek word which comes from the Assyrian-Babylonian word *sharu* = repetition

---

SEVERAL ECLIPSE TRACKS FROM THE SAME SAROS SERIES
From Eclipse by Brian Brewer, Seattle: Earth View Books

In a typical saros cycle 48 or 49 lunar eclipses occur within a period of 865 years and 70 or 71 solar eclipses in a period of about 1,200 years. This means nearly every year you can see a lunar eclipse from where you live. The next group of eclipses takes place about 120° west of the longitude where you saw the first group because the Earth has turned ⅓ of a revolution on its own axis during that time. After every three cycles the eclipses return to the original longitude where they were at the start of the cycle 54 years before. The latitude will be farther north or south depending on whether the series started at the Earth's north or south pole.

Draconic Month   The length of time it takes for the Moon to return to a node is 27.2 days. To the ancients this was the month of the dragon or the **draconic month.** The ascending node was the mouth of the dragon, the descending node was its tail. We still use the symbol ☊ for the dragon's head or ascending node, and the symbol ☋ for the dragon's tail or descending node. Some people think the symbols show the head and tail swallowing the Sun.

---

draco = comes from the Latin word *draco* = dragon or serpent

---

Solar Eclipses   The earliest record of a solar eclipse is in the ancient Chinese document *Shu Ching.* The date was October 22nd, 2134 B.C. when "the Sun and Moon did not meet harmoniously." The two royal astronomers **Hsi** and **Ho** failed to predict the event, which meant that people weren't prepared to make noise and shoot arrows into the sky to frighten away the Sun-eating dragon. For neglecting their duty the Emperor had the astronomers beheaded.

People all over the world have taken the idea of eclipses very seriously. Some cultures (India, Japan, China) consider the temporary loss of the Sun or Moon to be a bad omen. In the absence of the light and the forces of life, the forces of death and darkness are free to roam. Other cultures (Tahitians, Eskimos, Aleuts, and Tlingits) see eclipses as the Sun and the Moon leaving their places to visit each other or to see that things are going all right on the Earth.

Solar eclipses can only occur at the time of the new moon. The minimum number of solar eclipses in any calendar year is two. The maximum is five. A total eclipse takes place on the same spot on the Earth only once every 360 years. A total solar eclipse usually lasts only two or three minutes, the longest it can last at any one place is seven and one half minutes. You can only see a total solar eclipse from a point on the narrow path of totality the eclipse makes on the Earth as it passes by.

A total solar eclipse, Okinawa, Japan, September 23, 1987.

Total   If a solar eclipse occurs when the Moon is closest to the Earth and farthest from the Sun the disk of the moon completely covers the Sun, blocking out all its light. The stars and brighter planets come out, birds stop chirping and the temperature drops. This is a **total eclipse.**

Annular   If a solar eclipse occurs when the Moon is at its greatest distance from the Earth, and nearest the Sun, the Moon looks slightly smaller than the Sun and does not cover it completely. The uncovered outer ring of the Sun continues to shine as a ring of light around the blacked out area. We call this kind of solar eclipse an **annular eclipse.** During an annular eclipse, the sky remains bright and you cannot see the Sun's corona.

---

annular comes from the Latin word *annulus* = ring

Partial   When a solar eclipse occurs, the Moon is not directly in front of the Sun but very close, the Moon's disk will "bite" a little piece out of the Sun as it passes by. This is a **partial eclipse.**

Stonehenge   **Gerald Hawkins** and **Fred Hoyle** have suggested that people used Stonehenge to predict eclipses. There are 56 holes around Stonehenge called **Aubrey holes** after John Aubrey, a seventeenth century researcher of ancient history who discovered them in 1666. These chalk-filled holes are about 3 feet (1 meter) deep and were dug about 300 years before the stones of Stonehenge went up.

One complete Moon node revolution is $3 \times 18.6 =$ almost 56. Moving a marker in the Aubrey holes, three holes each year = one complete journey around the circle of 56 holes in 18⅔ years. Two markers on opposite sides of the Aubrey ring would always show the position of the Moon nodes.

If a Sun marker moved two holes every 13 days, it would take 364 days (56/2 × 13) or only 1¼ days less than a full year to go completely around. This would measure the length of the year. If a Moon marker moved two holes every day, it would take 28 days (56½) to go completely around. This would measure the length of the lunar month.

If a marker moved three holes every day until it went around the circle twice (2 [56/3]) this would measure the length of the **eclipse year.** Figuring out when the Moon was at its most southern or northern part of its orbit was one of the purposes of the architecture of Stonehenge and other stone circles and lines. One-fourth of a month later the Moon would be crossing one of its nodes. All of this information gave potential dates for eclipses.

Maya Calendar   Two Maya Sacred Rounds (see Chapter 1, Section 4) of 260 days each = 520 days. The line of the Moon's nodes points to the Sun every 173.31 days. 3 × 173.31 = 519.93 days, or about 2 hours less than 2 Maya Rounds. Here is another means for predicting eclipses.

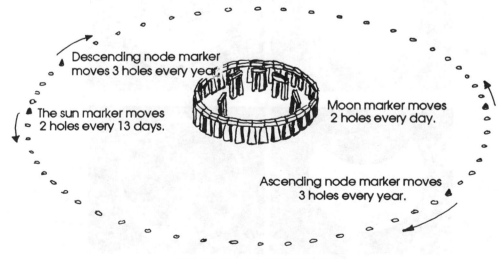

Descending node marker moves 3 holes every year.

The sun marker moves 2 holes every 13 days.

Moon marker moves 2 holes every day.

Ascending node marker moves 3 holes every year.

THE CIRCLE OF AUBREY HOLES

Composition   The Moon has no atmosphere, nor any traces of water on its surface. The crust of the Moon appears to be thicker than the Earth's. It is covered with craters, mountains, plains, and valleys. The Moon's surface contains about 58% oxygen, 20% silicon with aluminum, calcium, iron, magnesium, and titanium. Samples from the Moon's surface contain basalt and volcanic minerals such as plagioclase and pyroxene as well as some minerals which don't exist on Earth. One of these is the mineral **armalcolite** which is named for the crew of Apollo 11, *Arm*strong, *Al*drin and *Col*lins.

On Earth we only see one side of the Moon. Soviet space probes have provided us with views of the "dark side of the Moon." In this next project you will be sketching the "near side of the Moon" using a technique that makes your drawing look real.

Astronaut Alan Bean examining *Surveyor 3* on the Moon, 1969.
Photo courtesy of Johnson Space Center, NASA

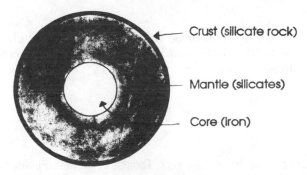

Crust (silicate rock)

Mantle (silicates)

Core (iron)

THE INTERIOR OF THE MOON

——————— Project 74: Sketching the Moon ———————

MATERIALS

telescope
pencil (soft lead)
file or fine sandpaper
tissue paper
drawing paper (smooth surface)
soft eraser
clipboard

small flashlight
dowel
tape
2 rubber bands
stiff paper
brown paper bag
photograph of Moon

PROCEDURE

1. Wedge the dowel into the hole at the top of the clipboard and mount the flashlight on it with a rubber band. This will be your drawing lamp.

2. Draw a circle about 3½–4 inches (10 centimeters) in diameter.

3. File or sand your pencil so you can collect some powdered "lead." Pick up some lead with a piece of tissue paper placed over your finger. Rub the lead on the circle so it becomes an even light grey all over.

4. Put the paper onto the clipboard and take it outside on a clear night when you can see the Moon's craters clearly through the telescope. Study the Moon for awhile noticing the light and dark areas.

5. Draw the outlines of the shapes you want onto the grey circle. Make sure the sizes and shapes of the craters and their positions near each other are correct. If you make a mistake, don't erase—just redraw. Use the flashlight to help you see your drawing.

6. Erase the grey background to indicate bright areas.

7. Darken the grey background to indicate dark shadows and emphasize crater edges. Don't outline the white areas.

8. Bring your drawing indoors and touch up using a photograph of the Moon as a guide. Remember, the photograph may have been taken at a different phase so the light and dark areas will be different.

OBSERVATIONS

You can use this technique later to draw the planets seen through the telescope.   This project is adapted from *Modern Astronomy: An Activities Approach* by R. Robert Robbins and Mary Kay Hemenway, Austin: University of Texas Press, 1982. Used with permission.

READING MORE

Alter, Dinsmore. *Pictorial Guide to the Moon.* New York: Thomas Y. Crowell, Publishers, 1973.
Brewer, Brian. *Eclipse.* Seattle: Earth View, Inc., 1978.

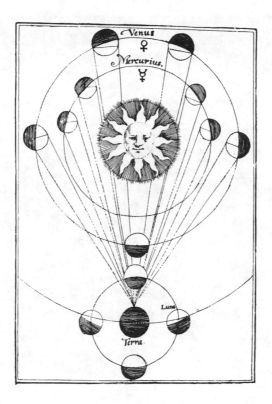

Section 3: THE INNER PLANETS

Mercury   Have you ever noticed a bright object in the early evening sky, raying out with such intense light that you wondered if it was an airplane? Some people have mistaken this bright light for a spaceship from another planet. This "star" is actually a planet, the planet Venus. Together with Mercury, the planet Venus travels in between the orbit of the Earth around the Sun. For this reason, these two planets are called the **inner planets.** The closeness of these two planets to the Sun helps make them shine so brightly. Because they pass in between the Earth and the Sun, the inner planets go through phases like the Moon. While Mercury and Venus share these features in common, they are two very different planets.

Names   The Greeks associated Mercury with the god Hermes and called it Stilbon "the twinkler." Hermes-Thoth invented astrology, astronomy, mathematics, geometry, medicine, grammar, and music. The Polynesians called Mercury Na-holo-holo which means "running to and fro."

Stilbon comes from the Greek word στιλβω *(stilbo)* = to shine, glitter or glisten

---

The names of the cliff lines (scarps) of Mercury come from historic ships of discovery and exploration, such as Endeavour (Captain Cook's ship), Santa Maria (Columbus' ship), and Vostok (a Soviet spacecraft). Some plains have the name of Mercury in different language such as Tir (ancient Persian), Odin (in ancient Scandinavia), and Suisei (in Japan). The sea which is nearest to the spot where the Sun is overhead when the planet is closest to it is Caloris (heat). The names of craters come from nonscientific authors, composers, and artists, as well as scientists such as Kuiper (astronomer).

Early Observations   Mercury appears for eight weeks as a morning object, rising just before sunrise and then eight weeks as an evening object, settling just after the Sun does. This cycle occurs three times during the year. The Greeks saw these two appearances of Mercury as two separate aspects of the gods. The Mercury that appeared in the morning they called Apollo and the evening appearing planet was Hermes.

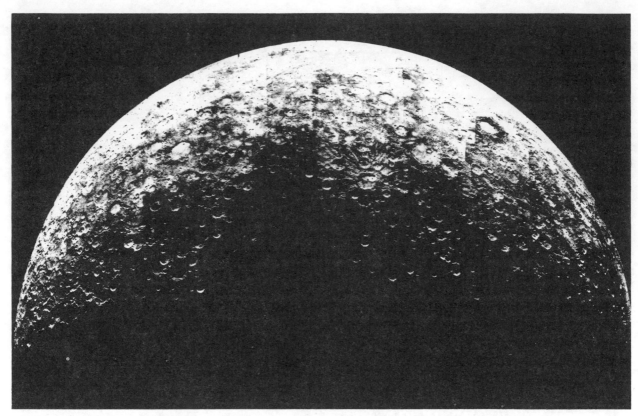

A photomosaic of Mercury (*Mariner* 10, 1974). *Photo courtesy of NASA*

Since the Earth is turning at a rate of 15° an hour, the Sun always rises or sets within about two hours of Mercury's rising or setting. Mercury's closeness to the Sun (it's never more than 28° away) makes it difficult for us to get a good look at it. The sky is often too full of sunlight and the planet is very close to the horizon. For these reasons, many people have never seen Mercury. Even Copernicus, who lived to be 70, sadly regretted on his deathbed that he never saw the planet. In Northern Europe where Copernicus worked, you can only see Mercury occasionally in the misty twilight.

The best time to observe Mercury is when it is farthest from the Sun (aphelion) and when it appears farthest east or west of the Sun (elongation). At these times Mercury is 28° from the Sun as seen from the Earth. The most visible eastern elongation times occur in August and September when Mercury appears in the east before sunrise as the morning star. The most visible western elongation times occur in March and April when Mercury appears in the west as the evening star just after sunset. Even at these times you can only see Mercury for about a half hour.

The View From Earth   Mercury is brighter than any star, except Sirius, and brighter than any object in the solar system except the Sun, the Moon, Venus, Mars, and Jupiter. Like the Moon and Venus, Mercury goes through phases from new to full. When it is full, it is farthest away from the Earth so that the brilliance you would expect becomes dimmer because of the distance. You can only see the gibbous and crescent phases of Mercury.

Except for Pluto, Mercury has the most elliptical orbit of all the planets. Mercury and Venus are both within the orbit of the Earth around the Sun. This means that as each planet travels around the Sun it passes in between the Earth and the Sun for part of its journey. When Mercury is exactly in between, we call its location an **inferior conjunction.**

---

inferior comes from the Latin word *inferior* = lower, further down or underneath

---

As the planet continues along in its orbit around the Sun, it goes behind the Sun and out of our view. When it is exactly on the outside of a line-up of the Sun in the middle and the Earth on the inside, we call its position a **superior conjunction.**

Mercury is in its new phase at inferior conjunction, and full at superior conjunction. Unlike the Moon, when Mercury or Venus are at the new phase, they are closer to the Earth and appear larger. At the full phase, they are farthest away from the Earth and appear much smaller.

During an inferior conjunction, Mercury sometimes crosses directly in front of the Sun. Because of the variation (inclination) of their orbits from the ecliptic, Mercury and Venus pass directly in front of the Sun only rarely. This crossing is a **transit.**

If the planet were bigger or farther away, a transit would cause a solar eclipse. Instead, you can only see a small dark spot moving across the face of the Sun. You need Sun filtering equipment to detect this dot without harming your eyes. The complete transit of Mercury takes up to four hours as the planet moves from east to west across the Sun. In the United States, the Naval Observatory records transits of Mercury to accurately monitor the Earth's rotation and to correct clocks. Transits of Mercury occur either in May or November every seven or thirteen years. The next transit of Mercury will be on November 14, 1999.

Both Mercury and the Moon have thousands of craters on their surface. In this next project you can make some of those craters yourself.

Project 75: Making Craters on Mercury

MATERIALS

metal pie pan
plaster of paris
small stones
corn starch or white flour
water

newspaper
fine dirt or coffee granules
camera or pencil and paper
chair you can stand on

PART 1
PROCEDURE
1. Spread newspaper on the floor and place a pie pan in the middle.
2. Cover the bottom of pie pan with a layer of dirt or coffee granules.
3. Cover the dirt layer with a layer of white flour or cornstarch.
4. Drop small stones one by one onto the flour while you kneel, stand, and stand on a chair.
5. Throw a stone carefully onto the flour straight down and then at an angle.
6. Photograph or draw your results.

PART 2
PROCEDURE
1. Empty the pie pan and return it to newspaper.
2. Mix enough plaster of paris to fill the pie pan almost to the top. The mixture should be as thick as syrup.
3. Fill the pie pan almost to the top with plaster of paris. Gently tap pan onto floor to remove air bubbles.
4. Repeat steps #4 and #5 from Part 1.
5. Photograph or draw your results.
6. Let the plaster of paris harden for about 10 minutes and repeat steps #4 and #5 again.
7. Photograph or draw your results.

OBSERVATIONS
Compare the photographs or drawings of your craters with photographs of the surface of Mercury. What does this project tell you about the effects of meteors on soft and hard surfaces of the planets?

Composition   Craters cover half of Mercury's surface. The other half is mostly smooth plains. There is a covering of fine dust on the planet's surface at least several inches or centimeters deep. If you look very carefully at the craters on Mercury, compared to those on the Moon you will notice that there are several important differences.

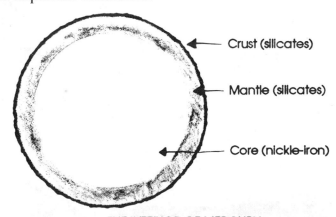

THE INTERIOR OF MERCURY

MERCURY
1. There are plains or smooth areas between craters and basins.
2. There are not many large craters with diameters between 12–30 miles (20–50 kilometers).
3. You can still see the results of early cratering
4. There are shallow cliffs (scarps) which run for hundreds of miles or kilometers.
5. When an object strikes Mercury and makes a crater on the planet's surface, the rocks and dust that are sent out will only cover 1/6 the area they would cover on the Moon. This is because the force of gravity on Mercury is twice as strong as it is on the Moon.
6. On Mercury, smaller craters tend to cluster more around larger craters than they do on the Moon.

MOON

1. The highland plains show densely packed and overlapping craters.
2. There are many large craters.
3. Rocks and dust scattered from recent impacts have covered much of the earlier craters.
4. There is stretching rather than cliffs.

While Mercury appears to be like the Moon on the outside, it is more like the Earth on the inside. Mercury's interior may have a core of iron which takes up about 50% of the planet's volume or 70% of its mass.

Around the planet there is a veil-like blanket of helium gas, far thinner than the atmosphere around the Earth. There is no real protective atmosphere around Mercury. There is, as around the Earth, a magnetosphere. Mercury does not rotate fast enough to create a magnetsophere, but somehow the planet generates one of its own. The solar wind is not the source.

Temperature   Because one-half of Mercury faces the Sun for 176 Earth days, while the other half faces away from it and is in darkness, Mercury has the strange combination of being the hottest and the coldest planet in the solar system. It lives up to its name, mercurial, which means changeable.

The sunlit side of Mercury reaches temperatures of 660°F or 350°C. When the planet's orbit brings it close to the Sun (perihelion) this temperature can get as high as 775°F or 412°C, hot enough to melt lead. The side of Mercury that is in darkness is not far from −459°F or −273°C. This is even colder than the temperature on the planet Pluto, the planet farthest from the Sun. These extreme temperature ranges are greater than those of any other planet.

Venus

Gods and Goddesses   The name Venus comes from the Roman goddess of love and beauty. Her Greek name was Aphrodite. The Phoenicians called her Astarte.

The ancient Babylonians worshipped Venus first as Inanna and later as Ishtar. During the reign of **King Ammisadugua** (1646–1626 B.C.) at the time of the great lawgiver **Hammaurabi** (1792–1750 B.C.) and his dynasty, astronomer-priests recorded regular observations of the dates when Venus was the Morning and Evening Star.

To the Maya of Central America, Venus was the god Quezalcoatl. Certain Mexican creation stories and epic tales describe the soul of a deceased hero passing to the east. There it descends into the underworld. This visit to the land of the dead lasts for eight days, the period during which Venus is invisible between her appearances as the Evening Star and the Morning Star. The resurrected hero then rises from the underworld to climb up the steps of the sky. Finally, the hero joins the creator in the "heart of heaven" at the zenith or noonday position of the Sun directly above the Earth. Compare this 8-day journey with the 72-day journey of the soul after death in ancient Egypt. See Chapter 1, Section 4.

Adjectives used to describe Venus include Venusian, Venerian, Cytherian (from the island Cythera, where Aphrodite lived). The names of plateaus on Venus come from different titles for the goddess Venus. There is an Ishtar Terra (Babylonian) and an Aphrodite Terra (Greek).

Early Observations   In Central Mexico in the buildings at Uxmal, there are buildings directed towards Venus. The axis of the front of the Palace of the Governor is 29° east of north. Every eight years, the astronomer-priest standing in the doorway of the Palace of the Governor would see Venus as Morning Star rising at its farthest position to the south.

In 1980, archeo-astronomers **Anthony Aveni** and **Horst Hartung** measured a perpendicular line to the front of the Palace. They found that their line was within 1/30 of a degree of the exact position of Venus at her maximum southern rising position.

The planet rose over the top of a pyramid nearly 100 feet (30 meters) high, about 6 miles (10 kilometers) east of Uxmal in the town of Nohpat. You can see the top of the pyramid from the doorway of the Palace. The facade of the Palace displays over 350 sculptured Venus signs like the one shown below. The two circles may represent Venus as the Morning and Evening Stars. There are 584 "X" shapes between the horizontal bars on the buildings. The number 584 was important to the Maya because it was the number of days it took Venus to complete her orbit.

To the ancient Greeks, Venus as morning star was Phosphorus or Lucifer—the light bearer. To the ancient Egyptians, the morning star was Tioumoutiri, the evening star was Quaiti. To the Quiche of Guatemala, Venus as the morning star is Santiago, and Raskap (thing of night or something late). The evening star was Hesperus. Observers (perhaps Pythagoras was the first in the sixth century B.C.) later realized that these two stars were actually one planet—Venus.

The View From Earth   We sometimes call Venus our sister planet because of all the planets, Venus seems most like our Earth, at least in size, mass, and density. Photographs of the two cloud-covered planets often resemble each other. Venus also approaches the Earth more closely than any other planet (30 million miles or 40 million kilometers away). You can see it for a longer time than Mercury. Due to Earth's rotation of 15° every hour, you can only see Venus three hours before sunrise or three hours after sunset.

Venus commands attention. Her beauty radiates with more visible light than any star or planet in the sky except for the Sun and Moon. Venus shines with a steady white light with an apparent magnitude of −4.4. At night, light from Venus can cast a shadow. If you know where to look, you can even see Venus in the daytime. This next project shows you how.

——————— **Project 76: Finding Venus Morning, Noon, and Night** ———————

MATERIALS

empty papertowel holder or roll of stiff paper

flat black paint

astrolabe or quadrant/azimuth measuring instrument (from Projects 34 and 36)

planetary table (available from *Sky and Telescope* or *Astronomy* magazine, planetarium or astronomy department at local high school or college)

PROCEDURE

1. Blacken the inside of a paper tube with flat black paint.
2. Consult the planetary table to find out where Venus is:

a. If Venus is behind the Sun, you can't see her yet.

b. If Venus is the morning star, face east before sunrise, raise your arm in front of you about 45° above the horizon. The brightest star you are pointing to is Venus.

c. After the sun rises, locate her position in the daytime sky from the planetary chart. Use your astrolabe or quadrant to find the number of degrees above the horizon. Venus, like the Sun, will move 15° every hour. Aim your paper tube to a position between the Sun and the Eastern horizon that is at the indicated altitude.

d. If Venus is the evening star, face west just after sunset, raise your arm in front of you 45° above the horizon. The brightest star you are pointing to is Venus.

OBSERVATION

How can you be sure that you are looking at Venus and not a star?

Like Mercury, Venus goes through a complete cycle of phases. Galileo was the first to report these phases in 1610. Galileo announced this discovery, which his former pupil **Beneditto Costelli** had probably shared in making, to **Giuliano de'Medici** in Prague. He made his announcement in a code called an anagram. It said: *Cynthiae figuras aemulatur mater amorum,* which means "the mother of love (Venus) imitates the shape of Cynthia (the Moon)."

Like Mercury, Venus also experiences inferior and superior conjunctions. These affect the apparent size of the planet's disk. When Venus is at full phase during its superior conjunction, you cannot see the planet because the Sun blocks your view. At the new phase and inferior conjunction, the Sun shining from behind the planet makes it impossible to see Venus. Your usual view of Venus, like that of your view of Mercury, is during its gibbous or crescent phases. Venus is at her brightest during the crescent phase about 36 days before and after an inferior conjunction. The angle between Venus and the Sun (elongation) at these times is about 39°, which gives the planet plenty of distance away from the light of the Sun. The combined movement of the Earth and Venus means that you would need almost 20 months to see Venus go through all of its phases. Venus cloud cover makes for terrific reflection of the Sun's light. More than 70% of the light received is reflected back. At every inferior conjunction, Venus presents the same face to Earth.

Transits of Venus across the Sun are rare, occurring in 1874, 1882, and then 2004 and 2012.

Composition: **Interior** The *Mariner 2* spacecraft launched by the United States in August 1962 passed within 22,000 miles or 35,200 kilometers of Venus. It recorded yellowish-white clouds completely covering the planet. The *Mariner 10* came within 4,000 miles or 6,400 kilometers of Venus in February 1974. It recorded that clouds swirl around the planet at speeds faster than 150 miles or 240 kilometers per hour. Large convection currents also occur in the clouds on the side of Venus which faces the Sun. On October 22, 1975, the Soviet spacecraft *Venera 9* landed on Venus sending photographs and other information back to Earth for 53 minutes. Three days later *Venera 10* landed and sent more information for 65 minutes. The photographs from these two unmanned probes were the first ever taken from the surface of another planet.

A view of Venus (*Mariner 10*, 1974). *Photo courtesy of Jet Propulsion Laboratory*

225

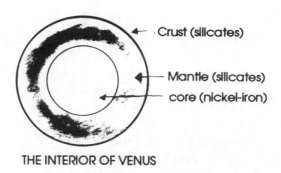

Crust (silicates)

Mantle (silicates)

core (nickel-iron)

THE INTERIOR OF VENUS

Most of our recent ideas about Venus come from the information we received from these two spacecraft. We know almost nothing about the interior of Venus. Astronomers assume that the mean density of Venus is similar to that of Mercury and the Earth. Because of its place in the solar system and the similarity of much of its physical characteristics to Mercury and the Earth, astronomers also assume that Venus' interior is also similar. We have looked for and have not detected much of a magnetic field around the planet.

Plateaus, canyons, mountain ranges, and volcanoes seem to make up only 5% of the surface of Venus, most of the planet is level. There are mountains in the **Maxwell Montes** range which we have calculated to be 2.22 miles or 3.7 kilometers taller than Mt. Everest.

Exterior The thick blanket of clouds around Venus move across the planet's surface once every four days. These clouds are part of a four-layered atmosphere surrounding the planet. The tops of the clouds may be a mixture of droplets containing sulfuric acid and water.

In 1761, observations suggested that Venus had an atmosphere. Studies in 1937 suggest that the atmosphere of Venus is 98% carbon dioxide. 0.3% of water vapor is in Venus' lower atmosphere. This combination of a thick layer of carbon dioxide and water vapor creates a condition between the atmosphere and the surface of Venus where heat energy from the Sun enters but cannot escape. This situation reminded people a little of what takes place in a greenhouse. The two conditions aren't really the same, but there is a similar quality of collecting and holding solar energy so that the temperature inside is greater than the temperature outside. This is the **greenhouse effect.** In the case of the greenhouse, the closed glass panels hold the warm air in and prevent cold air from the outside from entering. The clouds over Venus hold in the infrared energy once it enters the lower atmosphere, preventing it from returning out into space. In this next project you can create the greenhouse effect.

The **greenhouse** effect also takes place inside your car on a sunny day when all of the windows are up.

Project 77: Demonstrating the Greenhouse Effect

MATERIALS

aquarium
glass or plastic wrap to fit top of
   aquarium
dry ice (frozen carbon dioxide)
2 thermometers

light source
aluminum foil pan
flat black paint
water

PROCEDURE

1. Paint the aluminum foil pan flat black.
2. Put a block of dry ice in the pan and set the pan at the bottom of the aquarium. Pour a little water on the dry ice.
3. Place a thermometer at the bottom of the aquarium near one of the sides so you can read it.
4. Cover the top of the aquarium with a glass lid or plastic wrap.
5. Place the other thermometer on top of the glass or plastic.
6. Shine a light down onto the top of the aquarium.
7. Read and record the temperatures inside and outside.

OBSERVATIONS

What do the two temperatures tell you is happening? Are the clouds of smoke from the dry ice collecting in one area more than another?

Venus has water, light and carbon dioxide. As you saw in Chapter 4, Section 1, these are the ingredients needed for photosynthesis to occur. For this reason, some people feel that Venus could possibly support some form of life. What do you think?

READING MORE

Asimov, Isaac. *Venus, Near Neighbor of the Sun.* New York: Lothrup, Lee and Shepard Books, 1981.

Briggs, Geoffrey, and Frederick Taylor. *The Cambridge Photographic Atlas of the Planets.* Cambridge: Cambridge University Press, 1982.

Motz, Lloyd. *On the Path of Venus.* New York: Random House, 1976.

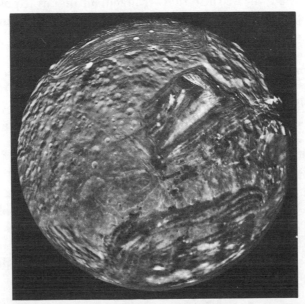

A computer-assembled mosaic of Uranus' moon, Miranda, Voyager 2, January 26, 1986.
Photo courtesy of NASA

Section 4: THE OUTER PLANETS

Mars   Beyond the Earth, heading out away from the Sun, are the orbits of the outer planets, Mars, Jupiter, and Saturn. Together with the Earth, Moon, inner planets and the Sun, the outer planets formed the boundary of the universe as people knew it from the beginning of time until as recently as 1781. We know more about these three planets than we know about any of the others. You can observe the planets Mars, Jupiter, and Saturn easily with your naked eye.

   Names   To the Greeks, Mars was Ares, the god of War and lover of strife, the son of Zeus and Hera. The Romans called Ares "Mars." The Babylonians called the planet Nergal, the "Star of Death." The red color of Mars has added to the picture of the anger and bloodshed which war brings.

   Most of the names of the canals and the dark and light areas on Mars come from Schiaparelli who chose names of places around the Mediterranean sea. In those days, planetary mapmakers named dark areas on the planets after bodies of water, as in the mare (seas) on the Moon, sinus (bay or gulf), lacus (lake), lucus (grove or wood), fretum (strait or channel), and palus (swamp).

   More recently people have chosen the names of scientists for craters and even the Mariner spacecraft for the largest canyon: **Valles Marineris**—the Valleys of Mariner.

   Early Observations   Mars was Tycho Brahe's favorite object, even without the benefit of a telescope. Tycho set Kepler to work to find a satisfactory theory of planetary motion based on observation. To do this, Kepler used Tycho's vast records of 38 years of observations of Mars.

   The first person to see Mars through a telescope was probably Galileo. In 1610, he wrote that he could see the planet as a disk and that it had phases. In 1666, **Giovanni Domenico Cassini** (1625–1712) discovered the rotation period of Mars. In 1830, **Sir John Herschel** (1792–1871) noted,

"In this planet we frequently discern, with perfect distinctness, the outlines of what may be continents and seas . . . (and) the appearance of brilliant white spots at its poles . . . which have been conjectured . . . to be snow."

   In 1869, **Father Angelo Secchi** in Rome drew a map of Mars. On his map, Father Secchi drew streak-like markings which he called **canali.**

Canali comes from the Italian word for channels.

   Because the orbit of Mars is an ellipse, Mars is almost twice as close to the Earth around August when it is in opposition to the Sun. Because this arrangement makes it possible to see Mars better, we call it a "favorable opposition." Most of our information about Mars, including the discovery of its two moons, came during these favorable oppositions. These occur every 15 or 17 years. The most recent one was in September 1988. Mars is farthest away from the Earth in February.

   In 1877, there was a favorable opposition of Mars which made it possible to make detailed observations of the planet. That year **Giovanni Schiaparelli** (1835–1910), the director of an observatory in Milan detected what appeared to be a number of long narrow lines on the surface of Mars. These dark lines seemed to come from the "ocean" areas on Mars. They cut across the "continents" forming a network which connected the various "seas" together. Schiaparelli popularized Father Secchi's term **canali** for these lines.

   To English-speaking people, the word canali suggested the word canals. The word canals suggested that some one or some thing had built them. The person who took this suggestion most seriously was **Percival Lowell** (1855–1916). With his own money, Lowell built an observatory in the exceptionally clear air of Mars Hill in Flagstaff Arizona to study Mars and to look for other planets. In his second book, *Mars and Its Canals and Mars As the Abode of Life*, Lowell put forth his ideas about the planet and the Martians who built the canals to irrigate their desert homeland. Several other observers in different locations also noted the canals. Surprisingly, the canals have never showed up in any of the photographs taken by the spacecraft which have mapped the entire surface of Mars. Like many other things about Mars, the canals remain a mystery.

Percival Lowell's map of Mars. *Photo courtesy of Lowell Observatory*

The View From Earth   Of all the planets, Mars is in the best location for observers on the Earth. Mars is the only planet whose solid surface you can see with a telescope. Mercury is too near the Sun and the other planets are either covered with clouds or too far away. The best telescopes show Mars to be a patchwork of red, grey, white, and yellow. The red areas are probably deserts and occur mostly in the northern hemisphere covering about 60% of the planet's surface. The grey areas (about 40% of the planet) occur mostly in the southern hemisphere.

The north and south poles take turns having a white polar cap during the winter, depending on which pole is pointing away from the Sun. The white cap builds up in several days extending 20° to 30° from the pole. Then it remains one size for the rest of the winter season. In the spring, the polar cap gradually breaks up until, in the summer, it is completely gone. The south polar cap usually becomes larger than the northern one.

Sir William Herschel was the first to carefully study these polar caps. Herschel noticed that the caps were largest from three to six months after the winter solstice on Mars. They then got smaller until they reached their smallest size about three to six months after the summer solstice.

From the point of view of an observer on Earth, it looks like Mars' orbit makes loops. During these loops, the planet appears to be going backwards. You can demonstrate how this happens in this next project.

November 20, 1979

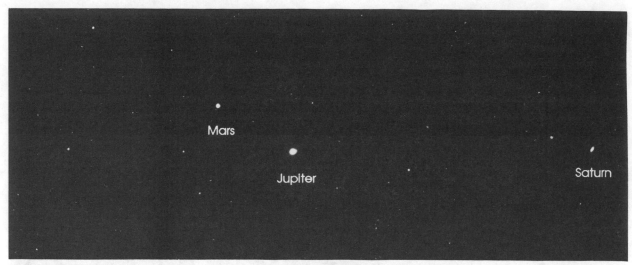

December 4, 1979

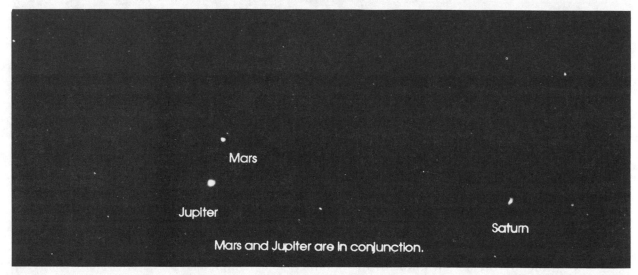

Mars and Jupiter are in conjunction.

December 13, 1979

January 10, 1980

The Retrograde Motion of Mars. *Photographs by Richard Moeschl*

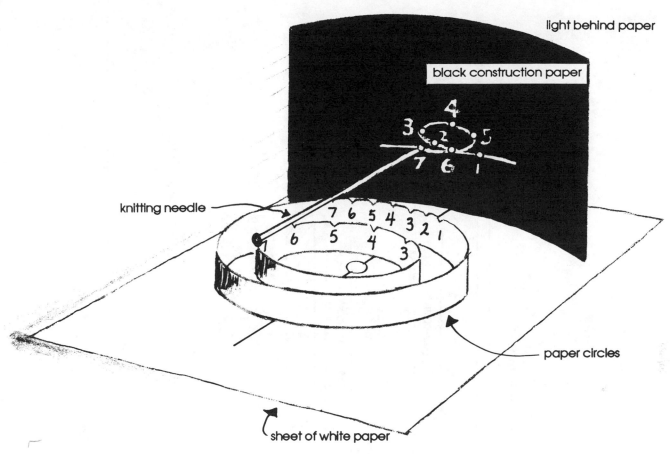

light behind paper

black construction paper

knitting needle

paper circles

sheet of white paper

— Project 78: Showing How Mars "Goes Backwards" (Retrograde Motion) —

MATERIALS

stiff paper
knitting needle
pencil
scissors
colored felt-tip pens (red and green)
white colored pencil
black construction paper

paper glue
ruler
sheet of cardboard
straight pins
tape
light source

PROCEDURE

1. Draw the two patterns from the following page onto stiff paper. Color the longer one red for Mars and the shorter one green for Earth. Cut them out and glue each into a circle.

2. Draw a straight line down the middle of the sheet of cardboard. Place the *Earth* circle in the middle so that the number four is above the line. Pin the circle to the cardboard. Pin the *Mars* circle into place on the cardboard so that the space between it and the Earth circle is even all around.

3. Stand the black construction paper up a few inches from the Mars circle in a curved position. Mark this curve on the cardboard and tape the construction paper in place.

4. Lay the knitting needle down on the two circles so that it lines up with the slot numbered one in each circle.

5. Bring the point of the needle right up to the black construction paper and push it through the paper. Mark this hole "1" in the construction paper with the white colored pencil.

6. Repeat step #5 for all the numbered slots. (In the illustration the needle is lined up with #7.)

7. Shine a light on the back of the black construction paper to see how the path of Mars appears to go backwards.

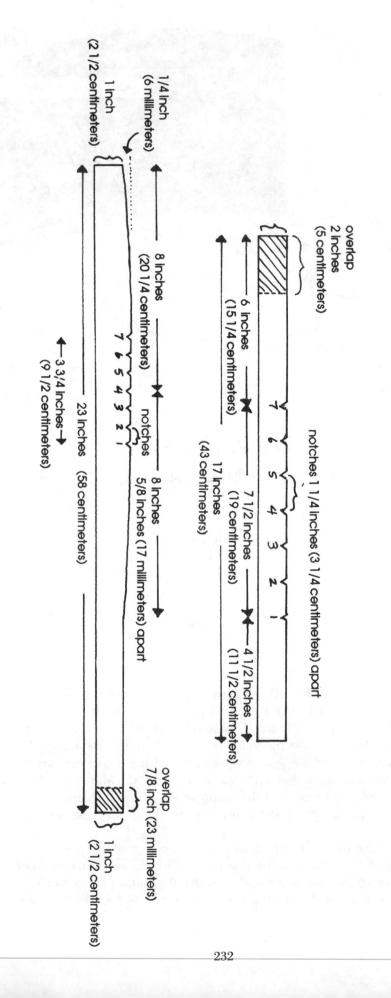

overlap
2 inches
(5 centimeters)

1/4 inch
(6 millimeters)

1 inch
(2 1/2 centimeters)

8 inches
(20 1/4 centimeters)

6 inches
(15 1/4 centimeters)

notches 1 1/4 inches (3 1/4 centimeters) apart

7 1/2 inches
(19 centimeters)

17 inches
(43 centimeters)

4 1/2 inches
(11 1/2 centimeters)

notches
8 inches
5/8 inches (17 millimeters) apart

3 3/4 inches
(9 1/2 centimeters)

23 inches   (58 centimeters)

overlap
7/8 inch (23 millimeters)

1 inch
(2 1/2 centimeters)

OBSERVATION

How would an ancient astronomer explain the backward movement of Mars from the point of view of a centrally placed, nonmoving Earth?   This project is adapted from *Everybody's Guide to Astronomy* prepared by the editorial staff of *Popular Science Monthly*, New York: Popular Science Publishing Company, 1934.

The View From Space   Exactly seven years after the first human set foot on the Moon, the first spacecraft landed on the surface of Mars on July 20, 1976. Called the *Viking 1*, this landing probe and the one after it, *Viking 2* have provided us with photographs and much information about the surface of Mars, its atmosphere and temperature.

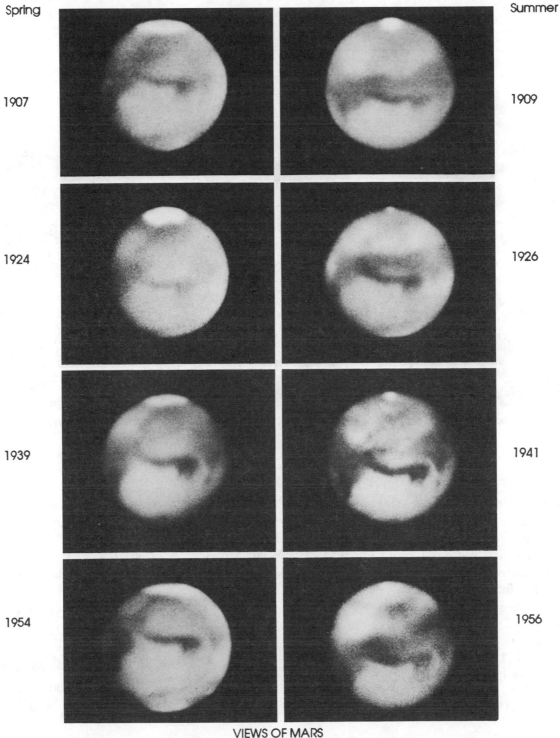

Spring   Summer

1907   1909

1924   1926

1939   1941

1954   1956

VIEWS OF MARS
Photo courtesy of Lowell Observatory

Composition   Mars appears like a rusty version of the Moon with fewer craters and bigger mountains. The red surface of Mars is from the iron dust that blows across the face of the planet at 100 miles or 160 kilometers per hour. Every ten years, a hugh dust-filled hurricane sweeps over the planet, eroding craters, covering rocks, hiding mountains, filling in craters and valleys. Sometimes the storms expose layers of darker rocks under the red dust. There are large smooth areas on Mars where lava once flowed from one of the planet's twelve volcanoes. The largest of these volcanoes is **Olympus Mons,** the biggest volcano we know of anywhere in the universe. It is 15 miles (25 kilometers) high and 360 miles (580 kilometers) across. Mt. Everest on Earth is about 5 miles (9 kilometers) above sea level, Mauna Kea, the largest volcano on Earth would almost fit into the 42 mile (70 kilometer) opening at the top of Olympus Mons.

The old name for Olympus Mons was **Olympus Nix** (the snows of Olympus).

Taking samples from the surface of Mars (*Viking 1*, 1978). *Photo courtesy of Jet Propulsion Laboratory*

Valles Marineris is a huge canyon on Mars almost as long as the width of the United States. Its branches are bigger than the Grand Canyon. Valles Marineris is only one example of many dry river beds, streams and even islands which show that there may have been running water on Mars. Now the planet is dry and wind-swept much like the North American Southwest.

From information gathered by the Viking missions in 1976, the atmosphere of Mars appears to contain the following:

Carbon dioxide, 95%
Nitrogen, 2 to 3%
Argon, 1 to 2%
Oxygen, 0.1 to 0.4%
Water, 0.01 to 0.1%
Krypton, less than 0.0001%
Xenon, less than 0.0001%

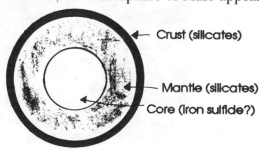

← Crust (silicates)

← Mantle (silicates)

← Core (iron sulfide?)

The Martian sky is pink, not blue.

THE INTERIOR OF MARS

Mars (Viking 2, 1976). Photo courtesy of NASA

Temperature The cloudiness surrounding Mars makes for incredibly high humidity. The thin atmosphere is almost saturated. Ground fog is everywhere. Because of this thin atmosphere, the temperature plummets very quickly after sunset to well below zero.

The maximum temperatures at the Martian equator are about 86°F or 30°C. The temperatures at the equator are much lower, around −40°F or −40°C at sunrise and −4°F or −20°C at sunset. At night the temperature drops to nearly −104°F or −75°C. The temperature at the South polar cap is about −238°F or −150°C.

In some ways the seasons on Mars are like those on the Earth. Venus, Earth, and Mars share many qualities. These have earned them the name **terrestrial planets,** since they are in many ways, Earth (*terra*)-like.

Moons Two small moons travel around Mars. In 1610, Kepler predicted they were there. **Jonathan Swift** (1667–1745) described them in 1726 in his book *Gulliver's Travels* and the French author **Voltaire** (1694–1778) wrote about them in 1752 in his book *Micromegas.* All of this is amazing since the two satellites weren't discovered until 1877! In August of 1877, **Asaph Hall** (1829–1907) of the U.S. Naval Observatory found the satellites when he was looking through what was the largest telescope in the world, a 66 centimeter refractor. He named the moons for the two sons of Mars: **Phobos** (fear) and **Deimos** (panic). Hall also named the largest crater on Phobos, **Stickney,** after his wife's maiden name. The other children of Mars are Terror, Trembling, and Ruiner of Cities.

Phobos is 5,800 miles or 9,380 kilometers from the center of Mars and takes 7 hours and 39 minutes to travel once around the planet. Phobos rises in the west and sets 4½ hours later. An unevenly shaped, pockmarked rock, Phobos is about 10 miles (25 kilometers) wide. Phobos goes around Mars three times in the time it takes Mars to turn around once. This appears to be the only place in the universe where such a relationship exists. For every complete journey of the Moon around the Earth, the Earth rotates 27 times. Even the Sun rotates several times before even the fastest moving planets have orbited once around the Sun.

Deimos is 14,600 miles (23,500 kilometers) from the center of Mars and takes 30 hours and 18 minutes to circle the planet. Deimos rises in the east and goes through two complete phases before it sets in the west. Like Phobos, Deimos is a slightly elongated, pockmarked rock made of dark materials and is very old. Deimos is 7 miles (13 kilometers) wide.

Mariner 9 launched in November 1971 is also a satellite of Mars. The first man-made satellite to orbit a planet, Mariner's orbit ranges from 1,025 to 10,610 miles (1,640 to 16,976 kilometers) above the surface of Mars.

Kepler was the first to use the word **satellite** as a name for a moon going around a planet. Satellite comes from the Latin word *satelles* = attendant or bodyguard.

Asteroids

Names   There are other orbiting bodies in our solar system. Because they look star-like, John Herschel named them **asteroids.** They are not stars. They are more like small planets which makes their other names **planetoids** or **minor planets** more accurate.

---

asteroid comes from the Greek word ἄστερ *(aster)* = star

Most asteroids lie in the asteroid belt between the orbits of Mars and Jupiter. Others have their own orbits which cross the orbits of the Earth and Mars. Some are in two swarms along Jupiter's orbit. An asteroid has two parts to its name: a number for the order in which it was discovered and a proper name. The proper names come from Greek and Roman mythology, heroines from **Richard Wagner's** (1813–1883) operas, wives of discoverers, friends, flowers, cities, colleges, pets, even favorite desserts and a computer (NORC). There are over 2,300 named minor planets. There are probably 100,000 more waiting to be charted and named.

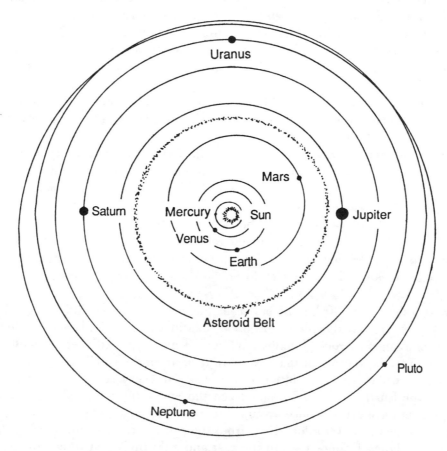

THE ASTEROID BELT
From Teaching with NightStar by Richard Moeschl

236

Asteroid 2005 is named in honor of **Karl Hencke** (1783–1866) postmaster and amateur astronomer who discovered the fourth asteroid, **Astraea** in 1845. Asteroid 1000 is named **Piazzia,** number 1001 is **Gaussia,** 1002 is **Olbersia.** Olbers also has a crater on the Moon named after him. Vesta is the only minor planet you can see without a telescope.

Early Observations   According to the Titius-Bode Law, there "ought" to be a planet in the space between Mars and Jupiter, two Astronomical Units from the Sun. In 1800, **Baron Francis Xavier von Zach** assigned a team of astronomers their own sections of the zodiac to search for the "missing planet." One of the astronomers, **Guiseppi Piazzi** (1746–1826) hadn't received his assignment yet when he discovered a new object on January 1, 1801, the first night of the nineteenth century. Piazzi felt certain that the object was moving and thought he had found a new comet.

Since the object was 2.8 Astronomical Units from the Sun, von Zach was sure the moving object was the "missing planet." He needed to know the object's orbit, but to do that would take nearly a year of continued observation. The object moved in the sky near the Sun and wouldn't be visible again for eight months. Everyone was afraid that it would never be found again. A young mathematician in Germany, named **Karl Friedrich Gauss** (1777–1855), invented a new way to calculate orbits and in November sent his results to von Zach. Using these calculations, von Zach saw the object on December 7th and again on December 31st, right where Gaus said it would be. On January lst, 1801, one year after Piazzi had first seen the new object, a doctor and amateur astronomer in Prussia named **Heinrich Wilhelm Mattias Olbers** (1758–1840) also found the object. The object was clearly not a comet, it was a small planet. At Piazzi's request the object received the name **Ceres,** the goddess of agriculture and the protecting goddess of Piazzi's native Sicily.

While tracking Ceres, Olbers discovered a second asteroid on March 28, 1802. He named it **Pallas.** In 1803, **Carl Harding** (1765–1834) discovered **Juno.** All three of these asteroids are about 2.8 Astronomical Units from the Sun. For this reason Olbers thought they might be the remains of a planet which had exploded. Astronomers today challenge this theory because asteroids contain different minerals, and there don't seem to be enough pieces to form a planet. Some observers believe instead that these particles were going to combine to become a planet and didn't.

Jupiter

Names   Jupiter is the Roman name for the Greek god Zeus. The Romans also called him Jove. It is by this name that the British swear when they say, "By Jove!".

Early Observations

1610—Galileo was the first to see the face of Jupiter through telescope.

1664—**Robert Hooke** (1635–1703) first recorded the Great Red Spot.

1672, 1691—Drawings by Cassini showing the Great Red Spot.

1831—The first time anyone saw the Great Red Spot through a telescope.

The View From Earth   Moving at a slow, regal pace, shining with a dazzling white brilliance, Jupiter was obviously the king. Jupiter is the second brightest planet after Venus. It reflects back a little more than half of the light it receives even though the amount it receives is far less than what Venus receives. Jupiter radiates out about 2.5 times as much energy as it receives from the Sun. If Jupiter were as near to the Sun as Mars, it would be the brightest planet in the sky and we could see it in the daytime. Because it is so far from the Sun, Jupiter appears fully lit to us, even though it has a gibbous phase.

Jupiter spins around faster than any of the other planets. We can tell this by timing the movement of certain patterns in the outer clouds. Jupiter's quick rotation has caused the planet to flatten at the poles and to spread out at the equator. You can notice this flattening when you look at the planet through a telescope.

The View From Space   The *Voyager* space probe took many images of Jupiter from 1977 to 1981. These images have provided us with our most recent and detailed glimpses of the giant planet. Jupiter appears to be a world of swirling clouds of gasses and molten metals. These clouds get thicker as you approach the center, gradually forming into a mushy "soup." The storms which create the swirls appear to occur regularly. They form the bands on the planet with distinctive markings of blue, orange, green, red, white, yellow, and grey.

Voyager 1 revealed much information about Jupiter, including a few surprises. One of the surprises was that Jupiter had a thin ring around it, an honor previously reserved only for Saturn. Jupiter's ring is much thinner and narrower, about 18 miles (30 kilometers) thick and apparently made up of very tiny particles. The most notable marking on Jupiter is the Great Red Spot, which received its name in 1887. It is about 8,400 miles × 18,000 miles (14,000 kilometers × 30,000 kilometers). It is thought to be a giant storm center circulating counterclockwise, which travels around the planet at its own rate, in six days. It is 3°C cooler then the surrounding atmosphere.

The surface of Jupiter, including the Giant Red Spot
(*Voyager 1*, March 1979). *Photo courtesy of Jet Propulsion Laboratory*

Composition Jupiter is the biggest of the gas planets. For its size, physical properties, and numbers of satellites, Jupiter is its own solar system, with a "Sun" of gas and liquid rather than fire.

Jupiter gives off more heat energy than it receives from the Sun. The center of the planet seems to be very hot, about 54,000°F or five times the temperature of the surface of the Sun. It is not clear whether this center is solid or liquid. The core may be about the size of the Earth and made from molten iron silicate. Above the core are two thick layers composed mainly of hydrogen. We don't really know what is happening in the interior of Jupiter. Some of the conditions that people have suggested, such as liquid metallic hydrogen, do not exist on Earth.

We know more about the wildly swirling clouds of Jupiter's multicolored atmosphere. We can copy some of these conditions in the laboratory. There are a great number of charged particles around Jupiter as part of the planet's magnetic field. Jupiter also has radiation belts, much like the Van Allen belt around the Earth. Jupiter has an extremely large and complex magnetosphere which extends 450 million miles (720 kilometers) around the planet. Jupiter's magnetic field is about 20 to 30 times more powerful than that of the Earth. Like the Earth's magnetic field, Jupiter's north and south magnetic poles are tilted from the planet's axis. We call the bright horizontal bands around the planet **zones.** They are usually light tan or yellowish. The dark horizontal bands are **belts.** They are usually brown, reddish, or greenish.

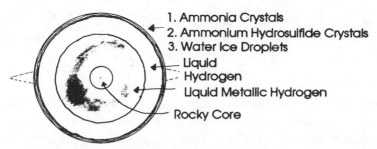

1. Ammonia Crystals
2. Ammonium Hydrosulfide Crystals
3. Water Ice Droplets
Liquid
Hydrogen
Liquid Metallic Hydrogen

Rocky Core

THE INTERIOR OF JUPITER

Jupiter has several layers of clouds, possibly containing hydrogen, helium, methane, and ammonia. The amounts of hydrogen and carbon (in various chemical combinations) compared to each other are very close to the ratio of the same elements found in the Sun. Clouds swirl around the planet in a continuous 300 miles (480 kilometers) per hour storm. The colors and patterns are so bright and so large you can see them through a telescope.

Jupiter's atmosphere is more like the oceans on Earth rather than its winds. Jupiter's atmosphere includes:

GAS	ESTIMATED PERCENT BY MASS
Hydrogen	60%
Helium	36%
Water	0.9%
Ammonia	.05%
Argon	.03%
Methane	.02%

Views from *Voyager* of Jupiter's dark side showed auroras and giant lightning bolts. In mythology, Zeus (Jupiter) often hurled lightning bolts.

The planet's outer atmosphere is quite cold, about -184°F or -119°C.

Moons In 1610, Galileo observed Jupiter through his telescope and found four satellites. They were traveling around Jupiter like planets around the Sun, like a miniature solar system. This discovery supported the heliocentric model of the Sun and the planets that Copernicus had suggested. In it, the Earth was not the central point for all revolutions.

The Galilean Moons of Jupiter (*Voyager 1*, 1979).
Photo courtesy of Jet Propulsion Laboratory

"I had now decided beyond all question that there existed in the heavens three stars wandering around Jupiter just as Venus and Mercury do around the Sun . . . there were not only three such stars; four wanderers complete their revolutions around Jupiter."—Galileo in *The Starry Messenger*

Simon Marius (1517–1624) a German astronomer, also observed the four moons of Jupiter. He gave these satellites their present names **Io, Europa, Ganymede,** and **Callisto** after friends and lovers of Jupiter (Zeus). See the Chart of Gods and Goddesses in Sky Files. We call these four largest of Jupiter's moons the **Galilean Satellites** after Galileo. These moons are equal to or larger than our Moon. You can easily see them with binoculars as a string of tiny pearls next to the giant planet. Jupiter has at least 11 more moons, which you can only see with a telescope or with the aid of cameras on a space probe.

The views which the Voyager cameras made of the Galilean satellites provided us with incredible sights and perplexing mysteries.

Jupiter has 16 moons. They are, in order of distance from the planet, closest first: Adrastea, Metis, Almalthea, Thebe, Io, Europa, Ganymede, Callisto, Leda, Himalia, Lysithea, Elara, Ananke, Carme, Pasiphae, and Sinope.

In this next project you can do what Galileo and Marius did and watch Jupiter's moons circle around the great planet.

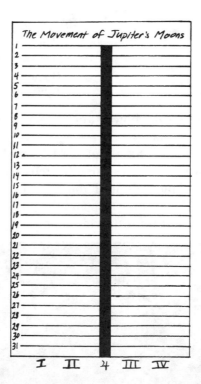

—————— **Project 79: Charting the Movement of Jupiter's Moons** ——————

MATERIALS

    telescope or binoculars   colored pencils and paper

PROCEDURE

1. Draw a chart like the one shown, one line for every day of the month.
2. Number each starting point from left to right beginning with Roman numeral I.
3. Choose a color for each number (use the ones suggested below or choose your own):

      I = blue   III = purple

      II = brown   IV = green

4. Observe the movements of each moon every night for a month. Enter the positions in color on the chart. If a night is cloudy, don't mark the positions for that date.

5. Draw the pattern or trail made by the movement of each moon as it appears on the chart at the end of the month. Use the same colors and lightly connect the changing positions of each moon. If you can, show where the moon went in front or behind Jupiter.

6. Write the names of each moon next to the number which shows its path based on what you know about these four satellites.

OBSERVATION

Charts like this one often appear in astronomy magazines like *Sky and Telescope* for all the planets and Earth's Moon as well as the moons of Jupiter.

Saturn

Names   **Saturn** is the father of Jupiter in Roman mythology. The Greeks knew him as Cronos. Saturn or Cronos ruled over time. To the ancients, Saturn or Cronos was the great grandfather of all the gods, the farthest of all the planets from the Earth and the nearest to heaven.

Early Observations   Through his telescope, Galileo observed two strange shapes on either side of Saturn. Either the planet's face had ears or else there were two large moons, one on each side.

"I have discovered a most extraordinary marvel, which I want to make known to their Highnesses and to your Lordship, but I want it kept secret until it is published in the work which I am going to have printed. . . . The fact is that the planet Saturn is not one alone, but is composed of three, which almost touch one another and never move nor change with respect to one another. They are arranged in the form o O o, as I will show their Highnesses this autumn, when it will be very easy to observe the celestial object with all the planets above the horizon."—Galileo, July 30, 1610.

Galileo was astonished when he saw Saturn two years later. The two satellites on either side had vanished.

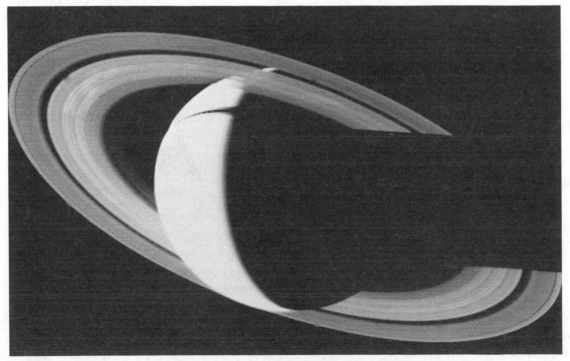

Saturn (*Voyager 1*, November 16, 1980).
Photo courtesy of Jet Propulsion Laboratory

In 1655 **Christian Huygens** (1629–1695), using a more powerful telescope than Galileo had, announced that Saturn's two large moons were in fact one large ring which surrounded the planet. Huygens also discovered the first satellite of Saturn, **Titan. Giovanni Domenico Cassini** noticed a division which separated the ring into two unequal parts. We still call this division, **Cassini's division.** Cassini also discovered the second, third, fourth, and fifth satellites of Saturn before becoming blind in 1710.

The sight of Saturn surrounded by its rings is a strangely beautiful one. Even though the ancients knew and saw Saturn well, they never shared this view which requires a telescope.

The View From Earth From the telescope, Saturn's rings appear to have three sections, called the "A" (outer), "B" (middle) and "C" (inner) rings. Cassini's division is between the A and B rings. The rings are thin and probably mostly ice. Because of the planet's tilt, you see the rings either from above or from below as Saturn makes its 29 year journey around the Sun. The rings are so thin (about 2 miles or 3.6 kilometers) that when they are facing you edge on as they do every 15 years, you can't see them. This is what happened when Galileo was watching them. Saturn is inclined 27° to its orbit, giving the planet seasons with a temperature of −292°F (−180°C). Saturn glows as a bright yellowish spot, the size of a star. At opposition, Saturn shines as bright as a 7th magnitude star.

The View From Space From the *Voyager* spacecraft, we have seen five ring sections, A through E. Each ring has many thousands of tiny ringlets and spaces in between. The surface of Saturn shows the same kinds of swirls that we saw on Jupiter. See Project 48, Interpreting Patterns of Movement in Water.

Composition The inside of Saturn is very similar to that of Jupiter, probably with a rocky core. Saturn's atmosphere is also very similar in chemical composition to that of Jupiter and the Sun.

Like Mercury, Earth, and Jupiter, Saturn has a magnetic field. Saturn's field is about 500 times

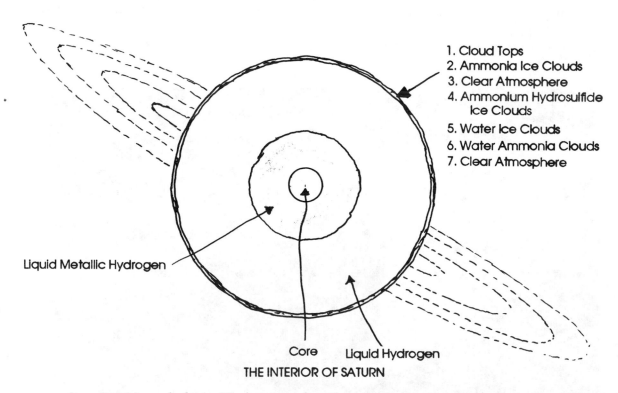

1. Cloud Tops
2. Ammonia Ice Clouds
3. Clear Atmosphere
4. Ammonium Hydrosulfide Ice Clouds
5. Water Ice Clouds
6. Water Ammonia Clouds
7. Clear Atmosphere

Liquid Metallic Hydrogen

Core   Liquid Hydrogen

THE INTERIOR OF SATURN

stronger than Earth's and about 35 times weaker than Jupiter's. As with Jupiter, Van Allen belts of radiation surround the planet.

Winds blow across Saturn at 400 miles (1,700 kilometers) per hour, which is four times faster than on Jupiter. The atmosphere contains: hydrogen, helium, methane, ammonia. The whole planet is so light that it could float on water.

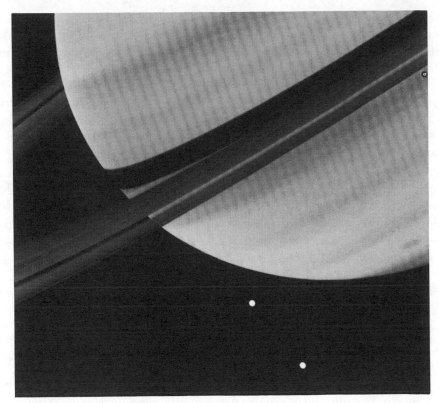

Saturn with two of its moons, Tethys (above) and Dione (below). Taken by *Voyager 1*, November 3, 1980.
Photo courtesy of Jet Propulsion Laboratory

Moons   Saturn has 17 moons. They are, in order of distance from the planet, closest first: Atlas, Inner F Ring Shepherd Moon, Outer F Ring Shepherd Moon, Epimetheus, Janus, Mimas, Encledaus, Tethys, Telesto, Calypso, Dione, S XII, Rhea, Titan, Hyperion, Iapetus, and Phoebe.

Saturn is such an fascinating planet to look at that its picture appears everywhere. Everyone knows what Saturn looks like with its famous rings. In this next project you can build a model of this amazing planet that can hang from the sky in your room.

—————————— **Project 80: Making A Model of Saturn** ——————————

MATERIALS

hollow ball about four inches in diameter

paints

felt-tip pens

plastic sheet

thin fishing line

thumb tack

razor blade or knife

rubber band

protractor

straight pin

electrical tape

drawing compass

PROCEDURE

1. Divide the ball in half with a rubber band. Make sure it is even all around. Make a mark ⅛ inch (3 millimeters) above and below the rubber band all the way around. Cut through both of these lines as carefully as you can so that your cuts are straight.

2. Paint the ball to look like Saturn. Use a photograph of the planet as a guide.

3. Put a protractor next to top half of the ball and make a mark on the top 27° from the center.

4. Push a straight pin through 27° mark. Remove the pin and thread the fishing line through the hole. Tie the end inside the ball into several knots and tape it down with electrical tape.

5. Cut out an 8 inch (20 centimeter) diameter circle from the plastic sheet.

6. Place one of the ball halves on a piece of paper and trace its outline. Draw another circle around it with a 5½ inch (14 centimeter) diameter. Remove the ball and place the clear plastic circle on the paper with the outline of the ball in the center.

7. Put a colored felt-tip pen in the compass (or tape it to the side of the compass) and draw concentric circles on the plastic sheet. Show the dark divisions between the rings. Use lighter colors to fade towards the outer circle on the paper. There should be no color from this circle to the center circle.

8. Glue both halves of the ball to the plastic circle. When it is dry, hang Saturn from your ceiling using the fishing line and the thumb tack.

OBSERVATION

Notice that when the rings are facing you edge on, you can't see them. The same thing happens when viewing Saturn through a telescope from Earth.

Uranus

Names   In the Greek story of the origin of the universe Ouranos (the Greek word for Uranus) was heaven. His wife was Gaea, the Earth. Their children included the Titans among whom was Cronos (Saturn), the father of Zeus (Jupiter). See Chapter 4, Section 1.

Discovery   Starting in the year 1690, people had noticed the planet and marked it on their star charts, thinking it was a star. In 1781, William Herschel was "sweeping the skies" with his telescope as part of a project to examine the whole sky. By March, he had reached the Gemini section. On March 13th, he spotted an object that appeared as a disk rather than as a glowing star. Herschel thought it was a comet and followed it for several weeks. After a few months and several calculations of its orbit, Herschel decided that the orbit was circular and his object was not a comet but a planet. This made William Herschel the first person we know of to discover a planet.

Herschel suggested that the name of the new planet should be **Geogium Sidus** (George's Star) in honor of the king of England, George III. Some people wanted to name the planet Herschel in honor of its discoverer. Johann Bode was very excited about the discovery because it was further proof of his law based on Johann Daniel Titius' series of numbers. See Chapter 5, Section 1 for more about the Titius-Bode Law. Bode suggested the name **Uranus** for the new planet in keeping with the Greek names of gods and goddesses.

"It has generally been supposed that it was a lucky accident that brought this new star to my view; this is an evident mistake. In the regular manner, I examined every star of the heavens, not only of that magnitude but many far inferior, it was that night its turn to be discovered . . . had business prevented me that evening I must have found it the next, and the goodness of my telescope was such that I perceived its visible planetary disc as soon as I looked at it; and by the application of my micrometer, determined its motion in a few hours."—William Herschel

The View From Earth   You can see Uranus on a clear night with your unaided eyes. It looks like a dim star. Binoculars help to show it more clearly. Through the telescope, Uranus looks greenish. At opposition Uranus has a magnitude of 5.5. Uranus is tilted 82° from its orbit. This means that

Uranus is practically lying on its side. When you look at the planet, at different times during its orbit you are seeing either its north or south pole.

The rotation of Uranus and the revolution of its satellites are in the opposite direction of all the other planets except Venus. This arrangement could make for extreme seasons. When the north pole is pointing toward the Sun, the Northern hemisphere has a 21 year summer of continual light and heat while the Southern hemisphere experiences 21 years of cold and darkness. In between would be 21 year periods when the Sun would be shining on the planet's equator, bringing day and night to the whole planet every 23 hours much like we experience on Earth. Compare this to the six months of light followed by six months of dark in the northern parts of the Earth.

In March 1977, 96 years after Herschel discovered the planet, observers planned to watch Uranus move in front of a bright star. When this happens, astronomers can use the star's dimming light to reveal information about the atmosphere of the planet. When Uranus came near the star, the star dimmed and then brightened again before dimming once more. This happened several times at an equal distance on both sides of the planet's disk. Why? The observations suggested that there might be a ring around Uranus which passed in front of the star before the planet did, causing the star to dim. When the ring passed, it uncovered the star.

Unlike the rings of Saturn which are wide with narrow gaps in between, the rings of Uranus appear to be narrow with wide gaps in between. These rings are invisible to Earth-bound telescopes. Their diameter is about 63,382 miles (102,000 kilometers).

The View From Space *Voyager 2* showed us views of the rings of Uranus and glimpses of the planet's moons.

Uranus (*Voyager 2, January 25, 1986*)
Photo courtesy of Jet Propulsion Laboratory

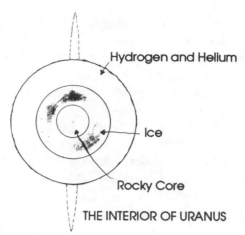

THE INTERIOR OF URANUS

Composition The ability of Uranus to reflect a large amount of light could mean that there is a reflective cloud layer or mist around the planet. The atmosphere contains hydrogen, helium and considerable amounts of methane. The interior is probably similar to Jupiter and Saturn. It seems that the atmosphere around Uranus is clearer than Jupiter's. A rocky and icy core could make up about half of the planet's interior. The outer layers are probably mostly hydrogen. The temperature is below 90° K which is $-298°F$ or $-183°C$.

Moons Herschel found the first two moons. Kuiper found the last and the smallest in 1948. Uranus has five moons. They are, in order of distance from the planet, closest first: Miranda, Ariel, Umbriel, Titania, and Oberon.

Miranda has places on its surface called **ovoid regions** which contain strange features that do not exist anywhere else in the solar system.

The names of the moons of Uranus come from Shakespearean characters from "The Tempest" and "A Midsummer Night's Dream."

Neptune and Triton, one of its moons.

Neptune

Names Neptune is the Roman name for the Greek god Poseidon, God of the Sea. He is the son of Cronos (Saturn) and brother of Zeus (Jupiter).

Discovery The mathematical calculations of Kepler and Newton did not fully explain the motions of Uranus. Some people suggested that there might be another planet pulling at Uranus. In 1840, two young scientists, set out independently to find this "unknown planet." One of the two scientists was a French mathematician, **Jean Joseph Leverier** (1811–1877), the other was an English astronomer, **John Couch Adams** (1819–1892). Both hoped the unknown planet would be where the Titius-Bode Law said it would be. It wasn't because the original figures used to calculate the planetary distances weren't completely accurate.

In 1913 **Mary Blagg** (1858–1944) used a slightly different number combination to revise the Titius-Bode Law. Using these revised figures, the unknown planet follows the Titius-Bode Law almost exactly. The same is true of all of the other planets including the asteroid belt, Uranus, and Pluto.

Adams finished his calculations first in September of 1845. He had neither the equipment nor the skill to check out his calculations with a large telescope. When he went to those who had both, they were either not there or only slightly interested. Two months after Adams completed his calculations, Leverrier finished the first part of his own and published them. The following August Leverrier completed his final calculations and like Adams, he needed the instrument and skill of others to test his mathematical predictions. Unable to get help in France, he wrote to the assistant at the Berlin Observatory in Germany. The young assistant manager, **Johann Gottfried Galle** (1812–1910), director of the observatory agreed to let him search for the unknown planet the very night he received Leverrier's letter. That was September 23rd, 1846. With the help of a young student astronomer, **Heinrich Louis d'Arrest,** (1822–1875) Galle looked into the predicted position. d'Arrest looked at a star chart while Galle looked through the telescope, calling out stars and their positions. d'Arrest searched for the stars Galle described. Finally Galle called out an 8th magnitude star that d'Arrest couldn't find on the charts. They had found the unknown planet after more than two years of research and half an hour at the telescope. The honor of the discovery belongs to both Adams and Leverrier.

The View From Earth   **Joseph Lelande** had seen Neptune on May 8th and 10th in 1795 but he didn't recognize the object as a planet. It is also possible that Galileo observed Neptune in 1613 while he was looking at Jupiter and its satellites. Galileo recorded seeing an 8th magnitude star near Jupiter and it appeared to be moving. Through a telescope, Neptune looks greenish, a bit like Uranus. Neptune has an apparent magnitude of 7.8.

Composition   Neptune's strong light reflecting ability suggests that the planet has a reflecting atmosphere of clouds or gas like Uranus. Hydrogen, helium, and methane help make up this atmosphere. Inside Neptune there is probably a rocky core like the one inside Uranus with large amounts of water surrounded by liquid hydrogen and helium. The temperature on Neptune is around 60°K which is −353°F or −251°C.

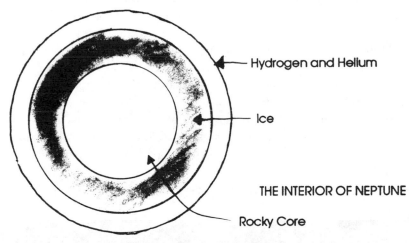

Hydrogen and Helium

Ice

THE INTERIOR OF NEPTUNE

Rocky Core

Moons   Neptune has two moons that we know of. **Triton,** the larger of the two, takes its name from the son of Neptune. It is about 211,800 miles or 353,000 kilometers from Neptune and travels from east to west. **Nereid,** the smaller of the two moons, is named for the Nereids which were sea-nymphs. Discovered in 1949, Nereid has the most eccentric orbit of any satellite in the solar system. Its distance from Neptune varies from 10 to 20 million kilometers.

Pluto

Names   Pluto is the Roman name for the Greek god Hades. Hades is the brother of Jupiter (Zeus) and Neptune (Poseidon). He is the Lord of the Underworld and ruler of the spirits of the dead. Pluto had a helmet which made him invisible. He also had a fork, like Neptune's, but Pluto's fork had only two prongs not three. An 11-year-old girl, **Venetia Burney,** the daughter of an Oxford astronomy professor suggested the name Pluto for the new planet. At school, she had learned about

Venetia Burney, the 11-year-old girl who gave the planet Pluto its name.

the old Greek and Latin mythologies and the distances of the planets. Her grandfather's brother had named Deimos and Phobos, the two satellites of Mars. The initials *P*ercival *L*owell and the first two letters in the planet's name *Pl*uto appear in the symbol for the planet ♇.

Discovery The discovery of Neptune helped explain some of the peculiar movements of Uranus. There were still some unanswered questions. Once again, people considered the pull of another planet beyond Neptune. Three scientists in the early years of the twentieth century set out to find this new, unknown planet, Planet X: **Gaillot** in 1909, **Percival Lowell** in 1915, and **W. H. Pickering** in 1928.

Lowell searched for the missing planet for 10 years (1906–1916) using the telescopes at his observatory in Arizona. After Lowell died in 1916, his brother gave the observatory a 13 inch (33 centimeter) photographic telescope that could record on a single photograph a 12 × 14 inch (31 × 36 centimeter) area of the sky. Observers began using the new camera in 1929 to continue the search for "Planet X." Lowell had suggested that the unknown planet was in the Gemini region of the sky. This area is rich in stars, so the photographs contained about 300,000 star images on each plate. If a planet was among the stars, it would look the same as every other speck of light. You would have to compare several photographs of the same part of the sky taken several days apart. If one of the 300,000 specks appeared in a different place on the plates, it meant that it had moved and was not a star. How can you do this without going crazy?

Fortunately, someone invented a device called the blink comparator or the blink microscope. To use this instrument, you place side by side two photographs of the same part of the sky taken a few days apart. Looking through the two eyepieces of the blink microscope, you see first one photograph then the other. If nothing has changed position on the plates since the two photographs were taken, what you see appears to be one photograph. If something has moved in the sky, what you will see through the blink microscope is a speck of light jumping back and forth as your eye moves from one photograph to the next.

This is just what **Clyde Tombaugh** saw in February 1930. He was looking at two plates, one made

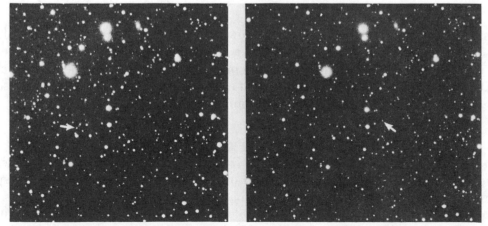

The photographic plates Clyde Tombaugh used to discover Pluto. *Photo courtesy of Lowell Observatory*

on January 23rd and one on January 29th, and saw an object move very near the area where Lowell had predicted "Planet X" would be, following an orbit like the one Lowell had calculated. On March 13, 1930, the observatory announced the discovery of the ninth planet. Percival Lowell was born on this date 75 years before. On March 13, 1781, Sir William Hershel had discovered Uranus in the same constellation (Gemini) where Clyde Tombaugh found Pluto 200 years later.

"There it was, a most unimportant-looking dim, starlike object, which had moved from its plate position of the night before."—Clyde Tombaugh

The View From Earth   To see Pluto you need a good telescope and you need to know exactly where the planet is. Even in a highly enlarged photograph, Pluto looks more like a smudge than a disk. Pluto's brightness varies every 6.39 days with a magnitude of 15.1.

The View From Space   Pluto has the most irregular (eccentric) orbit in the solar system. It is tilted 17° from the ecliptic compared to the Moon's 5°. Pluto's orbit brings it 2,800 million miles (4,500 million kilometers) close to the Sun (perihelion) and as far away as 4,350 million miles (7,000 million kilometers) at its greatest distance from the Sun (aphelion).

One theory about Pluto's wild orbit is that Pluto isn't really a planet. It was once one of Neptune's moons that was pushed out of orbit by the giant satellite Triton. This may also explain why Triton has such an unusual orbit. Once freed from orbiting around Neptune, Pluto was "captured" into an orbit around the Sun where it has remained.

Pluto's orbit crosses in front of Neptune's orbit at one point carrying the planet in front of Neptune's orbit for about 20 years. That is where Pluto is right now. In 1999 Pluto will reach the part of its orbit which continues beyond the orbit of Neptune which will return Pluto to its position as the farthest planet from the Sun. You can see for yourself why Pluto and Neptune don't crash into each other by making a 3-dimensional model of their orbits in this next project.

— Project 81: Making a Model of the Orbits of Uranus, Neptune, and Pluto —

MATERIALS

stiff paper
razor blade
pencil or marking pen
drawing compass
paper glue

small paper circles
scissors
drawings from this book
tape
access to a photocopier

PROCEDURE

1. Draw three complete circles the same size as the ones included with this project. Use the compass. Draw a dark line on the outer rim of the circle for the planet's orbit. Glue or draw the circles onto stiff paper and cut them out.

2. Photocopy the orbit lines from this project and glue the photocopied sheet onto stiff paper. Cut out the dark parts of the lines with the razor blade.

3. Slide one end of each orbit circle into its proper slot on the photocopied sheet. Feed the orbit circle through to the slot. Tape the ends of the orbit circles together.

4. Make planets from two small paper circles. Slice each circle *slightly* more than halfway through. Slide the two circles together and glue one of the halves of the circles down onto the outer part of an orbit circle.

OBSERVATION

Pluto doesn't crash into Neptune when they cross each other's orbit because the high inclination of Pluto's orbit never brings it closer to Neptune than 240 million miles (385 million kilometers).

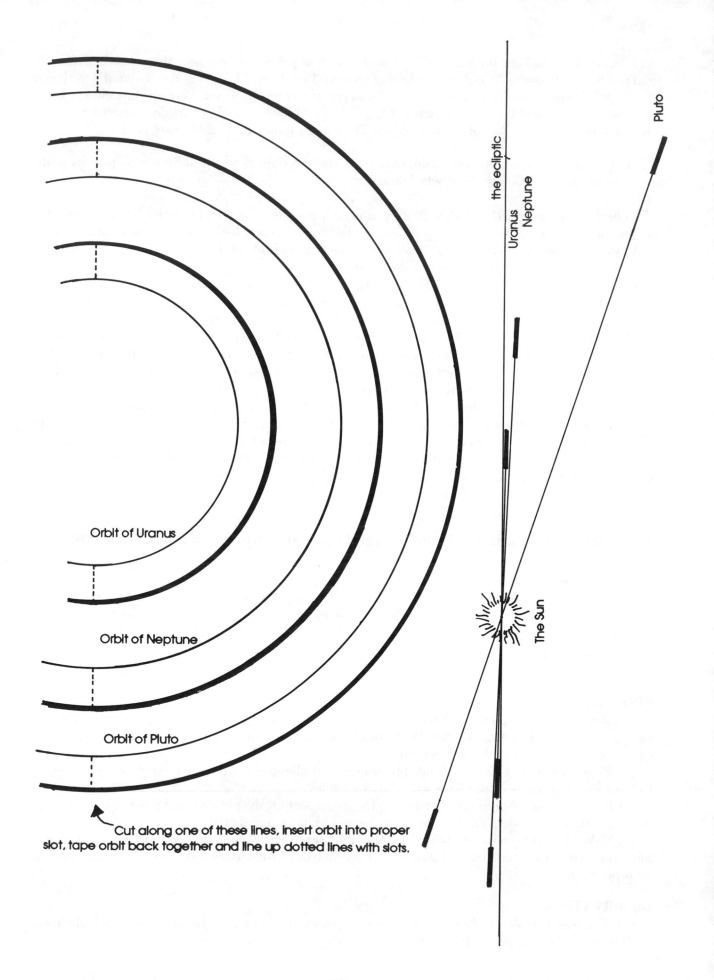

Orbit of Uranus

Orbit of Neptune

Orbit of Pluto

Cut along one of these lines, insert orbit into proper
slot, tape orbit back together and line up dotted lines with slots.

the ecliptic

Uranus

Neptune

Pluto

The Sun

Composition We know very little about Pluto. Our best guesses come from observations made from Earth in 1980. These suggest that Pluto is a small planet, probably 2,000 miles (3,400 kilometers) across or slightly smaller than Mercury. The surface of Pluto is most likely covered by a frost of frozen methane with a very thin atmosphere of methane. Pluto's temperature is 40°K.

Moons On July 2, 1978, **James W. Christy** of the U.S. Naval Observatory in Flagstaff, Arizona saw a strange "bump" on a photograph of Pluto. Checking on the photographs of the planet, Christy noticed that the bump appeared in some of them and wasn't there in others. Christy concluded that the bump was a moon orbiting around Pluto. The satellite takes 6 days, 9 hours, and 17 minutes, or 6.39 days, the same amount of time that Pluto's brightness varies. Now people knew why.

A sketch of Pluto and its moon, Charon taken from the photograph.

The name of Pluto's moon is **Charon,** the boatman who ferried the souls of the dead across the river Styx. Charon travels from east to west (backwards) around Pluto and is about one-third the size of the planet.

The Planets The solar system is much larger than Copernicus, Tycho, Kepler, and Galileo imagined. We have seen pictures of the planets taken at fairly close range. Some of these images actually came from space craft which landed on the planet's surface. Our understanding of the planets grows with each new discovery. In this next project, you can put together all the information you have about the planets and design travel brochures for each one.

The moons of Uranus (Voyager 2, January 24, 1986). Photo courtesy of Jet Propulsion Laboratory

Project 82: Designing Interplanetary Travel Brochures

MATERIALS

paper
glue
colored pencils, crayons, paints
old magazines

video equipment (optional)
colored transparent plastic sheets
travel brochures and posters

PROCEDURE

You and your friends run an interplanetary travel agency. Your job is to encourage people to visit any of the nine planets (including Earth) for a "unique vacation." You need to describe weather conditions, how much people would weigh, what sights they would see, what activities there are (climbing, windsailing, etc.), what to bring, etc. You might even suggest some short side trips to neighboring satellites. Describe each planet the way a travel brochure describes a country. You might want to make a poster or a video. You could listen to the symphony, "The Planets" by Gustav Holst to give you some creative ideas.

READING MORE

Simon, Tony. *The Search for Planet X.* New York: Scholastic Book Services, 1969.

Washburn, Mark. *Distant Encounters: The Exploration of Jupiter and Saturn.* New York: Harcourt Brace Jovanovich, 1983.

North American Nebula (NGC 2000).

Chapter 7:   CHANGING VIEWS OF THE SKY

Section 1:   SPACE AND TIME

The Chinese term **yu-chou** for the universe is similar to the modern idea of space-time. "All time that has passed since antiquity is called **chou;** all space in every direction is called **yu.**"

"From this hour on, space as such and time as such shall recede to the shadows and only a kind of union of the two retain significance."—H. Minkowski (1908)

Measurement of Distance   How far away are the stars? The ancients thought the stars occupied the farthermost regions of the celestial sphere, beyond the planets. When you look at stars through the most powerful telescopes they are still too far away to look like anything but points of light. Their distances are truly "astronomical." How can you possibly measure an object that far away?

Parallax   Look at something that is as far away as possible, like a distant hill, tree, or building. While looking at this object, quickly blink from one eye to the next. Does the object seem to move from one side to another? Now hold your finger at arm's length in front of the object. Quickly close one eye and then the next. What did your finger do? Try blinking again with your finger closer to you, then closer so your finger is almost touching your nose. How would you describe what you saw each time?

This changing position of your finger in front of a distant object whenever you blink your eyes we call **parallax.** The Sun, Moon, and planets are close enough to the Earth to change their position in front of the much more distant stars. The Greeks observed this change and made allowance for it in their calculations. Aristotle knew that if the Earth moved through space, nearby stars ought to show parallax.

---

parallax comes from the Greek word $\pi\alpha\rho\alpha\lambda\lambda\alpha\xi$ *(parallax)* = alternately

---

Tycho Brahe also searched for parallax among the stars. Galileo pointed out in 1632 that "by extremely accurate observations of [the fixed stars] there may be discovered those tiny changes that Copernicus took to be impossible to detect." Copernicus knew that the stars were so far away that you couldn't notice any parallax with your eyes.

Friedrich Wilhelm Bessell (1784–1846) believed that the stars nearer to us would appear to move slightly in front of the more distant background stars if you compared observations made from opposite sides of the Earth's orbit. Your observations would be 186,000,000 miles (297,600,000 kilometers) and six months apart. Bessell chose the star 61 Cygni since he figured it was very close to the Earth. He made a series of photographs six months apart and found that the star actually showed a change in its position.

Your finger represents a nearby star. Your right eye represents the view from Earth at one phase in its orbit. Your left eye represents the view from Earth six months later in its orbit.

The parallaxes of stars are extremely small angles. The nearest star angle, a Centauri, has α parallax of only .756 seconds of a degree. This is much smaller than the angle a small coin would make at a distance of 1 mile (1.6 kilometers).

Triangulation The most direct method for measuring the distance to the stars is the one the Egyptians and Greeks used and the one used to map the city of Paris. (See Chapter 3, Section 2.) This method requires constructing a triangle from the star to a baseline the width of Earth's orbit around the Sun and then back to the star, similar to the parallax triangle. In the next project you can do some measuring using triangulation.

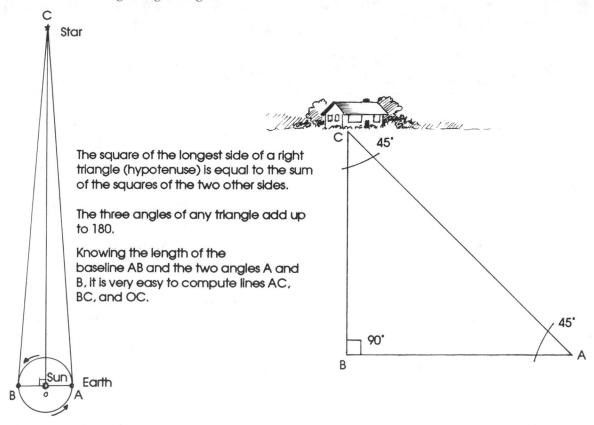

The square of the longest side of a right triangle (hypotenuse) is equal to the sum of the squares of the two other sides.

The three angles of any triangle add up to 180.

Knowing the length of the baseline AB and the two angles A and B, it is very easy to compute lines AC, BC, and OC.

Baseline of 186,000,000 miles (297,600,000 kilometers).

————— **Project 83: Surveying with Triangles (Triangulation)** —————

MATERIALS
protractor

PROCEDURE
1. Go outside and find a distant object (C) such as a mountain, a tree, or a building.
2. Line up the object (C) so that it is straight in front of your observation point.
3. Walk in a straight line, at a right angle (90°) from point B toward point A.
4. Sight object C as you walk until the protractor shows your line of sight to be 45° (or half of a right angle) from the direction you are walking from point B.
5. Measure the distance from point A to point B. If angle C and angle B are each 45° and angle A is 90°, then line AB = line AC, which is the distance from point A to the object, point C.

OBSERVATION
Can you see how triangulation makes it easy to measure long distances including the stars without having to leave your room?

The distances to stars are so great that our ordinary units of miles and kilometers are impractical. The nearest star is 25,000,000,000,000 miles (40,000,000,000,000 kilometers) away. These numbers are difficult to write, remember, and use. Instead, you can use three other ways of measuring:

1. The Astronomical Unit
2. The Parsec
3. The Light Year

The Astronomical Unit   This is the distance from the center of the Earth to the center of the Sun—93 million miles (150 million kilometers). The abbreviation for *Astronomical Unit* is A.U. You use astronomical units when you are measuring a distance within the solar system.

The Light Year   This is the distance a beam (ray) of light travels in one year. 1 light year = 6 trillion miles or 9.6 trillion kilometers. α Centauri = 4.2 light years away.

The Parsec   This is equal to 19.2 million, million miles or 30.7 million, million kilometers or 206,265 A.U. **Parsec** means parallax of one second (1/3600 of a degree). This is about the angle a coin ¾ inch (18 millimeters) in diameter would appear to make from a distance of 2.3 miles (3.7 kilometers). You use parsecs to measure extremely large distances. 1 parsec = 3.26 light years.

Sirius is 8.6 light years away. How far away is Sirius in parsecs? In A.U.'s? In miles? In kilometers?

The Doppler Effect   What would you have to do to your voice to make it sound like a car coming from far away, getting closer and zooming by? For which direction do you make your voice lower? Higher?

By making the pitch (not the volume) of your voice higher, you made the car sound like it was far away, but getting closer. The soundwaves for such a pitch are compressed. The closer together they are the higher the pitch. The longer the wavelength, the lower the pitch. As the car approaches you, the distance between you and the car (including its soundwaves) is constantly getting shorter. The sound waves become more and more compacted, striking your car at a faster rate than if the car were not moving. When the car passes you, the distance between you and the car (including its soundwaves) is constantly getting longer. The soundwaves spread out striking your car at a slower rate.

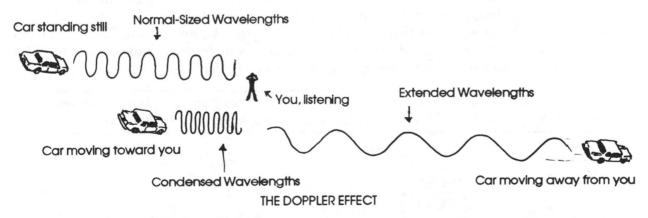

Car standing still — Normal-Sized Wavelengths

You, listening

Extended Wavelengths

Car moving toward you

Condensed Wavelengths

Car moving away from you

THE DOPPLER EFFECT

In 1842, **Christian Doppler** (1803–1853) noticed this effect when listening to trains passing and explained what was happening. The changing wavelength due to motion is called the **Doppler Effect.** This term also applies to lightwaves as well as soundwaves. Lightwaves from a moving object shorten as the object moves toward you and lengthen as the object moves away. You can *hear* the sound change, how can you *see* the light change? To make the lightwaves visible you look at the spectrum they create. If the object is moving toward you, a given line in the spectrum will condense. This will make the line in the spectrum appear to shift from its normal position to a position closer to the blue end of the spectrum. We call this a **blue-shift.** If the object is moving away from you, a given line in the spectrum will lengthen. This will make the line in the spectrum appear to shift from the normal position to a position closer to the red end of the spectrum. We call this a **red-shift**. If the object is a star, you can tell by looking at its spectrum whether the star is approaching or moving away from you and how fast it is traveling. The amount the wavelength changes on the spectrum depends on how fast the star appears to be traveling, seen from Earth.

__The Speed of Light__   During a thunderstorm, the sky flashes with a jagged bolt of lightening. Moments later, "Crack!" comes the sound of thunder. What you saw came to your eyes the moment it happened. What you heard took longer to arrive. Sound travels at about 240 miles (547 kilometers) per second. The French mathematician **Marin Mersenne** (1588–1648), came close to finding that out in 1640, by timing echoes over a known distance. In 1710, the Englishman, **William Derham** (1657–1735) refined Mersenne's calculations by comparing the time between the sight and sound of cannons firing 12 miles or 20 kilometers apart.

How did we figure out how fast light travels? In 1683, Galileo suggested having two people stand about a mile away from each other, each holding a covered lantern. As soon as one person uncovered his or her lantern, the other person would immediately uncover theirs. The amount of time it took should be the speed of light, except that Galileo realized that light moved too fast for someone to measure it his way.

In 1676, **Ole Romer** (1644–1710) from Denmark used the times in between the eclipses of Jupiter's moons to come up with 141,000 miles (226,916 kilometers) per second as the speed that light travels After centuries of very imaginative experiments, we have clocked the speed of light to 186,000 miles (298,000 kilometers) per second.

How long does it take light from the Moon to reach us? Earth-Moon distance = 238,857 miles (384,404 kilometers)/186,000 miles (298,000 kilometers) = 1.3 seconds.

How long does it take light from the Sun to reach us? Earth-Sun distance = 93,000,000 miles (150,000,000 kilometers)/186,000 miles (298,000 kilometers) = 500 seconds 500/60 = 8 minutes. It takes 8 years for the light from Sirius to reach us.

Since 1969, lasers attached to telescopes have sent light pulses to mirrors left on the Moon by U.S. astronauts and Soviet lunar probes. The light pulses are partially reflected back to the Earth. When we are able to determine the speed of light more accurately we will be able to calculate the distance to the Moon within a few inches or centimeters.

__Relativity__   What would happen, the 16-year-old Einstein wondered, if I could move at the speed of light and catch up with a beam of light? Since we were both traveling at the same speed, when I looked at the beam of light it would seem to be standing still.

Einstein's way of looking at the light beam is something you take for granted. Galileo came up with the idea about 300 years ago, that all motion depends on its relation to something else. This is the **principle of relativity** and it all depends on your frame of reference.

In 1905, when he was 26, Einstein published his thoughts on the speed of light in a paper entitled "The Special Theory of Relativity." Eleven years later, he developed his General Theory of Relativity.

Albert Einstein

When you ride in a car or train next to another car or train moving at the same speed it looks like you are both standing still like Einstein's light beam. If one of you goes a little faster or slower it is hard to tell just from looking, whose speed has changed or if one of you is going backwards. While all of this motion is going on outside the car, inside all is motionless. You can toss a ball straight up into the air and catch it just as if you were standing still. You have no sense of motion.

The same is true of your experience of the much faster speed of the Earth traveling through space at 18 miles (30 kilometers) per second. You don't feel it. Your hair doesn't blow back in the strong wind created by this motion. Neither do the trees. For these reasons, people long ago found it difficult to accept that the Earth was moving.

There has been research into the possibility of a particle that can travel faster than light. It is called a **tachyon.**

Einstein added **time** to the three dimensions of length, width, and height. A point of space at a point of time, he called a "world-point," and all the possible world points put together he called the "world." In the relativity theory, every object is a four-dimensional structure travelling along a world-line in the four dimensional world of space-time. Anything (a particle or a person) that exists in time creates a chart or graph of its position in time. This is called a "world-line."

In this next project, you can plot a world-line of your own travels.

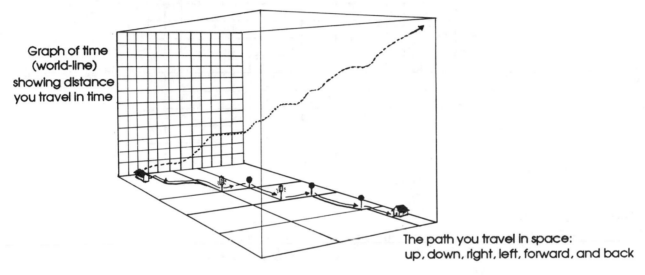

Graph of time (world-line) showing distance you travel in time

The path you travel in space: up, down, right, left, forward, and back

World-line: a journey from your house to a friend's house shown in both space and time.

———— Project 84: Plotting a World Line ————

MATERIALS

colored pencils
ruler
paper
clock or watch

pedometer, odometer, or map
graph paper
tracing paper

PROCEDURE

1. Draw a map of how to get to your friend's house from your own house. Use graph paper. Try to be as accurate as possible. Draw the map to scale so that each square equals a certain distance (e.g., 500 feet, 1 mile, 3 kilometers, etc.). Use a pedometer, the odometer in a car, or a street map to figure the distance.

2. Draw a line with a red pencil showing how to get from one place to the other, indicating all the turns and hills.

3. Use a clock or watch to time or estimate how long it takes to make the whole trip. As you time yourself, be aware of your traveling speed. Where on the map do you travel the fastest? Where do you slow down or speed up (hills, curves)? Where do you stop (lights, stop signs, etc.), and for how long?

4. Place the tracing paper over the map. Using a colored pencil (other than red), draw a straight line next to the map marked off in minutes. Use the squares showing through the tracing paper to indicate distance.

5. Make a graph of how far you went each minute. If you went faster, show that you covered more distance by drawing a line more horizontal. As you slowed down, the line should become more vertical. If you stopped, you aren't moving but the clock is so show this by continuing the timeline straight up.

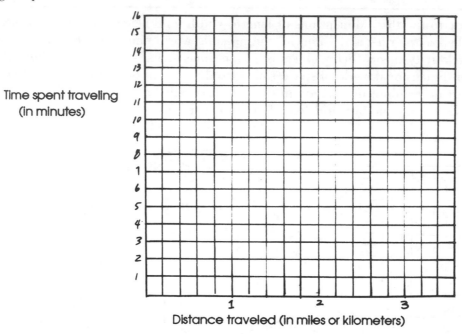

Time spent traveling (in minutes)

Distance traveled (in miles or kilometers)

OBSERVATIONS

The curved line you will have when you finish is the world-line for your travels in space-time. How does this compare with a regular road map version of your trip?

The Twin Paradox Gravity and speed affect time. According to this idea, if you could travel at or near the speed of light, your personal time would be much slower compared to someone who was not moving. When people imagined this possiblity they came up with the **"twin paradox"** or "Clock paradox" which Einstein first suggested in 1905. A paradox is an apparent contradiction, something that should be impossible, yet it seems to be happening. In the twin paradox there are two twins, let's call them Maria and Mark. Maria leaves on an expedition out into space traveling at or near the speed of light. Mark stays at home on Earth. After awhile, Maria turns around and heads home at the same speed. When the two meet again, they are in for a big surprise.

Each twin's clock and body has recorded the normal passage of time for that person only. The other twin is living in a completely different time frame. By traveling near the speed of light, Maria has slowed down her clock, calendar, and life rate compared to Mark's. According to the Lorentz-FitzGerald contraction formula, at 0.9999995 the speed of light, Maria's clock would be running at 1/1,000 the rate it would have if she were on Earth. The closer you approach the speed of light, the greater the effect on time. Each twin has the impression that he/she is at rest and the other person is moving. In addition, the other person's time seems to be going extraordinarily slowly; 1,000 times slower than normal. Imagine what their voices would sound like when they called each other on the phone. If they checked each other's heartbeats that used to occur once every second, they would have to wait 17 minutes between each one. They would have to wait 4 days in between hourly beeps on their watches.

Now for the surprise after the journey. As far as Maria is concerned, everything in her world was going along at a normal rate. She was gone for 2 weeks, so naturally she will be 2 weeks older when she returns. Since everything in Maria's world was actually happening at 1/1,000 the speed that things were happening to Mark on Earth, Maria will have aged far less compared to her brother. After 2 weeks, Maria will return to Earth 2 weeks older but her brother will be 38 years older!

You can see where the twin paradox leads your imagination. A voyage to α Centauri would take about 115,000 years in Earth time. If the space craft traveled at or near the speed of light, the journey would take about 4 years.

> There once was a young lady named Bright
> who traveled much faster than light,
> She started one day
> in the relative way,
> and returned the previous night.

Warped-Space-Time   According to relativity physics, an object moves on the straightest possible path along a line following the contours of a surface (geodesics), unless something acts upon it. This includes anything that moves in time, including vibrations of light or sound. The strong gravitational field around the Sun should slow down the frequency of light near the Sun shifting it very slightly toward the red.

Such a slowing down or shift would be due to the light following the contours of the warping or curve of space-time. Einstein predicted that the light traveling from stars near the Sun would follow a curve. He also said that you could detect such a curving by measuring the positions of stars close to the rim of the Sun during a total solar eclipse. In 1919, **Sir Arthur Stanley Eddington** (1882–1944), the English astronomer, set out for Africa with a group of scientists to observe a total eclipse of the Sun and to look for the predicted deflection of light. Their observations convinced them that such bending did occur. In this next project, you can visualize the warping of space-time with a model representing the "fabric of the universe."

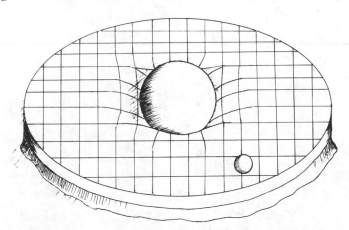

Project 85: Making a Model of Warped Space-Time

MATERIALS

large square piece of rubber cut from a
   tire tube
white paint
straight edge
large metal ball or an orange

ruler
small paint brush
marble
embroidery hoop
several books

PROCEDURE

1. Cut out a square piece of rubber from a tire tube.
2. Draw a grid on the piece of rubber using the ruler. Paint the lines white.

3. Stretch the piece of rubber onto the frame of the embroidery hoop.
4. Set some books under the edges of the embroidery hoop.
5. Place the heavy ball in the center of the painted grid.
6. Roll the marble across the piece of rubber to the other side.

OBSERVATIONS

Notice what happens to the lines of the grid as you place the heavy ball in the center. What kind of path does the marble follow as it rolls across the contours of the grid?

Space doesn't actually warp. What changes or bends are the coordinates you use to measure space.

Reading More

Apfel, Necia H. *It's All Relative: Einstein's Theory of Relativity.* New York: Lothrup, Lee and Shepard Books, 1981.
Calder, Nigel. *Einstein's Universe.* New York: Penguin Books, 1980.

Photo courtesy of Observatoire de Haute Provence

Section 2: STARS

In the second chapter, you looked at stars from the point of view of their names, what they look like, and where they live. This is as much information as you usually have about people when you first meet them. Later, as you get to know them better, you begin to learn about how they live. In this section, you are going to meet the stars again and see what they tell you about their lives, how they are born, go through infancy, mature, grow old, and eventually die. Most of what we know about the stars we have learned from their light.

Why Do Stars Twinkle?   The light from the stars is not constant, so the whole night sky shimmers. The colors of stars like Arcturus and Sirius seem to pulsate, changing into the colors of the rainbow. To the ancients, the stars were flickering fires from the torches or campfires of the gods.

One theory about the stars is that they really are fires. These fires send their light out into space which gradually passes through the air in the atmosphere surrounding us on Earth. This air is often in movement with warm currents rising up to meet cold currents coming down. Layers of air also sweep across the sky filled with tiny particles of dust. When you look at the light coming from a star, what you are seeing is what the light looks like after it has managed to pass through all of the different movements and layers of the atmosphere. The result is that the starlight itself does quite a bit of moving and bouncing around in the process and arrives twinkling instead of in a steady stream of light.

The Moon and planets do not usually twinkle. The sunlight reflected off the surface of the Moon and the planets has a shorter journey to make than the light from a star. It also travels differently and at different times. The result is a clear and steady light.

Olbers' Paradox   If the stars are like Suns and everywhere you look there are billions and billions of stars, why isn't the night sky filled with light? This mystery had puzzled scientists for over a hundred years when **Heinrich Wilhelm Olbers,** who discovered the first asteroid, began working on it in 1823. People soon called this puzzle **Olbers' paradox.** Like Einstein's twin paradox, Olbers' paradox made sense but it didn't. The answer that seems to explain the situation the best so far has to do with distant galaxies red-shifting to a point in space where their light hasn't reached us yet. This has a dimming effect on the total amount of light reaching the Earth.

Spectral Class   In 1872, **Henry Draper** (1837–1882) took the first photograph of the spectra of stars. In the 1880s, at Harvard College Observatory, astronomer **Edward C. Pickering** (1846–1919) began classifying the spectra of stars. **Annie Jump Cannon** (1863–1941) completed the task with a group of dedicated young women assistants. Together they invented a system of **spectral classes** based on the number and appearance of spectral lines. The classes started with "A" for the spectra with strong hydrogen lines, then "B," "C," up to "O." When Annie Cannon published the *Henry Draper Catalog* from 1918 to 1924, it contained spectral information on 225,320 stars. This catalog became the basis for all modern astronomical spectroscopy.

Annie Jump Cannon

SPECTRAL CLASS	TEMPERATURE K	COLOR	STARS
O	40,000°	very blue	Alnitak (ζ Orionis)
B	18,000°	bluish-white	Spica (α Virginis)
A	10,000°	white	Sirius (α Canis Majoris)
F	7,000°	yellowish-white	Procyon (α Canis Minoris)
G	5,500°	yellow	The Sun
K	4,000°	orange	Arcturus (α Bootes)
M	3,000°	red	Antares (α Scorpii)

The Birth, Life, and Death of a Star (Stellar Evolution)   What a star will go through in its life and how long it will live depends on its mass and how much hydrogen and helium it contains. The more massive stars will have shorter lives. Most stars go through the following stages:

1. Birth
2. Childhood
3. Adolescence
4. Maturity

5. Middle Age
6. Old Age
7. Death

Birth (Protostar)   The assumed starting point for the life of a star is a vast cloud of swirling stardust in space called a **nebula.** (See Section 3 in this chapter for more about nebulae.) Nebulae are the nurseries for billions of stars. Right now stars are being born in the Orion Nebula and the Lagoon Nebula.

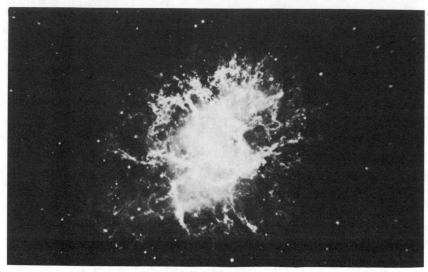

The Crab Nebula.

---

nebula comes from the Latin word *nebula* = mist or cloud
The plural of nebula is nebulae.

A nebula contains mainly hydrogen with traces of helium and other natural elements. The temperature in the nebula is just a few degrees above absolute 0. Slight motions within the nebula gather some of the matter together. Particles of dust and gas fall towards this center of condensation. As more matter keeps falling inward, it creates gravitational forces which further pack the matter together until it takes on an enormous mass of billions of tons. This mass is a **protostar** and is the "embryo" of a star. Heat and pressure build up as more and more matter is attracted to the protostar. At first, the protostar is too cold to send out any visible light. It might send out radio waves. Then it begins to shine dimly in the dust of the nebula. A star is born.

---

protostar comes from the Greek word πρωτος *(protos)* = before

---

Childhood (Contraction)   The process of condensing continues within the newborn star. Its own gravitational pull shrinks the star which changes its potential energy into heat.

Adolescence (Pre-main Sequence)   The heat in the star moves by convection first, then by radiation. (See Chapter 6, Section 1 for more on convection and radiation.) The star's radiation changes from radio to infrared, so the star is now an **infrared star.** The star contracts from a radius 100 times the radius of the Sun to a radius about 1½ times the radius of the Sun.

The temperature at the star's core rises to about 28 million degrees absolute. The temperature is high enough to start the thermonuclear transformation of hydrogen as well as deuterium, lithium, beryllium, and boron, into helium and carbon into nitrogen. This is **nuclear fusion** and it is how stars "burn." The nuclear energy in a star comes from its mass, according to Einstein's formula $E = mc^2$.

Maturity (Main Sequence)   You can now see the star shining. Gravitational contraction has stopped and now the proton-proton chain of thermonuclear reactions provides the star's energy In this reaction, four protons fuse into a helium nucleus releasing energy. The star's temperature is about 10 million degrees. Stars spend most of their lives as mature stars. The Sun is a mature star.

Middle Age (Red Giant)   To produce energy, stars either use hydrogen for fuel or else they go back to their childhood habit of depending on gravity. During middle age, some stars rely on gravity to produce energy when their supply of hydrogen runs out. This increases pressure at the core makes it get hotter. The carbon-nitrogen cycle thermonuclear reaction begins in which four hydrogen atoms fuse into helium. The combination of gravity acting on the helium core and thermonuclear reactions on the hydrogen-burning surface cause the outer layers of the star to swell up to several times their original diameter, forming an outer shell.

Since it is so far from the core which is the source of heat, the temperature of the shell drops. The star becomes cooler and glows as a **red giant** or a **red supergiant,** depending on the mass of the star. Aldebaran, Betelgeuse, and Antares are red giants.

Old Age (Variables)   While the star is expanding and its helium core is contracting, the temperature at the core continues to rise. When the core's temperature reaches a certain level, its helium fuses into carbon. The star again begins to rely on gravity for its energy and starts contracting. The gasses of the star compress so tightly that the star begins to resemble a solid. As this process continues, the star will start to become unstable. It will pulsate and become a **Cepheid variable.**

Death

White dwarf   The fate of a star depends on its mass. If the mass of the star is less than 1.4 times the mass of the Sun, the star will become a **white** or a **black dwarf.** Most stars become white dwarfs. When the star is out of fuel it shrinks to 1/100 its original diameter. It is now about the size of a planet. At this size, since brightness depends on the size of the star's surface, whatever brightness the star may have is lost to sight. The star is white hot. Because of its color and size, we call it a **white dwarf. W. S. Adams** in 1915, determined that Sirius B, the star orbiting Sirius that Friedrich Bessell studied in 1844 and that **Alvin Clark** had detected with his telescope in 1862 was a previously unknown type of star. It was a white dwarf, the first one to be discovered. Procyon in Canis Minor also has a white dwarf companion.

The helium at the core of a white dwarf has already changed to carbon in an earlier stage. The star has run out of energy sources: no hydrogen and no gravity. The negatively charged particles are not able to supply any energy. Energy provided by the positively charged nuclei produces heat and light for awhile. When they can no longer be an energy source no light comes from the star. It is then a **black dwarf.** You can't see it. The only way you will know that the star is there is by noticing its gravitational pull on other stars.

Some white dwarfs are actually yellow. We call them white dwarfs because the first one discovered (Sirius B) was white.

Nova   If the mass of the star is slightly more than 1.4 times the mass of the Sun, its internal pressure drops and the star can no longer support its own weight. The star will explode so it can shed a part of its mass and become a **nova.** It may have to go through this process several times.

The word **nova** in Latin means "new." To Brahe and Kepler this was a good word to describe their situation when they looked up at a sky they knew very well and found a star that wasn't there the night before! Actually, the star had been there, only they couldn't see it. The star had generated more energy than its surface could radiate into space. To get rid of the excess energy, the star "let off steam" and with an explosion, cast off its thin outer shell. Such an explosion is also necessary for some stars to lose excess mass before entering the white dwarf stage. What Brahe and Kepler saw was the moment of explosion. Star explosions are extremely powerful. Most novae only have to explode like this once. Then they calm down into the condition they were in before. Some explode again. After most of the star has been blown away, what is left is the very hot, dense core of a **white dwarf.**

Supernova If the mass of the star is far more than 1.4 times the mass of the Sun, it will explode violently and shed most of its mass as a **supernova.** A supernova, as you might guess from the name, is the most powerful of all stellar explosions. Supernovae can reach an absolute magnitude as high as -20, radiating as much energy in one year as the Sun does in a billion.

Supernovae are as rare as they are mighty. People have recorded only three in our galaxy. The first appeared in 1054. The Chinese and Japanese reported it naming it the "guest star." On July 4th, 1054, Chinese records describe the supernova this way: "It was visible by day, like Venus; pointed rays shot out from it on all sides; the color was reddish white. Altogether it was visible for 23 days." The native North Americans in Zuni, New Mexico recorded what we believe to be an image of this event. Arab astronomers noted it. So far, we have found no European record of this supernova.

The second supernova appeared in 1572 in the constellation Cassiopeia. This the the bright "new star" Tycho Brahe saw. It was possible to see this supernova for two years.Tycho Brahe describes his encounter with the supernova of 1572 like this:

"One evening, when, as usual, I was contemplating the heavenly dome whose face was so familiar to me, I saw with inexpressible astonishment . . . a radiant star of extraordinary magnitude. Struck with surprise, I could hardly believe my eyes. . . . Its brightness was greater than that of Sirius, and Jupiter. It could only be compared with that of Venus. People gifted with good eyesight could see this star in daylight, even at noon."

The third and last supernova seen in our galaxy appeared in 1604 in the constellation Ophiuchus. Kepler studied this one.

A supernova is the death cry of a very massive star which has run out of its main sources of fuel. It expands to 100 million times its size. Being too massive to collapse smoothly into the white dwarf stage, its pent-up energy bursts forth in an explosion that sends most of the star out into space. What is left is a highly dense core with a mass greater than the Sun compressed into an area the size of an asteroid. The supernova explosion results in the loss of 50% of the supernova's mass. What remains is a **neutron star** or **black hole.**

Neutron Star As the star continues to lose energy into space, it turns slower. After awhile this type of star will lose all its energy (like the white dwarf), and will move through space (like a black dwarf), with no light and only a gravitational field around it to let you know it is there. A neutron star can be a compact ball of subatomic particles (neutrons) left as a core of a supernova explosion. Having no charge, these particles don't repel each other and can be tightly packed together. A neutron star four times as big as the Sun can shrink to 6 miles (10 kilometers) in diameter. They can rotate 30 times a second on their axis. A rotating neutron star is a **pulsar.** (See Section 3 of this chapter for more about pulsars.)

Black Holes Depending on how far a particle is from the center of a gravitational field, the least speed (velocity) it can have at that place for it to be able to move away is called the **velocity of escape.** You would use the velocity of escape to figure out how much thrust a rocket or spacecraft would need to leave the surface of a planet by escaping its gravitational field.

In a star which has a gravitational field, there is a point where the velocity of escape is the speed of light. Since no known material particle can go this fast, this point forms a barrier, trapping all matter (including light) from escaping. This barrier point is the Schwartzchild radius, named after **Karl Schwartzchild** (1873–1916), who described it a few years after Einstein introduced general relativity. Already in 1796, **Pierre Simon, Marquis de Laplace** (1749–1827) had thought about what it would be like if there was an object with such a strong gravitational field that it would take more than the speed of light in order to escape. In such a place, since light couldn't escape, it would be bent back into itself and head back towards the object instead of away from it. From a distance, you would not see the object. Its body would be hidden. For this reason, Laplace called such objects "**corps obscurs**" (hidden bodies). **John A. Wheeler,** a physicist at Princeton came up with the same conclusion years later and named these objects "black holes."

Another name that people suggested for a black hole was **collapsar.**

In the words of one astronomer, a black hole is matter that dug a hole, jumped in, and pulled the hole in afterwards. A black hole is no longer a star.

The size of the Schwartzchild radius is proportional to the mass of the star. For a star the mass of the Sun, the black hole would have a radius of about 1.86 miles (3 kilometers) or a diameter of 3.73 miles (6 kilometers) which is ⅓ the size of a solar-mass neutron star.

Are there any black holes? If there are and you can't see them how would you find them? What is left behind that can tell you that they are there is the star's gravitational field. This field will have an effect on other stars nearby. The stars nearest to each other are those in a binary system. If one of the stars is invisible, has a mass too high to be a white dwarf or a neutron star, and is a collapsed object of extremely small size, it could be a black hole. Matter falling into the region of the Schwartzchild radius will be traveling at an incredible speed and therefore will be generating very high temperatures (up to 100 million°K or more). Such hot matter emits radiation in the form of X-rays, which you can detect with X-ray telescopes on Earth or from satellites in space.

In the inner part of the accretion disk, the matter attracted or gas blown by solar wind is revolving around the black hole so fast that internal friction heats it up to the temperature where it emits X-rays. This may be what is happening to the Cygnus binary system. Cygnus X-1 is an invisible X-ray star with a mass nearing 10 times that of the Sun. If it were a small, collapsed object, this star could be a black hole. If it is, the strong X-ray activity could be due to gas heated by spiralling into the black hole.

In this next project you can get an idea of what happens to the material in a star next to a black hole by making a model of a black hole.

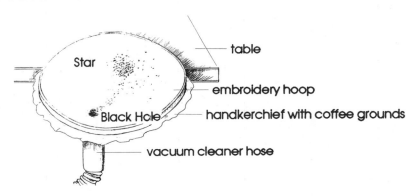

Project 86: Making a Model of a Black Hole

MATERIALS

embroidery hoop (or wooden frame)
white handkerchief or part of a sheet
instant coffee granules

table
vacuum cleaner

PROCEDURE

1. Stretch the handkerchief tightly over an embroidery hoop or a wood frame.
2. Sprinkle about one teaspoon of coffee granules (*the star*) onto the handkerchief.
3. Rest part of the hoop on the edge of a table. Hold the vacuum cleaner hose (*the black hole*) in one hand under the hoop a few inches away from the coffee granules. Turn on the vacuum cleaner. Make a small space between the vacuum cleaner hose and the handkerchief with your finger and thumb so that the star begins to vibrate and move toward the black hole.

OBSERVATIONS

Notice how the black hole concentrates the mass of the star. Notice the trail left as the star is drawn into the black hole.

The Hertzsprung-Russell Diagram In the 1900s, two astronomers, each working alone, drew up a chart on which they could plot the life history of a star. In 1911, the Danish astronomer, **Ejnar Hertzsprung** (1873–1967), compared colors and luminosity, and in 1913, the American astronomer, **Henry Norris Russell** (1877–1957), compared absolute magnitude and spectral classes. Independently, they came up with the charts design. Therefore, we call the chart by both of their names, the **Hertzsprung-Russell,** or the **H-R Diagram.**

In the H-R Diagram you indicate each star with a dot. The star's luminosity and spectral class determines where the dot will appear on the chart. Dots of neighboring stars show up at various places on the diagram. These places have nothing to do with where the stars are in the sky. What they show are stages in the life cycle of a star. Whatever stars are in this particular stage of their life will show up on the H-R Diagram in the section for that stage. In this next project, you can plot a number of stars in the H-R Diagram yourself to see how it works.

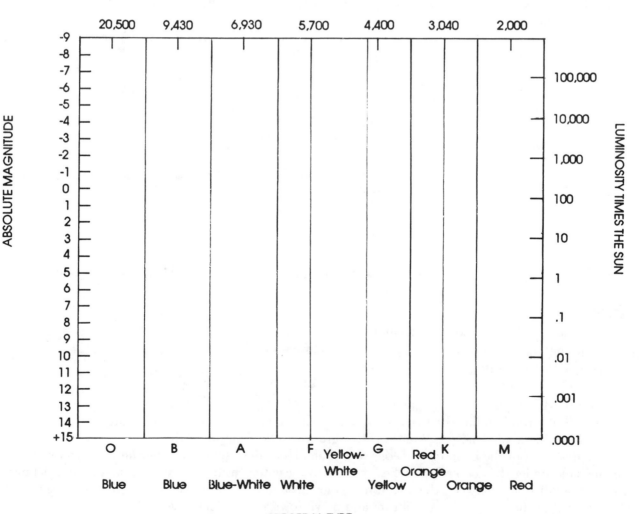

MATERIALS

graph
table of stars
colored pencils

pencil
access to photocopier

PROCEDURE

1. Photocopy the graph on the opposite page.
2. Lightly shade in the colors mentioned in the chart, using colored pencils.
3. Plot each star from the table onto the graph by making a dot and writing the name of the star next to it.

OBSERVATIONS

How does our Sun compare with other stars in terms of brightness and temperature? Which stars are young and which are old?

H-R DIAGRAM

STAR	SPECTRUM	ABSOLUTE MAGNITUDE	SURFACE TEMPERATURE
1. Sirius	A1	1.4	9500
2. Procyon	F5	2.8	6500
3. Sun	G2	5.0	5000
4. Barnard's Star	M5	13.2	2600
5. Vega	A0	0.5	9700
6. Van Maanen's Star	F0	14.2	5800
7. Canopus	F0	−4.6	6400
8. Deneb	A2	−7.1	9400
9. Pollux	K0	1.0	4100
10. Mintaka	O9.5	−5.1	21000
11. Altair	A5	2.4	7700
12. Regulus	B8	−0.7	13000
13. Luyten 745−6	F0	14.3	5900
14. Antares	M1	−3.0	2700
15. Rigel	B8	−6.2	11000
16. Betelgeuse	M2	−5.6	2700
17. Aldebaran	K5	−0.5	3500
18. Capella	G0	−0.5	5000
19. Arcturus	K1	−0.0	3900
20. Spica	B1.5	−2.2	19500
21. Acrux	B1	−2.7	19000
22. Fomalhaut	A3	2.1	8900
23. Rigel Kentaurus	G0	−0.5	5800
24. Wolf 424 A	M6	14.4	2500
25. Alnitak	O9.5	−5.9	23000

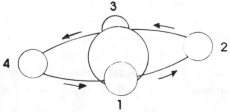

A Binary Star System with One Star Orbiting Around Another

Binaries   In 1650, **John Baptist Riccioli** (1598–1671) accidentally discovered that the star Mizar in the handle of the Big Dipper was part of a **two-star system,** one revolving around the other like a planet around the Sun. Up until then people assumed two stars near each other only looked that way from our viewpoint on the Earth. They were must likely one far behind the other, the farther one, therefore appearing dimmer. William Herschel thought such stars were good examples to measure for the parallax between the two. He published three catalogues listing more than 800 "double stars." He was amazed to find out that most of these were actually two stars revolving around each other. Herschel's son, John, continued his father's search for multiple stars from his observatory in South Africa. His search located 1,202 double and multiple stars, mostly in the Southern hemisphere. Another famous father and son team, **Friedrich Georg Wilhelm Von Struve** (1793–1864) and **Otto Wilhelm Von Struve** (1819–1905) working at their observatory near Leningrad, catalogued 3,110 double stars from the Northern hemisphere.

It's likely that at least one star in twenty among the brighter stars is a **visual binary star,** the name given to two-star systems. This is how the path of a star around another in a binary star system looks. The star with the greater mass becomes the focus of an ellipse which the star with the smaller mass travels.

Sometimes when the traveling star is behind the stationary one, you can't see it from the Earth. The larger star eclipses it. In a lesser way, the traveling star can partially block the stationary one. The change from eclipsing to being visible also changes how bright the stars appear to us.

Variable Stars   Over 18,000 stars have brightnesses and spectral characteristics which change over time. They do this either by expanding and contracting regularly or exploding part of their mass into space. Observers of these pulsating and exploding variable stars have used information from these stars and made important discoveries about the nature of stars in general. There are several groups of variable stars:

The Pulsating Stars: Cepheids I, Chepheids II, RR-Lyrae variables, Long-period variables
The Exploding Stars: Novae, and Supernovae.

Cepheid Variables   get their name from the star δ Cephei. The other Cepheid variables come from different constellations. Polaris, for example is a Cepheid variable. These stars have a moment of maximum light and a moment of minimum light. The time between two maximum or two minimum moments is called the period. Cepheid variables have periods of from one to fifty days. In 1784, a 19-year-old deaf English astronomer, **John Goodricke** (1764–1786), discovered that a Cepheid varies from magnitude 4.4 to 3.7 with a period of 5.4 days.

In 1912, **Henrietta Swan Leavitt** (1868–1921), while working at the Harvard College Observatory, discovered a remarkable relationship between the periods of Cepheid variables and their absolute magnitudes. When she plotted the periods of the Cepheids in the Small Magellenic Clouds of the Southern Hemisphere with their magnitudes, she found that when the periods of the Cephieds increase, their apparent magnitudes also increase. Those with the same periods have the same absolute magnitude.

Henrietta Swan Leavitt

Since we know how to find distance by using the inverse square law, we can find the distance to this star or to any groups of stars the star happens to be in. Suppose you find that a certain Cepheid has a period of 10 days, you look at the chart and find the period listed at the bottom. Then you would find the apparent magnitude of the star, also on the chart. You would calculate the absolute magnitude. From this information you could calculate the distance of the star.

In this next project, you can actually determine the **period** (the time between the two brightest or two dimmest dates) and **luminosity** (amount of light) of a Cepheid variable from your own observations.

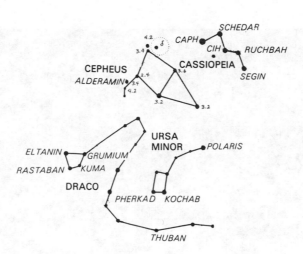

— Project 88: Calculating the Changing Brightness of a Cepheid Variable —

MATERIALS

paper   chart
pencil   star chart

PROCEDURE

1. Observe the apparent magnitude of Delta Cephei every night for two months. Use the star chart to locate this star.

2. Compare Delta Cephei with other stars in Cepheus, one brighter, one dimmer, to help you decide on the magnitude of Delta Cephei to the nearest 10th. (You saw this method back in Chapter 2, Section 3.)

3. Record the date, time, and magnitude for each observation.

4. Plot your results on the graph. This shows the star's changing *luminosity*.

5. Find the interval between the two brightest or two dimmest dates. That is the star's *period*.

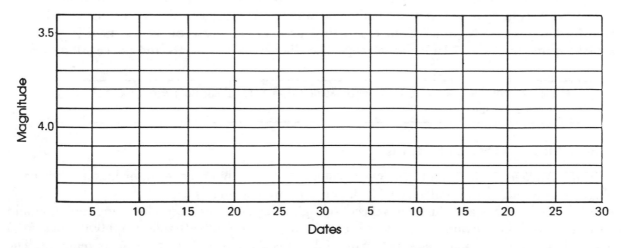

OBSERVATIONS

By how many magnitudes does Delta Cephei vary? Can you see any pattern or relation between the star's period and luminosity?

READING MORE

Branley, Franklyn M. *Black Holes, White Dwarfs and Superstars.* New York: Thomas Y. Crowell Co., 1976.
Degani, Meir H. *Astronomy Made Simple.* New York: Doubleday, 1976.
Kaufmann, William J. III. *Black Holes and Warped Spacetime.* San Francisco: W. H. Freeman and Co., 1979.

Two Galaxies, M81 and M82. *Photo courtesy of Observatoire de Haute Provence*

Section 3: THE GALAXY

Comets In 1950, astronomer **Fred Whipple** described **comets** as "dirty snowballs." Most people believe comets to be a mixture of ice and dust frozen out of the solar mix of gas (hydrogen, oxygen, and nitrogen becoming frozen methane, ammonia, and water)—the same material which we theorize makes up Uranus and Neptune. Comets remain frozen while their orbit keeps them in the outer solar system past the trans-Saturnian planets. The Chinese called comets and novae **guest stars.**

---

comet comes from the Greek word κομητησ *(kometes)* = long haired, from κομη *(kome)* = hair which is *coma* in Latin

---

The Structure and Origin of Comets

Head *Nucleus* is the bright center of a comet made mostly of ice—bright because it reflects sunlight. It is about ½ to 6 miles (1 to 10 kilometers) in diameter.

Coma is made of gas and dust and reflects sunlight. Gas floureses from absorbing radiation and ultra violet rays from the Sun. The coma has an enormous size of 62,140 miles (100,000 kilometers) or more. Every time a comet passes the Sun and forms a coma, it loses part of its material. The coma shrinks as it forms the tail. After passing close by the Sun nearly a thousand times, the coma uses itself up.

Tails develop only when a comet approaches the Sun, if at all. The tails face away from the Sun. Chinese comet observers noticed this first. The tail is made from material ejected from the nucleus and pushed away by solar radiation and solar wind. Most comets have two tails. One is nearly straight and is made of ionized particles. The other is covered and made mostly of dust. As a comet approaches the Sun its tails get longer. Ion tails can be as long as 190 million miles (300 million kilometers).

Comet Abe.

Origin Most astronomers think that comets come from a nonvisible cloud of orbiting comets and meteors surrounding the solar system at about 150,000 A.U. from the Sun. This idea came from **Ernst Opik** in 1932, and in 1952, the Dutch astronomer **Jan Oort** refined it. Gravity from stars passing within a few light years of the Sun and in between the **Oort Cloud** forces millions of comets out of the cloud. Some comets head out beyond the solar system. Others change their orbits but remain within the cloud. Still other comets stop their motion and lacking the momentum of their own orbit, fall towards the Sun in a new, slow orbit through the solar system. The planets (especially Jupiter) and the Sun exert pulls and deflections on the comets which further shape their orbits. These orbits are so large that you can only see a comet for the short time when it travels near the Sun. The rest of its orbit is beyond the range of our visibility. The time between when you can see the comet again would be so long that you might think you were seeing a new comet instead of the return of an old one.

In the next project you can make a model of a comet.

In 1744, when he was 14, **Charles Messier** (1730–1817) observed a brilliant comet. From that day on, comets became the focus of his whole life. He drew up a catalog of objects which at first may seem to be comets but were really star clusters and nebulae. His list was an effort to help him find more comets. Today, astronomers still use the **Messier Catalogue** for this and other purposes. There is a copy of Messier's Catalogue in Sky Files. Messier found Comet Halley within a month after it was first seen.

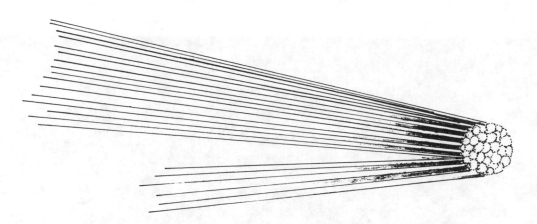

Project 89: Making a Model of a Comet

MATERIALS

cotton balls
crepe paper (two colors)
tape

glue
paint (two colors)

PROCEDURE

1. Using glue to stick the cotton balls together, make a ball the size of a softball (4 inches or 10 centimeters in diameter).

2. Paint the nucleus and coma two different colors. The nucleus is a tiny dot compared to the coma.

3. Cut each color of crepe paper into long strips (about 25 felt or 8 meters).

4. Tape or glue one end of each of the crepe paper strips to the cotton balls.

5. Tape the entire comet to the wall with one tail nearly straight and one at a slight angle. Both tails should spread out at the ends.

OBSERVATIONS

Your comet is a scale model: 1 inch = 75,000 miles (1 centimeter = 50,000 kilometers). How does the head of the comet compare in size to the tail? On which side of your comet would the Sun be? This project is adapted from a project developed by Dennis Schatz of the Pacific Science Center. Used with permission.

The first person to discover a comet that you could only see through a telescope was the American astronomer **Maria Mitchell** (1818–1889). In 1848, she won a medal from the King of Denmark for her discovery and the honor of having the comet named after her. Inscribed on the medal in Latin were the words, "Not in vain do we watch the setting and rising of the stars." **Caroline Herschel** (1750–1848) was the first woman to discover a comet (in 1786). Over the years, she discovered seven more. The most recent comet discoveries by a woman are being made by **Carolyn Shoemaker,** who has discovered 13 comets so far.

Maria Mitchell

Caroline Herschel

Meteors and Meteorites Have you ever been outside at night looking at the stars when suddenly a thin line of light darts across the sky then disappears as quickly as it came? It's a delightful surprise to see these "shooting" or "falling stars." What you're seeing is a **meteor,** not a star. We have found out what meteors are by finding them when they fall to the ground. On the ground we call them **meteorites.** Before they appear in our atmosphere as streaks of light, they travel through spare as **meteoroids.**

---

meteor comes from the Greek word $\mu\varepsilon\tau\alpha$ (meta) = beyond, and $\grave{\alpha}\varepsilon\iota\rho\omega$ (aeiro) = raise, or any thing raised beyond the atmosphere
The study of watery meteors (rain, hail, snow, etc.) = **meteorology**

Meteoroids A meteoroid is a rocky scrap of rubble, smaller than an asteroid, moving through space in orbit around the Sun. It can weigh as little as a grain of sand or as much as several tons. In 1866, G. V. Schiaparelli and **Hubert Anderson Newton** (1830−1896) discovered that the Perseid meteor shower occurred whenever the Earth crossed the orbit of Comet 1862 III. Checking other meteor showers and comet paths, people came to the conclusion that meteroids must be small particles of rubble scattered from the wreckage of comets and asteroids. Meteroids travel in their own orbits.

Meteors The Earth regularly journeys through areas thick with orbiting meteoroids, Meteoroids that don't pass through the Earth's atmosphere skim across it, burning up in the friction. They light up their paths like sparks from a firework before they disappear. You can see this as a streak of light that lasts for a few seconds. These brief sparks of light are meteors. They collide and burn up in Earth's upper atmosphere so regularly that people have named and dated their "showers." The names of the showers are the constellations from which the showers seem to be coming. The best time to observe meteors is 6:00 A.M., but there is too much sunlight then; 4:00 A.M. is the second best time but the least practical for most of us. Any time after midnight is fine since the side of the Earth we are on after midnight sweeps up most of the meteoroids.

Seeing a meteor shower is an exciting event which most of us "just happen" to see. In the next project you can plan ahead so you can observe and record one or many meteor showers.

METEOR SHOWERS CHART

NAME OF CONSTELLATION FROM WHICH SHOWERS APPEAR TO COME	NUMBER OF DAYS SHOWER OCCURS	DAY OF PEAK ACTIVITY	RELATED COMET	METEORS PER HOUR
Quadrantids*	4	January 3	No Known Parent Comet	28
Lyrids	4	April 21	Thatcher 18 GY I	7
Eta Aquarids	8	May 4	Halley	7
Delta-Aquarid	3	July 30	No Known Parent Comet	27
Perseid	25	August 11	1862 III	50
Draconid	1	October 9	Giacobini-Zinner	10
Orionid	14	October 20	Halley	21
Taurid	10	October 31	Encke	?
Andromedid	2	November 14	Biela	10
Leonid	7	November 16	1866 I	21
Geminid	14	December 13	No Known Parent Comet	50

* This meteor shower occurs in what was once the old constellation Quadrans Muralis (the Mural Quadrant formed by LeLande 1n 1795). This constellation is no longer recognized. It is now between the right foot of Hercules, the left hand of Boötes and the Constellation Draco.

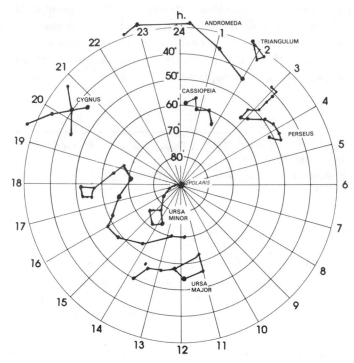

Barringer Meteorite Crater, Arizona, U.S.A. *Photo courtesy of NASA*

──── Project 90: Tracking and Photographing a Meteor Shower ────

PART 1
MATERIALS

meteor showers chart
polar map from this project

colored pencils
access to a photocopier

PART 2
MATERIALS

red felt-tip pen or colored pencil
camera (use fast lens f/2.8 or better)
tripod

film: tri-X (ASA 400) or
2475 Recording Film (ASA 1,000)

PART 1
PROCEDURE
1. Photocopy the polar map.
2. Locate where the first meteor trail begins and ends.
3. Connect the two points using a colored pencil.
4. Draw an arrow head on the line at the point where it ends.
5. Draw similar lines for all the other meteor tails. The arrow heads should show the direction meteor is moving. The point at which all the trails seem to begin is the *radiant*.
6. Mark the radiant with a red "R."

PART 2
PROCEDURE
1. Set your camera up on the tripod on a night when you know a particular meteor shower is expected and the sky is dark.
2. Aim the camera about 50° above the horizon and 45° from the radiant.
3. Expose the film for 10 to 20 minutes.
4. Develop and print the film.
5. Draw arrow heads on the meteor trails to indicate the direction they are moving.
6. Mark the radiant as in Part One, using a red felt tip pen.

OBSERVATION
Can you tell from which constellation the shower is coming?

Meteorites   The Earth's atmosphere prevents most meteoroids from reaching our planet's surface. Those which actually survive their passage through the Earth's atmosphere and fall to the ground are **meteorites.** The larger ones such as the one in Arizona about 15,000 to 40,000 years ago, have left craters 4,150 feet (1,265 meters) across and 560 feet (170 meters) deep. You can also see spectacular cratering on Mercury and the Moon.

Not all meteorites make craters. Most don't. Instead they become part of the mixture of sand and soil on Earth's mantle adding about four million tons of matter to the Earth each year. The largest meteroite ever found is in Nambia, Africa. It weighs about 60 tons and is about 4.2 cubic feet (7 cubic meters). Some meteorites are heavy since they are about 85% to 95% iron and the rest mainly nickel. Most meteorites, however, have more silicate and stone and only 10% to 15% iron and nickel.

About 100 tons of meteorite dust fall into Earth's atmosphere each day. There are enough flakes of iron and nickel in even the tiniest meteorite for you to be able to pick them up by brushing a magnet across the ground. Of the particles you collect, about 20% will be meteorite particles.

Quasars, Pulsars, and Cosmic Rays   In 1960, two radio astronomers, **Allan Sandage** and **Thomas Matthews** were hoping to see what they had only been able to detect as radio source 3C–48 (which means that in the 3rd Cambridge Catalogue of Radio Sources, this is the 48th object in the list). So far the only objects people had found in both the visible and the radio sky had been the Sun, Jupiter, and objects the size of a galaxy. Sandage and Matthews aimed the 200 inch Polamar telescope in the direction of 3C48. What they found on the photographic plates from the was a pale, bluish "star." Optical and radio astronomers working together found other photographic images of faint blue starlike objects which gave off radio signals. These objects were clearly not stars. They were almost like stars so optical astronomers began calling them "quasi-stellar objects." Radioastronomers preferred the name "quasi-stellar radio sources." In 1964, **Hong-Yee Chiu** of Columbia University invented the word **quasar** for *qua*si-s*tar* which is the name people use today.

---

quasi comes from the Latin word *quasi* = as if

Quasars show considerable red shift in their spectra. Today, astronomers estimate that 25% of all radio sources in the sky are quasars. We have found over 1,500 of them, which we have named, photographed, and studied. We still wonder exactly what they are, where this energy comes from, and how far away they are. Could quasars come from supernovae? From collisions? From our galaxy or other galaxies? From blackholes? These are a few of the ideas astronomers are looking into including the possibility that quasars follow physical laws that we haven't discovered yet. As British-born astrophysicist **Geoffrey Burbridge** once said, "We're egomaniacs to say that we know all there is to know about physics."

Quasar 3C 273

Horrid quasar, Near or far, This truth to you I must confess:
My heart for you is full of hate.
O superstar, Imploded gas, You glowing speck upon a plate,
Of Einstein's world you've made a mess!
                    —written by Jesse Greenstein on blackboards at the California Institute of Technology

Pulsars   In the summer of 1967, **Jocelyn Bell,** a graduate student from Northern Ireland, studying at Cambridge University was studying surveys of radio sources in the constellation Vulpecula. The weekly surveys appeared on 400 feet (122 meters) of paper charts. Bell's charts kept showing that her radio telescopes were picking up regular pulses of stray radio interference. The pulses came every night at a regular rate of about 1/30 of a second every 1.33728 seconds. Radio astronomers pinpointed the source as coming from a fixed point in space well beyond the solar system which rose and set with the stars. Whatever was causing the signals had an accuracy equalling some of the best clocks on Earth. Could they be signals from intelligent beings on another planet? For a few weeks, radios astronomers even called the pulsating source LGM (*Little Green Men*). After more sources turned up, it became clear that these sources weren't sending messages. Their new name became **pulsars** (*pulsa*ting *r*adio *s*ources).

A **pulsar** doesn't really pulse. It is only the impression you have of its radiation when you see it from the Earth. By calling it a pulsar, you are describing the object by what you *see*, by what *appears* to be happening rather than what may actually be happening. This is similar to describing the stars as part of a moving celestial sphere and the Sun as rising and setting.

Jocelyn Bell Burnell

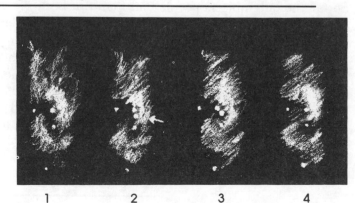

1   2   3   4

What are pulsars? One theory states that pulsars are rotating neutron stars, formed in supernovae explosions. This theory came about in the 1930s from **Walter Baade** (1893–1960) and **Fritz Zwicky** (1898–1974), the codiscoverers of supernovae. The British astronomer, Thomas Gold (who worked with Fred Hoyle on the Steady State Theory) further developed the ideas of Baade and Zwicky. The pulsar found in the heart of the crab nebula, the remains of a supernova, helped prove the neutron star theory. The force of a supernova explosion would cause the core of the dying star to cave in, driving the charged particles into the nucleus combining with the other charged particles. The result would be a tiny, densely packed clump of neutrons: a neutron star that spun very fast throwing off charged particles which leaked from the star's surface. These particles would eventually send out beams of radiation from the poles of the star. When one of the poles faces the Earth, we detect the radiation as a radio pulse just as we see the steady light on top of a police car as a flashing light.

Radio astronomers have found over 150 pulsars.

Cosmic Rays   You cannot see **cosmic rays** and the charged particles accompanying them. They are usually harmless, but once every several years, they leave the Sun during a solar flare in such large concentrations as to cause considerable damage to the structure of living cells. On the Earth our atmosphere protects us and the magnetic field surrounding the Earth deflects and absorbs lethal particles.

In the next project, you will be able to "see" cosmic rays.

The bacteria **micrococcus radiodurans** can withstand 10,000 times the radiation dose fatal to humans. How could we make use of this bacteria?

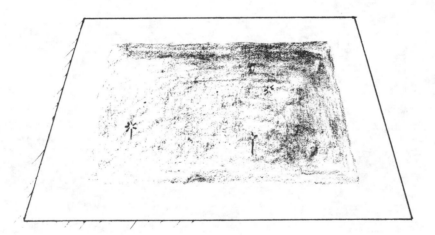

——————— **Project 91: Detecting Cosmic Rays (Scintillation Counter)** ———————

MATERIALS

sheet of cardboard or stiff paper   zinc sulfide
glue

PROCEDURE

1. Spread a thin layer of glue on one side of the cardboard.
2. Sprinkle the zinc sulfide on the wet glue. Let the glue dry.
3. Take the cardboard into dark closet.

OBSERVATIONS

The flashes of light you see are electrical particles in the air striking the zinc sulfide. When this occurs, the electrical particles change the form of their energy from movement to light. Satellites have scintillation counters on board to record these flashes of light.

Nebulae   In space, like on Earth, there are clouds. The clouds in space are **nebulae** and they come in three forms: **emission, reflection,** and **dark.**

Emission   The **Orion nebula** is an example of this kind of nebula where the ultraviolet light from the stars in it excites the hydrogen and oxygen present causing the nebula to "light up."

Reflection   The whispy clouds around the **Pleiades** are an example of a reflection nebula. The cloud itself is not emitting light, but it is reflecting light from the stars in it.

Dark   The **Horsehead nebula** in Orion is a wonderful example of a dark nebula which, containing no light, can be seen in front of an illuminated nebula behind it. (See Section 2 of this chapter for more information about nebulae.)

Nebulae provide some of the most beautiful astronomical photographs of any object in space. The Orion nebulae could easily be the most photographed celestial object. Other objects beyond our solar system like distant galaxies and clusters of stars are fascinating objects to view and photograph. Because they are so far away from Earth that you often need a fairly powerful telescope to see them, we call them **deep sky objects.** In this next project you can see these wonderful sights yourself.

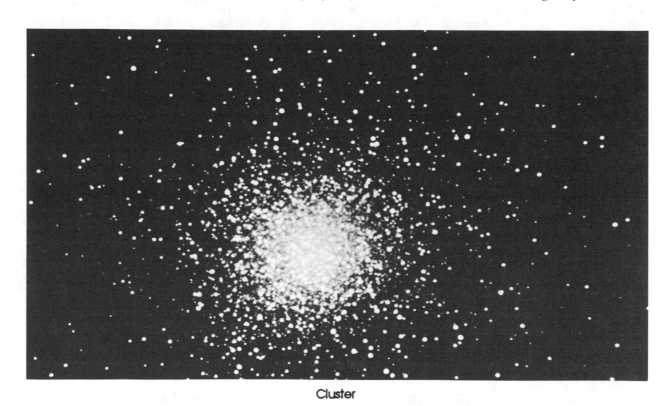

Cluster

—— Project 92: Viewing Galaxies, Nebulae, and Clusters with a Telescope ——

MATERIALS

binoculars or telescope

list of Messier Objects (galaxies and
    nebulae) from Sky Files
    M13 (Hercules)
    M42 (Orion)
    M31 (Andromeda)
    NGC 513A (Centaurus)
    Magellanic Clouds
    The Pleiaedes–Taurus
    The Hyades–Taurus

M33 (Triangulum Galaxy)
M3 (Globular Cluster)
M99 (Pinwheel Galaxy)
M51 (Whirlpool Galaxy)
M104 (Sombrero Galaxy)
M20 (Trifid Nebula)
M27 (Dumbell Nubula)
Veil Nebula
North America Nebula
M81 (Galaxy)

PROCEDURE

1. Use a low-power eyepiece and locate the objects listed. Sometimes it is easier to find things by looking a little to one side of the object rather than directly at it.
2. Make a log of your observations using the form shown here or make up one of your own.
3. Make a careful sketch of one example of a cluster, one nebula or galaxy.
4. Record for each object: name of object R.A. Dec. power of eyepiece

Time: Date:

OBSERVATIONS

Try to observe at least one example of each of the following kinds of objects:

1. Open star cluster
2. Globular star cluster
3. Galactic nebula
4. Planetary nebula
5. Galaxy

The shape of the spiral arms of a galaxy are similar to many of the spirals which occur elsewhere in nature. You can see these spirals everywhere: the heads of daisies and sunflowers, elephant tusks and the horns of wild sheep, whirlpools, the webs of certain spiders, the canals in the human ear. Descartes, who invented coordinate geometry, discovered that in these spirals, the arms are spaced farther and farther apart as they wind outward. The width of the spaces increases in a regular order. If you measure the widths, you will find that the order follows a progression in which the measurement of the third width is equal to the first and second widths multiplied together. The measurement of the fourth is equal to the second and third widths multiplied together, and so on. We call this process of growing larger by multiplication a **geometric progression.** This relationship has given the spirals in nature researched by Descartes the name **logarithmic spirals.**

An **arithmetic** spiral would be one whose spaces in between the spiral arms are equal. An example would be a phonograph record.

The logarithmic spiral is the geometric expression of organic growth and movement. It appears in the microscopic world in the trail left by subatomic particles. On Earth it appears in winds, water, plants, and animals. In the sky it appears in the solar system, wind storms on planets, and the shape of galaxies.

In this next project you can draw a logarithmic spiral and create the shape of galaxies, daisies, and all kinds of spiralled things.

——— Project 93: Drawing the Shape of the Galaxy (Logarithmic Spirals) ———

MATERIALS

tracing paper
white paper
straight edge
drawing compass

colored pencils
polar graph paper (photocopy from Sky Files)
access to a photocopier

PROCEDURE

1. Photocopy the polar graph paper from Sky Files and place it under a sheet of tracing paper. Draw a 4 inch (10 centimeter) diameter circle in the center of the page using the compass and the polar graph paper as your guide.

2. Divide the circle into 12 equal sections, 30° each.

3. Draw lines radiating from the center to all 12 points. Number each of the lines. Remove the polar graph from underneath. Replace it with a blank sheet of white paper.

4. Draw a line from point 12 to the radius at point 1 so that it meets the radius at 90° (perpendicular—a right angle).

5. Draw a perpendicular line to radius 2 from the point on radius one where the first line you drew formed a right angle.

6. Continue drawing lines from each radius until you reach the center.

7. Draw lines the same way starting from points 3, 6, and 9.

8. Extend lines as shown on drawing to points 2, 5, 8t, and 11.

9. Color each spiral with a lighter shade on the outside getter darker as it approaches the center.

10. Color the dark spaces blue on the outside of the spirals, with a **lighter shade** as you approach the spirals.

OBSERVATION

Compare your drawing with photographs of galaxies and other living things.

READING MORE

Berendzen, Richard, Richard Hart and Daniel Seeley. *Man Discovers the Galaxies.* New York: Science History Publications, 1976.

Branley, Franklyn M. *Mysteries of the Universe.* New York: E.P. Dutton, 1984.

The Editors of World Book. *The Heavens.* Chicago: The World Book Press, 1985.

The launch of *Voyager 1, 1977. Photo courtesy of Jet Propulsion Laboratory*

Section 4: *GETTING THERE*

Life Elsewhere

"Open wide the door for us, so that we may look out into the immeasurable starry universe; show us that other worlds like ours occupy the ethereal realms."

—Giordano Bruno (1548–1600)

(Medieval philosopher burned at the stake for this and other comments)

"It is not improbable, I must point out, that there are inhabitants not only on the Moon but on Jupiter too. . . . But as soon as somebody demonstrates the art of flying, settlers from our species of men will not be lacking. . . . Given ships or sails adapted to the breezes of heaven, there will be those who will not shrink from even that vast expanse."—Kepler

---

Does life, intelligent or otherwise, exist anywhere else in the universe? Life on Earth includes all the varieties of the kingdoms of nature which thrive under Earth's atmosphere and in her changing seasons. Life *as we know* it may or may not be present on other planets. There may also be a life-form unique to that planet and its particular conditions. What are the conditions required for what we call life?

1. **A cell,** the basic unit of living things
2. **DNA** (deoxyribonucleic acid) and **RNA** (ribonucleic acid), two carbon containing molecules which control the process of heredity
3. **Chemicals** necessary for the synthesis of **amino acids** (the building blocks of life)
4. **Water**
5. An **energy** source

What do living things do that qualifies them as being alive?

1. Take in food
2. Make use of what they eat to grow
3. Break down part of what they eat to produce energy
4. Eliminate waste materials
5. Reproduce
6. React to changes around them

What conditions must a planet meet in order to support life?

1. The central star (Sun) should not be more than about 1.5 solar masses.
   a. It must last long enough for life to evolve (at least two eons).
   b. It must not kill evolving life with too much ultraviolet radiation.
2. The central star should have at least 0.3 solar masses to be warm enough to create a large enough orbital area in which a planet could have liquid water.
3. The planet must orbit at the right distance from the star, so that liquid water will neither evaporate nor permanently freeze.
4. The planet's orbit must be near enough to circular to keep it that proper distance and to prevent too drastic seasonal changes.
5. The planet's gravity must be strong enough to hold a true atmosphere.

---

eon *(aeon)* = large, unmeasurable geological time period

Some astronomers figure that there is the possibility that 0.001% of the stars may have a planet that has life on it. The nearest civilized planet won't be as close as 15 to 250 light years away. Other astronomers figure that as few as 1 star in 100 million million may have a planet which supports life. The nearest of these planets would be about 10 million light years away.

Is there an intelligent life-form anywhere else in the universe? There are receivers listening in on our nearest stars. A giant radio telescope in Arecibo has been sending a coded message out into space toward the globular cluster M13 in the Milky Way since 1974. Various other programs such as the *S*earch for *E*xtra*t*errestrial *I*ntelligence (SETI) continue to attract attention and support from around the world.

We have sent two "letters of hello" into space. One is a 6 × 9 inch (15 × 23 centimeter) gold plaque on the outside of *Pioneer 10* with a drawing of a man and a woman, and a map showing where Earth is in the solar system. The other "letter" is a gold record and a collection of slides on the outside of *Voyager II* containing sights and sounds from all over the world as well as messages of greeting and friendship in many languages.

What about intelligent life visiting us? The possibility of visitors from outer space arriving in spacecraft and flying saucers has captured headlines and our imagination for years. Many people report that they have seen or photographed alien spacecraft. Since what they have seen has not been identified as ordinary planes or rockets, people call these craft **unidentified flying objects** (UFOs). Others describe meeting with **aliens.**

Flying Saucer is a term which a newspaper reporter invented to describe the object Kenneth Arnold saw above the Rocky Mountains in 1947. In January 1878, a Texas farmer saw a fast-moving object in the sky "looking like a large saucer."

alien comes from the Latin word *alienus* = foreign or an outsider

Alien can also mean someone or something that is to be excluded or even disliked. Can you think of a kinder word for people who come from another country or another planet?

Suppose you were to meet an astronaut from another planet. Do you think it would look like a human? Would it be friendly? Writers and movie-makers over the years have had fun coming up with answers to this question. Two thousand years ago, the Greek philosopher **Lucian of Samos** wrote the *True History* in which he describes a giant waterspout suddenly flinging a sailing ship from the Earth. The crew and the ship arrived on the Moon safely after an eight day journey. There they discovered a race of alien beings. In some of our modern stories, creatures from space have come to our planet to warn us about our own safety if we continue to build and use nuclear weapons. Sometimes the aliens are warlike and seek to conquer the Earth. Friendly or not, the aliens in our literature and films seem to have a much further advanced technology which makes it possible for them to travel through space and time to reach us. They may even be able to change their shape and language to match ours. Some of the aliens are living beings. Others are robots.

Robot from the Czech word *robota* = forced hard work.

In his play *R.U.R.,* the Czechoslovakian writer, **Karel Capek,** (1890–1938) made up the word "robot" to describe an artificial being that was made of organic molecules and looked like a human. We use the word **android** which comes from the Greek word ἀνδρος *(andros)* = man, to describe such a creature and use the word robot or automaton to mean a nonliving mechanical device shaped like a human being and usually made out of metal.

Flight   The dream of generations since ancient times has been to leave our planet to explore others. The Greek myth of Icaraus and Daedalus tells the story of a father and his son who escaped imprisonment by applying wings to their arms with molten wax.

Steam Motors   People have been hard at work to develop the technology to make flight possible. One of the first heat engines converted steam pressure into jet reaction. Its inventor was **Hero,** a Greek mathematician and physicist working in Alexandria between the first century B.C. and the third century A.D. Hero named his invention the **aeolipile** after Aeolus, god of the winds. The Viking rockets and X–15 rocket aircraft use similar steam jet reaction methods for their flight control.

In this next project you can make your own aeolipile out of a can. If you want your aeolipile to be a sphere like Hero's was, use a round float from the back of a toilet.

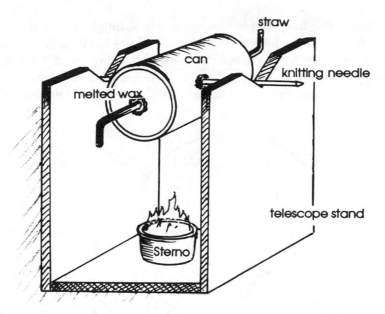

Project 94: Building a Steam Motor (Aeolipile)

MATERIALS

empty tin can
canned heat (Sterno)
candle
three pieces of wood
two drinking straws, hollow glass tubes
   or copper pipe
water

matches
nail
hammer
knitting needle
lubricating oil
the telescope stand from Project 61,
     Making a Reflecting Telescope.

PROCEDURE

1. Fill the can with enough water to reach ¼ of the way to the top when it lies on its side.
2. Put a hole in the center of the top and bottom of the can, using the hammer and the nail.
3. Push a flexible straw into each of the holes so it sticks out about 6 inches, curve straw as close to right angles as possible without creasing it. Put melted candle wax around straws where they meet the holes in the can.
4. Put holes on opposite sides of can.
5. Push the knitting needle through the holes making sure it extends at right angles to straws. Seal the places (with candle wax) where the knitting needle comes through the can. Use the needle to set the can in the telescope stand from Project 61, Making a Reflecting Telescope or build a cradle of three pieces of wood: one on the bottom, two for sides. Make sure the walls are set apart about 1½ times the size of the can. The walls should also be 4 inches (10 centimeters) taller than the canned heat container. Put a few drops of oil into each of the cradles so that the needle will rotate easily.
6. Use the canned heat flame to warm the side of the can. *Be careful to keep from burning the straws or melting the candle wax.*

OBSERVATION

As effective as the aeolipile was, no one took it seriously enough to put it to use for anything.

Leonardo da Vinci experimented with a number of flying machines. One was the first helicopter.
helicopter comes from the Greek words ελικοσ *(helikos)* = spiral, and πτερον *(pteron)* = wing

Hot Air Balloons   The first people to move freely through the air did so in 1783 in a balloon designed by two paper makers, **Joseph Montgolfier** (1740–1810) and his brother **Jacques Etienne** (1745–1799). This five mile flight across Paris lasted 25 minutes. By 1859, balloonists were able to travel as far as 804 miles. The Montgolfier brothers called their balloon an **aereostatic machine.**
In this next project you can make and launch your own aereostatic machine.

Project 95: Making a Hot Air Balloon

MATERIALS

6 sheets of light tissue wrapping paper
(at least 8 × 4 inches or 20 × 10
centimeters)
2 paper clips
scissors
paper glue

newspaper
small tin can
large tin can
canned cooking heat
hair dryer

PROCEDURE

1. Fold each sheet of tissue paper in half lengthwise and stack the folded sheets on top of each other with all the folded edges on the left. Use paper clips to hold the stack together.
2. Draw the pattern on top sheet. (See illustration.) Cut along line.
3. Place one cut out sheet of tissue paper on top of a newspaper and glue along one edge of tissue. Place the edge of another piece of tissue on top of glued piece. Continue until you have glued all six pieces together into a balloon shape open only at the bottom.
4. Let the balloon dry, then inflate it using a hair dryer.
5. Remove both ends of the smaller can.
6. Assemble the burner by cutting a hole in the big can so the smaller can fits inside.
7. Set a container of canned heat inside the burner and light the fuel.
8. *Carefully*, hold the balloon above small can so hot air goes inside the balloon without the burner touching the paper. When the balloon is full of heated air, let it go.

OBSERVATIONS

People still go up in hot air balloons. How do you think they steer and come to a landing?   This project is adapted from *Intermediate Science Curriculum Study, Winds and Weather* unit, Florida State University, 1972. Used with permission. Illustrations courtesy of Silver Burdett & Ginn, copyright 1972.

Rockets In the 1200s, the Chinese and Japanese used rockets made of bamboo sticks packed with gunpowder both as fireworks and short-range weapons ("arrows of flying fire"). British versions of these caused the "rockets red glare" which Francis Scott Key saw over Fort McHenry in 1814 and described in "The Star Spangled Banner."

In this next project you can make a very simple and very effective solid fuel rocket.

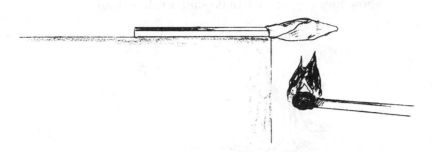

——————— **Project 96: Demonstrating How a Solid Fuel Rocket Works** ———————

MATERIALS
wooden kitchen matches   needle
aluminum foil   pin

PROCEDURE
1. Completely wrap the head of a large wooden kitchen match with aluminum foil.
2. Wrap the foil tightly around the matchstick.
3. Leave a small space all around the head, tapering to a point at the end.
4. Use the pin to poke a small hole at the tip of the end.
5. Go outside and set the match on a ledge so the head extends over the edge.
6. Place a lit match under the head of the covered match, keeping your face away from the match. *Be Careful.*

OBSERVATION
The hot gasses inside the aluminum foil had only one place they could escape. In their rush to get out, the gasses pushed the match in the opposite direction.

Airplanes Two brothers, **Wilbur** (1867–1912) and **Orville Wright** (1871–1948) built and flew more than 1,000 gliders before they decided to put a motor on one. The Wright brothers were bicycle makers in Dayton, Ohio. Their first successful "Flyer l" flight took place at Kill Devil Hill in North Carolina, at 10 o'clock in the morning on December 17th, 1903. This is the birthday of the age of the airplane.

---

airplane or aeroplane comes from the Greek words $\dot{\alpha}\varepsilon\rho o$ (aero) = air, and $\pi\lambda\alpha\nu o\varsigma$ (planos) = to wander

---

In their open cockpits, the first fliers experienced the air on their faces, the sights and sounds of their engines in front of them, and the Earth below them. Some of them put their experience into words which burst into poetry:

"With an aeroplane you do a man's work and experience a man's cares. You are in touch with the wind, the stars, the night, with the sand and the sea. You outwit the forces of Nature. You await the dawn as a gardener awaits spring. You await the next stop like a Promised Land, and in the stars you look for truth."— **Antoine de Saint-Exupery** (1900–1944), *Terre Des Hommes*

Airplane wings are curved on the top. When a plane is flying, the air on top moves faster than the air underneath and has less pressure. The slower air underneath has more push and helps to lift the plane and hold it up.

The engine of an airplane drives a wooden or metal blade which churns up the air and drives or propels the airplane forward. This blade, the **propeller,** can have two, three, or more blades. The blades each have a slight twist in them which helps the propeller scoop out the air in front of it and push it behind.

In this next project, you can show how a propeller makes an airplane move.

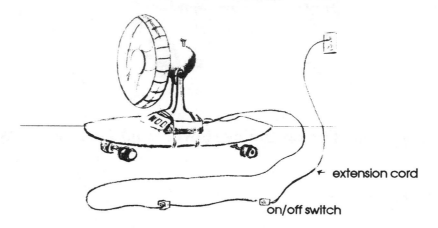

extension cord

on/off switch

———— Project 97: Demonstrating How an Airplane Works ————

MATERIALS

electric fan   skateboard
extension cord with switch   rope or twine

PROCEDURE

1. Clear a space of about 30 feet (9 meters) on the floor of a room or a hallway.
2. Tie the fan to the skateboard.
3. Plug the fan into an extension cord. Turn off the switch on the extension cord. Turn on the fan.
4. Set the skateboard on the floor and turn on the extension cord switch. To stop the skateboard, turn the fan off.

OBSERVATIONS

The skateboard is like a grounded airplane, moved by the fan. Rubber band wind up model airplanes show how the propeller can move airplanes through the sky.

Rockets Into Space   In 1634, Kepler wrote *Somnium* (The Dream) which tells of another journey to the Moon complete with the first descriptions of the Earth's gravity air above the atmosphere. A few years later, **Francis Godwin** (1562–1633) told of a trip to the Moon in which he described weightlessness in space for the first time. In the 1800s, the Russian scientist, **Konstantin Eduardovick Tsiolkovsky** (1857–1935) was the first one to write about how rockets could be used to carry people into space rather than kill them in a war. Tsiolkovsky had scarlet fever when he was ten, which made him totally deaf. He went on to pursue his scientific research and became a high-school physics and math teacher. His favorite subject, however, was space travel and he wrote several books on the subject, including a novel, *Outside the Earth.* Many of Tsiolkovsky's ideas about space travel have come true, including spacesuits, taking showers in space capsules, artificial satellites, space medicine, and solar energy.

Jules Verne, in 1865, wrote his first space novel, *From the Earth to the Moon* and joined the growing ranks of writers imagining trips to our satellite. Once in space, Verne's travelers observed that "the constellations shone with a soft lustre; they did not twinkle, for there was no atmosphere to produce scintillation. These stars were soft eyes, looking out into the dark night, amidst the silence of absolute space." When the space travelers returned safely to Earth in their metal projectile, they landed in the Pacific Ocean, three miles from the spot where a century later *Apollo 13* was to splash down. Verne was quite clear in his writing that people needed to keep a healthy attitude toward the technology which made all of this possible and not get carried away with it. People are far more important.

In 1901, the British writer, **H. G. Wells** (1866-1946), sent people to the Moon in his book, *The First Men in the Moon.* His later work, *The War of the Worlds*, presented a terrifying picture of Martian monsters attacking the Earth. When Orson Welles (no relation to H. G.) broadcast this book as a play on the radio, it caused a panic sending many people fleeing from their homes.

Two years after the publication of *The First Men on the Moon,* the first real men went up in the sky on a real flying machine. The writings of Jules Verne inspired **Robert Hutchings Goddard** (1882–1945). He was fourteen when he decided to dedicate his life to making the dream of space flight a reality. Goddard's efforts to use robots to help balloons go higher won him the title "father of American rocketry." Goddard's contributions include:

1. designs for both solid and liquid fuel rockets;
2. plans for rockets to investigate the upper atmosphere (described in his 1919 pamphlet "A Method of Reaching Extreme Altitudes");
3. the first liquid-fuel rocket in history, which he built and launched on March 16, 1926. The rocket took 2.5 seconds to reach 41 feet (12½ meters) and traveled 184 feet (56 meters) down range at the top speed of 60 miles (97 kilometers) per hour;
4. 11 foot (3 meter) rockets able to travel over 500 miles or 805 kilometers per hour;
5. first rocket with gyroscopic control system;
6. first multi-stage rockets;
7. first rocket with variable thrust engine;
8. the suggestion that a rocket could carry people to the Moon.

Robert Goddard with his first solid fuel rocket which he launched on March 16, 1926.
Photo courtesy of NASA

People recognized Goddard's work only after his death in 1945. NASA named its **Goddard Space Flight Center** in his honor.

In 1927, a group of amateur rocket engineers in Germany had formed the (*Verein Fur Raumschiffsfart* or V.F.R.) **Society for Space Travel.** During World War II, the German military called the top members of the Society to work on a special research project on the island of Usedom, off the coast of the Baltic Sea, near a small town called Peenemunde. Among the Space Travel Society members to work at the secret Peenemunde site were **Wernher von Braun** and **Hermann Oberth** from Romania.

Oberth was only one of three pioneers who lived to see the dawning of the space age. Like Tsiolkovsky and Goddard, Oberth was a teacher. These two joined many other rocket engineers. Together, they built, experimented, refined, and developed rocket techniques to the point where they were able to successfully launch 46 foot (14 meter) long, 12 ton (10,886 kilogram) liquid-fuel rockets 60 miles (97 kilometers) high with a range of 500 miles (805 kilometers) at speeds of 360 miles (579 kilometers) an hour.

The most advanced of these rockets, the **V2** became the ancestor of the modern rocket.

"Do you realize what we accomplished today? Today the space ship was born!"
—General Walter Dornberger to Dr. Wernher von Braun, October 3, 1942

After the war, the Peenemunde rocket engineers split up. Some of them went to the Soviet Union, others to the United States, where they continued to work in much the same kind of research facilities that they had enjoyed in Germany. Their efforts produced the rocket technology that has made Soviet and American space flight possible.

Rockets In the 14th century, the Italian **Muratori** made up the word *rocchetta* which comes from the Italian word *rocca* = a staff for holding the flax or wool from which thread is made by spinning.

How does a rocket work?

A **rocket** is a jet-propelled object that carries its engine and fuel along with it and whose functioning does not depend on the presence of an atmosphere.

payload could be passengers or objects, limited by the amount of space required by fuel;

oxidizer is necessary for fuel to burn, especially if a rocket will be traveling beyond atmosphere, such as liquid oxygen nitrogen tetroxide, fluoride, LOX (short for liquid oxygen);

liquid fuel is ethyl alcohol, such as gasoline, kerosene, and liquid hydrogen;

combustion chamber is where oxidizer and liquid fuel mix and are ignited, burning rapidly, generating hugh volumes of hot gases. The pressure in the chamber builds up with vents above the gases to escape outward through the engine's nozzle. The mass of gas released its exceptionally high speed of escape thrusts the rocket forward in the opposite direction of the outrushing gases;

thrust is the force which propels a rocket;

propellant is the substance or substances used to provide thrust for rocket;

solid fuel is such as potassium nitrate, sulfur, and charcoal packed tightly;

combustion chamber is where the fuel is limited and burns explosively;

vent or opening is where last gases are expelled causing a forward thrust;

In this next project you can see how a jet works.

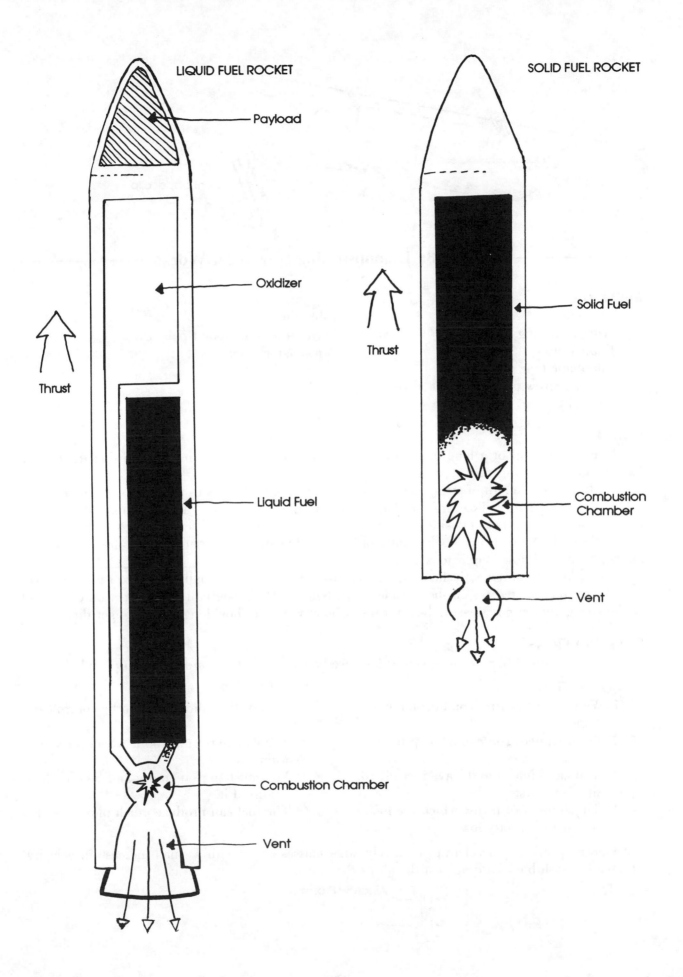

LIQUID FUEL ROCKET

Payload

Oxidizer

Thrust

Liquid Fuel

Combustion Chamber

Vent

SOLID FUEL ROCKET

Thrust

Solid Fuel

Combustion
Chamber

Vent

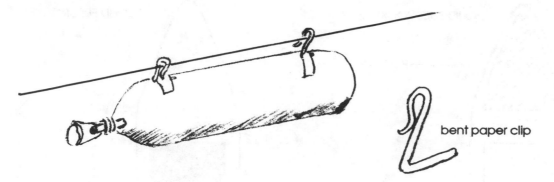

bent paper clip

—————— **Project 98: Demonstrating How a Jet Works** ——————

MATERIALS

long balloon
string or fishing line
2 paper clips
cellophane tape
drinking straw or small, light piece of
metal tubing

rubber band
barrel from a ballpoint pen or a
mechanical pencil

PROCEDURE

1. Place the end of a long balloon over a small section of a drinking straw using the rubber band to keep them together.

2. Run a long length of string across the room. Attach both ends to the wall or to chairs.

3. Bend two paper clips into the shape shown in the illustration. Tape them onto the inflated balloons so they face the opposite way (just as in the illustration).

4. Blow the balloon up, hook it onto one end of the string, and let go. Measure how far the balloon went and how long it took to get there.

5. Replace the straw with the plastic barrel from the outside of a ballpoint pen or a mechanical pencil with the pointed tip on the outside of the balloon. Re-inflate balloon, hook it onto one end of the string and let go. Measure how far the balloon went and how long it took to get there.

OBSERVATIONS

Was there any difference in speed or distance between the straw and the pen tip? Why?

SOLID FUEL

1. You cannot control combustion and flight.

2. Once ignited, you cannot stop it.

3. You can build it and leave it ready to fire for years.

4. The amount of thrust which the fuel produces is pretty low.

LIQUID FUEL

1. Combustion and flight can be controlled.

2. You can start and stop it whenever you want

3. You must store it empty and fuel it when you need it.

4. The fuel can produce much more power.

Airscrew (propeller) accelerates relatively large masses of air with a small increase in velocity. The blades push backward against the air as they turn.

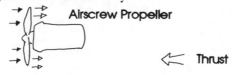

Airscrew Propeller

Thrust

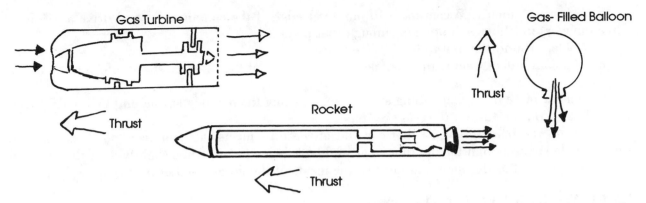

Gas Turbine

Thrust

Rocket

Thrust

Gas- Filled Balloon

Thrust

Gas Turbine accelerates the gas masses (air and combustion) with a relatively large increase in velocity. Uses air to burn its fuel. Can only work in the atmosphere.

Rocket accelerates masses at rest (propelled or combustion products) to a very high exit velocity. With its self-contained oxygen supply, the rocket is useful anywhere.

In this project you can see how a jet turbine works by making a model of one yourself.

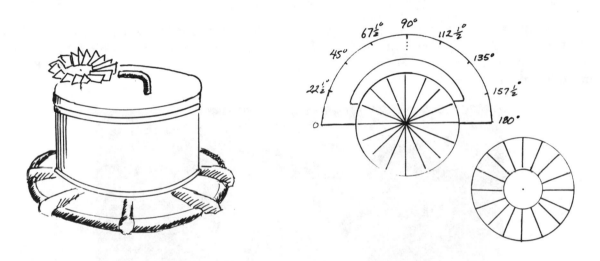

Project 99: Building a Model Jet Turbine

MATERIALS

felt-tip pen
cookie container with tight-fitting lid
scissors
aluminum foil pie tin
protractor
drawing compass
3 long finishing nails

solder and soldering tool
hammer
thin copper tubing ¼ × 3¼ inch
 (6 × 83 millimeters)
glass of water
stove
tube bending spring

PROCEDURE

1. Cut a 3 inch (7½ centimeter) diameter disk from the pie plate.
2. Divide the disk into 16 equal parts, 22½°, each using compass and protractor and felt-tip pen.
3. Draw a 1 inch (2.5 centimeter) circle in the center of the disk.
4. Cut along each line in the disk up to the inner circle.
5. Twist each section of the disk to a 45° angle. (This is the *rotor*.)

6. Measure 1 inch (2.5 centimeter) from outer edge of the container lid and drive a 1½ inch (4 centimeter) finishing nail upward through that point.

7. Solder around the nail to hold it into place.

8. Make an indentation with a nail point in the center of the rotor. Rest the rotor on top of the nail.

9. Bend a piece of copper tubing at right angles using the bending spring and two nails driven into a board. Be careful not to crease the pipe.

10. Hold the bent tubing so that one end of the tube meets the container top. Use a nail to make a hole large enough for the tube to fit in. Flare the end of the tube slightly with the nail and pull the flared end of the tube tight against the inside of the lid and solder it into place.

USING YOUR MODEL JET TURBINE

Fill the container with ½ glass of water, put the lid on tightly, and place the container on a burner of a stove. Heat the water until it makes enough steam to come out of the tube and drive the rotor.

OBSERVATION

Is this use of steam more effective than the aeolipile in Project 94, Building a Steam Motor (Aeolipile)?

Living in Space   Traveling in space is a remarkable experience. No weight. No noise. It also presents problems. Our bodies and our form of life require certain conditions which do not exist in space. You have to be inventive if you want to reproduce these conditions in space, especially if you want to live there.

U.S. Astronaut Bruce McCandless using his jetpack to move in weightless space, February 7, 1984.
Photo courtesy of NASA

The history of space travel has meant preparing both people and machines to be capable of such a journey. The history of rocketry lists the events in the development of a rocket capable of leaving the Earth's atmosphere. Wings, fins, and propellers make use of the air in our atmosphere to move airplanes and jets once outside the atmosphere. Where there is no air, these devices no longer work. To enter this airless environment you must develop enough speed to escape the pull of Earth's gravity. To do this, you need to travel 25,000 miles (40,233 kilometers) per hour. This is the **escape velocity**. See the information charts on the planets in Sky Files for their escape velocity.

In order to develop the amount of energy necessary to move at speeds this fast, you need a powerful rocket with large amounts of fuel. At least 75% of a rocket's weight would have to be fuel. All of this hardware adds to the weight of the package you are trying to launch into space. To keep the weight of the rocket down and the quantity of the fuel up, the fuel tanks on the *Atlas* rocket are so thin-walled, they cannot even stand up under their own weight. The *Saturn 5* rocket which carried the *Apollo* astronauts to the Moon weighed 3,000 tons at lift off.

When it lifted off, the rocket's five engines burned off 4,400,000 pounds (1,995,840 kilograms) of LOX and kerosene-type fuel in 2½ minutes developing 7.5 million pounds (3.4 million kilograms) of thrust.

The Vehicle Assembly Building at Cape Canaveral is the world's largest building.

Gravity   As a creature of the Earth, you are used to walking with your feet on the ground and drinking from glasses whose liquid content stays at the bottom until we pour it out. On Earth, "what goes up, must come down," or as my friend used to say, "whatever is down, must have been up." In space, there is no up or down. This condition of no weight causes medical problems. You get motion sickness. Your red blood cell count drops for about a month and you produce less blood. Your pulse rate drops and your bones discard calcium. You also lose nitrogen and phosphorus. Space travel presents a real challenge to doctors, nurses, and medical research to understand and treat these conditions. The challenge to the engineers and architects is to recreate the forces of gravity within their space villages. To create an Earth-like gravity, the arm of a space station would have to spin 3½ times a minute.

At such a rate, you also get another Earth-like condition, the Coriolis affect. (See Chapter 4, Section 4.) This is the source of dizziness and motion sickness, when a person is rotating rapidly. Because we are small, compared to the Earth, the effects are larger. A space station which is bigger than a person but smaller than the Earth will have to deal with the Coriolis effect or else water or objects traveling in the air will have sharp curves in their paths.

For a variety of reasons, the most comfortable rotation rate for a space station has been set at 1 rpm. At this rate to achieve normal gravity (1.8), you would have to be a mile from the center. A popular design is the **torus design** which looks like a hugh bicycle tire, one mile (1.6 kilometers) in diameter and 400 feet (122 meters) wide.

The word **space station** comes from the science fiction novel *Between Two Planets* by **Curd Lasswitz** (1848–1910), published in 1897.

Gravity would be different at different places within the space station. There would be less at the center and more at the ends. This could have some curious effects on life within your own home. If you lived in a two-story space station home, gravity would be about .5% weaker in the second story. If you weighed 100 pounds (45 kilograms) you would loose a ½ pound (¼ kilogram) just by walking upstairs. Imagine the change in your weight if you lived near the center of the space station and visited a friend who lived at one of the ends!

In this next project, you can made your own model of a spinning space station.

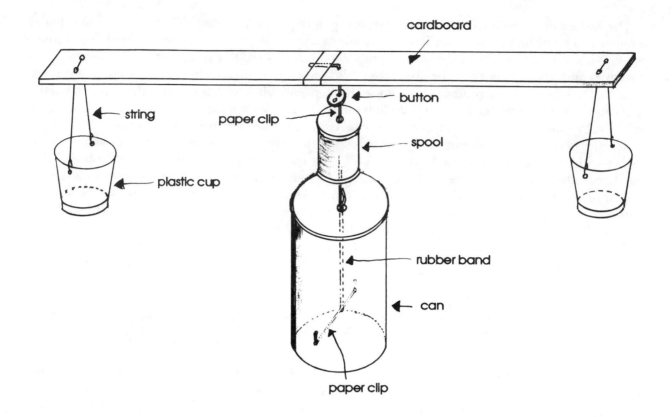

cardboard

button

string

paper clip

spool

plastic cup

rubber band

can

paper clip

—————— **Project 100: Demonstrating How a Space Station Rotates** ——————

MATERIALS

thick piece of cardboard, 20 x 1 inch
   (50 x 2½ centimeters)
strong tape
2 clear plastic drinking cups
modelling clay
knife (or razor blade)
long rubber band
empty tin or cardboard can

2 paper clips
button
nail
spool of thread
string
modelling clay
water

PROCEDURE

1. Poke a hole with the nail into the center of the lid of the can.
2. Put the button on top of the spool and the spool on top of the lid of the can.
3. Straighten out a paper clip. Bend one end into a hook and use it to hold one end of the rubber band inside the can. Push the other end of the paper clip through the hole in the can and up through the spool and the button. Bend about 1 inch (2½ centimeters) of the paper clip so that it doesn't slip through the button.
4. Use the nail to poke two small holes in the sides of the can opposite each other about 1 inch (2½ centimeters) from the open end of the can.
5. Straighten out the other paper clip and push it through one of the holes in the side of the can. Pull the rubber band down in front of the hole, push the paper clip through the opening in the rubber band and through the hole on the other side of the can. Bend both ends of the paper clip so that it doesn't slip through the can. The can is now the *power station*.
6. Put a small hole in the exact center of the long piece of cardboard and a hole ½ inch (12 millimeters) from each of the ends. The piece of cardboard is now the *arm*.

7. Push the paper clip wire from the top of the power station through the hole in the center of the arm. Rebend the paper clip (if necessary) and tape it securely to the arm. Wind the arm up and test it to see that it rotates freely and that the paper clip is secure.

8. Trim down the two plastic drinking cups using the knife (or razor blade) so the cups are each about 2½ inches (6 centimeters) tall. Punch two holes opposite each other in the sides of each drinking cup near their tops. The drinking cups are now the *cylinders*.

9. Tie a piece of string to one of the holes in one of the cylinders. Thread the string through the other hole in the opposite side. Repeat for the other cylinder.

10. Wind the arm up about 50 turns while holding your finger over the center to keep it from moving. Hold the power station from underneath and extend it away from you. Slowly remove your finger from the arm. It should turn. Hold the power station sideways so that the arm turns vertically. This is the orbiting position for a space station or space colony.

11. Wind up the arm again. Put a modelling clay person in each cylinder. Let the arm speed up slowly in the orbiting position. As the cylinders swivel up level with the arm, the people remain on their feet. If the cylinder was a space station, you could stand up and walk around.

12. Try the same experiment with water. Fill the cylinders about ½ full of water. Have the arm speed up at steady rate in the orbiting position. The water stays at the bottom of the cylinders. If the cylinder was a space station and there was a bathtub inside, you could take a bath.

OBSERVATIONS

Your project shows you how people imagine that it will be possible to recreate certain Earth conditions, such as gravity, in space. How would you equip a space station or space colony to provide all the materials humans need to live normal life?

1. How would you provide for food?
2. How would you provide for water?
3. How would you recycle oxygen and CO_2?
4. What would you do with human waste?
5. Draw a plan for a space station or a space colony. Include places for work, recreation, sleeping, food production and any other areas you feel would be needed.

Part of this project is adapted from *Holt Life Science*, New York: Holt Rinehart and Winston, Publishers, 1982.

As one science writer desribed it, the space colony will be small, like a medieval village. You could walk around it in an hour or so. Settlers there will raise families which will parent the first space children, children who know no other home. Perhaps one day, the colony may declare itself to be a new nation, independent of Earth, or even the Sun, as they set their course through space as citizens of the galaxy.

Soviet Cosmonaut Yuri Gagarin,
the first person in space.

READING MORE

Feldman, Anthony. *Space*. New York: Facts on File, Inc. 1980.

Harrison, Harry & Malcolm Edwards. *Spacecraft in Fact and Fiction*. New York: Exeter Books, 1979.

Osman Tony, *Space History*. New York: St. Martin's Press, 1983.

"When I looked toward the horizon I saw an unusual distortion, very distinctly. The Earth was ringed by a light blue halo, which gradually darkened, turned turquoise, dark blue violet, then coal black.

Trembling with excitement, I watched a world so new and unknown to me, trying to see and remember everything. Astonishingly bright cold stars could be seen through the windows. They were still far away—oh, how far away—but in orbit they seemed closer than the Earth. But the point was not the distance (my distance from the Earth was but a drop in the ocean compared to the light-years separating us from the stars) but the principle. Man had overcome the force of Earth's gravity and gone out into space."

—Yuri Gagarin (1934–1968), the first person to look at Earth from outer space

Photo courtesy of NASA

SKY FILES

HELPFUL NUMBERS FOR MEASURING

LENGTH

1 inch = 25.4 millimeters   1 centimeter = 0.3937 inches

1 inch = 2.54 centimeters   1 meter = 1.0936 yards

1 foot = 0.3048 meters   1 meter = 3.3 feet

1 yard = 0.9144 meters   1 kilometer = 0.6214 miles

1 mile = 1.6093 kilometers

1 Astronomical Unit (A.U.) = 92,960,116 miles (149,597,870,000 kilometers)

1 parsec = 2062265 A.U.

         3.262 light years

speed of light = 186,291 miles per second (299,792.458 kilometers per second)

1 light year = 5.88 trillion miles (9.46 trillion kilometers)

1 year = 365.242199 days

1 Å = 1 ten billionth of a meter

MASS

1 ounce = 28 grams   1 kilogram = 2.2046 pounds

1 pound = 0.4536 kilogram   1 gram = 0.0353 ounce

TEMPERATURE

Celsius (centigrade) = Fahrenheit° - 32 x 5/9

Fahrenheit = Celsius° x 9/5 + 32

Kelvin = Fahrenheit° + 459° x 5/9

Kelvin = Celsius ° + 273

Freezing Point (water)   Boiling Point (water)

     273 K   373 K

     32° F   212° F

     0° C   100° C

THE CIRCLE

one circle = 360° π = 3 1/7 or 22/7 or 3.14159

1° = 60 minutes of an arc = 60'   circumference = π x diameter or C = π d

1' = 60 seconds of an arc = 60"

THE GREEK ALPHABET

A α	alpha
B β	beta
Γ γ	gamma
Δ δ	delta
E ε	epsilon
Z ζ	dzeta
H η	eta
Θ θ	theta
I ι	iota
K κ	kappa
Λ λ	lambda
M μ	mu
N ν	nu
Ξ ξ	ksi
O o	omicron
Π π	pi
P ρ	rho
Σ σ	sigma
T τ	tau
Y υ	upsilon
Φ φ	phi
X χ	chi
Ψ ψ	psi
Ω ω	omega

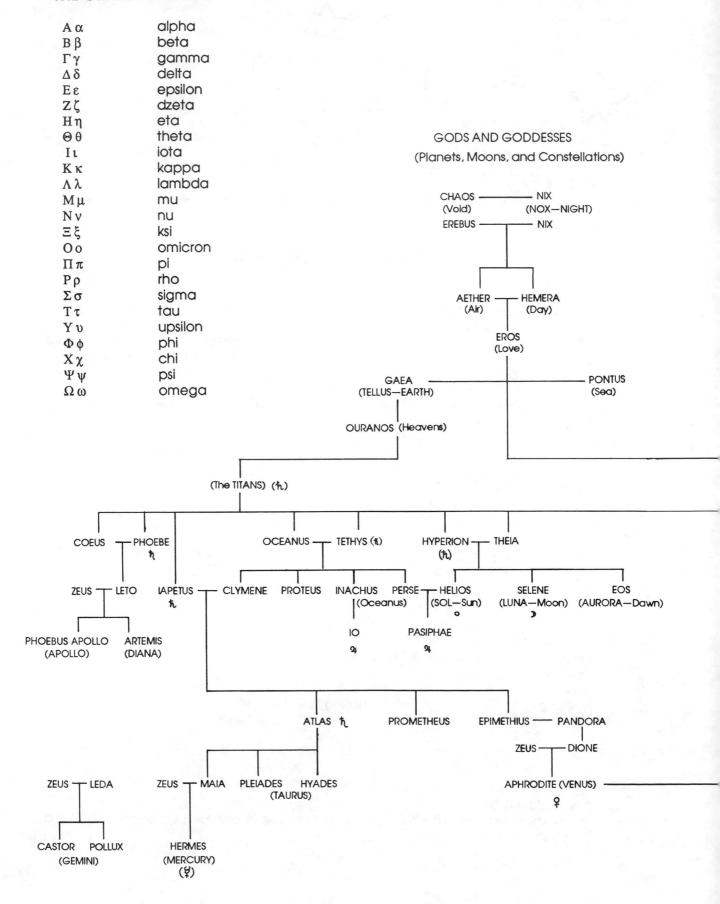

GODS AND GODDESSES
(Planets, Moons, and Constellations)

CHAOS (Void) —— NIX (NOX—NIGHT)

EREBUS —— NIX

AETHER (Air) —— HEMERA (Day)

EROS (Love)

GAEA (TELLUS—EARTH) —— PONTUS (Sea)

OURANOS (Heavens)

(The TITANS) (♄)

COEUS —— PHOEBE ♄   OCEANUS —— TETHYS (♄)   HYPERION (♄) —— THEIA

ZEUS —— LETO   IAPETUS ♄ —— CLYMENE   PROTEUS   INACHUS (Oceanus)   PERSE —— HELIOS (SOL—Sun) ○   SELENE (LUNA—Moon) ☽   EOS (AURORA—Dawn)

PHOEBUS APOLLO (APOLLO)   ARTEMIS (DIANA)   IO ♃   PASIPHAE ♃

ATLAS ♄   PROMETHEUS   EPIMETHIUS —— PANDORA

ZEUS —— DIONE

ZEUS —— LEDA   ZEUS —— MAIA   PLEIADES   HYADES (TAURUS)   APHRODITE (VENUS) ♀

CASTOR   POLLUX (GEMINI)   HERMES (MERCURY) (☿)

298

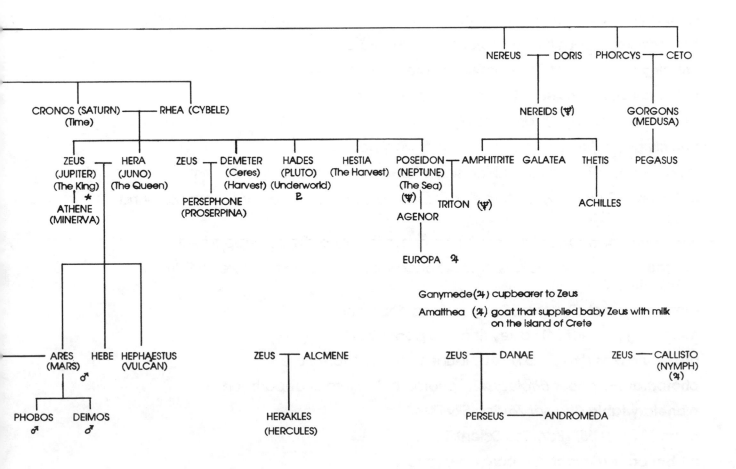

NEREUS —— DORIS   PHORCYS —— CETO

CRONOS (SATURN) —— RHEA (CYBELE)
(Time)

NEREIDS (♆)   GORGONS
(MEDUSA)

ZEUS   HERA   ZEUS   DEMETER   HADES   HESTIA   POSEIDON —— AMPHITRITE GALATEA   THETIS   PEGASUS
(JUPITER)   (JUNO)   (Ceres)   (PLUTO)   (The Harvest) (NEPTUNE)
(The King) (The Queen)   (Harvest)   (Underworld)   (The Sea)

ATHENE   ♇   (♆)
(MINERVA)   PERSEPHONE   TRITON (♆)   ACHILLES
                      (PROSERPINA)   AGENOR

                                                              EUROPA ♃

                                            Ganymede(♃) cupbearer to Zeus

                                            Amalthea (♃) goat that supplied baby Zeus with milk
                                                      on the island of Crete

ARES   HEBE   HEPHAESTUS   ZEUS —— ALCMENE   ZEUS —— DANAE   ZEUS —— CALLISTO
(MARS) ♂   (VULCAN)   (NYMPH)
                                                                                              (♃)

PHOBOS   DEIMOS   HERAKLES   PERSEUS ———— ANDROMEDA
♂   ♂   (HERCULES)

299

WHERE TO FIND MATERIALS FOR THE PROJECTS

You can find most of the materials required for the projects at discount stores, drug stores, hardware stores, flea markets, Sears, K-Mart, Goodwill, or Salvation Army stores.

There also are a number of science supply stores that provide items such as diffraction grating, magnets, prisms, etc. If there isn't one near your home, you may want to write to one for a catalog. A good one is Edmund Scientific Company, 101 East Gloucester Pike, Barrington, New Jersey, 08007.

bag of lime *(Project 8)* hardware store

ball bearing *(Project 59)* autoparts store, some gas stations

blueprint paper *(Project 9)* drafting supply store or a company that makes blueprints

bolt with wing nut and washer *(Project 34)* hardware store

cable release *(Project 63)* photography store or department

canned cooking heat *(Project 95)* Sterno, from grocery store

cellophane strips *(Project 22)* plastic wrap for food

clear glass globe *(Projects 27, 31)* light fixture department

copper pipe *(Project 94)* hardware store

diffraction grating *(Project 67)* Edmund Scientific Co.

drinking straws *(Projects 94, 95)* grocery store

dry ice *(Project 77)* ice-cream store

grease pencil/china marker *(projects throughout book)* art or office supply store

fine powder (lycopodium) *(Project 48)* drug store

finishing nail *(Project 95)* hardware store or department

flat black paint *(Project 62)* paint or hardware store

glycerine *(Project 48)* drug store

iron filings *(Project 37)* a soapless steel wool pad

lead weights *(Project 53)* fishing sinker from sporting goods department

lodestone *(Project 39)* nature store, science section of large toy store, or Edmund Scientific Co.

lubricating oil *(Project 94)* 3-in-1 oil from sewing or hardware department

magnet *(Project 39)* nature store, science section of large toy store, or Edmund Scientific Co.

metal grommet *(Projects 12, 18)* sewing department

metal ring *(Project 36)* a key ring or a paper clip

observing lens *(Project 61)* eye loupe from hardware store

photographic paper *(Project 62)* photography store or department

planetary table *(Project 76)* See Sky Files.

prism *(Project 65)* Edmund Scientific Co.

rubber caps *(Project 35)* hardware store

rubber cut from a tire tube *(Project 85)* gas station or tire store

rubber or plastic tubing *(Project 44)* sporting goods department

sheet of plastic *(Project 2)* report covers (the thicker the better) from stationery departments

sheet of plexiglass *(Project 32)* glass company or hardware store

solder and soldering tool *(Project 99)* hardware store or department store

styrofoam balls *(Project 80)* craft and hobby store or department

suspension wire *(Project 53)* hardware store

thermometers *(Project 77)* long, without a back, from housewares department

thin wire *(Project 58)* hardware store

tube bending spring *(Project 99)* hardware store

water plant *(Project 42)* pet shop

white pencil *(Project 35)* art or stationery department or office supply store

zinc sulfide *(Project 91)* drug store or a high school or college chemistry department

zodiac grid *(Project 16)* See Sky Files.

Polar Coordinate, Radius 20 Divisions 5th Accent, Circumference 1° 5° 15° Divisions

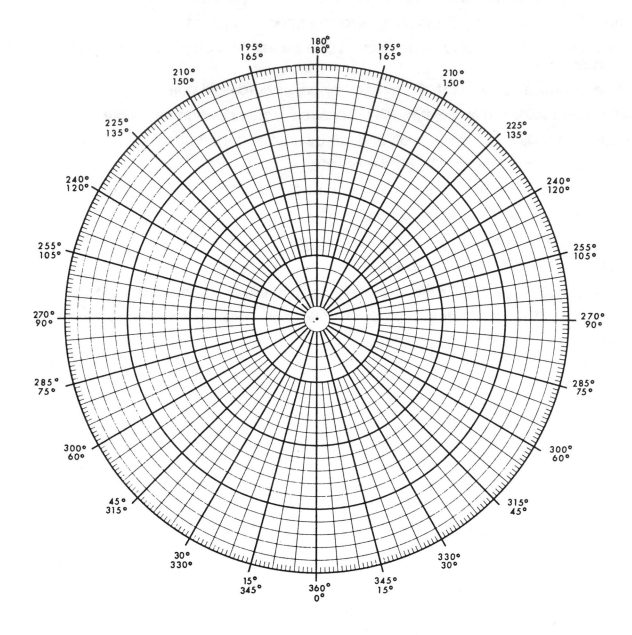

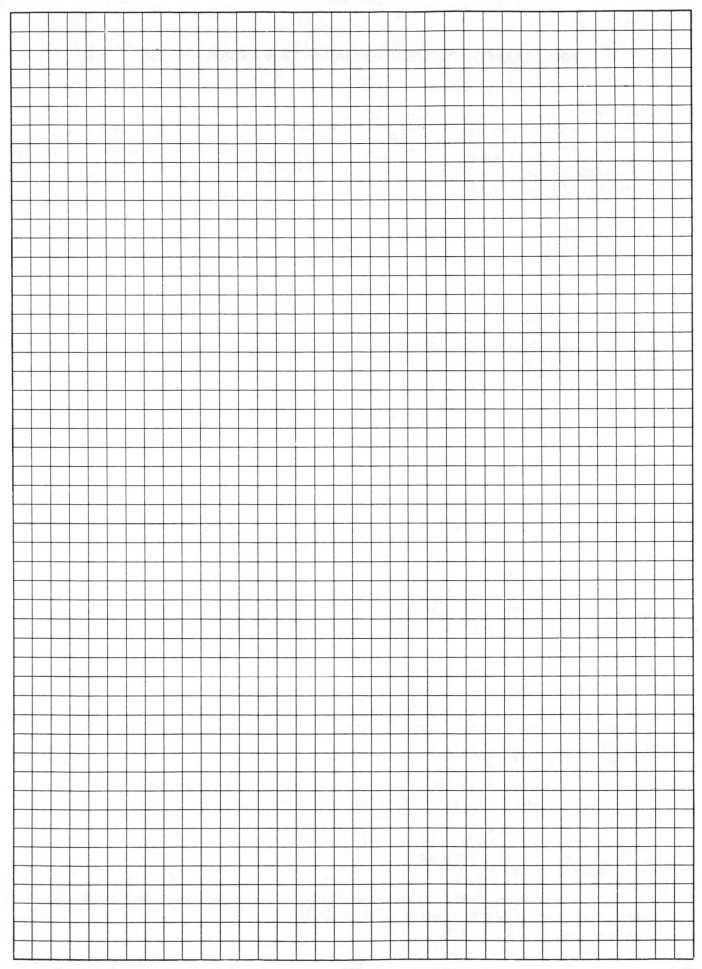

PROGRAM FOR PROJECT 36: MAKING AN ASTROLABE (IBM)

```
10 SCREEN 2: SCREEN 0:CLS:DIM H(1000), Y(1000), J(1000)
20 I=1:M=50+(80/11)
30 INPUT "calibration for which latitude?",A%
40 INPUT "radius for equatorial circle?",B%         (This can be in inches or centimeters.)
50 INPUT "step differential?",C%             (This is the number of degrees between coordinates.
60 FOR D=0 TO 90 STEP C%                              10 is usually enough.)
70 F=B%*COS(A%/M)
80 G=SIN(A%/M)+SIN(D/M)
90 H(I)=F/G
100 Z=B%*COS(D/M)
110 J(I)=Z/G
120 I=I+1:NEXT D
140 R(1)=B%*TAN(33.75/M)
150 R(2)=B%
160 R(3)=B%*TAN(56.25/M)
170 I=I-1:J(I)=0
190 X=-B%*TAN(A%/57.27273):V=1
200 FOR W=10 TO 180 STEP 10
210 Y(V)=-B%*1/TAN(W/M)*1/COS(A%/M)
220 V=V+1:NEXT W:V=V-1
230 INPUT "printer? (Y/N)",K$
240 IF K$="Y" THEN GOTO 340 :ELSE
250 CLS:LOCATE 1,16:PRINT"ASTROLABE CO-ORDS"
260 PRINT:PRINT"For Lat.",A%," Circle Size",B%
270 PRINT"Tropic of Cancer    ",R(1)
280 PRINT"Equator             ",R(2)
290 PRINT"Tropic of Capricorn",R(3)
300 PRINT:PRINT"        X-plot                        Radius":PRINT
310 L=L+1:IF L=I+1 THEN GOTO 430
320 PRINT SPC(5) H(L) SPC(20) J(L)
330 GOTO 310
340 CLS:LOCATE 1,16:LPRINT"ASTROLABE CO-ORDS"
350 LPRINT:LPRINT"For Lat.",A%," Circle Size",B%
360 LPRINT"Tropic of Cancer    ",R(1)
370 LPRINT"Equator             ",R(2)
380 LPRINT"Tropic of Capricorn",R(3)
390 LPRINT:LPRINT"        X-plot                        Radius":PRINT
400 L=L+1:IF L=I+1 THEN GOTO 430
410 LPRINT SPC(5) H(L) SPC(20) J(L)
420 GOTO 310
430 INPUT "More?",T$
440 IF T$="Y" THEN GOTO 450:ELSE GOTO 600
450 IF K$="Y" THEN GOTO 530 :ELSE
460 PRINT"              Arc co-ords"
470 PRINT:PRINT"The Y co-ord remains constant at ";X
480 PRINT"the X co-ord varies as follows:"
490 FOR T=10 TO 170 STEP 10
500 PRINT,Y(S):S=S+1
510 NEXT T
520 PRINT"Use each X co-ord as a positive and a negative":PRINT"value to determi
ne the co-ord for both sets of arcs.":GOTO 600
530 LPRINT"              Arc co-ords"
540 LPRINT:PRINT"The Y co-ord remains constant at ";X
550 LPRINT"the X co-ord varies as follows:":PRINT
560 LFOR T=10 TO 170 STEP 10
570 LPRINT,Y(S):S=S+1
580 NEXT T
590 LPRINT"Use each X co-ord as a positive and a negative":LPRINT"value to deter
mine the co-ord for both sets of arcs.":END

600 for F-1 To 9000: NEXT F: END
```

EQUATION OF TIME CHART

How many minutes is the Sun faster or slower than the clock?

Day	Jan.	Feb.	March	April	May	June	July	August	Sept.	Oct.	Nov.	Dec.
1	-3.0	-13.5	-12.5	-4.0	+3.0	+2.5	-3.5	-6.5	0.0	+10.0	+16.5	+11.0
2	-3.5	-13.5	-12.5	-3.5	+3.0	+2.5	-4.0	-6.0	0.0	+10.5	+16.5	+11.0
3	-4.0	-14.0	-12.0	-3.5	+3.0	+2.0	-4.0	-6.0	+0.5	+10.5	+16.5	+10.5
4	-4.5	-14.0	-12.0	-3.0	+3.0	+2.0	-4.0	-6.0	+1.0	+11.0	+16.5	+10.0
5	-5.0	-14.0	-12.0	-3.0	+3.5	+2.0	-4.5	-6.0	+1.0	+11.5	+16.5	+9.5
6	-5.5	-14.0	-11.5	-2.5	+3.5	+1.5	-4.5	-6.0	+1.5	+11.5	+16.5	+9.0
7	-6.0	-14.0	-11.5	-2.5	+3.5	+1.5	-4.5	-6.0	+2.0	+12.0	+16.5	+9.0
8	-6.5	-14.0	-11.0	-2.0	+3.5	+1.0	-5.0	-5.5	+2.0	+12.0	+16.5	+8.5
9	-7.0	-14.5	-11.0	-2.0	+3.5	+1.0	-5.0	-5.5	+2.5	+12.5	+16.0	+8.0
10	-7.0	-14.5	-10.5	-1.5	+3.5	+1.0	-5.0	-5.5	+3.0	+13.0	+16.0	+7.5
11	-7.5	-14.5	-10.5	-1.5	+3.5	+0.5	-5.5	-5.0	+3.0	+13.0	+16.0	+7.0
12	-8.0	-14.5	-10.0	-1.0	+3.5	+0.5	-5.5	-5.0	+3.5	+13.5	+16.0	+6.5
13	-8.5	-14.5	-10.0	-0.5	+3.5	+0.5	-5.5	-5.0	+4.0	+13.5	+16.0	+6.0
14	-9.0	-14.5	-9.5	-0.5	+3.5	0.0	-5.5	-4.5	+4.0	+14.0	+15.5	+5.5
15	-9.0	-14.5	-9.0	0.0	+3.5	0.0	-6.0	-4.5	+4.5	+14.0	+15.5	+5.0
16	-9.5	-14.0	-9.0	0.0	+3.5	-0.5	-6.0	-4.5	+5.0	+14.0	+15.5	+4.5
17	-10.0	-14.0	-8.5	+0.5	+3.5	-0.5	-6.0	-4.0	+5.0	+14.5	+15.0	+4.0
18	-10.0	-14.0	-8.5	+0.5	+3.5	-1.0	-6.0	-4.0	+5.5	+14.5	+15.0	+3.5
19	-10.5	-14.0	-8.0	+0.5	+3.5	-1.0	-6.0	-3.5	+6.0	+15.0	+14.5	+3.0
20	-11.0	-14.0	-8.0	+1.0	+3.5	-1.5	-6.0	-3.5	+6.5	+15.0	+14.5	+2.5
21	-11.0	-14.0	-7.5	+1.0	+3.5	-1.5	-6.5	-3.5	+6.5	+15.0	+14.5	+2.0
22	-11.5	-13.5	-7.0	+1.5	+3.5	-1.5	-6.5	-3.0	+7.0	+15.5	+14.0	+1.5
23	-11.5	-13.5	-7.0	+1.5	+3.5	-2.0	-6.5	-3.0	+7.5	+15.5	+14.0	+1.0
24	-12.0	-13.5	-6.5	+2.0	+3.5	-2.0	-6.5	-2.5	+7.5	+15.5	+13.5	+0.5
25	-12.0	-13.5	-6.5	+2.0	+3.5	-2.5	-6.5	-2.0	+8.0	+16.0	+13.0	0.0
26	-12.5	-13.0	-6.0	+2.0	+3.0	-2.5	-6.5	-2.0	+8.5	+16.0	+13.0	-0.5
27	-12.5	-13.0	-5.5	+2.5	+3.0	-3.0	-6.5	-1.5	+9.0	+16.0	+12.5	-1.0
28	-13.0	-13.0	-5.5	+2.5	+3.0	-3.0	-6.5	-1.5	+9.0	+16.0	+12.0	-1.5
29	-13.0	-12.5	-5.0	+2.5	+3.0	-3.0	-6.5	-1.0	+9.5	+16.0	+12.0	-2.0
30	-13.0		-4.5	+2.5	+2.5	-3.5	-6.5	-1.0	+10.0	+16.0	+11.5	-2.0
31	-13.5		-4.5		+2.5		-6.5	-0.5		+16.5		-2.5

TOTAL SOLAR ECLIPSES FROM 1988 THROUGH 2020

DATE		HOW LONG IT LASTS (minutes: seconds)	WHERE YOU CAN SEE IT (Path of center of eclipse)
1988	March 18	3:42	Phillipines, Indonesia
1990	July 22	2:33	Finland, Arctic, U.S.S.R.
1991	July 11	6:54	Hawaii, Central America, Brazil
1992	June 30	5:20	South Atlantic
1994	November 3	4:23	Bolivia, Brazil, South Atlantic
1995	October 24	2:10	India, S.E. Asia, Indonesia
1997	March 9	2:50	Siberia, Arctic
1998	February 26	4:08	Central America
1999	August 11	2:23	Central Europe, Middle East, India
2001	June 21	4:54	Southern Africa
2002	December 4	2:06	South Africa, Australia
2003	November 23	2:00	Antarctica
2005	April 8	0:42	South Pacific
2006	March 29	4:06	Africa, Turkey, U.S.S.R.
2008	August 1	2:24	Arctic, Siberia, China
2009	July 22	6:36	India, China, South Pacific
2010	July 11	5:18	South Pacific
2012	November 13	4:00	Northern Australia, South Pacific
2013	November 3	1:42	Atlantic, Central Africa
2015	March 20	4:06	North Atlantic, Arctic
2016	March 9	4:30	Indonesia, Pacific
2017	August 21	2:42	U.S.A., Pacific, Atlantic
2019	July 2	4:30	South America, South Pacific
2020	December 14	2:12	South America, South Pacific, South Atlantic

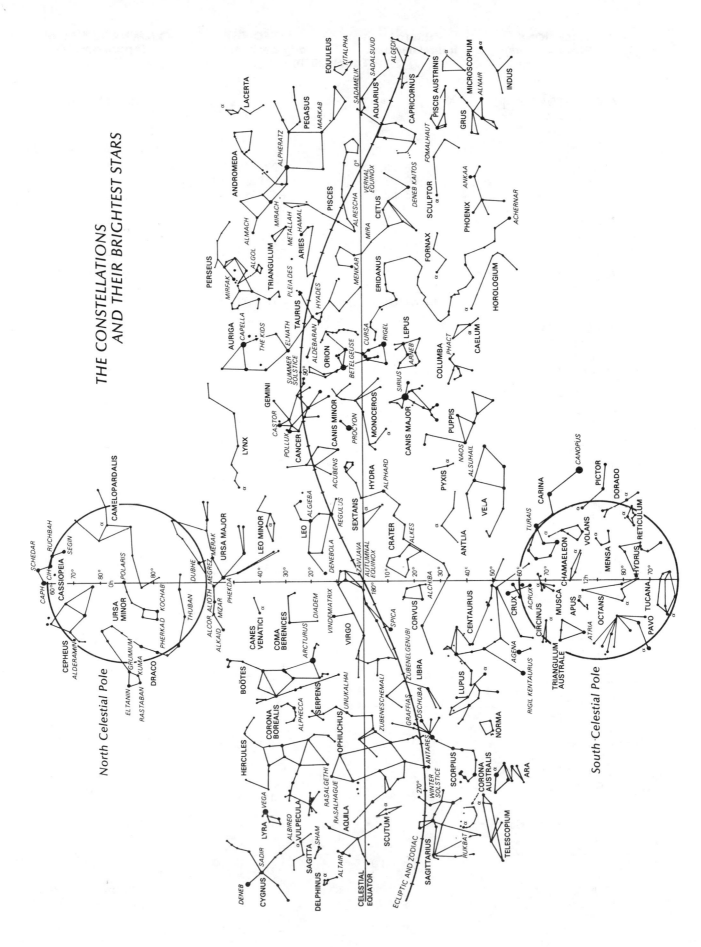

THE CONSTELLATIONS
AND THEIR BRIGHTEST STARS

North Celestial Pole

South Celestial Pole

CONSTELLATIONS (Stars—Greek Letters)	R.A.(α) hours/min./sec. (Epoch 2000)	DEC. (δ) degrees/min./sec.	CULMINATION AT 9:00 (Approximate)
1. ANDROMEDA [And] (Andromedae)			November 23
(α) Alpheratz	0 08 23.7	+29° 05' 26"	
(β) Mirach	1 09 43.8	+35° 37' 14"	
(γ) Almach	2 03 53.9	+42° 19' 47"	
2. ANTLIA [Ant] (Antilae)			April 10
(α)	10 27 09.1	−31° 04' 04"	
3. APUS [Aps] (Apodis)			July 5
(α)	14 47 51.6	−79° 02' 41"	
4. AQUARIUS [Aqr] (Aquaril)			October 9
(α) Sadalmelik	22 05 46.8	− 0° 19' 11"	
(β) Sadalsuud	21 31 33.3	− 5° 34' 16"	
5. AQUILA [Aql] (Aguilae)			August 30
(α) Altair	19 50 46.8	+ 8° 52' 06"	
6. ARA [Ara] (Arae)			July 25
(α)	17 31 50.3	−49° 52' 34"	
7. ARIES [Ari] (Arietis)			December 14
(α) Hamal	2 07 10.3	+23° 27' 45"	
8. AURIGA [Aur] (Aurigae)			February 4
(α) Capella	5 16 41.3	+45° 59' 53"	
9. BOOTES [Boo] (Bootis)			June 16
(α) Arcturus	14 15 39.6	+19° 10' 57"	
10. CAELUM [Cae] (Caeli)			January 15
(α)	4 40 33.6	−41° 51' 50"	
11. CAMELOPARDALIS [Cam] (Camelopardalis)			February 6
(α)	4 54 03.0	+66° 20' 34"	
12. CANCER [Cnc] (Cancri)			March 16
(α) Acubens	8 58 29.2	+11° 51' 28"	

APPARENT VISUAL MAGNITUDE (V) −1 = brightest +6 = dimmest	COLOR OF STARS	MEANINGS OF NAMES AND OTHER NOTES
		the daughter of King Cepheus and Queen Cassiopeia of Ethiopia, chained to a rock exposed to the sea monster Cetus as a punishment because Cassiopeia boasted that her daughter was more beautiful than the Nereids.
2.06	b-w	the horse's navel
2.06	o-r	the loins
2.18	white	the earth-kid
		Antlia Pneumatica, the air pump created by Lacaille
4.25	red	
		the bird of paradise, created by Keyser and de Houtman
3.83	o-r	
		the water carrier sky-god pouring the waters of eternal life from the highest heaven upon the Earth.
2.96	yellow	the lucky star of the king
	yellow	the luckiest of the lucky stars
		the eagle, a shape Zeus once appeared in to carry off Ganymede
0.77	y-white	the flying eagle or vulture
		the altar
2.95	blue	
		the ram that carried Phyrixus and his sister Helle on its back to Colchis so they could escape the wrath of their stepmother Ino. When the ram was sacrificed, its fleece turned to gold and became the object of the Argonaut's quest.
2.00	yellow-orange	the full grown lamb
		the charioteer, Erichthonius, son of Hephaestus and Gaea. Athene taught him how to harness horses to chariots. He became a king of ancient Athens.
0.08	yellow	the little she-goat
		the ploughman steering the plough (Ursa Major) or the herdsman or bear-driver.
−0.04	yellow-orange	the bear guard
		Sculptorium, the burning or engraving tool created by Lacaille
4.45	yellow	
		the giraffe or camel that brought Rebecca to Isaac created by Petrus Plancius.
4.29	blue	
		the crab which Herakles crushed for pinching his toes during the hero's contest with the Hydra in the marsh of Lerna.
4.25	blue-white	the claw

CONSTELLATIONS (Stars—Greek Letters)	R.A.(α) hours/min./sec. (Epoch 2000)	DEC. (δ) degrees/min./sec.	CULMINATION AT 9:00 (Approximate)
13. CANES VENATICI [CVn] (Canum Venaticorum)			May 22
(α) Cor Caroli	12 56 01.6	+38° 19′ 06″	
14. CANIS MAJOR [CMa] (Canis Majoris)			February 16
(α) Sirius	6 45 08.9	−16° 42′ 58″	
(β) Mirzam	6 22 41.9	−17° 57′ 22″	
15. CANIS MINOR [CMi] (Canis Minoris)			February 28
(α) Procyon	7 39 18.1	+ 5° 13′ 30″	
16. CAPRICORNUS [Cap] (Capricorni)			September 22
(α) Algedi	20 18 03.1	−12° 32′ 42″	
17. CARINA [Car] (Carinae)			March 17
(α) Canopus	6 23 57.1	−52° 41′ 44″	
(β) Turais (Aspidoske)	9 17 05.4	−59° 16′ 31″	
18. CASSIOPEIA [Cas] (Cassiopeiae)			November 23
(α) Schedar	0 40 30.4	+56° 32′ 15″	
(β) Caph	0 09 10.6	+59° 08′ 59″	
(χ) Cih	0 56 42.4	+60° 43′ 00″	
(δ) Ruchbah	1 25 48.9	+60° 14′ 07″	
(ϵ) Segin	1 54 23.6	+63° 40′ 13″	
19. CENTAURUS [Cen] (Centauri)			May 14
(α) Rigil Kentaurus	14 39 36.7	−60° 50′ 02″	
(β) Agena, Hadar	14 03 49.4	−60° 22′ 22″	
20. CEPHEUS [Cep] (Cephei)			November 13
(α) Alderamin	21 18 34.6	+62° 35′ 08″	
(μ) The Garnet Star			
21. CETUS [Cet] (Ceti)			November 29
(α) Menkar	3 02 16.7	+ 4° 05′ 23″	
(β) Diphda	0 43 35.3	−17° 59′ 12″	
(χ) Mira	2 19 20.6	− 2° 58′ 39″	

APPARENT VISUAL MAGNITUDE (V) −1 = brightest +6 = dimmest	COLOR OF STARS	MEANINGS OF NAMES AND OTHER NOTES
		the hunting dogs Asterion and Charra, hounds of Bootes, created by Hevelius.
2.90	white	the heart of King Charles I, first mentioned in 1725 by British Catholic royalist, Edward Sherburne.
		the greater dog of Orion
−1.46	blue	the dog star, the scorching one or Isis
1.98	blue-white	the announcer or proclaimer, the brightest star in the sky
		the lesser dog of Orion.
0.38	yellow-white	before the dog, i.e., the bright star that rises before Sirius.
		the horned sea goat. It could be Pan who, in his panic at the approach of the monster, Typhon, jumped into the Nik and turned himself into half a fish.
3.57	yellow	the kid
		the keel from the ship Argo Navis (Ruppis & Vela from the other parts) built by Argos for Jason and his 50 Argonauts to find the golden fleece.
−0.72	yellow-white	a city in Ancient Egypt named after the chief pilot of the fleet of Menelaus which destroyed Troy in 1184 BC. The 2nd brightest star in the sky.
2.25	pale yellow	the stern ornament of an ancient ship
		the Queen of Ethiopia, seated in her chair and forced to rotate around the North Pole as punishment for bragging about her daughter's beauty, "the lady of the chair."
2.23	orange-yellow	the breast
2.27	yellow-white	the stained hand
2.47	blue-white	in Cassiopeia's girdle
2.68	white	the knee of "the lady of the chair"
3.38	blue-white	near the foot
		the centaur, Chiron, son of Cronos. A helper of mortals and teacher of Herakles, he is said to be the inventor of the constellations.
0.00	(yellow-orange) white-yellow	the centaur's foot
0.61	blue	the centaur's knee
		the King of Ethiopia, husband of Cassiopeia and one of the Argonauts
2.44	white	the right forearm
	red	named by William Herschel. It is the reddest naked-eye star
		the sea beast descended from Pontus. Cetus was sent to devour Andromeda but was turned to stone at the sight of the Medusa's head which Perseus was holding
2.53	orange-red	the nostril
2.04	yellow-orange	the southern branch of the sea monster's tail
(3.04) variable	red	wonderful

CONSTELLATIONS (Stars—Greek Letters)	R.A.(α) hours/min./sec.	DEC. (δ) degrees/min./sec. (Epoch 2000)	CULMINATION AT 9:00 (Approximate)
22. CHAMAELEON [Cha] (Chamaeleonis)			April 15
(α)	8 8 31.7	−76° 55′ 10″	
23. CIRCINUS [Cir] (Circini)			June 14
(α)	14 42 28.0	−64° 58′ 43″	
24. COLUMBA [Col] (Columbae)			February 1
(α) Phact	5 39 38.9	−34° 04′ 27″	
25. COMA BERENICES [Com] (Comae Berenices)			May 17
(α) Diadem	13 09 59.2	+17° 31′ 45″	
26. CORONA AUSTRAUS [CrA] (Coronae Australis)			August 14
(α)	19 09 28.2	−37° 54′ 16″	
27. CORONA BOREALIS [CrB] (Coronae Borealis)			July 3
(α) Alphecca (Gemma)	15 34 41.2	+26° 42′ 53″	
28. CORVUS [Crv] (Corvi)			May 12
(α) Alchiba	12 08 24.7	−24° 43′ 44″	
29. CRATER [Crt] (Crateris)			April 26
(α) Alkes	10 59 46.4	−18° 17′ 56″	
30. CRUX [Cru] (Crucis)			May 12
(α) Acrux	12 26 35.9	−63° 05′ 56″	
(β) Becrux	12 47 43.2	−59° 41′ 19″	
31. CYGNUS [Cyg] (Cygni)			September 13
(α) Deneb	20 41 25.8	+45° 16′ 49″	
(β) Albireo	19 30 43.1	+27° 57′ 35″	
(χ) Sadir	20 22 13.5	+40° 15′ 24″	
32. DELPHINUS [Del] (Delphini)			September 14
(α) Sualocin	20 39 38.1	+15° 54′ 43″	
33. DORADO [Dor] (Doradus)			January 31
(α)	4 33 59.8	−55° 02′ 42″	

APPARENT VISUAL MAGNITUDE (V) −1 = brightest +6 = dimmest	COLOR OF STARS	MEANINGS OF NAMES AND OTHER NOTES
		the Chamaelion, created by Keyser & de Houtman
4.07	yellow	
		the pair of geometrical compasses named by Lacaille
3.19	white	
		the dove of Noah with a branch in its beak, created by the Dutch theologian and geographer Petrus Plancius
2.64	blue	the ring dove
		Berenice's hair. Berenice, queen of Egypt, cut off her amber hair as a sacrifice to Aphrodite to ensure her husband Ptolemy a safe return from a dangerous voyage. Created by Mercator.
4.32	yellow-white	
		the southern crown or wreath
4.11	blue-white	
		the northern crown or wreath of Ariadne
2.23	white	the broken or fractured one
		the crow, or raven, messenger to Phoebus Apollo
4.02	yellow-white	
		the cup
4.08	orange-red	
		the Southern Cross, created during Counter-Reformation times by Spanish and Portuguese navigators from stars at the hind feet of Centaurus
1.41	blue	a(lpha) Crucis = acrux
		the swan, and the Northern Cross
1.25	white	the hen's tail
3.08	yellow & blue	the hen's beak
2.20	yellow-white	the hen's breast
		the dolphin
3.77	blue-white	named after Nicolaus Venator by spelling his first name backwards. Venator was Piazzi's assistant at the Palerno Observatory.
		the goldfish (or swordfish) created by Keyser and de Houtman
3.27	blue-white	

CONSTELLATIONS (Stars—Greek Letters)	R.A.(α) hours/min./sec. (Epoch 2000)	DEC. (δ) degrees/min./sec.	CULMINATION AT 9:00 (Approximate)
34. DRACO [Dra] (Draconis)			July 8
(α) Thuban	14 04 23.2	+64° 22' 33"	
(β) Rastaban	17 30 25.8	+52° 18' 05"	
(χ) Eltanin	17 56 36.2	+51° 29' 20"	
(δ) Grumium	17 53 31.5	+56° 52' 21"	
(ε) Kuma	17 32 10.3	+55° 11' 03"	
35. EQUULEUS [Equ] (Equulei)			September 22
(α) Kitalpha	21 15 49.3	+ 5° 14' 52"	
36. ERIDANUS [Eri] (Eridoni)			December 25
(α) Achernar	1 37 42.9	−57° 14' 12"	
(β) Cursa	5 07 50.9	− 5° 05' 11"	
37. FORNAX [For] (Fornacis)			December 17
(α)	3 12 04.2	−28° 59' 13"	
38. GEMINI [Gem] (Geminorum)			February 19
(α) Castor	7 34 35.9	−31° 53' 18"	
(β) Pollux	7 45 18.9	+28° 01' 34"	
39. GRUS [Gru] (Gruis)			October 12
(α) Alnair	22 08 13.8	−46° 57' 40"	
40. Hercules [Her] (Herculis)			July 28
(α) Rasalgethi	17 14 38.8	+14° 23' 25"	
41. HOROLOGIUM [Hor] (Horologii)			December 25
(α)	4 14 00.0	−42° 17' 40"	
42. HYDRA [Hya] (Hydrae)			April 29
(α) Alphard	9 27 35.2	− 8° 39' 31"	
43. HYDRUS [Hyi] (Hydri)			December 10
(α)	1 58 46.2	−61° 34' 12"	
44. INDUS [Ind] (Indi)			September 26
(α)	20 37 33.9	−47° 17' 29"	
45. LACERTA [Lac] (Lacertae)			October 12
(α)	22 31 17.3	+50° 16' 57"	
46. LEO [Leo] (Leonis)			April 15
(α) Regulus	10 08 22.2	+11° 58' 02"	
(β) Denebola	11 49 03.5	+14° 34' 19"	
(χ) Algieba	10 19 58.3	+19° 50' 30"	

APPARENT VISUAL MAGNITUDE (V) −1 = brightest +6 = dimmest	COLOR OF STARS	MEANINGS OF NAMES AND OTHER NOTES
		the dragon which Athene snatched from the giants and whirled up to the sky. It became the monster which Herakles killed and whose teeth he sowed for a crop of armed men.
3.65	pale yellow	the serpent or dragon
2.79	yellow	the serpent's head
2.23	orange-yellow	the dragon's head
3.75	orange-yellow	the under jaw
4.88	white	
		the foal
3.92	yellow-white	the part or section of the horse
		the river, the longest constellation
0.46	blue-white	the end of the river
2.79	white	the foremost chair of Orion
		Fornax Chemica, the chemical furnace formed by Lacaille
3.87	white	
		the twins (the Dioscuri) sons of Leda
1.58	white	the mortal brother; the horseman, son of Tyndarus
1.14	yellow-orange	the immortal brother; the boxer, son of Zeus
		the crane (symbol of the star observer in Egypt) created by Keyser and de Houtman in 1595–1597
1.74	white	the bright one
		Herakles
3.19	orange-red	head of the kneeler
3.86	orange-red	a pendulum clock created by Lecaille
1.98	yellow-orange	the sea serpent (female) preventing the crow (Corvus) from drinking from the cup the solitary (star) of the serpent
2.86	white	the water monster (male) created by Keyser and de Houtman in 1595–1597
3.11	orange-red	the American Indian, created by Pieter Dirksz Keyser and Frederick de Houtman in 1595–1597
3.77	white	the lizard formed by Hevelius
		the Nemean lion which came from the Moon. Herakles carried it back to the heavens after he slayed it.
1.35	blue-white	the prince, named by Copernicus
2.14	white	the lion's tail
2.28	orange-yellow	the forehead

CONSTELLATIONS (Stars—Greek Letters)	R.A.(α) hours/min./sec.	DEC. (δ) degrees/min./sec.	CULMINATION AT 9:00 (Approximate)
		(Epoch 2000)	
47. LEO MINOR (LMi) (Leonis Minoris)			April 9
(β) Praecipua	10 27 52.9	+36° 42′ 26″	
48. LEPUS [Lep] (Lipi)			January 28
(α) Arneb	5 32 43.7	−17° 49′ 20″	
49. LIBRA [Lib] (Librae)			June 23
(α) Zubenelgenubi	14 50 52.6	−16° 02′ 30″	
(β) Zubeneschemali	15 17 00.3	− 9° 22′ 58″	
50. LUPUS [Lup] (Lipi)			June 23
(α)	14 41 55.7	−47° 23′ 17″	
51. LYNX [Lyn] (Lyncis)	9 21 03.2	+34° 23′ 33″	March 5
52. LYRA [Lyr] (Lyrae)			August 18
(α) Vega	18 36 56.2	+38° 47′ 01″	
53. MENSA [Men] (Mensae)			January 28
(α)	6 10 14.6	−74° 45′ 11″	
54. MICROSCOPIUM [Mic] (Microscopii)			September 18
(α)	20 49 57.8	−33° 46′ 47″	
55. MONOCEROS [Mon] (Monocerotis)			February 19
(α)	7 41 14.8	− 9° 33′ 04″	
56. MUSCA [Mus] (Muscae)			May 14
(α)	12 37 11.0	−69° 08′ 07″	
57. NORMA [Nor] (Normae)			July 3
(χ)	16 17 00.7	−50° 04′ 05″	
58. OCTANS [Oct] (Octanis)			Circum-polar
(α)	21 04 42.7	−77° 01′ 25″	
(δ)	21 08 44.9	−88° 57′ 24″	
59. OPHIUCHUS [Oph] (Ophiuchi)			July 26
(α) Rasalhague	17 34 55.9	+12° 33′ 36″	

APPARENT VISUAL MAGNITUDE (V) −1 = brightest +6 = dimmest	COLOR OF STARS	MEANINGS OF NAMES AND OTHER NOTES
		the lesser lion, formed by Hevelias in 1690
4.21	yellow	chief
		the hare, placed in the heavens to be close to its hunter, Orion
2.58	yellow-white	the hare
		the balance or scales
2.75	white	the southern claw
2.61	blue-white	the northern claw
		the wolf
2.30	blue	
		the tiger, created by Hevelius
3.13	orange	
		the harp or lyre invented by Hermes and given to his half-brother, Apollo who in turn passed it on to his son, Orpheus, the musician of the Argonauts.
0.03	blue-white	the falling eagle or vulture
		the table, formed by Lacaille. Named after Table Mountain which lies behind Cape Town, South Africa, where Lacaille worked.
5.09	white-yellow	
		the microscope, formed by Lacaille
4.90	white-yellow	
		the unicorn, created by Petrus Plancius
3.93	yellow-orange	
		the southern fly, or bee, created by Keyser and de Houtman
2.69	blue	
		the level, formed by Lacaille (originally, Norma and Regula, the architect's level and square)
4.99	yellow	
		Octans Halecianus, the octant or reflecting quadrant formed by Lacaille in 1752.
5.15	white	the star closest to the south celestial pole
5.47	blue-white	
		the medicinal serpent holder Aesculapius, the ship's surgeon of the argo
2.08	white (sapphire)	the head of the serpent collector or charmer

CONSTELLATIONS (Stars—Greek Letters)	R.A.(α) hours/min./sec. (Epoch 2000)	DEC. (δ) degrees/min./sec.	CULMINATION AT 9:00 (Approximate)
60. ORION [Ori] (Orionis)			January 27
(α) Betelgeuse	5 55 10.2	+ 7° 24' 26"	
(β) Rigel	5 14 32.2	− 8° 12' 06"	
(χ) Bellatrix	5 25 07.8	+ 6° 20' 59"	
(δ) Mintaka	5 32 00.3	− 0° 17' 05"	
(κ) Saiph	5 47 45.3	− 9° 40' 11"	
(λ) Heka (Meissa)	5 35 08.2	+ 9° 56' 02"	
61. PAVO [Pab] (Pavonis)			August 29
(α) Peacock	20 25 38.7	−56° 44' 06"	
62. PEGASI [Peg] (Pegasi)			October 16
(α) Markab	23 04 45.5	+15° 12' 19"	
(β) Scheat	23 03 46.3	+28° 04' 58"	
(χ) Algenib	0 13 14.1	+15° 11' 01"	
63. PERSEUS [Per] (Persei)			December 22
(α) Mirfak (Algenib)	3 24 19.3	+49° 51' 40"	
(β) Algol	3 08 10.1	+40° 57' 21"	
64. PHOENIX [Phe] (Phoenicis)			November 18
(α) Ankaa	0 26 17.0	−42° 18' 2"	
65. PICTOR [Pic] (α)	6 48 11.4	−61° 56' 29"	January 30
66. PISCES [Psc] (Piscium)			November 11
(α) Alrescha	2 02 02.7	+ 2° 45' 49"	
67. PISCIS AUSTRINUS [PsA] (Piscis Austrini)			October 9
(α) Fomalhaut	22 57 38.9	−29° 37' 20"	
68. PUPPIS [Pup] (Puppis)			February 22
(ζ) Lyn	8 03 35.0	−40° 00' 12"	
(χ) Naos	7 49 17.6	−24° 51' 35"	
69. PYXIS [Pyx] (Pyxidis) (α)	8 43 35.5	−33° 11' 11"	March 21
70. RETICULUM [Ret] (Reticuli)			January 3
(α)	4 14 25.5	−62° 28' 26"	

APPARENT VISUAL MAGNITUDE (V) −1 = brightest +6 = dimmest	COLOR OF STARS	MEANINGS OF NAMES AND OTHER NOTES
		Orion the giant, mighty hunter and warrior. He was the lover of the huntress-goddess Diana. Orion died from the sting of Scorpius, the Scorpion as punishment for bragging.
0.50	orange-red	the armpit of the white-belted sheep
0.12	blue-white	Orion's left foot
1.64	blue-white	the female warrior, the Amazon Star
2.23	blue	the belt
2.06	blue-white	the sword of the powerful one
3.39	yellow-white	the circle of hairs
		the peacock. Hera changed Argos, the builder of the ship Argo, into a peacock when the gods placed the Argo in the sky. Created by Keyser and de Houtman
1.94	blue	
		the winged horse. Poseidon commanded that Pegasus spring forth from the sea where blood from the severed head of Medusa had dropped.
2.49	blue-white	riding, or anything which carries a person
2.42	red	the leg
2.83	blue-white	the side
		the champion, rescued Andromeda by showing the severed head of Medusa to the sea monster Cetus who immediately turned to stone the elbow or the side
1.80	yellow-white	the demon's head
2.12	blue	
		the phoenix created by Keyser and de Houtman
2.39	orange-red	Equuleus Pictoris, the painter's easel, created by Lacaille
3.27	white	the fishes, possibly Aphrodite and her son Eros, who plunged into the Euphraetes to protect themselves from the monster Typhon the rope or cord
3.79	white	the southern fish, drinking the flow from Aquarius
		the month of the southern fish
1.16	blue-white	the stern of the ship Argo created by Lacaille in 1752
2.25	yellow	
3.34	yellow	Pyxis Nautica, the mariner's compass, created by Lacaille
3.68	blue	the net or rhombus in honor of the reticule or micrometer used to measure the position of stars created by Lacaille.
3.35	white-yellow	the arrow, shot by either Zeus or Herakles toward the Eagle or the Swan

CONSTELLATIONS (Stars—Greek Letters)	R.A.(α) hours/min./sec. (Epoch 2000)	DEC. (δ) degrees/min./sec.	CULMINATION AT 9:00 (Approximate)
71. SAGITTA [Sge] (Sagittae)			August 30
(α) Sham	19 40 05.6	+18° 00' 50"	
72. SAGITTARIUS [Sgr] (Sagittarii)			August 21
(α) Rukbat	19 23 53.0	−40° 36' 58"	
73. SCORPIUS [Sco] (Scorpii)			July 18
(α) Antares	16 29 24.3	−26° 25' 55"	
(β) Graffias (Acrab)	16 05 26.1	−19° 48' 19"	
(δ) Dschubba	16 00 19.9	−22° 37' 18"	
74. SCULPTOR [Scl] (Sculptoris)			November 10
(α)	0 58 36.3	−29° 21' 27"	
75. SCUTUM [Sct] (Scuti)			August 15
(α)	18 35 36.3	−29° 21' ??"	
76. SERPENS [Ser] (Serpentis)			July 21
(α) Unukalhai	15 44 16.0	+ 6° 25' 32"	
77. SEXTANS [Sex] (Sextantis)			April 8
(α)	10 07 56.2	− 0° 22' 18"	
78. TAURUS [Tau] (Tauri)			January 14
(α) Aldebaran	4 35 55.2	+16° 30' 33"	
(β) Elnath	5 26 17.5	+28° 36' 27"	
79. TELESCOPIUM [Tel] (Telescopii)			August 24
(α)	18 26 58.2	−45° 58' 06"	
80. TRIANGULUM [Tri] (Trianguli)			December 7
(α) Metallah	1 53 04.8	+29° 34' 44"	
81. TRIANGULUM AUSTRALE [TrA] (Trianguli Australis)			July 7
(α) Atria	16 48 39.8	−69° 01' 39"	
82. TUCANA [Tuc] (Tucanae)			November 1
(α)	22 18 30.1	−60° 15' 35"	

APPARENT VISUAL MAGNITUDE (V) −1 = brightest +6 = dimmest	COLOR OF STARS	MEANINGS OF NAMES AND OTHER NOTES
		the archer, a stern centaur with bow drawn and arrow aimed at the heart of the Scorpion.
4.37	yellow-white	the archer's knee
3.97	blue-white	
		the scorpion, slayer of Orion
0.96	red	the rival of Mars
2.64	blue	the crab
2.32	blue	the forehead or front of the scorpion
		the sculptor, the sculptor's studio or tools, created by Lacaille in 1751–1752. The south galactic pole lies in this constellation.
4.31	blue	
		Scutum Scobiescianum, the shield of John Scobiesci III, the Polish king who aided Hevelius when his observatory in Danzig burned to the ground.
3.85	yellow-orange	
		the serpent
2.65	yellow-orange	the serpent's neck
		Sextans Uraniae, or sextant, named by Hevelius in honor of the instrument which he used to measure the stars at Danzig from 1658–1679.
4.49	white	
		the bull into which Zeus changed himself to carry away Europa
0.85	yellow-orange	the follower (of the Pleiades)
1.65	blue-white	the one butting with horns
		Tubus Astronomicus, or the telescope, created by Lacaille
3.51	blue	
		the triangle, created by Keyser and de Houtman
3.41	yellow-white	
		the southern triangle
1.92	orange	entry-way into the main room
		the toucan, created by Keyser and de Houtman
2.86	orange-red	

CONSTELLATIONS (Stars—Greek Letters)	R.A.(α) hours/min./sec. (Epoch 2000)	DEC. (δ) degrees/min./sec.	CULMINATION AT 9:00 (Approximate)
83. URSA MAJOR [UMa] (Ursae Majoris)			April 25
(α) Dubhe	11 03 43.6	+61° 45' 03"	
(β) Merak	11 01 50.4	+56° 22' 56"	
(χ) Phekda	11 53 49.7	+53° 41' 41"	
(δ) Mergrez	12 15 25.5	+57° 01' 57"	
(ε) Alioth	12 54 01.7	+55° 57' 35"	
(ξ) Alkaid	13 47 32.3	+49° 18' 48"	
(ζ) Mizar	13 23 55.5	+54° 55' 31"	
(θ) Alcor	13 25 13.4	+54° 59' 17"	
84. URSA MINOR [UM] (Ursae Minoris)			June 27
(α) Polaris	2 31 50.4	+89° 15' 51"	
(β) Kochab	14 50 42.2	+74° 09' 19"	
(γ) Pherkad	15 20 43.6	+71° 50' 02"	
85. VELA [Vel] (Velorum)			March 30
(λ) Alsuhail	9 07 59.7	−43° 25' 57"	
86. VIRGO [Vir] (Virginis)			May 26
(α) Spica	13 25 11.5	−11° 09' 41"	
(β) Zavijava	11 50 41.6	+ 1° 45' 53"	
(ε) Vindemiatrix	13 02 10.5	+10° 57' 33"	
87. VOLANS [Vol] (Volantis)			March 4
(α)	9 02 26.9	−66° 23' 46"	
88. VULPECULA [Vul] (Vulpeculae)			September 8
(α)	19 28 42.2	+24° 39' 54"	

For each **hour** earlier than 9 PM, add 15 days.
For each **hour** later than 9 PM, subtract 15 days.

For each **week** earlier than dates given: add 28 minutes to 9 PM.
For each **week** later than dates given: subtract 28 minutes from 9 PM.

APPARENT VISUAL MAGNITUDE (V) −1 = brightest +6 = dimmest	COLOR OF STARS	MEANINGS OF NAMES AND OTHER NOTES
		the greater bear, who was once the beautiful Callisto until jealous Hera turned her into a bear
		People also know this constellation as "the wain" (the wagoner) or "the Plough."
1.79	yellow-orange	the back of the greater bear
2.37	white	the loins of the greater bear
2.44	white	the thigh of the greater bear
3.31	white	the root of the tail of the greater bear
1.77	white	the extremely bright one
1.86	blue-white	the leader or governor of the daughters of the bier.
2.27	white	the veil, trousers, or waist cloth
4.01	white	the abandoned or friendless one
		the lesser bear
2.02	yellow	the pole star since 300 AD
2.08	orange-yellow	the north star–named during the period when it was the brightest star near the pole, from about 1500 BC to 300 AD
		the sail, from the ship Argo
2.21	orange-red	
		the young woman, perhaps Persephone, daughter of Demeter
0.98	blue-white	the ear of wheat
3.61	yellow-white	the corner of the barking dog
2.83	yellow	the female grape gatherer
		Piscis Volans, the flying fish, created by Keyser and de Houtman
4.00	white	
		Vulpecula cum Ansere, the little fox with a goose, created by Hevelius.
4.44	orange-red	

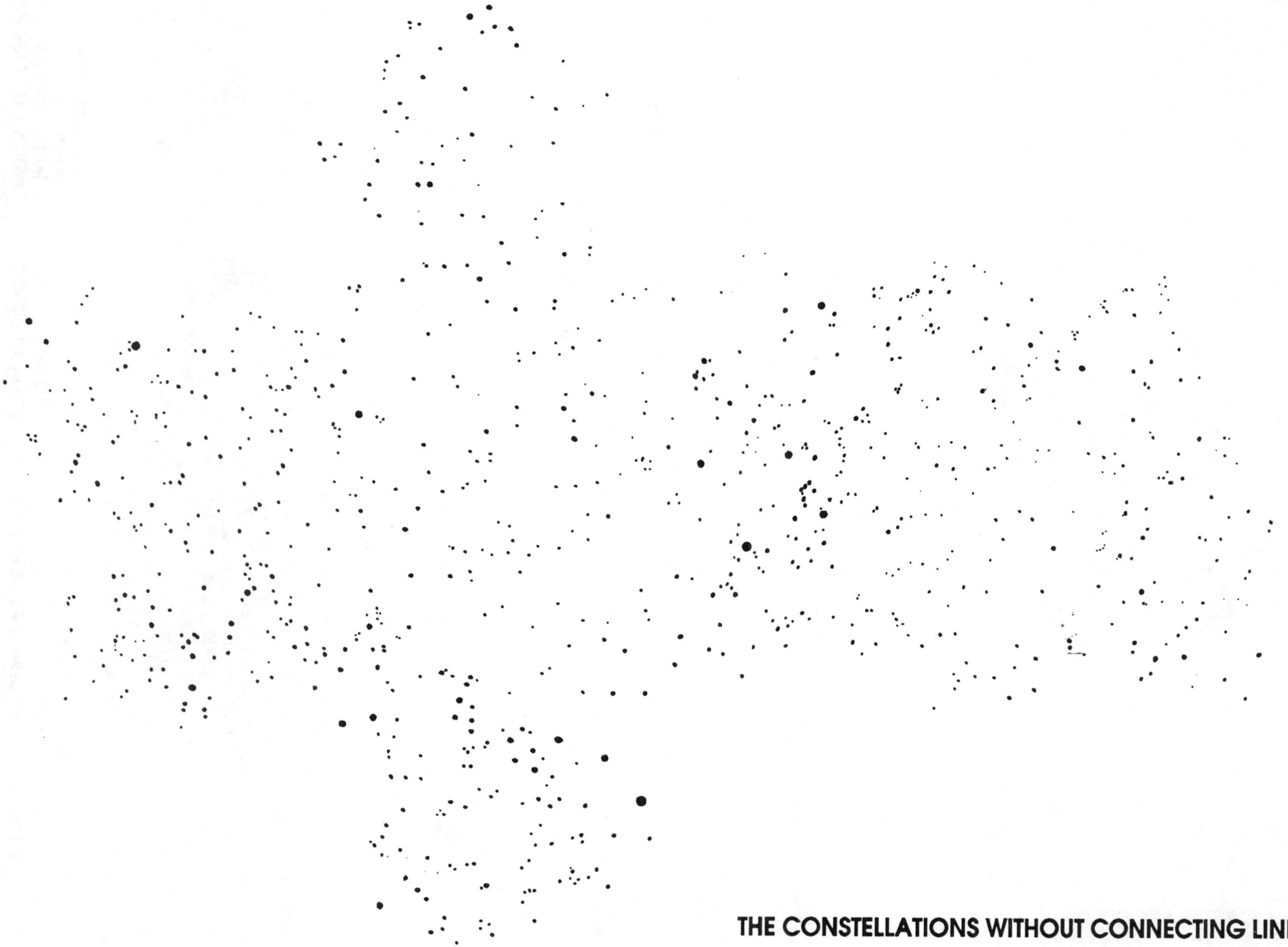

THE CONSTELLATIONS WITHOUT CONNECTING LINES

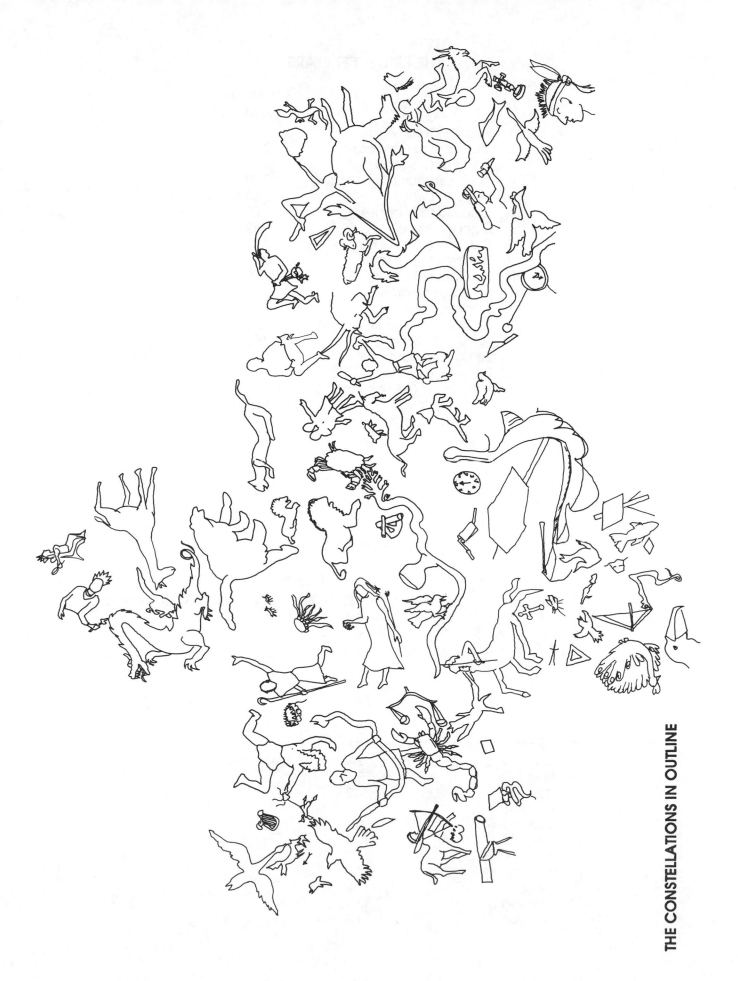

THE BRIGHTEST STARS

	STAR	APPARENT MAGNITUDE (V)
1.	Sirius (α Canis Majoris)	-1.46
2.	Canopus (α Carinae)	-0.72
3.	Arcturus (α Bootis)	-0.04
4.	Rigel Kentaurus (α Centauri)	0.00
5.	Vega (α Lyrae)	0.03
6.	Capella (α Aurigae)	0.08
7.	Rigel (β Orionis)	0.12
8.	Procyon (α Canis Minoris)	0.38
9.	Achernar (α Eridani)	0.46
10.	Betelgeuse (α Orionis)	0.50
11.	Hadar (α Centauri)	0.61
12.	Altair (α Aquilae)	0.77
13.	Aldebaran (α Tauri)	0.85
14.	Antares (α Scorpii)	0.96
15.	Spica (α Virginis)	0.98
16.	Pollux (β Geminorum)	1.14
17.	Fomalhaut (α Piscis Austrini)	1.16
18.	Deneb (α Cygni)	1.25
19.	Becrux (β Crucis)	1.25
20.	Regulus (α Leonis)	1.35

THE NEAREST STARS

	NAME	DISTANCE (IN LIGHT YEARS)
1.	The Sun	93,000,000 miles (150,000,000 kilometers)
2.	α Centauri A	4.3
3.	α Centauri B	4.3
4.	α Centauri C	4.3
5.	Barnard's Star	5.9
6.	Wolf 359	7.6
7.	Lalande 21185	8.1
8.	Sirius A	8.6
9.	Sirius B	8.6
10.	Luyten 726-8A	8.9
11.	Luyten 726-8B (UV Ceti)	8.9
12.	Ross 154	9.4
13.	Ross 248	10.3
14.	ε Eridani	10.7
15.	Luyten 789-6	10.8
16.	Ross 128	10.8
17.	61 Cygni A	11.2
18.	61 Cygni B	11.2
19.	ε Indi	11.2
20.	Procyon A	11.4
21.	Procyon B	11.4

THE MESSIER CATALOG OF NEBULAE AND STAR CLUSTERS

Messier number	NGC or (IC) (1980)	Right ascension	Declination (1980) magnitude	Apparent visual	Description
1	1952	5h 33.3m	+22°01'	8.4	Crab Nebula in Taurus; remains of SN 1054
2	7089	21h 32.4m	−0°54'	6.4	Globular cluster in Aquarius
3	5272	13h 41.2m	+28°29'	6.3	Globular cluster in Canes Venatici
4	6121	16h 22.4m	−26°28'	6.5	Globular cluster in Scorpio
5	5904	15h 17.5m	+2°10'	6.1	Globular cluster in Serpens
6	6405	17h 38.8m	−32°11'	5.5	Open cluster in Scorpio
7	6475	17h 52.7m	−34°48'	3.3	Open cluster in Scorpio
8	6523	18h 02.4m	−24°23'	5.1	Lagoon Nebula in Sagittarius
9	6333	17h 18.1m	−18°30'	8.0	Globular cluster in Ophiuchus
10	6254	16h 56.1m	−4°05'	6.7	Globular cluster in Ophiuchus
11	6705	18h 50.0m	−6°18'	6.8	Open cluster in Scutum Sobieskii
12	6218	16h 46.3m	−1°55'	6.6	Globular cluster in Ophiuchus
13	6205	16h 41.0m	+36°30'	5.9	Globular cluster in Hercules
14	6402	17h 36.6m	−3°14'	8.0	Globular cluster in Ophiuchus
15	7078	21h 28.9m	+12°05'	6.4	Globular cluster in Pegasus
16	6611	18h 17.8m	−13°47'	6.6	Open cluster with nebulosity in Serpens
17	6618	18h 19.6m	−16°11'	7.5	Swan or Omega Nebula in Sagittarius
18	6613	18h 18.7m	−17°08'	7.2	Open cluster in Sagittarius
19	6273	17h 01.4m	−26°14'	6.9	Globular cluster in Ophiuchus
20	6514	18h 01.2m	−23°02'	8.5	Trifid Nebula in Sagittarius
87	4486	12h 29.7m	+12°30'	8.7	Elliptical galaxy in Virgo
88	4501	12h 30.9m	+14°32'	9.5	Spiral galaxy in Coma Berenices
89	4552	12h 34.6m	+12°40'	10.3	Elliptical galaxy in Virgo
90	4569	12h 35.8m	+13°46'	9.6	Spiral galaxy in Virgo
91	Omitted				
92	6341	17h 16.5m	+43°10'	6.4	Globular cluster in Hercules
93	2447	7h 43.7m	−23°49'	6.5	Open cluster in Puppis
94	4736	12h 50.0m	+41°14'	8.3	Spiral galaxy in Canes Venatici
95	3351	10h 42.9m	+11°49'	9.8	Barred spiral galaxy in Leo
96	3368	10h 45.7	+11°56'	9.3	Spiral galaxy in Leo
97	3587	11h 13.7m	+55°07'	11.1	Owl Nebula; planetary nebula in Ursa Major
98	4192	12h 12.7m	+15°01'	10.2	Spiral galaxy in Coma Berenices
99	4254	12h 17.8m	+14°32'	9.9	Spiral galaxy in Coma Berenices
100	4321	12h 21.9m	+15°56'	9.4	Spiral galaxy in Coma Berenices
101	5457	14h 02.5m	+54°27'	7.9	Spiral galaxy in Ursa Major
102	5866(?)	15h 05.9m	+55°50'	10.5	Spiral galaxy (identification as M102 in doubt)
103	581	1h 31.9m	+60°35'	6.9	Open cluster in Cassiopeia
104†	4594	12h 39.0m	−11°31'	8.3	Spiral galaxy in Virgo
105†	3379	10h 46.8m	+12°51'	9.7	Elliptical galaxy in Leo
106†	4258	12h 18.0m	+47°25'	8.4	Spiral galaxy in Canes Venatici
107†	6171	16h 31.4m	−13°01'	9.2	Globular cluster in Ophiuchus
108†	3556	11h 10.5m	+55°47'	10.5	Spiral galaxy in Ursa Major
109†	3992	11h 56.6m	+53°29'	10.0	Spiral galaxy in Ursa Major
110†	205	0h 39.2m	+41°35'	9.4	Elliptical galaxy (companion to M31)

Continued on next page

THE MESSIER CATALOG OF NEBULAE AND STAR CLUSTERS

Messier number	NGC or (IC) (1980)	Right ascension	Declination (1980)	Apparent visual magnitude	Description
21	6531	18h 03.4m	−22°30′	6.5	Open cluster in Sagittarius
22	6656	18h 35.2m	−23°56′	5.6	Globular cluster in Sagittarius
23	6494	17h 55.8m	−19°00′	5.9	Open cluster in Sagittarius
24	6603	18h 17.3m	−18°26′	4.6	Open cluster in Sagittarius
25	(4725)	18h 30.5m	−19°16′	6.2	Open cluster in Sagittarius
26	6694	18h 44.1m	−9°25′	9.3	Open cluster in Scutum Sobieskii
27	6853	19h 58.8m	+22°40′	8.2	"Dumbbell" planetary nebula in Vulpecula
28	6626	18h 23.2m	−24°52′	7.6	Globular cluster in Sagittarius
29	6913	20h 23.3m	+38°27′	8.0	Open cluster in Cygnus
30	7099	21h 39.2m	−23°16′	7.7	Globular cluster in Capricornus
31	224	0h 41.6m	+41°10′	3.5	Andromeda Galaxy
32	221	0h 41.6m	+40°46′	8.2	Elliptical galaxy; companion to M31
33	598	1h 32.7m	+30°33′	5.8	Spiral galaxy in Triangulum
34	1039	2h 40.7m	+42°43′	5.8	Open cluster in Perseus
35	2168	6h 07.5m	+24°21′	5.6	Open cluster in Gemini
36	1960	5h 35.0m	+34°05′	6.5	Open cluster in Auriga
37	2099	5h 51.1m	+32°33′	6.2	Open cluster in Auriga
38	1912	5h 27.3m	+35°48′	7.0	Open cluster in Auriga
39	7092	21h 31.5m	+48°21′	5.3	Open cluster in Cygnus
40		12h 21m	+59°		Close double star in Ursa Major
41	2287	6h 46.2m	−20°43′	5.0	Loose open cluster in Canis Major
42	1976	5h 34.4m	−5°24′	4	Orion Nebula
43	1982	5h 34.6m	−5°18′	9	Northeast portion of Orion Nebula
44	2632	8h 39m	+20°04′	3.9	Praesepe; open cluster in Cancer
45		3h 46.3m	+24°03′	1.6	The Pleiades; open cluster in Taurus
46	2437	7h 40.9m	−14°46′	6.6	Open cluster in Puppis
47	2422	7h 35.7m	−14°26′	5	Loose group of stars in Puppis
48	2548	8h 12.8m	−5°44′	6	"Cluster of very small stars"; identifiable
49	4472	12h 28.8m	+8°06′	8.5	Elliptical galaxy in Virgo
50	2323	7h 02.0m	−8°19′	6.3	Loose open cluster in Monoceros
51	5194	13h 29.1m	+47°18′	8.4	Whirlpool spiral galaxy in Canes Venatici
52	7654	23h 23.3m	+61°30′	8.2	Loose open cluster in Cassiopeia
53	5024	13h 12.0m	+18°16′	7.8	Globular cluster in Coma Berenices
54	6715	18h 53.8m	−30°30′	7.8	Globular cluster in Sagittarius
55	6809	19h 38.7m	−30°59′	6.2	Globular cluster in Sagittarius
56	6779	19h 15.8m	+30°08′	8.7	Globular cluster in Lyra
57	6720	18h 52.8m	+33°00′	9.0	Ring Nebula; planetary nebula in Lyra
58	4579	12h 36.7m	+11°55′	9.9	Spiral galaxy in Virgo
59	4621	12h 41.0m	+11°46′	10.0	Spiral galaxy in Virgo
60	4649	12h 42.6m	+11°40′	9.0	Elliptical galaxy in Virgo
61	4303	12h 20.8m	+4°35′	9.6	Spiral galaxy in Virgo
62	6266	16h 59.9m	−30°05′	6.6	Globular cluster in Scorpio
63	5055	13h 14.8m	+42°07′	8.9	Spiral galaxy in Canes Venatici
64	4826	12h 55.7m	+21°39′	8.5	Spiral galaxy in Coma Berenices
65	3623	11h 17.9m	+13°12′	9.4	Spiral galaxy in Leo
66	3627	11h 19.2m	+13°06′	9.0	Spiral galaxy in Leo; companion to M65
67	2682	8h 50.0m	+11°53′	6.1	Open cluster in Cancer
68	4590	12h 38.4m	−26°39′	8.2	Globular cluster in Hydra
69	6637	18h 30.1m	−32°23′	8.0	Globular cluster in Sagittarius
70	6681	18h 42.0m	−32°18′	8.1	Globular cluster in Sagittarius
71	6838	19h 52.8m	+18°44′	7.6	Globular cluster in Sagitta
72	6981	20h 52.3m	−12°38′	9.3	Gilbular cluster in Aquarius
73	6994	20h 57.8m	−12°43′	9.1	Open cluster in Aquarius
74	628	1h 35.6m	−15°41′	9.3	Spiral galaxy in Pisces
75	6864	20h 04.9m	−21°59′	8.6	Globular cluster in Sagittarius
76	650	1h 41.0m	+51°28′	11.4	Planetary nebula in Perseus
77	1068	2h 41.6m	−0°04′	8.9	Spiral galaxy in Cetus
78	2068	5h 45.7m	0°03′	8.3	Small emission nebula in Orion
79	1904	5h 23.3m	−24°32′	7.5	Globular cluster in Lepus
80	6093	16h 15.8m	−22°56′	7.5	Globular cluster in Scorpio
81	3031	9h 54.2m	+69°09′	7.0	Spiral galaxy in Ursa Major
82	3034	9h 54.4m	+69°47′	8.4	Irregular galaxy in Ursa Major
83	5236	13h 35.4m	−29°31′	7.6	Spiral galaxy in Hydra
84	4374	12h 24.1m	+13°00′	9.4	Elliptical galaxy in Virgo
85	4382	12h 24.3m	+18°18′	9.3	Elliptical galaxy in Coma Berenices
86	4406	12h 25.1m	+13°03′	9.2	Elliptical galaxy in Virgo

COMPARING THE SIZES OF THE PLANETS

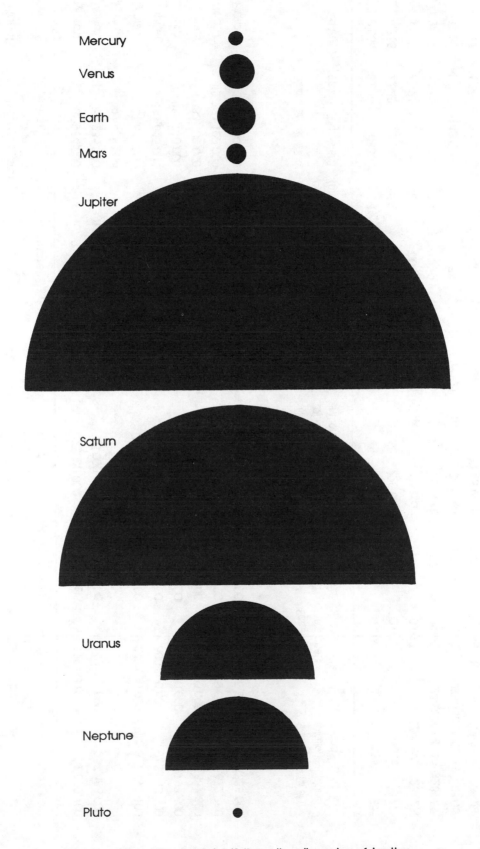

Mercury

Venus

Earth

Mars

Jupiter

Saturn

Uranus

Neptune

Pluto

The diameter of the sun = 9 1/2 times the diameter of Jupiter.

THE PLANETS

Symbol	Planet	Average distance from the Sun (miles)	(kilometers)	A.U.	Closest distance from the Earth (miles)	(kilometers)	Furthest distance from the Earth (miles)	(kilometers)
☿	Mercury	35,984,000	57,910,000	0.387	57,000,000	91,730,100	129,000,000	207,599,700
♀	Venus	67,236,000	108,200,000	0.7233	26,000,000	41,841,800	160,000,000	257,488,000
⊕	Earth	92,958,000	149,597,870	1.0000				
♂	Mars	141,640,000	227,940,000	1.5237	35,000,000	56,325,500	247,000,000	397,497,100
♃	Jupiter	483,640,000	778,320,000	5.2028	367,000,000	590,613,100	600,000,000	965,580,000
♄	Saturn	886,710,000	1,427,000,000	9.5388	741,000,000	1,192,491,300	1,032,000,000	1,660,797,600
♂, ♅	Uranus	1,783,100,000	2,869,600,000	19.1819	1,605,100,000	2,583,087,400	1,961,000,000	3,155,837,300
♆	Neptune	2,794,100,000	4,496,600,000	30.0578	2,675,100,000	4,305,038,400	2,911,000,000	4,684,672,300
P, ♇	Pluto	3,666,300,000	5,965,200,000	39.44	2,672,000,000	4,300,049,600	4,660,000,000	7,499,338,000

Planet	Mass (Earth =1)	Diameter (miles)	(kilometers)	Average density (gm/cm3)	Surface gravity (Earth =1)	Escape velocity (mi/sec)	(km/sec)	Number of known moons	Period of orbit	Inclination of planet's orbit to the ecliptic	Eccentricity of the planet's shape (circle = 0)	Sidereal rotation period	Tilt of the planet
Mercury	0.554	3,013	4,850	5.4	0.377	2 .58	(4.3)	0	88 days	7°	0.206	59 days	28°
Venus	0.815	7,543	12,140	5.2	0.905	6.24	(10.4)	0	225 days	3.39°	0.007	244 days	177°
Earth	1.000	7,926	12,756	5.5	1.000	6.72	(11.2)	1	365.26 days	0°	0.017	23h 56m 04s	23° 27'
Mars	0.107	4,219	6,790	3.9	0.379	3.18	(5.3)	2	1.88 years	1.85°	0.093	24h 37m 22.6s	23° 59'
Jupiter	317.89	88,980	143,200	1.3	2.54	36.12	(60.2)	16	11.86 years	1.30°	0.048	9h50m to 9h55m	3° 05'
Saturn	95.17	74,560	120,000	0.7	1.07	19.38	(32.3)	17	29.45 years	2.48°	0.056	10h14m to 10h38m	26° 44'
Uranus	14.6	32,190	50,769	1.7	0.86	13.5	(22.5)	5	84.07 years	0.80°	0.046	12h to 24h	97° 55'
Neptune	17.2	30,760	48,600	1.6	1.14	14.34	(23.9)	2	164.81 years	1.76°	0.010	15h48m	28° 48'
Pluto	0.0026	1,400	2,253	0.8	0.03	?		1	247.70 years	17.15°	0.249	6 days 9h 17m	60° ?

GLOSSARY

Aberration The apparent change in the position of a star or the difference in the focal points for light passing through a lens.

Absolute Magnitude The magnitude that a star would have if it were at a distance of 10 parsecs from the observer.

Absorbtion Lines Dark lines in the spectrum of light from a star.

Albedo The percentage of light an object (such as a planet) reflects compared to the total amount of light it receives.

Altitude The distance in degrees of the angle between the horizon and an object.

Aphelion The point in the orbit of a planet or a comet where it is farthest from the Sun.

Apogee The point in the orbit of the Moon or a planet where it is farthest from the Earth.

Apparent Magnitude The measurement of the brightness of a star or other object in the sky as we see it from the Earth.

Asteroid (Planetoid, Minor Planet) A small body in orbit around the Sun.

Astronomical Unit (A.U.) The average distance between the Earth and the Sun. 92,960,116 miles (149,597,870,000 kilometers).

Azimuth A coordinate used to measure the position of a star in degrees of the angle from north eastward along the horizon to the vertical circle which passes through the star.

Binary Star (Double Star) Two stars revolving around each other.

Black Hole A star which has collapsed under its own gravity with the result that not even light can escape.

Celestial Equator The projection of the Earth's equator onto the sky, creating a great circle around the middle of the celestial sphere that is 90 degrees from each of the poles of the celestial sphere.

Celestial Sphere The imaginary sphere out in space which surrounds the Earth and serves as a screen on which we see all of the objects in the sky.

Cepheid Variable A group of stars that pulsate, changing their brightness in a regular rhythm.

Circumpolar Stars The constellations that are around one of the poles of the celestial sphere.

Comet A swarm of ice and solid particles which orbits the Sun.

Conjunction The apparent line-up of two or more planets or the Sun and one or more planet.

Constellation The groups of stars that form 1 of 88 patterns which people have named for animals, heroes, and gods.

Cosmogony The study of the origin and evolution of the material in the Universe.

Cosmology The study of the organization and structure of the Universe and its evolution.

Culmination The position of a star when it is on the meridian.

Declination The distance of an object north or south of the celestial equator measured in degrees. It is like latitude in maps of the Earth.

Density The amount of matter contained in a given volume, measured in grams per cubic centimeter.

Doppler Effect The apparent change in the wavelength of sound, radio waves, or light due to the motion of the object toward or away from the observer.

Eclipse The blocking of light from the Sun by the Moon (solar) or the Moon by the Earth (lunar).

Ecliptic The apparent path of the Sun on the celestial sphere or the plane of the Earth's orbit projected onto the sky.

Ellipse The shape of all planetary orbits, more of an oval than a circle.

Elongation The apparent angle between the Sun and a planet.

Equinox One of the two points where the ecliptic and the celestial equator cross. When the Sun is at one of these points, the length of day and night are equal.

Galaxy A large island of stars, dust, and gas forming one system.

Geocentric System The system that describes the Earth as the center of the Universe.

Globular Cluster A collection of tens of thousands of stars forming a sphere which is usually part of a galaxy.

Heliacal Rising When a star or planet rises with the Sun.

Heliocentric System The system that describes the Sun as the center of the Solar System.

Hertzsprung-Russell (H.R.) Diagram A chart that shows the life cycle of the stars by graphing them according to their luminosity and temperature.

Inclination (of an orbit) The angle between the plane of the orbit of a planet and another plane, such as the celestial equator or the ecliptic.

Inferior Planets Those planets between the Earth and the Sun. They include Mercury and Venus.

Latitude The vertical lines on a map showing the distance north or south of the equator on the Earth.

Light-Year The distance that light travels in one year, about 5.88 trillion miles (9.46 trillion kilometers).

Local Group The clusters of about 20 galaxies to which the Milky Way belongs.

Longitude The horizontal lines on a map showing the distance east and west around the Earth from a north-south line running through Greenwich, England.

Main Sequence The diagonal band on the H-R diagram which contains most of the stars.

Mass The amount of matter contained in an object.

Meridian An imaginary line on the celestial sphere running north and south through the observer's zenith and nadir. On Earth maps, a meridian is a vertical line running from pole to pole and crossing the equator at right angles.

Meteor The bright streak of light that occurs when a particle from outside the Earth's atmosphere enters the atmosphere and the friction causes it to burn up.

Meteorite The part of a meteroid that makes it through the Earth's atmosphere and lands on the ground.

Meteoroid An interplanetary chunk of rock smaller than an asteroid.

Milky Way The speckled band of faint stars that forms the edge of our galaxy.

Nadir The point on the celestial sphere directly below the observer.

Nebula A cloud of gas or dust in space.

Neutron Star A dense, highly contracted star composed mainly of neutrons.

Node The point where one orbit crosses another.

Nova A dying star that suddenly brightens and then fades again as it throws off a shell of hot gasses.

Nutation The small variations in the movement of the Earth's poles.

Occultation When the Moon or another planet passes in front of a star or another planet temporarily hiding it.

Opposition When a planet is directly opposite the Sun or another planet as seen from the Earth.

Orbit The path of one body revolving around another.

Parallax (Stellar) The apparent shift of a star against the background of more distant stars due to the motion of the Earth around the Sun.

Parsec The distance of an object having a stellar parallax of one second of an arc. 1 parsec = 3.26 light years.

Perigee The point in the orbit of the Moon or a planet when it is nearest the Earth.

Perihelion The point in the orbit of a planet or celestial object when it is nearest the Sun.

Planet A celestial object that orbits a star and shines by reflecting light. There are nine known planets orbiting around the Sun in the Solar System.

Precession The slow wobble of the Earth's axis which sweeps out a circle in 26,000 years. This brings about a change in the position of the celestial poles and the celestial equator.

Precession of the Equinoxes The gradual falling back of the Equinox points along the zodiac due to the precession of the Earth.

Proper Motion The motion of a star across the background of the rest of the stars as seen from the Sun.

Pulsar An object that sends out rapid "pulses" of radio waves and sometimes light at regular intervals. It is possibly a very dense star, like a neutron star, spinning rapidly.

Quasar A "quasi-star" or "quasi-stellar object" that looks like a star but generates incredible amounts of energy. They are the most luminous objects known in the Universe and shine from enormous distances.

Radio Astronomy The branch of astronomy that studies objects that emit radio waves and little or no visible light.

Red Giant The stage in the life of a star when it expands to a huge size and cools to a red color.

Refraction The bending of a ray of light when it passes from one substance to another one with a different density.

Relativity The theory that all motion depends upon the observer's frame of reference and is therefore relative and not absolute.

Revolution The motion of one object around another. An orbit is the path a planet makes as it revolves around the Sun.

Right Ascension (R.A.) The distance of an object east or west along the celestial equator measured in degrees or hours. It is like longitude in maps of the Earth.

Rotation The motion of an object turning on its own axis. The spin of the Earth is a rotation which takes 24 hours.

Saros The eclipse cycle with intervals of 18 years, 11 days between two lunar or two solar eclipses of the same series.

Sidereal Time Time that is reckoned according to a planet's position compared to the stars instead of the Sun.

Solar System The system that includes all the objects which revolve around the Sun. The Solar System contains the Sun, the planets and their moons, comets, asteroids, meteoroids, etc.

Solstice One of the two points on the ecliptic farthest away above or below the celestial equator. When the Sun is above the celestial equator, the winter solstice occurs for the northern hemisphere and the summer solstice occurs for the southern hemisphere. When the Sun is below the celestial equator the summer solstice occurs for the northern hemisphere and the winter solstice occurs for the southern hemisphere.

Spectroscope An instrument that separates light from a star into its color wavelengths (spectrum) so that you can measure and analyze it.

Star A large sphere of intensely hot gas under great pressure that shines by the light of its own energy.

Superior Planets Those planets beyond the Earth heading away from the Sun. They include Mars, Jupiter, Saturn, Uranus, Neptune, and Pluto.

Synodic Period The time between two of the same alignments of planets (e.g., from conjunction to conjunction, Full Moon to Full Moon, etc.).

Terminator The line that separates the dark half of the Moon or a planet from the half that is lit.

Transit The passing of Mercury or Venus across the disk of the Sun as seen from the Earth. A transit is also the passing of a star across the meridian.

Universal Time (U.T.) The time at the 0 degree Meridian passing through Greenwich, England. Used as a world standard.

Variable Star A star whose brightness changes either regularly or irregularly.

White Dwarf The stage in the life of a star near death when the star has collapsed into a very dense, very hot mass with a small diameter and burning with a white light.

X-ray Stars Stars that send out radiation between the frequencies of ultraviolet radiation and gamma rays. These are the frequencies of X- rays that are not visible.

Zenith The point on the celestial sphere directly overhead.

Zodiac The band of 12 constellations centered on the ecliptic 18 degrees wide through which the Sun, Moon, and planets move as seen from the Earth.

INDEX